THE ROYAL PRIESTHOOD

DATE DUE

Demco, Inc. 38-293

The Royal Priesthood

Essays Ecclesiological and Ecumenical

JOHN H. YODER

Edited with an introduction by

Michael G. Cartwright

Herald
Press

Scottdale, Pennsylvania
Waterloo, Ontario

Library of Congress Cataloging-in-Publication Data
Yoder, John Howard, 1927-1997
    The royal priesthood : essays ecclesiological and ecumenical /
John H. Yoder ; edited with an introduction by Michael G. Cartwright.
        p.   cm.
    Originally published: Grand Rapids, Mich. : Eerdmans Pub. Co.,
c 1994.
    Includes bibliographical references and indexes.
    ISBN 0-8361-9114-5 (alk. paper)
    1. Church—Unity. 2. Church and the world.
3. Interdenominational cooperation.   I. Cartwright, Michael.
II. Title.
[BV601.5.Y63 1998]
262—dc21

                                                                    98-50878

This book, first published in 1994 by Wm. B. Eerdmans Publishing Co.,
is exclusively available from Herald Press, Scottdale, Pennsylvania 15683.

The editor and publishers gratefully acknowledge permission granted by
the publishers listed on page xii to reprint copyrighted material.

Contents

I. THEOLOGICAL PERSPECTIVES

II. ECUMENICAL PERSPECTIVES

CONTENTS

III. ECUMENICAL RESPONSES

IV. RADICAL CATHOLICITY

Foreword

The views contained in this book are not detestable. That may seem like a strange way to invite readers into a serious engagement with a stimulating volume of essays, but it is for me an important concession to make. As a Dutch Calvinist, my earliest assessment of Anabaptist thought and practice was formed by the stern judgment of my sixteenth-century spiritual ancestors, as they expressed it in the Belgic Confession: "We detest the Anabaptists and other seditious people, and in general all those who reject the higher powers and magistrates and would subvert justice, introduce community of goods, and confound that decency and good order which God has established among men."

I have come to realize that this verdict is seriously mistaken. And no one has influenced me more in coming to this realization than John Howard Yoder. His writings have been an important stimulus in the development of my own thinking about the contours of Christian discipleship. In the universe of discourse that I have inhabited as a teacher and scholar, Yoder's 1972 *The Politics of Jesus* has been an influential text. My own wrestlings with that book, even though I seriously disagree with some of its key arguments, have forever shaped the ways in which I think about questions of violence and the normativity of Jesus' redemptive ministry for the patterns of our social-political witness.

John Howard Yoder has also taught me that I have not seriously engaged the Anabaptist tradition if I merely allow myself to be "challenged" by its views about Jesus and peacemaking. There is a real danger that we former "detesters" of the Anabaptists will nurture a kind of condescending fondness for their views. We can easily come to see their perspective as a helpful "corrective" to our own tendencies, as reminding us of "aspects" of the gospel that we might otherwise ignore.

Such an outlook treats the Anabaptist perspective as if it were not so much a system of thought as a series of compensatory emphases whose ecumenical usefulness lies in their ability to modify other theological schemes. Of course, the Anabaptists have often left themselves open to this kind of treatment. They have not always placed a high premium on systematizing their theology; historical and biblical studies have often been preferred over systematic theology among the Mennonites and their kin. But there is another, more subtle factor at work when we attempt to tame the Anabaptist perspective by viewing it as a "necessary corrective": this means that we do not have to deal with the Anabaptist perspective as a systematic challenge to our own dogmatic designs.

John Howard Yoder has made it difficult for us to take refuge in this posture of condescending affection. He has led the way in setting forth the systematic challenge. And he has done so in a manner that makes it difficult for those of us in, say, the Reformed or Lutheran or Roman Catholic traditions — communities that take pride in a long history of systematic theological studies — to dismiss Anabaptist theology with faint praises.

The essays in this book set forth the challenge in boldly provocative terms. Michael Cartwright has served us well, not only by bringing these writings together in one volume, but also by giving us an insightful overview of the "Yoderian" project. The Anabaptist position we encounter here is no mere set of theological "reminders," nor is it just a laudable witness to the importance of "life-style" questions; rather, it is itself a full-fledged and coherent perspective on the crucial issues of theology. At the center of Yoder's focus in these essays is the doctrine of the church. Yoder not only presents the Anabaptist position as a consistent alternative to other ecclesiologies; in doing so he argues convincingly that, because this is a consistent alternative, we can no longer work with long-standing classificatory schemes for mapping out ecclesiological positions. This is a book that rightly calls for a rewriting of the ecumenical agenda.

I must admit that I find this unsettling. In one sense, of course, that is nothing new for a Calvinist. But when my spiritual ancestors felt unsettled by the Anabaptists, they responded by portraying the Anabaptist movement as a fanatical departure from the "decency and good order" of mainstream Christianity. John Howard Yoder has demonstrated the deep folly of this portrayal. He offers us an Anabaptist perspective that, in a decent and orderly manner, forces us to retrace our historical and theological steps as we take an honest look at questions that have long been ignored — yes, even suppressed — by those of us who have found it easy to marginalize the "free church" tradition. For many good and important reasons, this book is an important gift to all who care about honest and faithful theology.

RICHARD J. MOUW

Acknowledgments

From the beginning, this project has been a cooperative endeavor between the editor and several other scholars. As the author of the essays collected here, John H. Yoder has cooperated with this project from the beginning — providing materials, answering queries, making revisions where requested and reading drafts along the way — while never doing anything that could be construed as intruding on the editor's freedom. I would note here, for the record, that the views expressed in the editorial introduction are my own and do not necessarily reflect either Yoder's imprimatur or his disapproval. John welcomed various requests that I made concerning the elimination of language that would now be regarded by many readers as sexist. Although in several instances we decided that it would be too awkward to alter the original text, we did make such changes where it was feasible to do so.

I am also grateful to my students and colleagues in the community of learning at Allegheny College, which in various ways has supported this project. A modest grant four years ago from the Faculty Development Committee made it possible for me to extend my collection of John H. Yoder's writings and thereby begin to envision possible ways of providing a retrospective of Yoder's lifework. At that time, I could never have envisioned that I would one day edit a collection of Yoder's essays. More recently, James Sheridan, chairperson of the Philosophy and Religious Studies Department at Allegheny College, provided temporary office space and other financial support from departmental funds for the preparation of this collection for publication. Andrew T.

Ford, who until recently served as the provost and academic dean of Allegheny College, provided financial support for research assistant-ships for the summer of 1993. Most of all, I am grateful to the two research assistants, whose dedicated effort and interest in this project made it possible for me to complete this project. Jennifer Rychlicki '93 and Timothy J. Luoma '95 did much of the work of scanning, typing, and preparing the texts of these essays during the preliminary processes of editing. Their work made it possible for me to proceed with editorial tasks. Timothy J. Luoma was primarily responsible for completing the later stages of preparing the manuscript for submission to the publisher and assisted with proofreading. Tim is responsible for the topical index as well. Tim's willingness to work on all phases of this project has enabled me to concentrate my efforts on the conceptual issues discussed in the editorial introduction.

Others have also contributed to this project in various ways. Reinhard Hütter, Mark Nation, James Wm. McClendon, Jr., and Stanley M. Hauerwas contributed to the process of selecting the essays to be included in this collection and subsequently have served as an informal "editorial board" for me to consult about various editorial decisions ranging from "how wide the net should be" in determining the shape of this collection to recommendations about what issues should be discussed in the editorial introduction. L. Gregory Jones, while not formally involved in the process of consultation, as always proved to be a very insightful reader of my work and offered several timely suggestions about the editorial introduction. Mark Nation, a graduate student in theology and ethics at Fuller Theological Seminary, was kind enough to provide a selected bibliography of Yoder's writings on ecclesiology and ecumenism. All readers should be aware of the debt that we owe Mark Nation for his careful work over the past few years in cataloging Yoder's published and unpublished works. I also want to indicate my gratitude to Charles Van Hof and the editorial staff at William B. Eerdmans Publishing Company for their technical assistance at various stages of this project. I am especially grateful to President William B. Eerdmans, Jr., for his enthusiasm for and commitment to this project.

As the editor, I accept ultimate responsibility for the way this volume has been put together. However, I gratefully acknowledge that without the efforts of all of the people mentioned in the previous paragraphs this project would be significantly impoverished.

Finally, I am grateful to my wife, Mary Wilder Cartwright, who in the midst of changes in her own career in ministry undertook a disproportionate share of responsibility for the care of our children so that I could complete this project.

MICHAEL G. CARTWRIGHT

The editor and publisher gratefully acknowledge permission to reprint the following published material:

"Another 'Free Church' Perspective on Baptist Ecumenism," reprinted by permission of the *Journal of Ecumenical Studies*.

"Christ, the Hope of the World," from *The Original Revolution* by John H. Yoder, reprinted by permission of Herald Press, Scottdale, PA 15683.

"Christ, the Light of the World," from *The Original Revolution* by John H. Yoder, reprinted by permission of Herald Press, Scottdale, PA 15683.

"The Disavowal of Constantine: An Alternative Perspective on Interfaith Dialogue," reprinted by permission of the *Tantur Yearbook*, the Tantur Ecumenical Institute for Theological Studies, POB 19556, 91194 Jerusalem, Israel.

"The Free Church Ecumenical Style," reprinted by permission of *Quaker Religious Thought*.

"A 'Free Church' Perspective on Baptism, Eucharist and Ministry," from *Mid-Stream* [Indianapolis], Vol. 23, No. 3 (July 1984), Paul A. Crow, Jr., editor. Reprinted by permission.

"Let the Church Be the Church," from *The Original Revolution* by John H. Yoder, reprinted by permission of Herald Press, Scottdale, PA 15683.

"The Nature of the Unity We Seek: A Historic Free Church View," from *Religion in Life*, Vol. XXVI, Spring, 1957, No. 2. Copyright © 1957 by Abingdon Press. Excerpted by permission.

"The Otherness of the Church," from *The Drew Gateway*, vol. 30, no. 3 (Spring 1960), reprinted by permission of Drew University.

"Peace Without Eschatology?" from *The Original Revolution* by John H. Yoder, reprinted by permission of Herald Press, Scottdale, PA 15683.

"A People in the World," from *The Concept of the Believers' Church* by John H. Yoder, reprinted by permission of Herald Press, Scottdale, PA 15683.

"Sacrament as Social Process: Christ the Transformer of Culture," reprinted by permission of *Theology Today*.

"To Serve Our God and to Rule the World," reprinted by permission of *The Annual for the Society of Christian Ethics*.

Radical Reform, Radical Catholicity: John Howard Yoder's Vision of the Faithful Church

MICHAEL G. CARTWRIGHT

I. Introducing Yoder's Vision of the "Royal Priesthood" of the Church

As readers of this collection of essays will discover, it is not possible to disengage John H. Yoder's practice of ecumenical dialogue from his vision of the church. In fact, as I shall argue in this introductory essay, it is crucial to take into account the ways in which Yoder's approach to ecumenical dialogue correlates with his conception of the *faithfulness* of the church, especially in as much as he sees the latter displayed in the embodiment of apostolic practices of discipleship. In this respect Yoder reflects his Anabaptist heritage. However, this does not mean that Yoder is bound by the framework of the Mennonite tradition. Rather, his vision of the church poses challenges for Christians of *all* communions because he calls for disciplined dialogue and faithful servanthood that renders the confession of Jesus Christ's lordship meaningful. In turn, Yoder reminds contemporary Christians that discussion of doctrinal questions of "faith and order" require a willingness to engage questions of moral inadequacy. Thus Yoder's essays challenge all Christians to reassess what it means to call churches "reformed" and "catholic" if — as Yoder argues — fraternal admonition is the logical prerequisite for engaging in ecumenical dialogue.

To conclude, however, from these challenges that Yoder is postulating an "ideal" of the church that is divorced from the concrete reality of the church would be wrong. On the contrary, Yoder is very much concerned with the practical details of enacting the gospel corporately.

1

He believes that the New Testament writings describe the social practices that faithful Christianity embodies: basin and towel, eucharistic sharing, "binding and loosing," and martyrdom. In this sense, Yoder has argued that early Christian doxologies such as "The Lamb is worthy to receive power" should be understood as "performative utterances" that signify their corporate (political and ecclesiological) confession of the lordship of Jesus Christ. The apocalyptic writings of the apostolic communities of faith, Yoder argues, exhibit the awareness that there is "no crown without a cross" and, thereby, no sharing in the kingly reign of God without sharing in Christ's sacrificial servanthood. In *these* practices of discipleship the "royal priesthood" of the church is made visible in the world wherever Christians may gather.

This vision of the royal priesthood rests on a claim about the *theological* meaning of history itself under Jesus' lordship. With this claim in view, Yoder's vision of the faithful church can hardly be conceived as withdrawing from concrete engagements with the world; rather the church's witness *to* the world takes shape as "evangelical nonconformity" *in* and *for* the world. In this sense "royal" also *affirms* the historical effectiveness or "power" of the servant community, or church, to carry out its mission on behalf of the Lord of history. From this "gospel view of history," the church's royal priesthood is ultimately validated not by economic standards or efficacy but by its capacity to manifest "the continuing relevance" of the servantlike work of Christ as *the sign* of the lordship of Christ (see "Christ, the Hope of the World," 192–218).

It would, therefore, be a mistake to think that the significance of the title of this collection of essays is *limited to* the distinctive character of the community of faith in relation to the rest of the world. As Yoder has articulated in several contexts, the priestly character of the community of faith arises out of its very mission: the role of the church is *not* to serve itself but to be the bearer of reconciliation. The royal character of this community can be specified in terms of its participation in God's intentions for the direction of the world. In these senses, then, it is appropriate to the vocation of the church as a royal priesthood to conceive itself in terms of its dual vocation "to serve our God and to rule the world." Without such a self-understanding, the church will be tempted to presume either that it should make history come out right or, conversely, that it has *no role* in God's reign now or in the future. From Yoder's point of view, when the church yields to either temptation it forsakes its vocation as the royal priesthood.

This collection of essays on ecclesiology and ecumenism is intended to demonstrate the substantial unity of Yoder's work over the past four decades. I suspect that the incredible breadth of Yoder's life-work as historian, ethicist, theologian, seminary educator and adminis-trator, denominational agency executive, missiologist, "Bible lecturer," critic of the "just war" tradition, and proponent of Christian pacifism may constitute part of the reason why the inner unity of Yoder's scholar-ship has not been adequately recognized. Yoder's writings on issues related to the "just war" tradition of moral discourse alone could easily equal the lifework of some prominent Christian ethicists, and it may be that Yoder's prominence in discussions of war and peace issues have overshadowed his contributions to ecclesiology and ecumenism, partic-ularly with respect to the ongoing ecumenical engagement of churches from the "radical reformation" or "believers' church" traditions (see discussion below) with "mainstream" Protestants.

By contrast, Yoder's contributions within the arena of ecumenical affairs are widely recognized, even if they often have been characterized somewhat narrowly with reference to his membership in one of the historic peace churches and his consistent advocacy of Christian paci-fism. His witness to peace is a key feature of his approach to ecumenical dialogue, but Yoder's contribution to ecumenism is certainly not ex-hausted by his peace witness. Rather, Yoder's peace witness takes shape *within* a consistently articulated belief that the unity of the church is a gift of God's Holy Spirit, which *enables* Christians to embody God's *shalom* in the world. Thus, on the one hand, Yoder reminds ecumenists that the world Christian community "represents an agency of peacemaking in ways often underestimated" and, on the other hand, Yoder has raised questions about the extent to which the existing con-ciliar process needs to be re-ordered not only to reflect more inclusive participation of Christian peoples in the world but also to reflect "a restored vision of the wholeness shalom demands."[1]

In this sense Yoder's contribution to the ecumenical movement can be seen as part of a larger effort on the part of such groups as the Fellowship of Reconciliation (FOR) and the historic peace churches. These groups have striven both to make questions about peacemaking central in the conciliar process of the World Council of Churches and

---

1. John H. Yoder, "Peace" in *The Dictionary of the Ecumenical Movement* (Geneva, Switzerland: World Council of Churches Publications Office, 1991; Grand Rapids: Eerdmans, 1991): 786–89. For a discussion of Yoder's contribution to the hermeneutical discussion of the use of Scripture in the church ecumenical, see Michael G. Cartwright's article on "Hermeneutics," op. cit., 454–58.

to initiate ecumenical dialogues outside the conciliar process. For example, in 1991 representatives of FOR and the historic peace churches (Yoder included) published *A Declaration on Peace: In God's People the World's Renewal Has Begun,* an appeal "addressed to all Christians everywhere."[2] Although the authors of this volume do not indicate that Yoder's work was particularly influential on their process of discussion, it is interesting to note that the way the authors explicated "the unity and diversity" of the vocation of the Christian community bears a strong resemblance to some of Yoder's own theological writings where he has used the "threefold office" of Christ — prophet, priest, and king.[3]

This volume's placing Yoder's contributions to ecumenism side by side with his various articulations of the "free church" vision of the church should begin to correct a misunderstanding of Yoder's work. The editorial decision not to include essays on such topics as just war is quite deliberate. Discussions where issues of war and peace crop up in this collection are oriented toward an ecclesiological or ecumenical agenda. Accordingly, this introductory essay will explicate the "inner unity" of these various essays by sketching the conceptual background of Yoder's work, first as a historical theologian; second as an ecumenist and theologian who has engaged the proposals of major twentieth-century European and American writers (Barth, the Niebuhrs, Outler, etc.); and third as an articulate advocate of the free church or believers'

---

2. Douglass Gwynn, George Hunsinger, Eugene F. Roop, John Howard Yoder, *A Declaration on Peace: In God's People the World's Renewal Has Begun* (Scottdale, Penn.: Herald Press, 1991): 7, 8. A chronology compiled by Yoder, "40 Years of Ecumenical Theological Dialogue Efforts on Justice and Peace Issues by the Fellowship of Reconciliation and the Historic Peace Churches," appears as Appendix C, pp. 93–105.

3. E.g., see the titles of the four chapters in *A Declaration on Peace:* "The Priestly Role," "The Prophetic People," "The Discerning People," "The Royal Servant People." It is beyond the scope of this essay to offer an analysis of Yoder's theological method, but it should be noted that Yoder quite often will use classical Protestant rubrics (particularly where these can be said to be biblically grounded) for the purpose of explicating his arguments. E.g., see *Preface to Theology: Christology and Theological Method* (Elkhart, Ind.: Goshen Biblical Seminary, 1981): 170–285, where Yoder discusses the substance of the Christian faith under the rubrics "Christ the King: Last Things," "Christ as Priest: Atonement," and "Christ as Prophet: Revelation." And as readers of this volume and Yoder's early book, *The Priestly Kingdom* (1984), should recognize, Yoder's has shown a preference in titling collections of his essays in theology and ethics for the images of 1 Peter 2:9–10 (which in turn reflect imagery that carries over from the Old Testament into the writings of the New Testament writers).

church approach to church renewal before attempting to provide my own assessment of Yoder's contributions to ecumenism and ecclesiology in the last two sections of this editorial introduction.

II. The Conceptual Matrix of John H. Yoder's Writings on Ecclesiology and Ecumenism

A. *Reading the History of Christianity — and the World — with John Howard Yoder*

In ways that are both straightforward and strikingly subtle, Yoder's approach to ecclesiology and ecumenism is firmly grounded in historical scholarship. Yoder's Th.D. dissertation at the University of Basel focused on the "dialogues" or disputations between the Anabaptists and the "magisterial reformers" in Switzerland between 1523 and 1538.[4] Some of his earliest published articles focused on the struggles of the sixteenth-century Anabaptists to make their dissent from state-church reformations of Europe heard — often at the cost of their lives as *The Martyrs' Mirror* attests. Throughout his career, Yoder has contributed to historical studies of the sixteenth-century Anabaptist theologians such as Michael Sattler and Balthasar Hubmaier.[5]

There is no question that Yoder's approach to the history of Christianity (and of the world) is "revisionist," but specifying *how* it is revisionist and explaining *how* his reading of history correlates with his writings on ecclesiology and ecumenism are very important and challenging tasks. I would argue that delineating the *levels* in which his reading of history goes "against the grain" is especially important. First, unlike some contemporary Christian theologians, Yoder does not seek to make a virtue of contesting all categorizations, although he does recognize that categories such as "sectarian," which are ostensibly to be used in a descriptive sense, are more often used pejoratively in recent literature. Eschewing what he calls "contrarianism," Yoder argues for the importance of "evangelical revisionism" in the writing of history,

---

4. *Täufertum und Reformation in der Schweiz: I. Die Gespräche zwischen Täufern und Reformatoren 1523–1538.* Schriftenreihe des Mennonitischen Geschichtsvereins, no. 6. Karlsruhe: Buchdruckerei und Verlag H. Schneider.

5. See *The Legacy of Michael Sattler* (ed.) John H. Yoder (Scottdale, Penn.: Herald Press, 1973) and *Balthasar Hubmaier: Theologian of Anabaptism* (trans. and ed.) H. Wayne Pipkin and John H. Yoder (Scottdale, Penn.: Herald Press, 1989), both in the Classics of the Radical Reformation series.

and accordingly he admonishes peace church historians to maintain the "good news" quality of their stance in relation to "mainline historiography" by remembering that "love of the enemy must include love of the intellectual adversary, including intellectual respect for the holders of the positions one must in conscience reject."[6]

In this respect, as well as others, Yoder's historiographical perspective also diverges rather sharply from "the 'post-modernist' claim that 'everyone is biased,' as if that meant that all truth claims are equal." Rather, Yoder argues that the writing of history, "when rightly done, ought to somehow render the decisiveness of the choices people make" in the midst of human history.[7] In turn, the way historians assess particular "historical turning points" determines the possibilities for appropriating the "good news about the human condition."[8] For this reason Yoder takes great pains to point out the track record of radical reformation or free church contributions to church renewal. No less important is to call attention to the *historical patterns* by which Christians have engaged the alleged "primacy of politics." In this respect Yoder is more rigorously historical in locating a political phenomenon that political theorists like Jean Bethke Elshtain have noted is very important for understanding the origins of Western political constructions of the relationship of the "public" and the "private" spheres: "Christianity challenged the primacy of politics. It did not relegate secular power to silence and shadows as secular power had formerly relegated the private, but claims of the public political world no longer went unchallenged. Caesar now had to confront the formidable figure of Christ."[9] Whereas Elshtain and other political theorists seek to "deepen and extend the 'redemption of everyday life' in Christian doctrine against

6. John H. Yoder, "The Burden and Discipline of Evangelical Revisionism" in *Nonviolent America: History through the Eyes of Peace* (ed.) Louise Hawkley and James C. Juhnke (North Newton, Kans.: Bethel College, 1993): 21, 22.

7. Ibid., 22, 23.

8. Ibid., 24. The larger context in which Yoder summarizes his conception of "evangelical revisionism" is very important to take into account:

> The reason history needs to be reread is not merely that every generation must claim the right to begin writing world history over from scratch, nor that in particular the children of the bourgeois cannot get out of the nest without soiling it, but that at certain points there is specifiable good news about the human condition, the goodness or the newness of which those who hitherto have been controlling the storytelling had not yet appropriated.

9. Jean Bethke Elshtain, *Public Man, Private Woman: Women in Social and Political Thought* (Princeton, N.J.: Princeton University Press, 1981; second ed. 1993): 59.

gnostic disparagers past and present"[10] as part of the project of recon-
structing the public and private spheres, Yoder's project is to reconstruct
the church/world distinction ecclesiologically as well as politically —
by *locating* this distinction within particular historical moments — but
without thereby cutting off dialogue between Christians and non-Christians as if "church" and "world" were monolithic categories.

Characteristically, Yoder does not seek to demythologize what
New Testament writers described as the "principalities and powers."
Instead, he challenges readers to see the possible ways these apostolic
categories provide for engaging the contemporary political contexts as
well as imaginative means for contesting the ways in which governments, ideologies, and other religions characterize (and caricature) particular theological understandings of the church as "private" or "sectarian" or "apolitical." In so doing, Yoder reminds Christians and
non-Christians alike that there is nothing obvious or self-evident about
the way we read history in relation to sociological and political claims
about what is normal or mainstream for the church in relation to the
world.

Apocalyptic/Eschatology and the Framework of Normalcy

In all his writing, Yoder can be said to contest the adequacy of "the
frame of normalcy,"[11] which, in turn, can be said — explicitly or implicitly — to presuppose an ecclesiology that is normative for mainstream
Christians. One way that Yoder *contests* the frame of normalcy is by
treating the biblical metaphors of cosmic conflict as providing a viable
way of assessing the situation of the people of God in human history.
Characteristically, Yoder offers very little by way of theoretical justification for the "apocalyptic" perspective.[12] Instead, he calls attention to
the contemporary prevalence of apocalyptic perspectives in Western
culture while also calling attention to the very different, and ultimately

10. Ibid., "Afterword" to the second edition of *Public Man, Private Woman*,
355–56.
11. John H. Yoder, "Ethics and Eschatology" *Ex Auditu* 6 (1990): 124.
12. E.g., see Yoder's discussion of apocalyptic in "Armaments and Eschatology," 43–47, and "Ethics and Eschatology," 125–26. It should be noted that in both
of these instances, the topic of eschatology was justified by those who invited Yoder
to present his perspective. However, beyond the occasions of these and other papers,
it should be noted that Yoder does not provide foundationalist epistemological
justifications for using apocalyptic categories.

hopeful, perspective on the cosmos in the writings of the "seers" of Christian Scriptures.

Thus, Yoder makes no effort to "translate" apocalyptic perspectives into a vocabulary more compatible with contemporary world views. Rather, he treats these perspectives as a form of (political) reading of history "from below":[13]

> A community playing the victim role within a society needs first of all to know not what they would do differently if they were the rulers, nor how to seize power, but that the present power constellation that oppresses them is not the last word.
>
> The first word in the reaffirmation of the human dignity of the oppressed is thus to constitute in their celebrative life the coming Rule of God and a new construal of the cosmos under God. To sing "The Lamb is worthy to receive power," as did the early communities whose hymnody is reflected in the first vision of John, is not mere poetry. It is performative proclamation. It redefines the cosmos in a way prerequisite to the moral independence that it takes to speak truth to power and to persevere in living against the stream when no reward is in sight.[14]

This redefinition of the cosmos, however, *does not mean* that we should "substitute (as fundamentalism does) a literal reading of the scheme of Ezekiel, or of Mark 13 or of John of Patmos, for the scenarios of the Pentagon." Nor, Yoder warns, should we overdramatize "the church/world clash" in a time when or in a place where, in fact, a clash has been mitigated in some respects by favorable cultural changes.[15] Understanding the relationship of the church and the world in light of eschatology is crucial for Yoder; ultimately it is for the purpose of

13. Ibid., 124. Yoder goes on to correlate this view of history with what liberation theologians have called "the epistemological privilege of the poor" while correcting what some North Americans take this slogan to mean.

14. John H. Yoder, "Armaments and Eschatology," *Studies in Christian Ethics* 1/1 (T. & T. Clark, 1988): 53.

15. Ibid., 56. Yoder specifically mentions such writers as Vernard Eller (Church of the Brethren) and William Stringfellow (Protestant Episcopal) who offer "over simple statements of the dualism" of church and world. As he comments in an extended note: "To take seriously the basic validity of the apocalyptic stance need not imply disrespect for the concrete values attained by democratic government in (e.g.) the defense of religious liberty, limited government, the franchise, etc. Such a systematic dualism as would refuse the vote or reject public social services need not follow. Nonetheless the fundamental dualism remains valid at other points where neither moral nor institutional progress can be claimed . . ." (p. 61 note 37).

clarifying the church/world dichotomy that Yoder attempts to retrieve the idiom of apostolic apocalyptic.[16]

Church and World

Against that form of history-writing that accentuates frameworks of normalcy by an implicit appeal to a doctrine of divine Providence that blesses the present political regime, Yoder reads history from the vantage of the difference made by the life, ministry, death, and resurrection of Jesus Christ; in short, the writings of the New Testament, which bear witness to the resurrection as the central event in cosmic history.

> The New Testament sees our present age — the age of the church, extending from Pentecost to the Parousia — as a period of the overlapping of two aeons. These aeons are not distinct periods of time, for they exist simultaneously. They differ rather in nature or in direction; one points backward to human history outside of (before) Christ; the other points forward to the fullness of the kingdom of God, of which it is a foretaste. Each aeon has a social manifestation: the former in the "world," the latter in the church or the body of Christ. The new aeon came into history in a decisive way with the incarnation and the entire work of Christ. Christ had been awaited eagerly by Judaism for centuries; but when He came He was rejected, for the new aeon He revealed was not what people wanted. . . . Thus Christ's claims and His kingdom were to them scandalous. (see pp. 146–47)

Yoder goes on to explain in "The Otherness of the Church" that it is possible to discover the pre-Constantinian significance of the concepts "church" and "world" within the New Testament:

> "World" (*aion houtos* in Paul, *kosmos* in John) signifies in this connection not creation or nature or the universe but rather the fallen form of the same, no longer conformed to the creative intent. The state, which for present purposes may be considered as typical for the world, belongs with the other *exousiai* in this realm. Over against this "world" the church is visible; identified by baptism, discipline, morality, and martyrdom. It is self-evident for the early centuries as a part of this visibility of the fellowship of disciples, that the church's members do not normally belong in the service of the world and a fortiori in that of the pagan state.

16. Ibid., 47.

But behind or above this visible dichotomy there is a believed unity. All evidence to the contrary notwithstanding, the church believed that its Lord was also Lord over the world. The explicit paganism of state, art, economics, and learning did not keep the church from confessing their subordination to him who sitteth at the right hand of God. This belief in Christ's lordship over the *exousiai* enabled the church, in and in spite of its distinctness from the world, to speak to the world in God's name, not only in evangelism, but in ethical judgment as well. (see pp. 55–56)

This way of reading human history is displayed in most of the other essays in this collection. In turn, it informs his understanding of the history of the Christian church.

Before Constantine — After Christendom

Central to Yoder's approach to ecclesiology and ecumenism is his analysis of the historical and political role played by the "Constantiniani-zation" of the church. In one respect Yoder's argument is typically Protestant insofar as theologians from Martin Luther to H. Richard Niebuhr have deplored the "captivity" of the church in their time and culture. By seeking to "dismantle the notion that the ruler is the primary agent of divine movement in history,"[17] Yoder is not only questioning a way of writing history that conflates secular political narratives of legitimation with ecclesiastical justifications, but also he is insisting that the kind of consequentialist reasoning that blinds Christians to "other modes of moral reasoning"[18] distracts contemporary Christians from the kind of doxological confession that in the early church found expression in the *hope* of the Apocalypse of John. In other words, Yoder uses metaphors of cosmic conflict because they are "most apt" to break the "frame of normalcy" created by Constantinian regimes.

Some have argued that Yoder's critique of Constantinianism suffers from a lack of historical and sociological precision in his view of the pre-Constantinian church and of the subsequent "Constantinian" history of Christianity and in his description of the morally rigorous church.[19] This criticism actually constitutes a significant misreading of

17. Ibid., 53.
18. John H. Yoder, "Ethics and Eschatology," 123.
19. E.g., see Philip LeMasters, *The Import of Eschatology in John Howard Yoder's Critique of Constantinianism* (San Francisco: Edwin Mellen Research University Press, 1992).

Yoder's work in at least two senses. First, it does not engage Yoder's careful analysis of the historical and social circumstances of "Constantinianism old and new," which is laid out in "Christ, the Hope of the World" (see pp. 195–97). In fact, it could be argued that Yoder's understanding of the reality of Constantianism in the time of Constantine is closely related to his analysis of the patterns of "neo-Constantinianism" that emerged after the "wars of religion" had ended in 1648.

> It is a new phase of unity or a new kind of unity between church and world. This unity has lost the worldwide character of the epoch of Constantine, yet the fusion of church and society is maintained. We can even say that it is tightened, since the wars of religion linked particular national governments in a way that had not obtained in the Middle Ages. Now the church is servant, not of mankind at large but, of a particular society, not of the entire society, but of a particular dominating class. (see p. 195)

This social pattern, in turn, is historically and socially distinct from what Yoder describes as "neo-neo-Constantinianism," which is the circumstance "where the church blesses its society (and particularly its own national society) without a formal identification therewith, or without religious rootage in the common people" (p. 196). A third pattern, "neo-neo-neo-Constantinianism," describes the situation in cultures where secularization has occurred and the point is reached when Christians begin to argue that "the process of secularization can best succeed when favored and fostered by the church" (p. 196). Finally, when the future is predicated in terms of a particular political alliance or cause, such as in the revolutions of Latin America, Yoder notes that the groundwork is laid for a fourth pattern, "neo-neo-neo-neo-Constantianism" (p. 197).

Yoder's purpose in delineating these distinctions is precisely to situate these developments as *sociologically and historically different* while structurally similar in terms of their use of the established political mechanisms of control available in each cultural situation. This "anatomy of the Constantinian temptation" unfolds from the basic axiom that "the true meaning of history, the true locus of salvation is in the cosmos and not in the church. Then what God is really doing . . . is through the framework of society as a whole and not in the Christian community" (p. 198). Interestingly enough, Yoder's primary argument here is not so much an indictment of secularity as such but with "the progressive abandonment of the vision of catholicity" that occurs as

11

part of the various instances of the "Constantinianization" of the church (p. 201).

Second, critics of Yoder's conception of Constantinianism fail to take into account the extensive discussion of social practices (each of which, Yoder argues, is described in the New Testament writings) in relation to which Yoder's free church ecclesiology has been articulated over the past three decades. In addition to Yoder's earlier essay on "The Kingdom as a Social Ethic" published in *The Priestly Kingdom*,[20] the essays on "Binding and Loosing" (pp. 323–58) and "Sacrament as Social Process" (pp. 359–73) provide some of the most recently published examples of the way Yoder describes the sociological contextualization of faithfulness. Further, Yoder's recently published *Body Politics* (Discipleship Resources, 1993) specifies "five practices of the Christian community before the world." But it is important to note that this kind of sociological specification of Yoder's ecclesiology is by no means new. Yoder's brief essay (on Matt. 18:15–20) "Christian Discipline" appeared in *The Gospel Herald* as early as 1964; later in that same decade he prepared a "schematic summary of marks of the church" for a cooperative study project to develop a model for theological education in the free church tradition. This teaching aid includes "eight specific functions, each discussed in terms of its subjective meaning, the sacramental form, the process, and the underlying anthropology" (see the chart on p. 13).[21]

As Ross T. Bender paraphrases the findings of the seminar process to which Yoder had contributed some of these perspectives, in so far as this schematic vision assumes that there is a "biblical pattern" to be

20. John H. Yoder, *The Priestly Kingdom* (Notre Dame: University of Notre Dame Press, 1984): 80–101, esp. 93–94.

21. Ross Thomas Bender, *The People of God: A Mennonite Interpretation of the Free Church Tradition* (Scottdale, Penn.: Herald Press, 1971): 142–45. Yoder's schematic chart of the marks of the church was developed in relation to the ecumenical discussions current at that time, a discussion in which the marks of the church were being revised in the direction of recognizing the communal character of the church's life and functions. The chart has been altered in two ways from its use in Bender's book. The "Notae" are also listed as "Practices," whereas the original text on p. 143 of Bender had "Notae" only. For a similar discussion of the notae or marks of the church, see pp. 75–79 in Yoder's "A People in the World" essay. At other points, the chart has been revised for the purpose of being inclusive.

This volume, which is the "Report of the study project to develop a model for theological education in the Free Church tradition sponsored by the Associated Mennonite Biblical Seminaries of Elkhart, Indiana," was one of the byproducts of a three-year period of self-assessment by the faculty of the Associated Mennonite Biblical Seminaries from 1967 through 1970.

Nota or Practice	Meaning for Me	Sacramental Form	Meaning in Terms of Process	Underlying Anthropology "To be human is . . ."
Bind and Loose	Forgiveness Reconciliation	Fraternal Admonition Conversation	Discernment	To arise out of and to produce moral community
Love the Brothers and Sisters	Sharing	The Supper	Covenant Celebration	To share "food" with others
Teach	Homologia	Scripture (tradition)	Testing	To take up anew one's history
Follow Christ	Imitation Participation	The Plow Left Behind	Forsaking	To forsake the good for the best
Serve	Servanthood	The basin The cross	Suffering	To subject my freedom for the need of my brother or sister
Praise God	Reaffirmation	Psalter	Recital	To give thanks
Make Disciples	Witness	Baptism	Adding to the Church	To join a voluntary covenanting community
Greet the Brothers and Sisters	Unity	Kiss Sandal and Satchel	Mobility, "as you go" cosmopolitanism	To keep widening one's experience of Christian fellowship

identified, the practices in question are "drawn primarily from the injunctions of Jesus rather than from an analysis of the congregations of the New Testament church" understood as providing a "coherent social vision" for the early church.

This vision provided the pattern of life of the churches in the first century after Pentecost; it reflected the original simplicity of the gospel prior to the more highly institutionalized sets of structures, offices and ceremonies which developed later. It sees the potential spiritual significance in the ordinary things of life when pressed into the service of God and his people such as conversation, the basin and towel, the kiss, the sandal and the satchel as well as in baptism and the Lord's Supper. The latter were also initially an expression of the common life (water, bread and wine) symbolizing the interpenetration of the nature and the spiritual orders which was part of the early Christian genius.[22]

While on this level and at this point of their argument, Bender, Yoder, et al.'s reading of history is clearly restitutionist, they are quite clear in saying that

> Such a vision is not pre-institutional primitivism; it rather stands prior to the development of any institutional or sacramental forms and provides criteria by which to judge their appropriateness. It does not fix the shape of the forms for all times; neither, however, does it permit arbitrariness in determining them. The presence of the Holy Spirit in the original community and in the modern community of faith is the effective guarantee that form and essence in any age coincide faithfully.[23]

Here, in Bender's paraphrase of Yoder's presentation, we see how Yoder's reading of history correlates with a specifically *theological* affirmation of the activity of the Holy Spirit that enables *faithfulness* in the church's witness to the presence of the Kingdom of God in human history. Yoder's steadfast refusal to dehistoricize the role of the Holy Spirit in human history, or to divorce the work of the Spirit in the life of the church from the definitive character of the revelation of God in Jesus Christ, has shaped the way he has engaged the proposals of other theologians, ethicists, and ecumenicists over the past four decades.[24]

22. Ibid., 144.
23. Ibid.
24. For more extended reflections on the topic of the role of the Holy Spirit in human history, see Yoder's published lecture "Is There Historical Development of Theological Thought?" in *The Witness of the Holy Spirit: Proceedings of the Eighth Mennonite World Conference* (ed.) C. J. Dyck (Nappanee, Ind.: Evangel Press, 1968): 379–88.

B. Ecumenical Conversation Partners

Given what has already been said about Yoder's work, it is important to situate Yoder's ongoing conversations and disagreements with various theologians over the past four decades. In some instances Yoder builds upon the work of other theologians; in other cases, he clearly has felt the need to contest the very ways in which his interlocutors have characterized ecclesiological and ecumenical issues. Perhaps the best image to use to describe the significance of theologians such as Karl Barth, Reinhold and H. Richard Niebuhr, and Albert Outler for Yoder's own theological articulations is that of "ecumenical conversation partners." Other theologians, historians, ethicists, ecumenicists, and scholars — Harold Bender, Guy F. Hershberger, Franklin Littell, Richard Mouw, José Míguez Bonino, James Wm. McClendon, Jr., James Turner Johnson, and Stanley Hauerwas[25] — could also be identified in some sense as signifi-

---

25. Stanley Hauerwas is a theologian whose work is not discussed or engaged in the articles in this volume but whose work has had an effect on the ways in which Yoder's own work has been read in the past two decades. On several occasions, Hauerwas has described how he came to know Yoder's work (e.g., see "On What I Owe to Whom" in *The Peaceable Kingdom*, xxiv-xxv), and Hauerwas frequently cites Yoder's essays and books in his publications.

Given Yoder's somewhat self-effacing practice of dialogue, and given Hauerwas's interest in Yoder's work, over the past two decades (see Hauerwas's early essay on "The Nonresistant Church: The Theological Ethics of John Howard Yoder" in *Vision and Virtue* (Notre Dame: Fides Press [University of Notre Dame Press], 1974): 197–221) Hauerwas has represented Yoder's work in various contexts (see also Hauerwas's essay on "Messianic Pacifism," *Worldview* 16, 6 [June 1973]: 29–33). On one level, this representation has been helpful insofar as Yoder's work has become known to more people (graduate students, seminarians, laypeople) in diverse settings. But on another level, Hauerwas's representation has, indirectly, contributed to a misidentification of Yoder's work with Hauerwas's own position. While there is no question that Yoder and Hauerwas share many of the same theological concerns, it should not be assumed that Hauerwas's approach to ecclesiology and ecumenism is the same as Yoder's approach. For this reason, it may be useful to offer a brief explanation.

In part the difference is dispositional: Hauerwas is more of a contrarian than Yoder. But more substantively, the difference can be charted in terms of their location and biography. Hauerwas is a United Methodist who teaches at (the UMC denominationally affiliated) The Divinity School at Duke University; Yoder is a Mennonite. While Hauerwas is not averse to describing himself as "evangelical" in some contexts (while at the same time refusing any use of that label that excludes the catholicity of Christianity), he has never explicitly adopted the free church articulation of Yoder's ecclesiology. Rather, Hauerwas has refused to clarify his ecclesial stance in that way, preferring to describe himself on some occasions as a kind of "high

cant "conversation partners," but Yoder's dialogue and debate with these theologians are not as central for the essays in this collection as they would be for a collection of Yoder's essays on other topics.

Karl Barth

While working on his Th.D. in historical theology, Yoder studied with Karl Barth at the University of Basel in the 1950s during a time when Barth's own thinking about theological ethics arguably can be said to have been shifting. In the following decades Yoder has engaged Barth's work at several points for various purposes, in each case clearly building on what Barth had done but without agreeing with particular applications that Barth made of his own insights. By following this series of engagements, we can trace the emergence of Yoder's conviction that the conceptual basis of social ethics is found in (a free church) ecclesiology. Yoder's first engaging of Barth's work in relation to his own constructive interests appears in the 1964 Church Peace Mission pamphlet on *The Pacifism of Karl Barth.* Subsequently Yoder expanded another study into *Karl Barth and the Problem of War* (1970). In these works Yoder argued that had Barth followed his own best insights in III/4 of the *Church Dogmatics*, and not allowed the *Grenzfall* concept (the extreme case in which killing may be willed by God) to distract him, Barth's argumentation would have led him to a position that would best be characterized as Christian pacifism.[26]

In his earlier booklet *Christian Witness to the State* (1964, revised 1977), Yoder discusses the "politics" of the church, understood as a Christian community that is ordered in a particular way. In a footnote to his discussion of Barth's essay "Christian Community and Civil Community," Yoder comments:

---

church Mennonite" as a way of calling into question the helpfulness of the categories. Although he is every bit as interested as Yoder is in contesting the adequacy of the Troeltschian categories of the church-sect typology, Hauerwas, both in his rhetoric and in the substance of his argumentation, has chosen to emphasize the sectarian character of his theology (see *Resident Aliens,* for instance). Unlike Yoder, Hauerwas has not invested himself in such ecumenical engagements as the Faith and Order discussions or the Concept of the Believers Church conferences.

Other differences could also be indicated, but these comments may help the reader to grasp some of the important rhetorical and substantial differences in the way Hauerwas and Yoder approach ecclesiological and ecumenical questions.

26. John H. Yoder, *Karl Barth and the Problem of War* (Nashville: Abingdon, 1970): 118.

Karl Barth has advocated a form of "analogy" for relating church ethics derived from a faith commitment to the lower standards applicable to the civil community. In carrying out this undertaking Barth is not fully consistent; the Church side of the analogy is less important to him and less carefully developed than the civil side; with the *intention* of this approach by analogy we would, however, agree.[27]

While in *Christian Witness to the State,* Yoder draws upon J. H. Oldham's notion of "middle axioms"[28] to describe the way the church addresses the state,[29] in his subsequent work Yoder appears to move away from these formulations (although he does not explicitly repudiate the notion of "middle axioms") while moving progressively to make "the church side of the analogy" more explicit. In this sense, Yoder can be said to be struggling to identify ad hoc strategies for making discriminating ethical judgments while taking into account the ecclesiological significance of the church-world distinction.[30]

In Yoder's 1980 Stone Lectures "New World on the Way" at Princeton, he went beyond the "middle axioms" formula to articulate a more ecclesiologically specific conception. In the first Stone Lecture, "Why Ecclesiology Is Social Ethics" (see pp. 102–26), Yoder focuses on a passage from Karl Barth's discussion of "The Order of Community" in IV/2 of the *Church Dogmatics,* using it as a means of unfolding several claims. The most significant of the "Barthian insights" that Yoder explicates in the first of the Stone Lectures is that "the access to social ethics should consist in the exemplarity of the church as model/fore-taste/herald of the kingdom" (see p. 106). From this claim, Yoder goes on to argue that the originality of Barth's social ethics is located in his contention that the only necessary dualism for Christian ethics is the confession or non-confession of the lordship of Jesus Christ. By locating Barth as moving on a free church trajectory, Yoder is able to account for the tensions that surround Barth's use of analogies with respect to

27. John H. Yoder, *Christian Witness to the State,* Institute of Mennonite Studies Series No. 3 (Newton, Kans.: Faith and Life Press, 1964, rev. 1977): 17–18.

28. For a very helpful discussion of "Middle Axioms," and the origins of this notion in J. H. Oldham's preparatory work for the 1937 Oxford Conference on Life and Work, see the article on "Middle Axioms" by José Míguez Bonino in *The Dictionary of the Ecumenical Movement,* 675. As Míguez Bonino observes, "there is little reference to these axioms in recent ecumenical discussions" although "the question which this category addresses is still present" not only in European and American discussions but within the conversations spawned by Latin American liberation theologians.

29. See *Christian Witness to the State,* 32, 71–73.

30. I am indebted to Stanley Hauerwas for this way of putting the matter.

what he here calls "the wider wisdom" that exists in the civil community, while also explicating the narrative and doxological character of Barth's ecclesiological vision. In subsequent essays and a recent book, Yoder has gone on to explicate themes announced in the Stone Lectures, particularly the notion of "Sacrament as Social Process" (see the title of the last essay in this collection, pp. 359–73) and the ethical significance of biblical practices such as "binding and loosing," Eucharist, baptism, "the fullness of Christ," and "the rule of Paul," each of which are carried out "before the watching world."[31]

In his 1986 essay "Karl Barth: How His Mind Kept Changing," Yoder argued that after Vol. IV/2 of the *Church Dogmatics* "there is no refuting Barth's commitment to the free church vision."[32] But as Yoder would probably be the first to note, although Barth changed his mind on a number of issues (infant baptism, the specific character of God's transcendence, etc.), Barth never committed himself to a free church ecclesiology in the way in which Yoder has. In this respect, Yoder follows the theological — and specifically *ecclesiological* — implications that he has discerned in Barth's corpus within a different construal of the social embodiment of the church as Barth articulated it.

Reinhold Niebuhr

Reinhold Niebuhr's political ethical writings evoked some of Yoder's earliest arguments on war and peace. While Yoder and Niebuhr never directly exchanged views, and only rarely did their works appear in close proximity to one another,[33] there is no question that some of Yoder's most important essays from the 1950s through the early 1970s were constructed in relation to Niebuhr's arguments. For example, in his 1955 essay "Reinhold Niebuhr and Christian Pacifism" Yoder offered a respectful assessment and critique of Niebuhr's arguments in "Why the Christian Church Is Not Pacifist" (1939, 1940).[34] The first half

31. These five practices of discipleship are described in Yoder's recently published study *Body Politics* (Nashville: Discipleship Resources, 1993).

32. John H. Yoder, "Karl Barth: How His Mind Kept Changing" in *How Karl Barth Changed My Mind*, ed. Donald K. McKim (Grand Rapids: Eerdmans, 1986): 171.

33. In the August 18, 1954, issue of *The Christian Century* Reinhold Niebuhr and John Howard Yoder had articles printed next to one another. Niebuhr's essay, "Co-Existence or Total War?" appeared on pp. 971–73; Yoder's essay, "Let Evanston Speak on War!" was printed on pp. 973–74.

34. Niebuhr's "Why the Christian Church Is Not Pacifist" was published in

of his essay offers a careful summary and explication of Niebuhr's argument against Christian pacifism; the latter part offers a carefully reasoned evaluation of the merits of Niebuhr's argument in which Yoder notes agreements and disagreements with Niebuhr. Only in the last few pages of the article did Yoder unfold his own criticisms of the theological basis of Niebuhr's critique of Christian pacifism. There Yoder locates the heart of their disagreement in Niebuhr's conception of redemption, which Yoder argues is inadequate because of the absence of the doctrines of resurrection, the church, and regeneration, each of which Yoder describes as "works of the Holy Spirit."[35]

Although each of Yoder's arguments in refutation of Niebuhr's critique are important, here I will only call attention to the *ecclesiological* focus of Yoder's counter-argument. Yoder prefaced his comments about the church with the observation that the only time the word "church" is used in Niebuhr's essay is to "criticize the medieval synthesis of Catholicism." According to Yoder, this lacuna is central not only because it is inadequate on historical grounds but also because it exposes a central flaw in Niebuhr's political ethic.

> For the body of Christ differs from other social bodies in that it is not less moral than its individual members. If being a perfectly loyal American, a free mason, or a bourgeois identifies a man with that group egoism in such a way as to make him less loving than he would be as an individual, the contrary is true of being a member of Christ. Thus the thesis of *Moral Man and Immoral Society* falls down in the crucial case, the only one which is really decisive for Christian ethics.[36]

The significance of Niebuhr's argument, then, not only for how we understand Yoder's approach to social ethics and pacifist argumentation, but also for the way he proceeds to articulate his ecclesiology, is very great indeed. In his 1972 study of *The Politics of Jesus*, Yoder identifies Reinhold Niebuhr's role in articulating the six theses of "mainstream ethics" and goes on to juxtapose his own conception of "messianic ethics" with that of Niebuhr. While *The Politics of Jesus* was primarily a study of New Testament writings, very early in that work

1939 as a pamphlet and also as part of *Christianity and Power Politics* (New York: Charles Scribner's Sons, 1940): 1–32.

35. John H. Yoder, "Reinhold Niebuhr and Christian Pacifism," *Mennonite Quarterly Review* 29/2 (April 1955): 115–16.

36. Ibid., 115.

Yoder raised questions about "the authority of the hermeneutic assumptions" (such as those found in Niebuhr's argumentation) that suggest that "Jesus himself . . . is not normative for ethics."[37]

Later, in *Christian Attitudes to War, Peace, and Revolution: A Companion to Bainton* (1983) Yoder described the way in which Niebuhr influenced Mennonite theologians in the post–World War II era.[38] Yoder's summaries of the "Niebuhrian-influenced" articles of Donavan Smucker and John Mumaw indicate that, among other things, these Mennonite and Anabaptist writers had failed to see the degree to which the categories (non-resistance vs. non-violence) of Niebuhr's argumentation was undermining the basis of their own discipleship ethic. In contrast to these and other members of his own communion, Yoder has continued to argue against the usefulness of the Niebuhrian framework by contesting both its hermeneutic assumptions and its ecclesiological inadequacies.

H. Richard Niebuhr

Yoder's engagement with H. Richard Niebuhr has taken a slightly different form, although in some respects Yoder argues that the brothers Niebuhr share some of the same views. In the first essay of this collection, "The Otherness of the Church" (see pp. 53–64), Yoder argues against the "Christ and Culture" typology from the vantage that it is "unfair to history and unfruitful for ethics" (p. 62). Yoder argues that it is fallacious to assume that "culture 'as such' . . . is a tangible reality patient of being related to 'Christ' in one of the five typical ways. . . . This is to attribute to the world that intrinsic ontological dignity that neither the New Testament nor the Old allows it to claim" (p. 62). Here Yoder characteristically refuses to grant *autonomous* significance to the reality of the world, while he also argues that for theological reasons we should "affirm the reality of the world" both as God's creation and for what, by God's grace, it will become as part of the restitution of all things.

In his essay, "How H. Richard Niebuhr Reasons: A Critique of *Christ and Culture*" (1964, 1986), Yoder argues that the problem with the "Christ and Culture" typology can be located in terms of the "monolithic logic" by which data that might conceivably call into question the

---

37. John H. Yoder, *The Politics of Jesus*, 22–23.

38. John H. Yoder, *Christian Attitudes to War, Peace, and Revolution: A Companion to Bainton*, 356–69.

adequacy of the "types" are excluded. In this respect, many of Niebuhr's students and others who have appropriated this typology from him are not as careful as their teacher (at his best) was in recognizing the limits of the typology. Although Yoder provides additional criticisms of the theological and epistemological presumptions of Niebuhr's typology of "Christ and Culture," perhaps the most telling criticism comes where Yoder identifies the most important of "the standards of the ethicist's judgment" for Niebuhr, namely "his unquestioning commitment to the necessity of managing society from the top and his identification of political control with culture."[39]

Implicitly, Yoder's essay "Sacrament as Social Process: Christ the Transformer of Culture" (see pp. 359–73) provides an alternative to the Niebuhrian conception, particularly insofar as Yoder offers analysis that is compatible with the view that the Christian community is "a sociological entity in its own right," a contention that lies at the basis of Yoder's critique of Niebuhr.[40] Here again, Yoder is attempting to foster a conversation that centers not so much on traditions as on "apostolic practices" that can be identified within the writings of the Bible, particularly the New Testament writings. In this respect, Yoder is continually calling for a very different approach to catholicity than that found in mainstream approaches to ecumenism in the twentieth century.

Albert Outler

Yoder's "ecumenical conversation" with the veteran Protestant ecumenist and historical theologian Albert Outler is not as easy to describe as his relationship with the brothers Niebuhr. On the one hand, Yoder builds upon Outler's work insofar as the latter has articulated a rationale for using the "common traditions" of the church as a basis for proceeding with ecumenical dialogue. On the other hand, throughout his career Yoder has repeatedly insisted — as Outler never did in any explicit way — that part of what must be assessed in ecumenical dialogue is heresy and schism. These similarities and differences appear at several points in the career of each man. In 1957, Outler's book *The Christian Tradition and the Unity We Seek* was published. That same year, Yoder published "The Unity We Seek: A Historic Free Church View"

---

39. "How H. Richard Niebuhr Reasons: A Critique of *Christ and Culture*," in John Howard Yoder, Diane M. Yeager, and Glen H. Stassen, *Authentic Transformation: A New Vision of Christ and Culture*, forthcoming from Abingdon Press, 1995.

40. Ibid., pp. 48–49; see also "Sacrament as Social Process," below (359–73).

(see pp. 221–30) that argued for a conception of ecumenism that is centers on, among other things, a clearly specified linkage of church discipline to ethics as opposed to ethical pluralism.

Less than a decade later, Outler was a primary proponent of the "traditions and Tradition" formula found in the 1963 Faith and Order Assembly at Montreal. This formulation

> used "Tradition" with a capital T to refer globally to all that each Christian community and all the Christian communities together think and speak. It is a stream of handing-down processes which is prior to and wider than the tradition of any one denominational communion. Secondly, the "traditions" (small t) are the several sets of sectarian understandings. They may properly be cultivated in separate spaces, but by their nature do not justify dividing the church. Thirdly, "tradition" (singular with a lower case t) means the event or process of handing down the substance of a community's faith. Everyone affirms all three. Since it is fitting that local "traditions" (lower case plural) should differ, we can recognize one another without demanding uniformity or centralization.[41]

In his essay "The Authority of Tradition" in *The Priestly Kingdom* (1984) Yoder argues that this conception is insufficient to account for the problems presented in ecumenical dialogue:

> We are not plagued merely by a hard-to-manage diversity, by a wealth of complementary variations on the same theme. We are faced with error, into which believers are seduced by evil powers seeking to corrupt the church and disqualify her witness. To denounce those errors we must appeal to the common traditions from which those who fall into error are falling away, which they previously had confessed together with us.[42]

The problem, stated in Yoder's terms, is not one of "integration" into a richer pluralism, but rather Yoder wants to probe more deeply into the question of *how* tradition exercises authority, especially as this latter question evokes the related question of the authority of Scripture. Contrary to the way that Outler et al. structured the problem of "the traditions and the Tradition" at Montreal, Yoder contends that there is another, more fruitful way of characterizing this conundrum.

41. John H. Yoder, "The Authority of Tradition" in *The Priestly Kingdom*, 64.
42. Ibid., 69.

The clash is not tradition versus Scripture but faithful tradition versus irresponsible tradition. Only if we can with Jesus and Paul . . . denounce *wrong* traditioning, can we validly affirm the rest. Scripture comes on the scene not as a receptacle of all possible inspired truths, but rather as a witness to the historical baseline of the communities' origins and thereby as link to the historicity of their Lord's past presence.[43]

In one of Yoder's more recent essays (see "Catholicity in Search of Location," pp. 300–322) he returns to Outler's *Christian Tradition and the Unity We Seek* and builds upon Outler's discussion for the purpose of exploring the problems associated with "locating" the dialogical process in the midst of the various traditions of "catholicity," especially where it is not clear that Christian Scripture is given decisive authority.

Of course, both Outler and Yoder would emphasize the importance of scriptural authority in some sense. However, Outler's way of linking the authority of Scripture to a carefully defined notion of the "Great Tradition" ends up finessing the conflict among Scripture, reason, tradition, and experience (the so-called Wesleyan quadrilateral), whereas Yoder tries to engage the hard questions that arise when different conceptions of the witness of Scripture in relation to the Great Tradition clash. The similarities and differences between these two approaches to ecumenism are manifested in other ways as well, including the ways they assess the relative importance of restorationist traditions in church renewal and, in turn, their conceptions of catholicity.

C. The "Free Church" Vision of the Church

Yoder's ecclesiological and ecumenical essays have almost always been written in the awareness of the distinctiveness of "radical reformation" stance of the historic free church tradition. Historians such as George Hunston Williams and Roland Bainton used the term "free church," among other things, to designate the non-"magisterial" reformation churches. Unfortunately, the term "free church," while useful in many contexts to designate non-state church communions, eventually proved conceptually imprecise for the kind of ecclesiological focus that theologians from this broad tradition wanted to explore. The term "believers' church" originated in Max Weber's study of *The Protestant Ethic and*

43. Ibid.

the Spirit of Capitalism where he used it to describe the Anabaptists and Quakers.[44] In the middle-1960s, theologians began to use the term "believers' church" to discuss the commonalities and differences of churches that were, in some sense, neither Protestant nor Catholic in the mainstream uses of those designations. As James Leo Garrett, Jr., has observed, the use of the term "believers' church" arose as an attempt "to fashion an instrument of identification, however imperfect, for that segment of the Protestant Christian heritage which is distinct both from Classical Protestant and from Catholic — Roman, Eastern, Anglican, et al. — understandings of the church. . . ."[45]

Free Church and "Believers' Church" Conceptions

The origins of the "believers' church" conception of ecclesiology can be located in the context of the sixteenth-century Reformation in which various groups of believers' churches came into being. Some of these groups were labeled "Anabaptists" and were opposed by the "official reformers" who sought to implement reforms through governing authorities. Not as well known is the fact that some of the leaders of the magisterial reformation also envisioned believers' church orders. The best example of this phenomenon is found in Martin Luther's 1526 preface to "The German Mass and Order of Service,"[46] where the Wittenberg reformer describes three kinds of divine service. First, there is the mass in Latin, which Luther did not intend to change or abrogate. The second is the vernacular (German) mass and Order of Service, which should be arranged "for the sake of the unlearned layfolk" for use in public with "those who do not believe and who are not yet Christians"[47] in mind.

> The third kind of service should be a truly evangelical order and should not be held in a public place for all sorts of people. But those who want to be Christians in earnest and who profess the gospel with

44. Max Weber, *The Protestant Ethic and the Spirit of Capitalism* (trans.) T. Parsons (New York: Charles Scribner's Sons, 1958): 145–46. See also Donald Durnbaugh, *The Believers' Church: The History and Character of Radical Protestantism* (Scottdale, Penn.: Herald Press, 1985): Preface to First Edition, p. ix.

45. "Preface" by the editor (James Leo Garrett, Jr.), *The Concept of the Believers' Church*, 5.

46. Ulrich S. Leupold, ed., *Hymns and Liturgy*, Vol. 53 of *Luther's Works*, ed. Helmut T. Lehman (Philadelphia: Fortress Press, 1965): 61–90.

47. Ibid., 63–64.

hand and mouth should sign their names and meet alone to pray, to read, to baptize, to receive the sacrament, and to do other Christian works. According to this order, those who do not lead Christian lives could be known, reproved, corrected, cast out, or excommunicated, according to the rule of Christ, Matthew 18 [:15–17]. Here one should also solicit benevolent gifts to be willingly given and distributed to the poor, according to St. Paul's example, II Corinthians 9. Here would be no need of much and elaborate singing. Here one could set up a brief and neat order for baptism and the sacrament and center everything on the Word, prayer and love.[48]

Luther never worked out the "third order" sketched here, and ultimately he concluded that it was impractical to create such a believers' church given the mixture of people, some of whom were believing Christians and some of whom were not. As Roland Bainton has observed: "Luther's dilemma was that he wanted both a confessional church based on personal faith and experience, and a territorial church including all in a given locality. If he were forced to choose, he would take his stand with the masses, and this was the direction in which he moved."[49]

While Luther elected to secure the Reformation by consolidating the *territorial* church in concert with the prince and other governing authorities, other Christians — in Europe and elsewhere — sought to establish "free churches," i.e., not sponsored by the state. As Donald Durnbaugh and other historians have shown, over the past four centuries various groups ranging from Separatist Puritans in the seventeenth century to Lutheran pietists and Wesleyan Methodists in eighteenth-century England to Disciples of Christ in nineteenth-century America to the Confessing Church in Germany and Pentecostal churches in Latin America in the twentieth century have displayed the believers' church pattern that Luther himself articulated but did not, strictly speaking, attempt to put into practice.[50]

The Concept of the Believers' Church Conferences

While it is possible to identify a common set of characteristics that, more or less, can be found in particular communions of the believers'

48. Ibid. Brackets from original of English translation in *Luther's Works.*
49. Roland H. Bainton, *Here I Stand: A Life of Martin Luther* (Nashville: Abingdon Press, 1950): 311, as cited in Durnbaugh, *The Believers' Church,* 4.
50. For a survey of various historical expressions of the believers' church concept, see Donald Durnbaugh, *The Believers' Church,* 39–204.

church paradigm, this *does not mean* that there are no tensions between these communions. On the contrary, participants in one of the ongoing Conferences on the Concept of the Believers' Church would find significant disagreements among the representative theologians from communions as different as the Assemblies of God, Churches of Christ, Church of the Brethren, Mennonite, Mennonite Brethren, Society of Friends, and various kinds of Baptists. Since 1967, these similarities and differences have been discussed on a semi-regular basis in the series of Conferences on the Concept of the Believers' Church, gatherings in which Yoder has played an active role. In fact, Yoder's involvement with this ongoing series of theological discussions provides another example of the way he engages, fosters, and participates in ecumenical discussion.

The first of these conferences was held on the campus of Southern Baptist Theological Seminary, Louisville, Kentucky, June 26–30, 1967. As Yoder recalled in a recent article narrating the evolution of this series of exploratory conversations,

> The planners of that conference limited its study objectives to clarifying a concept. . . . We did not ask whether infant baptism is justified biblically or according to this or that system of sacramental theology. We went a step deeper, asking not about the theory of ordinances but about the lived ecclesiology. We asked not whether the believers' church vision is theologically correct but whether it is a helpful tool of classification and interpretation, usable alongside or in contrast to traditionally more dogmatic or systematic differentiae.[51]

This concentration on ecclesiology has remained the focus of the conferences over the past quarter century.

The keynote speaker for that first conference was Dr. Franklin Littell, a United Methodist theologian and the author of *The Anabaptist View of the Church: The Origins of Sectarian Protestantism* (1954, rev. 1961). Littell also happened to be the person whose opening address on "The Historic Free Church Tradition" for the Seminar on the Church in the World at Earlham College, Richmond, Indiana, in June 1964, had provided the occasion for an earlier gathering of theologians from the Mennonite, Quaker, and Church of the Brethren traditions that laid the basis for the Louisville Conference.[52] Littell's address highlighted the

51. John H. Yoder, "The Believers' Church Conferences in Historical Perspective," 8.
52. See editorial comment at the beginning of Littell's address in Garrett, *The*

26

"basic principles" of the Believers' Church paradigm: voluntary membership, believers' baptism, separation from the world, mission and witness of all members, church discipline, the rejection of the state-church alliance, which in this instance Littell interpreted in terms of the importance of understanding the *secularity* of government in the wake of the collapse of Christendom.[53]

Yoder's own Louisville address, entitled "A People in the World" (see pp. 65–101) constituted one of the principal attempts to offer a "theological interpretation" of the concept of the believers' church. Characteristically, Yoder links the vocation of the church to the meaning of history itself.

> The work of God is the calling of a people, whether in the Old Covenant or the New. The church is then not simply the bearer of the message of reconciliation, in the way a newspaper or a telephone company can bear any message with which it is entrusted. Nor is the church simply the result of a message, as an alumni association is the product of a school or the crowd in the theater is the product of the reputation of the film. That men and women are called together to a new social wholeness is itself the work of God that gives meaning to history, from which both personal conversion (whereby individuals are called into this meaning) and missionary instrumentalities are derived. (see p. 74)

This discussion, which reflects Yoder's reading of Ephesians 2–3 (esp. 3:10), once again illustrates the distinctiveness of Yoder's way of interpreting human history in relation to Christian Scripture.

It would be a mistake to think that Yoder's interpretation of the theological significance of the church as a *visible* people in the world met with no dissent at Louisville.[54] However, there is reason to believe that this essay, which up until the present has only been available as part of the proceedings of the conference, has proved to be provocative for a new

---

Concept of the Believers' Church, 15. Of course, Littell was not the only theologian whose efforts were crucial in bringing about the 1967 gathering at Louisville. As Yoder notes in his essay "Another Free Church Perspective on Baptist Ecumenism" (see pp. 262–76), the initiatives of the Dutch Mennonite Jan A. Oosterbaan were also very important in bringing about the first Conference on the Concept of the Believers' Church.

53. Ibid., see especially 27–32.

54. For example, see Garrett's commentary on the response of C. Emanuel Carlson, then the executive director of the Baptist Joint Committee on Public Affairs, to Yoder's presentation in *The Concept of the Believers' Church,* 250–52.

generation of theologians and ethicists from Reformed, Lutheran, and United Methodist traditions interested in renewal of the church.[55] In this respect, Yoder's work — like some of the Conferences on the Concept of the Believers' Church, which have "reconnoiter[ed] the border between radical and moderate reformation"[56] — has encouraged a few theologians in mainstream Protestant traditions to reconsider the validity of traditional mainstream suspicions about the radical reformation stance.

Shortly after the Louisville conference, Yoder proposed that a group of believers' church theologians convene to expand the discussion. In the proposal Yoder provided "An Inventory of the Situation" — namely that the believers' church stance was not only of continuing, perhaps even "increasing relevance," but also that there was evidence that "some thinkers within the believers' church denominations" were becoming more ready to overcome the silence in which they had been living ecumenically.[57] After calling attention to some of the practical difficulties facing such a proposed group, Yoder proceeded to identify the theological task of the proposed group. The first item on that list was to "test and to clarify the central witness that is common to the believers' churches and to do so in the form that this must take in the encounter with other traditions."[58] Such a group did convene on the margins of the 1968 Assembly of the World Council of Churches at Uppsala, but no continuing body resulted from that consultation. However, the (North American) Conferences of the Believers' Church have continued on and off since 1968,[59] the most recent one — on the topic of "The Rule of Christ" (Matthew 18:15–20) — having taken place at Goshen College, Goshen, Indiana, in May 1992.

55. E.g., see George Hunsinger's discussion of Yoder's address in "Where the Battle Rages: Confessing Christ in America Today," *Dialog* 26 (1987): 264–74; Reinhard Hütter, "The Church: Midwife of History or Witness to the Eschaton?" *The Journal of Religious Ethics* 18/1 (Spring 1990): 27–54; Michael G. Cartwright, "The Practice and Performance of Scripture: Toward a Communal Hermeneutic for Christian Ethics," *The Annual for the Society of Christian Ethics 1988* (Georgetown University Press, 1988): 31–53.

56. Yoder uses these words to describe the focus on the 1989 Conference on Balthasar Hubmaier.

57. "Proposal for a group of 'Believers' Church' Theologians" drafted by John H. Yoder, August 1968, unpublished manuscript, typescript p. 1.

58. Ibid., typescript p. 3.

59. For a helpful review of the quarter-century history of the Conferences on the Concept of the Believers' Church, see John H. Yoder "The Believers' Church Conferences in Historical Perspective" in *The Mennonite Quarterly Review* 65 (January 1991): 5–19.

Typologies and Ecclesiology

As the preceding discussion indicates, Yoder's approach to ecclesiology and ecumenism is clearly grounded in the ongoing discussion of the distinctiveness of the radical Protestant stance that some have called "free church" and others designate as the "believers' church" tradition. Each of these ways of proceeding involves the use of a typology as a heuristic device for the purpose of clarifying ecclesiological questions. To his credit, while Yoder has employed these typologies for the purpose of clarifying the historical dimension of the debate between mainstream and radical Protestants and thereby to "locate a stance" within the spectrum, he has never placed much stock in the typologies themselves. In fact, as he has noted on numerous occasions in various contexts, some typologies tend to falsify reality and some typologies serve the useful purpose of clarifying reality. In sum, there are good uses of typologies and bad uses of typologies; we simply must exercise care when we use them.

One of Yoder's primary concerns about the use of any given typology is whether it will advance the discussion, i.e., allow honest disagreements, or will it obscure the issues that are at stake and lead to the kind of agreements that are illusory, if not dishonest. As he indicated in a note to his essay "The Hermeneutics of Peoplehood" in *The Priestly Kingdom*, "At the same time that I yield to historical typology in order to locate a stance, I must object to the way such typologies tend to freeze the conversation." Elsewhere Yoder has (on his own[60] and with others[61]) argued about the confusing uses to which such typologies can be put and the consequences for evangelical ethics. At the same time, Yoder does continue to use typologies and acknowledges that in some sense it is necessary to identify "types" for the purpose of clarifying ecclesiological disagreements.

Yoder has never used *any one typology* exclusively in his ecclesiological writings, although in the essays in this volume the "free church" designation is used in many of the essays from the 1950s to 1970s. However, throughout his career Yoder has been very thorough in laying out the conceptual juxtaposition of the Constantinian vision of the church, "Christendom," with the free church vision that questions the

60. John H. Yoder, "Reformed Versus Anabaptist Social Strategies: An Inadequate Typology," *TSF* [Theological Students' Fellowship] *Bulletin* 8 (May–June 1985): 2–10.
61. Richard J. Mouw and John H. Yoder, "Evangelical Ethics and the Anabaptist-Reformed Dialogue," *The Journal of Religious Ethics* 17 (Fall 1989): 121–37.

faithfulness of the Christendom model. As Yoder describes in his essay on "The Disavowal of Constantine: An Alternative Perspective on Interfaith Dialogue" (see pp. 242–61), the anti-Constantinian critique is substantial.

> Without seeking completeness, a few of the recurrent accents of the anti-Constantinian critique should be noted:
> - its concern for the particular, historical, and therefore Jewish quality and substance of New Testament faith in Jesus;
> - its holistic inclusion of communal and cultural dimensions of "way of life" within the faith (decision-making patterns, e.g., or economics) as religious issues, rather than making them peripheral behind the priority of spirituality or dogma;
> - its insistence on the voluntariness of membership in the visible church, usually expressed in the baptism of people old enough to confess responsibly their own faith;
> - its rejection of the support, defense, and control of the church by the civil rulers;
> - its relativizing of the hierarchical dimensions of the church in favor of maximum freedom and wholeness in the local congregational fellowship.
>
> Behind these more evident, formal distinctives lie a specific view of the place of Scripture in the church, a specific eschatology, specific views on certain ethical issues, a specific approach to sacraments, ministry, and on down the line. (pp. 247–48)

Clearly, as this passage demonstrates, from Yoder's perspective there is an *ongoing* argument between those churches that bear witness to a vision of radical reform and those churches whose conception of reform is more moderate or less thoroughgoing. In this respect, Luther's ambivalence about the need for a "third order" has spawned a debate about whether twentieth-century American Protestant churches are examples of "Protestantism without reformation."[62] However, because in the American context there is no "state church" as such — and, therefore, all churches are in some technical sense "free churches" — the

---

62. George Hunsinger, "Barth, Barmen, and the Confessing Church Today," *Katallagete* (Summer 1985): 14–27. Hunsinger borrows the phrase "Protestantism without reformation" from Dietrich Bonhoeffer, whose essay by that title was published in *No Rusty Swords: Letters, Lectures, and Notes . . . from the Collected Works of Dietrich Bonhoeffer*, Vol. 1, ed. Edwin H. Robertson and trans. Edwin H. Robertson and John Bowden, 92–118.

debate about the character of reformation of the church has taken shape in relation to the *theological integrity* of what it means to be a free church in relation to the wider culture. Because the absence of moral integrity is one of the primary ways in which the *faithfulness* of the church is undermined, the free church critique calls into question those structures, dispositions, and justifications that deny the necessity of accountability in Christian discipleship. Divergent conceptions of catholicity, in turn, are enfolded within this debate about the character of the reformation in the life of the church.

III. Radical Reform *and* Radical Catholicity: An Alternative Approach to Ecumenism

Given the challenges posed by the believers' church conception, it is not surprising that theologians from mainstream Protestant traditions have sometimes taken offense at arguments that question the faithfulness of historic Christian practices. In response, these theologians have sometimes bristled at the very notion of a believers' church ecclesiology. What has often gone unnoticed in assessments of the free church critique by mainstream Christian theologians, whether Protestant or Catholic, is that the "free church position is intrinsically unfinished,"[63] in the sense of the classic phrase *ecclesia semper reformanda,* as Yoder has noted in another connection. Arguably one of Yoder's greatest contributions over the past four decades has been to display the *unfinished* character of free church ecclesiology in his various essays where he has engaged ecumenical themes. For example, as Yoder states in "Binding and Loosing" (see pp. 323–58):

> The position suggested here may seem to gather together the dangers of several ecclesiastical scarecrows. It gives more authority to the church than does Rome, trusts more to the Holy Spirit than does Pentecostalism, has more respect for the individual than humanism, makes moral standards more binding than puritanism, is more open to the given situation than the "new morality." If practiced it would change the life of churches more fundamentally than has yet been suggested by the perennially popular discussions of changing church structures." (p. 325)

63. John H. Yoder, "How Karl Barth's Mind Kept Changing," 171.

That the preceding comments occur in the context of a discussion of fraternal admonition is no more accidental than the implicit argument is for the renewal of the church. For, very often, Yoder's approach to ecumenicity takes the form of admonition, and he in turn has invited "mutual correction" from others, thereby seeking to elicit the kind of ongoing dialogue between the various communions which he would argue always characterizes the church, in the fullest and most ecclesiologically specific sense of the word.

Dialogue

There is no question that John Yoder writes in the awareness of significant others while refusing to treat interlocutors wholly as Other. As this introductory essay has already demonstrated, Yoder's primary strategy of engagement involves the attempt to call the churches into a conversation about those things that, like Christian Scripture, they arguably already share in common. Readers of Part Three — " 'Free Church' Responses" — of this volume will find Yoder engaging a variety of different ecclesiological perspectives — Quaker, Methodist, Church of England, Roman Catholic, Baptist, Faith and Order — often in response to invitations that he has received to represent the historic free church tradition in various ecumenical symposia, but also in diverse cultural (Latin American, the Middle East, Pacific Islands) and linguistic (German, French, Spanish) as well as ecclesial (Protestant, Catholic, Free Church) settings.

What is most fascinating about the articles in Part Three is that Yoder always writes for a *particular* audience. Unlike many contemporary writers who are so adept at twisting the agenda of a given conference or symposium into an opportunity for presenting their own agenda that they effectively evade or subvert the questions even at the cost of *thwarting* possibilities for further dialogue, Yoder typically accepts as a given the agenda of whatever group has asked him to speak, write, or respond.

One of the reasons for including the different responses included in Part Three (some of which overlap with one another in significant ways) is to show how Yoder's way of articulating the free church perspective has occurred in significantly different cultural, linguistic, and ecclesial contexts of dialogue, and in the midst of diverse agendas for discussion and dispute, thereby exhibiting a consistency and constancy that goes beyond mere restatement of one's views. If, after taking these factors into account, one then factors in the fact that Yoder, being a polyglot, has given some of these same lectures and presentations in several different languages, it becomes clear that questions of "translation" and "dialogue" are by no means merely abstract theoretical notions for Yoder's ecclesiological and ecumenical explorations.[64] Nor would it be correct to assume that Yoder is unaware of the theoretical issues, at the levels of epistemology, ontology, and validation,[65] involved in trying to communicate the good news about "the new world on the way."

It is equally important to note that the notion of ecumenical dialogue also includes the communion within which Yoder holds membership, the Mennonite Church. Yoder's lecture on "The Imperative of Christian Unity" (see pp. 289–99) offers but one of several examples of the kinds of arguments Yoder has made within his own denomination over the past four decades for the importance of engaging the ecumenical movement in disputation and dialogue. Yoder's earlier pamphlet on *The Ecumenical Movement and the Faithful Church* (1958) illustrates many of the same themes as the lecture cited, although the context of discussion is twenty-five years earlier.

Mission and Translatability

One of the most difficult decisions that I have faced as editor of this collection of essays has been the question of what to leave out of it.

64. Although, this same point could be made with respect to other instances in which Yoder's way of engaging in response or rebuttal creates new possibilities for dialogue and disagreement in the disciplines of history, ethics, and biblical studies, these contributions are beyond the scope of what I am attempting to assess in this introductory essay. A memorable example of this can be found in Yoder's contribution to the symposium on James M. Gustafson's *Ethics from a Theocentric Perspective* (Chicago: University of Chicago Press, 1984, 1986) held at Washington and Lee University, 26–28 September 1985. In his contribution on "Theological Revision and the Burden of Particular Identity" Yoder deliberately "represented" not himself, or other interests, but "the classical mainstream of Western Protestant moral thought," which he noted was not otherwise represented by the participants in the panel discussion. For the published version of Yoder's essay, see *James M. Gustafson's Theocentric Ethics: Interpretations and Assessments*, ed. Harlan R. Beckley and Charles M. Swezey (Macon, Ga.: Mercer University Press, 1988): 62–89. Thanks to the good offices of Harlan R. Beckley and Charles M. Swezey, the oral discussion of Yoder's presentation has also been made available, op. cit., 89–94.

65. E.g., see Yoder's essay "On Not Being Ashamed of the Gospel: Particularity, Pluralism, and Validation," *Faith and Philosophy: Journal of the Society of Christian Philosophers* 9/3 (July 1992): 285–300.

Nowhere is this more notable than with respect to Yoder's publications in the area of missiology, which arguably should be paired with his contributions to ecclesiology and ecumenism. For, it must also be said that Yoder's commitment to dialogical process as a form of discipleship can be specified in a correlative commitment, which for lack of a better phrase can be described ás his conviction of the "translatability" of the good news of Jesus Christ. Here again, Yoder's characteristic way of proceeding is not only relevant to contemporary discussions of trans-latability in Christian ethics and moral philosophy[66] but also his body of work can be said, at least implicitly, to provide a contrasting model in the sense that Yoder engages all invitations for dialogue *as if* trans-lation is possible but with an openness to taking seriously the objections that others might present about the problems faced by the task of being a missionary in a world of seemingly incommensurate perspectives, ideologies, cultures, and histories.

Of course, Yoder's working assumption — that translation can continue in the face of manifold problems related to inculturation, homogeneity, etc. — is not intended as a way to ignore the difficulties. Rather, in line with the previous discussion of his disposition to the apocalyptic writings of Christian Scripture, Yoder simply insists that we take each problem as it comes, without assuming that any one problem is ultimately formidable in some global or monolithic sense. Nor does it mean that understanding is always the result of the ex-change. In fact, Yoder has had to confront numerous misunderstandings of his work and of his comments, and invariably he patiently addresses and tries to remove the misunderstandings. In this respect, Yoder's own transdisciplinary practice, i.e., his refusal to give to any one discipline explanatory privilege — whether one is talking about the epistemologi-cal status of apocalyptic perspectives, or the cosmological vision that is presumed by consequentialist reasoning, or the foundationalist con-cern to settle all questions a priori, or the "public concern" for having nothing scandalous to say — can also be seen to be anchored in a commitment to translation for the purpose of carrying out the church's mission in, to, as well as *for* the world.

---

66. See the recent discussions of Alasdair MacIntyre, *After Virtue: An Essay in Moral Theory* (Notre Dame: University of Notre Dame Press, 1984); Jeffrey Stout, *Ethics After Babel: The Languages of Morals and Their Discontents* (Boston: Beacon Press, 1988); and Stephen Fowl, "Can Horace Talk with the Hebrews? Translatability and Moral Disagreement in MacIntyre and Stout," *Journal of Religious Ethics* 19/1 (Spring 1991): 1–20.

Postmodern?

In a sense, the previous comments can be taken as an indication of why Yoder has been identified by at least one prominent literary critic as a postmodern theologian,[67] precisely because Yoder's work has *not* been determined by "modernist" hermeneutical strategies ranging from Rudolf Bultmann's "demythologizing" project to the "therapeutic religion"[68] of Norman Vincent Peale, Robert Schuller, et al. If Yoder's work is in some sense postmodern it is precisely because he *does not assume* that his discourse is context independent, any more than he assumes that the Bible is to be interpreted as if the context does not matter. Finally, although Yoder probably would never put it this way, even the style of Yoder's engagement in dialogue and disputation reflects the awareness of the "politics" of writing itself. Yoder's work is always *political* in the sense that he is always engaged in the production of discourse that should matter — for the church *and* for the world.[69]

This last point is particularly important. One way to describe the difference between Stanley Hauerwas and John Yoder is that Yoder prefers to think of himself as disposed to be "for the nations" (in the missiological sense of the phrase) and not "against the nations" (to borrow the title of one of Hauerwas's earlier books). Thus, in contrast to Hauerwas, Yoder does not want to say or imply that *one has to be converted* to a particular way of thinking in order to understand an argument or position. Conversion may or may not occur, Yoder would argue, but the intelligibility of one's arguments or communication of the good news of the gospel does not necessitate conversion *prior* to understanding.

Characteristically, Yoder has no more interest in claiming to be postmodern than he does in claiming to be modern; the labels simply do not apply. However, Yoder's insistence upon the viability of apocalyptic views of history and the cosmos, without arguing either that it is fundamentally discontinuous with modernity — on epistemological or foundationalist grounds — or that it is not, distinguishes him from a variety of contemporary theologians and philosophers, many of

67. See Fredric Jameson, *Postmodernism Or, the Cultural Logic of Late Capitalism* (Durham, N.C.: Duke University Press, 1991): 390–91. It should be noted that Jameson not only misidentifies Yoder as an "Amish pacifist" but uses the word "fundamentalist" in a very idiosyncratic sense in his discussion of Yoder's work.

68. I borrow this phrase from Roger Betsworth's discussion of "therapeutic religion" in *Social Ethics: An Examination of American Moral Traditions* (Louisville: Westminster/John Knox Press, 1990): 92–98.

69. I am indebted to Stanley Hauerwas for this insight.

whom *would* claim to be modern or postmodern. Here as elsewhere, Yoder invites those who want to raise such questions to present them one at a time, without presuming that any one form of the query constitutes the means for a global assessment of the problem of continuity and discontinuity.[70]

Retrieval and Tradition

Over the past decade, interest has renewed in the role of "living traditions" in shaping moral discourse in all spheres of society.[71] In his study *After Virtue: An Essay in Moral Theory*, Àlasdair MacIntyre has contested the Enlightenment tradition's claims of objectivity and exposed the fragmentation of contemporary moral discourse in relation to the influence of logical positivism. In his more recent study *Three Rival Versions of Moral Enquiry*, MacIntyre has contested the adequacy of the modernist project of the encyclopedia and the postmodernist genre of genealogy as traditions of moral inquiry.[72] MacIntyre's own project, which can essentially be described as a project of retrieval, is cast within a reconstruction of the Aristotelian tradition of ethics and, more specifically, within the Thomistic version of that tradition of moral inquiry. As such, MacIntyre's attempted reconstruction of a teleological ethic is designed not only as an alternative to Nietzsche's genealogical approach to morality, but also as a theoretical alternative to the sociological substructure of consequentialist ethics that pervades Western culture.

70. See for example, Yoder's discussion in "Armaments and Eschatology," 51, where he comments: "There is not and there never has been within Christianity a single sober, solid, universally self-evident rational base line cosmology, in contrast with which 'apocalyptic' thought constitutes a departure. Some of the marks of what such a system might be are recognizable within what some call 'modernity,' but some are not. 'Modernity' as a label for something clear seems to be a firm concept mostly in the minds of those who today doubt its adequacy or welcome its passing.

"We do better, then, not to ask a priori how to play off an 'apocalyptic' cosmology as a whole against 'reality,' in order to study its oddity as we do an exotic culture. We should rather investigate in what setting the 'apocalyptic vision of things, or specific elements of it, would make sense. There must after all have been some context in which the documents of an apocalyptic genre, including the cosmology they presupposed, communicated coherently."

71. See, for example, Robert Bellah et al., *The Good Society* (New York: Alfred Knopf, 1991): 174 as well as elsewhere.

72. Alasdair MacIntyre, *Three Rival Versions of Moral Enquiry: Encyclopedia, Genealogy and Tradition* (Notre Dame: University of Notre Dame, 1990).

Although it is beyond the scope of this essay to offer an adequate discussion of the differences between MacIntyre's project and Yoder's work, a few comments are necessary for the purpose of clarifying Yoder's own project of retrieval. First, Yoder offers no explicit moral theory in the way that MacIntyre does. Second, Yoder's conception of practical reason — oriented as it is within what he has called "The Hermeneutics of Peoplehood" — is much more narrowly focused in terms of what might be called a discipleship ethics, whereas MacIntyre's agenda is broader and more all-encompassing. Third, whereas MacIntyre wants to reconstruct the "local communities" in the midst of "the new dark ages," as we have already seen, Yoder's contention is that the church should be seen as "a sociological entity in its own right." Fourth, MacIntyre is so broadly concerned with foundations in theory that he does not discuss such issues as the love of enemies, war, money, whereas Yoder would argue that such issues as these in relation to the messianic kingship of Jesus are the substance of ethics. Finally, where MacIntyre's interest in the church appears not to exclude the possibility of Christendom-type alliances, Yoder's free church is juxtaposed against any version of Christendom, if "Christendom" means the alliance of church and state for the purpose of governance. In these respects, Yoder's attempt to retrieve the idiom of apostolic apocalyptic as a resource with which to interpret both social and cosmic structure appears to offer a very different way of approaching moral inquiry in contrast to the three approaches MacIntyre identifies, although Yoder's project, like MacIntyre's, is one of recovery or retrieval.

Reading Scripture

Yoder's project of retrieval or "appropriation" is specified in a hermeneutic disposition toward Christian Scripture that is quite different than the Thomistic mode of appropriating the sacred writings of the church presupposed by MacIntyre. Yoder's conception of appropriation acknowledges that there is mediation, but Yoder believes that where the free church is concerned the mediation involved in the recovery of the apostolic idiom remains *integrally related* to the way Scripture has been appropriated in the past by the "faithful" church:

> . . . the believing community today participates imaginatively, narratively, in the past history as her own history, thanks to her historians, but also thanks to her poets and prophets. As that story becomes her

own story she retrieves the posture of her precursor generations and discovers in her own setting something quite original yet essentially like what the faith had meant before."[73]

As James Wm. McClendon, Jr., has stated elsewhere, this orientation to Scripture presumes that "the story *now* echoes the story *then, is the story then*. . . ."[74] But this should not be taken to be so much an effort to return to "pre-modern" reading strategies as it is an effort to embody apostolicity. Rather, to use the phrase given currency in the writings of Hendrikus Berkhof, Paul Minear, and others a quarter century ago, this way of reading Scripture can best be described as "biblical realism" or, as more recent scholarship has described it, following Paul Ricoeur, a "second naiveté."

It is beyond the scope of this essay to offer a full assessment of Yoder's use of Scripture; it should be noted, however, that throughout his work Yoder has been attentive both to the issues of the hermeneutic distortions of Scripture by contemporary categories and to the need to maintain the perspicuity of Scripture within the believing community.[75] The same John Yoder who writes "Bible lectures" for laypeople (see *He Came Preaching Peace* [1985]) has written essays such as the first chapter of *The Politics of Jesus* (1972), which could be classified on some levels as exercises in philosophical hermeneutics. Further, Yoder is unusually adept at uncovering the axiomatic assumptions, whether acknowledged or not, that determine the use of Scripture in theology and ethics. As Stanley Hauerwas has remarked elsewhere, one of the most intriguing features of Yoder's *Christian Attitudes to War, Peace, and Revolution: A Companion to Bainton* (1983) is that Yoder does not begin to address the question of how Scripture should be interpreted until near the end of this very large book. The difference this makes is made clear in a passage from Yoder's study outline on "Binding and Loosing":

> To speak of the Bible apart from people reading it and apart from the specific questions that those people reading need to answer is to do violence to the very purpose for which we have been given the Holy Scriptures. There is no such thing as an isolated word of the Bible carrying meaning in itself. It has meaning only when it is read by someone and then only when that reader and the society in which

73. John H. Yoder, "Armaments and Eschatology," 51.

74. James Wm. McClendon, Jr., *Ethics: Systematic Theology*, Vol. 1 (Nashville: Abingdon, 1986): 84.

75. See also Yoder's notion of "resourceful selectivity" in his essay on "The Hermeneutics of Peoplehood" in *The Priestly Kingdom*, 15–45, esp. 30–32.

he or she lives can understand the issue to which it speaks. (see p. 353)

The larger context of this essay makes clear that Yoder believes that reading Scripture is a disciplined activity that occurs in relationship to other practices of discipleship such as that described in "Binding and Loosing." As Yoder has said in a different context, "the Bible functions as a fount or fulcrum for a constantly renewed, nondogmatic, critical, and recreative debate. This is . . . the point of Puritan John Robinson's 'The Lord has much more light and truth to break forth from His holy Word.' "[76]

Terminological Shifts and Conceptual Developments

Over the course of four decades, Yoder has used different phrases to convey the same basic point. For example, in some of his earlier essays, such as those collected in *The Original Revolution*, Yoder used the term "other light" to refer to "channels of revelation" whereby imperatives contrary to the work and words of Jesus Christ are used to structure social-ethical and ecclesiological conceptions. In his 1972 study of *The Politics of Jesus* he refers to some of these same assumptions as the "axioms" that provide the substructure of "mainstream ethics." More recent essays such as "Why Ecclesiology Is Social Ethics" used a different phrase, "the wider wisdom," to refer to the same structure of thought, and a similar phrase, "wider world," is used in some essays in *The Priestly Kingdom* to designate this way of relativizing the authoritative significance of Jesus and the Kingdom.

Another example of a shift in vocabulary that also constitutes a conceptual development is the way Yoder discusses eschatology, not only in relation to ethics, but with respect to ecclesiology. Early in his career, Yoder's discussions of eschatology were in response to themes raised in the wider ecumenical discussions of Faith and Order. For example, Yoder's essay "Peace without Eschatology?" was informed by the prominence of the theme of eschatology at the 1954 Evanston Assembly of the World Council of Churches in response to developments in biblical studies in the aftermath of World War II. Over the past thirty years the debate about eschatology has changed in certain ways, and Yoder's most recent articles in this collection reflect this shift. For

76. John H. Yoder, "Karl Barth: How His Mind Kept Changing," 169.

example, in his 1988 presidential address to the Society of Christian Ethics, "To Serve Our God and to Rule the World" (see pp. 127–42), Yoder used apocalyptic categories much more than he did in the essays in this collection dating to the 1950s and 1960s. More recently, Yoder has addressed the question of eschatology in conversation with scholarly developments in biblical studies while prescinding from the conflicting scholastic claims made about genre distinctions among apocalyptic, eschatology, and prophecy.[77]

At a different level, one can discern a development in Yoder's conception of ecumenicity or catholicity in as much as Yoder has tried to articulate his vision of catholicity in recent essays. At one time, Yoder would have been content to emphasize the importance of "locating" practices of discipleship in the community of faith while cautioning against an inappropriate sense of the congregation as "closed" in its communion.

> *The process of binding and loosing in the local community of faith* provides the practical and theological foundation for the centrality of the local congregation. It is not correct to say, as some extreme Baptist and Churches of Christ do, that only the local gathering of Christians can be called "the church." The Bible uses the term church for all of the Christians in a large city or even in a province. The concept of local congregational autonomy has, therefore, been misunderstood when it was held to deny mutual responsibilities between congregations or between Christians of different congregations. (see p. 352)

In one of his most recent essays, "Catholicity in Search of Location" (see pp. 300–320), Yoder probes the tension between "catholicity" and "location" in ways that should challenge both the conciliar movement, particularly as found in Faith and Order discussions, and also the churches of the free church tradition, some of which do not appear to be overly concerned about catholicity.

> The logical alternative to someone else's design for merger is not my design for a merger; it is rather a search for modes of dialogue that do not begin by asking which structures are right. . . . It is thus fitting not only procedurally but also substantially that we begin with the role of discernment. It is not as if liturgy or works of love were less

---

77. See Yoder's discussion of these issues in his essay "Armaments and Eschatology," 47–51; see also the discussion of these same questions in his related essay on "Ethics and Eschatology," 120.

characteristic of catholic faith than is discerning dialogue; yet, they are less representative of the challenge of location. Catholic existence will not be achieved by one decisive act, but asymptotically, cumulatively, through communication processes that fulfill more or less our common calling. (see p. 309)

As Yoder is quick to point out, "This conversation must, as an activity of the *ecclesia semper reformanda*, denounce present and future as well as past unfaithfulness. . . ."

> Catholicity is not "looking for a home" in the sense of a vagabond who "once lodged will no longer roam"; it is a lived reality that will have its place or "location" wherever all comers participate, in the power of the Triune God, in proclaiming to all nations (beginning where they are) all that Jesus taught. Only if the avowed agenda is that broad and that open can we claim the promises of the Lord who pledged that he would accompany us to the end of the age. (see p. 320)

By repeatedly insisting on the "unfinished" character of the church, ecclesiologically *and* ecumenically, in the particular way that he does, Yoder has articulated a vision of the church that is, at one and the same time, radically *reformed* and radically *catholic*.

IV. "The Otherness of the Church" Revisited: Assessing John Howard Yoder's Contribution to Ecclesiology and Ecumenism

In 1960 Yoder offered his initial articulation of "the otherness of the church" by providing a careful evaluation of the statement that "[t]he assumption that we live in a Christian world no longer holds" (see p. 55). In that lecture, first delivered at the School of Theology at Drew University, Yoder offered his refutation of the doctrine of the invisible church while providing an initial argument about the ecclesiological and ecumenical importance of recovering a "believing church" as the *visible* manifestation of Christian peoplehood. Interestingly enough, much of what Yoder argued in that lecture turns out to be supported by proposals being advanced in various quarters today. In the remainder of this essay, I want to call attention to seven such developments.

    1. The juxtaposition between so-called mainline American religion and the free churches has altered in several significant ways. Historio-

graphically, over the past decade more and more historians of religion in American life have narrated the dis-establishment of mainline Protestant traditions. Today, historians are more likely to accent the role of "religious outsiders" in the construction of American identity[78] than they were a generation ago. Correlatively, the necessity of articulating the ecclesiological basis for one's own communion is now more common as the cultural privilege of being mainline fades.

2. Sociologically speaking, the reality of the collapse of the American version of "the Christendom myth" is gaining recognition not only among intellectuals but institutionally within the various mainline denominations. For example, a major study of the Presbyterian Church (U.S.A.) recently described this mainline Protestant church as "The Re-forming Tradition."[79] The transition from Christendom to life "After Christendom," which has been described anecdotally by Stanley Hauerwas and William H. Willimon in their book *Resident Aliens* (1989), has recently been given the imprimatur of congregational analysis in Loren Mead's study of *The Once and Future Church* (1991). Each of these studies, in its own ways, with its particular demurrers, qualifications, and rhetorical challenges, confirms what Yoder and others have been saying for the past four decades: the only viable way to proceed with church renewal and ecumenical exploration in the present and future is to declare the myth of Christendom invalid not only for pragmatic reasons but for specifically *theological* reasons.[80]

3. Yoder's emphasis on the *particularity* of the sociology of the church has recently become creditable in light of the work of Alasdair MacIntyre and other philosophers and theologians. MacIntyre's contention that every morality has a correlative sociology, and therefore every moral discourse presupposes some kind of community, lends support — if only indirectly — to Yoder's repeated contention that the church should be taken seriously not simply as an institution but as exhibiting a different sociology. While not everyone will be persuaded

78. E.g., see the title of R. Laurence Moore's study of *Religious Outsiders and the Making of Americans* (New York: Oxford University Press, 1986).

79. Milton J. Coalter, John M. Mulder, and Louis B. Weeks, *The Reforming Tradition: Presbyterians and Mainstream Protestantism* (Louisville: Westminster/John Knox Press, 1993).

80. Unfortunately, some of the same books that declare the end of Christendom are shifting to yet another form of what Yoder would call "neo-neo-neo-neo-Constantinianism" insofar as they predicate a future of continuing mainstream Protestant influence on American culture or of continuing subservience to "public" value consensus.

by Yoder's individual arguments on behalf of particular social practices — binding and loosing, etc. — the work of MacIntyre et al. lends more plausibility in the 1990s to the substance of Yoder's arguments. In fact, Yoder is no longer the only theologian raising questions about the adequacy of the social theory that informs theology in general and, in particular, what has served (implicitly and explicitly) in the stead of ecclesiology. John Milbank's major study of *Theology and Social Theory* (1990) has raised many of the same questions while articulating an essentially different ecclesiology.

4. Yoder's work now stands in a slightly different relationship to the work of some theologians in the American context than it did nearly forty years ago. The past two decades have seen several notable developments in the debate among Christian theologians in the American context. Interventions by Hans Frei, in particular, have posed new questions about the adequacy of the foundations of the (rationalist) biblical interpretation that fails to keep the "identity of Jesus Christ" hermeneutically central in its construal of Christian Scripture. While it probably obscures more than it helps in this instance to speak of a "new Yale theology,"[81] there is no question that Hans Frei's colleague George Lindbeck has also raised questions about the theological bases for ecumenical dialogue that make it clear that the *confessional* alternative that Yoder espouses is one of the proposals that must be taken seriously by any "postliberal theology."[82] While Lindbeck himself has drawn back from his earlier prognosis concerning the "sectarian future of the church"[83] and more recently has begun to reassert the classical vision of the "indefectability" of the church,[84] the typology of doctrinal perspectives that he presented in *The Nature of Doctrine* (1984) ultimately did reassert the importance of approaching theology *as if faith makes a difference* in the way one views the cosmos and history.

81. Mark I. Wallace popularized this designation in his study *The Second Naiveté: Barth, Ricoeur, and the New Yale Theology* (Macon, Ga.: Mercer University Press, 1990), see especially the chapter on "The New Yale Theology," 87–125.

82. George Lindbeck, *The Nature of Doctrine: Religion and Theology in a Postliberal Age* (Philadelphia: Westminster Press, 1984), see especially 128–135.

83. George Lindbeck, "The Sectarian Future of the Church," in Joseph P. Whelan (ed.) *The God Experience* (Newman Press, 1971): 226–43.

84. E.g., see Lindbeck's Fourth Kershner Lecture entitled "Re-Envisioning the Church," given at Emmanuel School of Religion, March 8–11, 1988, where Lindbeck contends that even "communal degeneracy cannot erase election. . . . Similarly, the apartheid churches in South Africa are no less churches than the black ones they oppress. Just as sixteenth century Protestants and Catholics were part of the same elect people as the Anabaptists they both persecuted."

5. While there is a great deal of interest in church renewal at present in the United States, there is no real consensus about the direction of that renewal. One group of congregational analysts propose to redescribe "the vital congregation"[85] while others, adopting an ethnographic model, propose to describe the "stories and structures"[86] that account for renewal in congregational life. Meanwhile, denominational executives and councils of bishops are issuing pastoral letters that decry the nostalgia for the Protestant establishment while exhorting the membership of their communion to nurture "vital congregations and faithful disciples."[86] In short, there is a great hunger for church renewal but little direction. In this kind of circumstance, ecclesiology becomes all the more important if also more highly contested.

In general, at least within the world of American Protestant theological discourse, ecclesiology remains rare, and where it does appear it has been remarkably thin. Over the past decade several American Protestant theologians, including those of a Barthian bent, have called for the equivalent of a "confessing church" in America; the model for this has been the 1934 Barmen Declaration.[87] Significantly, these calls typically begin by questioning "American exceptionalism," which often gets expressed within myths of American benevolence, which in turn seduce American Christians into some form of what Yoder has called the "Constantinian temptation." However, for all the rhetorical eloquence of these incisive diagnoses of the American Protestant penchant for "Protestantism without reformation"[88] — which typically results in the validation of one or another form of "culture religion" — there has been no more interest in the free church alternative that Yoder has continued to articulate than there was in Germany at the time of

85. Herb Miller, *The Vital Congregation* (Nashville: Abingdon, 1990). James F. Hopewell, *Congregation: Stories and Structures* (Philadelphia: Fortress, 1987).

86. E.g., see the 1990 pastoral letter of the Council of Bishops of the United Methodist Church, *Vital Congregations — Faithful Disciples: Vision for the Church.*

87. George Hunsinger, "Barth, Barmen and the Confessing Church Today," *Katallagete* (Summer 1985): 14–27. See also the recent book by Robert T. Osborn, *The Barmen Declaration as a Paradigm for a Theology of the American Church* (San Francisco: Edwin Mellen Research Press, 1992).

88. Dietrich Bonhoeffer coined this phrase; it also serves as the title of a report on American Christianity that he wrote in 1939. For the full text of this report, see the collection of Bonhoeffer's writings, *No Rusty Swords*, pp. 92–118. I am indebted to George Hunsinger's article, "Barth, Barmen, and the Confessing Church Today," in *Katallagete* (Summer 1985): 18, for calling this article by Bonhoeffer to my attention.

the Barmen declaration.[89] In fact, there is significant evidence that at least some proponents of a "confessing church in America" remain captivated by the desire for cultural influence.[90] Whether this constitutes yet another version of what Yoder has described as the Constantinian temptation ("neo-neo-neo-neo-neo Constantinianism"?) or is but another variant on one of the four historical types that he has already identified is not a question to resolve here.

6. Nevertheless, it is significant that more and more mainline voices are raising questions that arguably fall within what Yoder has identified as the free church trajectory. For example, it was not Yoder but Loren Mead, an Anglican priest and church consultant at The Alban Institute, who in his book *The Once and Future Church* (1991) called for the mainline Protestant and Catholic churches to "rethink what the churches mean by baptism and how they structure their life to bring the young to faithful maturity."

> In the time of Christendom, infants were assumed to be born into and nurtured by a parish that was a community of faith. Baptism of infants made sense in many different denominations. . . . In this age, when we cannot assume that a child will be nurtured within a faith community . . . [t]his rethinking involves deeply loved practices and long-held theological positions. It requires something more than tinkering with the age of baptism and admission to communion. It requires more than a Saturday afternoon hour with lovely pagan godparents! The problem is acute right now for those who practice infant baptism, but it is no less important for those whose practice is different.[91]

If Mead's book is representative, then it may be that the questions Yoder has been raising about the ecclesiological coherence and pastoral adequacy of mainstream practices such as *indiscriminate* infant baptism (see "A Free Church Perspective on Baptism, Eucharist and Ministry" pp. 282–85) are more likely to be regarded as productive than in the past.

89. Franz Hildebrandt called attention to the fact at Barmen that the declaration may have had a free church form but the Confessing Church was not living up to the implications of its confession. For more about Hildebrandt's role in the Confessing Church and his relationship and occasional disagreements with Dietrich Bonhoeffer, see Eberhard Bethge's biographical study *Dietrich Bonhoeffer: Man of Vision — Man of Courage* (New York: Harper and Row, 1970).

90. E.g., see the articles in the "Confession: Facing the Demons Within and the Darkness of the Historical Moment" issue of *The Witness* 74/9 (September 1991).

91. Loren Mead, *The Once and Future Church: Reinventing the Congregation for a New Missionary Frontier* (An Alban Institute Publication, 1991): 52.

At the same time, the kind of reassessment of Yoder's work that I have suggested may also pave the way for renewed engagement with ecclesiological and ecumenical issues at other levels — including the issue of infant baptism. As Yoder himself has argued on occasion, "Mutual recognition as Christian ecclesial fellowships need not be identified with or boiled down to the narrower questions of the recognition of specific ordained ministries or of other sacramental practices."[92] Potentially this suggestion could open the way for pedobaptists and non-pedobaptists to reengage the issue of infant baptism in ways that might avoid past quagmires. Like many of the Anabaptists of the sixteenth century (e.g., Balthasar Hubmaier), Yoder has not been so much concerned with *the decision* to be baptized as with the capacity of candidates for baptism to participate in the congregational process of "binding and loosing." In this regard, Hauerwas's provocative suggestion that one of the criteria by which to assess the *faithfulness* of congregations is whether churches are *able to welcome* mentally retarded children and adults into our congregations may also assist in refocusing the debate about infant baptism. Hauerwas argues that the only kinds of congregations that are *capable* of sustaining *the corporate discipline* needed to welcome the retarded — or to support the practice of infant baptism — are congregations formed by the practice of "binding and loosing." Yet, it has been *pedobaptist* churches that have taken the strongest stand for baptizing mentally retarded adults![93] This highlights the error of detaching the question of infant baptism from other practices of discipleship.

Loren Mead's final comment in the passage quoted above also constitutes an important observation. For correlative to the upheaval in the world of mainline Protestants in American culture is the contemporary upheaval within the believers' church traditions. As Calvin Redekop and other Mennonite sociologists have argued in recent years, Mennonites in America may have a different pattern of acculturation —

92. John H. Yoder, "Could There Be a Baptist Bishop?" (editorial) in *Ecumenical Trends* Graymoor Ecumenical Institute 9 (July/August 1980): 105. As Yoder goes on to elaborate, these issues "may still need debate and adjudication in particular cases. A Baptist congregation can recognize an Anglican congregation as a body of Christian believers and not necessarily have to grant that infants baptized in the Anglican communion are fully qualified for adult membership in a Baptist congregation without further confession of faith. . . . The ongoing debate about specific orders and sacraments is, then, subsequent to, rather than prior to, the affirmation of parish-to-parish commitment. . . ."

93. Hauerwas made these observations in the context of his lectures in the CHE 33 "Christian Ethics" class at Duke Divinity School, Durham, N.C. (Spring 1987).

one that has peculiarities that stand out from the acculturation of mainstream Protestants, on the one hand, and American Catholics, on the other — but there is no question that acculturation has occurred.[94] Therefore, if there is a "pathos" about the lack of missional character in the mainstream traditions of Christianity, there is a comparable if distinctly different pathos in many of the communions of the historic free church tradition as well. That is why it is important to read Yoder's essays not only as a challenge to whatever group is regarded as "the mainstream" at any given time but also as a kind of admonition to those communions, including his own Mennonite Church, which, by virtue of their practices, are recognizably free church in polity, but which in practice may be as debased as the mainstream churches that they regard as "Protestantism without reformation." The moribund state of *both sets* of communions — free church and mainstream Protestants — constitutes its own special set of reasons for a very different kind of ecumenical engagement.

7. Finally, there is a seventh set of reasons why Yoder's essays may be regarded in a new light. In his book, *Unbaptized God: The Basic Flaw in Ecumenical Theology* (1992), Robert Jenson has voiced the "strange frustration" that he and other veteran ecumenists have felt about their involvement in ecumenical dialogue over the past three to four decades.

> As the dialogues have worked down the program of controversies, and as each traditional controversy has in the event been mitigated, its divisive power has seemed merely to rise from it and settle elsewhere; nor is the process terminated by completing the program, since the process seemingly proved circular. On each traditionally disputed item, the dialogues have sought what has come to be called convergence, a narrowing of the distance between differing positions to the point where a particular dispute can no longer be incompatible with fellowship inside one churchly communion. And such convergence has, with almost monotonous consistency, been regularly achieved. But from each remaining small and apparently tolerable divergence, an urgent reference has emerged to some other topic of the agenda, causing a newly virulent division within that topic. And with that topic it has gone the same way, and so on, back to the beginning.[95]

94. Calvin Redekop, *Mennonite Society* (Baltimore: Johns Hopkins University Press, 1989). As Redekop comments on p. 246: "Mennonite peoplehood exists and is struggling for renascence."

95. Robert Jenson, *Unbaptized God: The Basic Flaw in Ecumenical Theology* (Minneapolis: Augsburg Fortress, 1992): 3.

This brief excerpt from Jenson's argument should not be taken to mean that he would endorse Yoder's proposals for how ecumenical dialogue should be engaged any more than it should be read as an endorsement of Yoder's free church ecclesiology. Not only would Jenson and Yoder very likely disagree about the constructive implications of ecclesiology for the doctrine of God, but Jenson would also question the viability of a free church ecclesiology on other grounds. However, the general lines of Jenson's frustration about (and critique of) the way ecumenical dialogue has been pursued do converge with some of the objections, cautions, and admonitions that Yoder has raised.

It would appear, then, that the appearance of this collection of Yoder's writings on ecclesiology and ecumenism is timely in a way that it may not have been more than three decades ago when Yoder first presented "The Otherness of the Church" as a lecture at the School of Theology at Drew University. Although there have been conceptual shifts — changes in vocabulary, different conversation partners to engage, and new occasions and challenges to address — and a dramatically different context of discussion, Yoder's way of articulating the ecclesiological and ecumenical significance of the "otherness" of the church remains a distinctive alternative to the kind of mainstream ecclesiological reflection that is current today. In 1939, Dietrich Bonhoeffer asserted: "The decisive task for today is the dialogue between Protestantism without Reformation and the churches of the Reformation."[96] Bonhoeffer's comments on this occasion focused on the churches in America (and did not include the radical reformation churches) in relation to those churches that allegedly still confessed faith in Jesus Christ as the "sole ground of radical judgment and radical forgiveness."[97] Fifty years after Bonhoeffer's assessment, Yoder continues to articulate a vision of the otherness of the church that is centered precisely on the claim that any church that confesses Christ must be a church where the radical (apostolic) practices of judgment and forgiveness are embodied as evidence of ongoing reformation and visible catholicity.

As I have tried to suggest in this essay, ultimately, the importance of Yoder's essays on ecclesiology and ecumenism lies in the *different kind of dialogue* about the future of the church in relation to the past that he continues to foster within as well as between the various communions. By insisting that ecumenical discussions be anchored in a clear

96. Bonhoeffer, *No Rusty Swords*, 118.
97. Ibid., 117–18.

conception of the *faithful* church, and thereby demanding that Christians be candid with themselves and the world about those times when the Christian communities have been *faithless,* Yoder pushes Christians to be accountable for discipleship. In the process, Yoder has taught us that the way forward is not — contra Loren Mead — to *reinvent* "the once and future church," as if the apostolic paradigm were no longer viable, but rather to re-imagine the possibilities for the social embodiment of precisely the same apostolic practices in relation to which the *otherness* of the church was not only visible once upon a time but can become visible again as "the new world of the Kingdom on its way" in our own time and place.[98]

98. I am grateful to Mary Wilder Cartwright, Stanley Hauerwas, L. Gregory Jones, Timothy J. Luoma, Mark Nation, and John H. Yoder for their comments on earlier drafts of this essay. Each has contributed in important ways to the final product, but probably none of them would agree fully with the way I have characterized the significance of Yoder's essays on ecclesiology and ecumenism.

I. Theological Perspectives

The Otherness of the Church

"The Otherness of the Church" originated in a lecture delivered at Drew University in the winter of 1959–60. Subsequently, it was published in *The Drew Gateway* 30 (Spring 1960): 151–60. Later it was reprinted in the pamphlet series *Concern* 8 (May 1960): 19–29, and the *Mennonite Quarterly Review* 35 (October 1961): 286–96. Apart from a few minor changes, the present text is substantially the same as the version that was published in the *Concern* pamphlet.

This essay offers a succinct statement of the major themes of Yoder's approach to ecclesiology and ecumenism. For example, Yoder's historical and theological analysis of the "Constantinianization" of the church, while not articulated for the first time, is clearly and succinctly presented in this essay. The essay begins with conceptual analysis of the relationship of the church to the world "in their pre-Constantinian significance" and proceeds to explicate the sense in which prior to Constantine, the church was *visibly distinct* from the world even, from the church's point of view, as the *unity* of the church and the world were presupposed under the lordship of Jesus Christ. With Constantine's conversion, a transformation in the life of the church occurs in which "the two visible realities, church and world, were fused."

The emergence of the doctrine of the "invisibility of the church" must be seen against the backdrop of these developments, Yoder argues. Throughout the Medieval and Reformation periods, a "residual awareness" of the "otherness of the church" can be detected, but the specificity of the dimensions of this visible distinction were abandoned by the magisterial Reformers of the sixteenth century. As a result of these historical develop-

53

ments, a different configuration of the relationship of "church" and "state" emerges in which church discipline is handed over to agents of the state. Therefore, Yoder argues, it is not surprising to find that the Constantinian approach is constitutionally "incapable" of "making visible Christ's lordship over church and world."

Here also, we see Yoder's initial critique of H. Richard Niebuhr's *Christ and Culture* typology, which by the 1960s had already received widespread acceptance in both church and academy in the American context. A few years later, in his [as yet unpublished] essay, "How H. Richard Niebuhr Reasons: A Critique of *Christ and Culture*" (1964, rev. 1986), Yoder offered a more thorough analysis of the critique announced in this essay. Here and elsewhere, Yoder attacks the very structure of ethical reasoning that emanates from those constructions of the church-world relationship that locate the source of Christian unity *outside* the church's relationship to Christ and thereby erode the "otherness" of the church as a visible community in the world. "The basic theological issue is . . . between those for whom the church is a reality and those for whom [it] is the institutional reflection of the good and bad conscience . . . of the religion of a society."

Given this historical and theological analysis of the relationship of the church and the world, Yoder argues that the more recent process of the disestablishment or "deconstantinianization" of the church should not cause the church of Jesus Christ to fear; rather, it is an opportunity for the free church to "be the church," that is, to live out its vocation as a visible people in the world bearing witness to the lordship of Jesus Christ over the world.

The Otherness of the Church

That the "Constantinian era" is coming to an end has become one of the commonplaces of European social analysis. The fact that this breakdown has at some points been anticipated in North America (in the disestablishment of religion) and at other points is evolving differently here (rising church membership) hides from no one the fact that the framework of thought about the church and the world and their mutual interrelations, which for centuries was shared by all mainline Christian theologies, Protestant and Catholic, orthodox and rationalist, has fallen in the last two generations. The assumption that we live in a Christian world no longer holds.

The predominant theological response to this development has been to face the fact without evaluating it. Apart from a few clericalists and monarchists who are still working to restore the past, most thinkers simply make their peace with the new situation as they had with the old, assuming that the total process is of God's doing. For the first three centuries Christians were persecuted by the world; that was as it had to be. For over a millennium Christians ruled the world; that was as it should be. In the modern age the world again faces the church as an autonomous, articulate, partly hostile party; that is as it should be. The Lord gave, the Lord takes away, blessed be the name of the Lord. The early church was right in facing persecution courageously, the church of the fourth century was right in making its peace with the world, the churches of the Middle Ages and the Reformation were right in leaning on the state; and now that that is no longer possible, the church is again right in making the best of a bad deal.

But we can no longer so simply identify the course of history with Providence. We have learned that history reveals as much of Antichrist as of Christ. We are no longer sure that we are edging upwards at the top of a progression of which every preceding step must have been right for its time, since it has led us to this pinnacle. Above all we have learned to ask if it can really be the will of the Lord of history that his church should be limping after history, always attempting to adapt to a new situation that it assumes to be providential, always a half-step behind in the effort to conform, being made by history instead of making history. We, therefore, cannot say whether the deconstantinizing of the church — be it in the form of possible disestablishment in East Germany, in that of defecting membership in Western Europe, or in the more complex forms taken by post-Christian paganism elsewhere — is a bane or a boon, until we have sought on a deeper level an understanding of the roots of modern secularism, of the *Mündigkeit*, the coming-of-age of the world. In this search we shall expect no new answers but shall attempt to illuminate some old answers with a modified question.

We begin by seeking to isolate the concepts "church" and "world" in their pre-Constantinian significance. "World" (*aion houtos* in Paul, *kosmos* in John) signifies in this connection not creation or nature or the universe but rather the fallen form of the same, no longer conformed to the creative intent. The state, which for present purposes may be considered as typical for the world, belongs with the other *exousiai* in this realm. Over against this "world" the church is visible; identified by baptism, discipline, morality, and martyrdom. It is self-evident for the early centuries as a part of this visibility of the fellowship of disciples that the church's members do not normally belong in the service of the world and a fortiori in that of the pagan state.

But behind or above this visible dichotomy there is a believed unity. All evidence to the contrary notwithstanding, the church believed that its Lord was also Lord over the world. The explicit paganism of state, art, economics, and learning did not keep the church from confessing their subordination to him who sits at the right hand of God. This belief in Christ's lordship over the *exousiai* enabled the church, in and in spite of its distinctness from the world, to speak to the world in God's name, not only in evangelism but in ethical judgment as well. The church could take on a prophetic responsibility for civil ethics without baptizing the state or the statesman. The justice the church demanded of the state was not Christian righteousness but human *iustitia*; this it could demand from pagans, not because of any belief in a universal, innate moral sense, but because of its faith in the Lord. Thus the visible distinctness of church and world was not an insouciant irresponsibility; it was a particular, structurally appropriate way, and the most effective way, to be responsible. This attitude was meaningful for the church because it believed that the state was not the ultimately determinative force in history. It ascribed to the state at best a preservative function in the midst of an essentially rebellious world, whereas the true sense of history was to be sought elsewhere, namely in the work of the church. This high estimation of the church's own vocation explains both its visible distinctness from the world and the demands it addressed to the world. The depth of the church's conviction that its own task was the most necessary enabled it to leave other functions in society to pagans: the church's faith in Christ's lordship enabled it to do so without feeling that it was abandoning them to Satan.

It follows from the "already, but not yet" nature of Christ's lordship over the powers that there is no one tangible, definable quantity that we can call "world." The *aion houtos* is at the same time chaos and a kingdom. The "world" of politics, the "world" of economics, the "world" of the theater, the "world" of sports, the under-"world," and a host of others — each is a demonic blend of order and revolt. The world "as such" has no intrinsic ontological dignity. It is creaturely order in the state of rebellion; rebellion is, however, for the creature estrangement from what it "really is"; therefore, we cannot ask what the world "really is," somehow "in itself." This observation is borne out by the New Testament's use of a multiplicity of terms, most of them in the plural, when speaking of the world. All that the Powers have in common is their revolt, and revolt is not a principle of unity. Since the Prince of the Power of the Air is a liar from the beginning, he cannot even lie consistently. Only the lordship of Christ holds this chaos of idolatrous "worlds" together.

We have seen that for the early church, "church" and "world" were visibly distinct yet affirmed in faith to have one and the same Lord. This pair of affirmations is what the so-called Constantinian transformation changes (I here use the name of Constantine merely as a label for this transformation, which began before A.D. 200 and took over 200 years; the use of his name does not mean an evaluation of his person or work). The most pertinent fact about the new state of things after Constantine and Augustine is not that Christians were no longer persecuted and began to be privileged, nor that emperors built churches and presided over ecumenical deliberations about the Trinity; what matters is that the two visible realities, church and world, were fused. There is no longer anything to call "world"; state, economy, art, rhetoric, superstition, and war have all been baptized.

It is not always recognized in what structural connection this change, in itself self-evident, stands with a new distinction that now arose. It was perfectly clear to men like Augustine that the world had not become Christian through its compulsory baptism. Therefore, the doctrine of the invisibility of "the true church" sprang up in order to permit the affirmation that on some level somewhere the difference between belief and unbelief, i.e., between church and world, still existed. But this distinction had become invisible, like faith itself. Previously Christians had known as a fact of experience that the church existed but had to believe against appearances that Christ ruled over the world. After Constantine one knew as a fact of experience that Christ was ruling over the world but had to believe against the evidence that there existed "a believing church." Thus the order of redemption was subordinated to that of preservation, and the Christian hope turned inside out.

The practical outworkings of this reversal were unavoidable. Since the church has been filled with people in whom repentance and faith, the presuppositions of discipleship, are absent, the ethical requirements set by the church must be adapted to the achievement level of respectable unbelief. Yet a more significant reason for moral dilution lies in the other direction. The statesman, who a century earlier would have been proud to declare that his profession was unchristian by nature, now wants to be told the opposite. What he does is the same as before, if not worse. Yet since there are no more heathen to do the work (correction: of course there are heathen; everyone knows with Augustine that most of the population is unbelieving, but unbelief has become invisible, like the church), since there are no more confessing heathen, every profession must be declared Christian. Since Christian norms for the exercise of some professions are difficult to find, the norms of pagan *iustitia* will be declared to define the content of Christian love. The autonomy of the state and of the other realms of culture is not brought concretely under the lordship of Christ, with the total revision of form and content which that would involve: it has been baptized while retaining its former content. An excellent example is Ambrose's rephrasing of Cicero's political ethics.

And yet the medieval church maintained significant elements of otherness in structure as in piety, which are generally underestimated. When under the influence of men like Troeltsch we speak of the "medieval synthesis" and of a fusion of church and world such that the salt had lost *all* its savor, the risk of caricature is great. Whatever was wrong with the basic confusion we have just described, the church in the Middle Ages retained a more than vestigial consciousness of its distinctness from the world. The higher level of morality asked of the clergy, the international character of the hierarchy, the visibility of the hierarchy in opposition to the princes, the gradual moral education of barbarians into monogamy and legality, foreign missions, apocalypticism and mysticism — all of these preserved an awareness, however distorted and polluted, of the strangeness of God's people in a rebellious world. Will the Reformation unearth and fan into new flame these smoldering coals, or will it bury them for good?

Despite many insights and initiatives which could have led in another direction, the Reformation, deciding between 1522 and 1525 in favor of political conservatism, decided at the same time not to challenge the Constantinian compromise. The Reformers knew very well of the "fall of the church"; but they dated this fall not in the fourth century but rather in the sixth and seventh. They did not see that the signs of fallenness to which they objected — papacy, Pelagianism, hagiolatry, sacramentalism — were largely fruits of the earlier confusion of church and world.

For this reason there remains a fundamental inconsistency in the work of the Reformers. They decided in favor of the Middle Ages. They wanted nothing other than the renewal and purification of the *corpus christianum.* And yet they were driven, for reasons partly of tactics, partly of principle, to shatter that unity which they sought to restore. We have already noted that the hierarchy, the higher ethical commitment of the orders, the missionary and international character of the Roman Church, had preserved, even though in a distorted form, a residual awareness of the visible otherness of the church. All of these dimensions of specificity were abandoned by the Reformation.

In the face of monasticism the Reformation affirmed the ethical value of the secular vocation. Through the imprecision of their terms this affirmation, right in itself, amounted to the claim, as wrong as the other was right, that every calling is its own norm, thereby heightening immeasurably (and unintentionally) the autonomy of the several realms of culture. Proper behavior in a given vocation is decided not by Christ but by the inherent norms of the vocation itself, known by reason, from creation, despite the Fall. The Reformers did not intend thereby to secularize the vocations and declare the order of creation independent of Christ; this is demonstrated by their continued efforts to give instructions to statesmen and by their claim that certain professions are unchristian (not those of prince, mercenary, and hangman, but those of monk, usurer, and prostitute); nevertheless the autonomy of state and vocation was mightily furthered by what they said, so that even today many German Lutherans will argue that faithfulness to Luther demands that they let the state be master in its own house.

When the church of the fourth century wished to honor Constantine, it interpreted him in the light of its eschatology. For Eusebius, the Christian *Imperator* stood immediately under *Christos Pantokrator;* the state was unequivocally in the realm of redemption. The Reformation, however, placed the state in the realm of creation. Theoretically this meant decreasing the state's dignity; practically it meant increasing its autonomy. The prince in the sixteenth century is a Christian, the noblest and most honored member of the church; but the work he does as prince is a purely rational one, finding its norms not in Christ but in the divinely fixed structure of society; it is a work a reasonable Turk could do as well.

Further: the Reformers did not call on "the state" abstractly, on the state as such, or on the state *universal* (Charles V), but on the *territorial* state — on the Elector of Saxony and Milords of Zürich — to carry through the Reformation. The territorial state was thereby loosed from the network of imponderable political and ecclesiastical forces and counterforces, which in their complex entirety had formed and held together the *corpus christianum* and given an immediate, unequivocal, uncontrollable divine imperative, subject to no higher earthly authority. Previously political action in God's name had been possible only in the name of "the Church Universal"; now religiously motivated political struggle is possible between Christian peoples. The Thirty Years' War was the last crusade — on both sides.

The conviction that the center of the meaning of history is in the work of the church, which had been central in the pre-Constantinian church and remained half alive in the Middle Ages, is now expressly rejected. The prince is not only a Christian, not only a prominent Christian; he is now the bishop. True faith and "the true church" being invisible, the only valid aims of innerworldly effort are those that take the total secular society of a given area as the object of responsibility. The prince wields not only the sword but all other powers as well. The church confesses in deed and sometimes in word that not it but the state has the last word and incarnates the ultimate values in God's work in the world. What is called "church" is an administrative branch of the state on the same level with the army or the post office. Church discipline is applied by the civil courts and police. It is assumed that there is nothing wrong with this since the true church, being invisible, is not affected.

It cannot be said that this turn of events was desired by the Reformers. Their uniform intention was a renewal of the visible, faithful body of believers. But the forces to which they appealed for support, namely the drives toward autonomy that exist in the state and the other realms of culture, were too strong to be controlled once they had been let loose.

In the context in which the Reformers made this decision there is much that we can understand and even approve. Their faith in the all-powerful Word of God, which will not return void if it but be rightly preached, and their awareness of the divine ordination of the secular order, which were their conscious points of departure, were true in themselves. But they did not succeed in bringing up for examination the Constantinian synthesis itself. Thus their decisions, which in their minds were conservative, reveal themselves in a broader socio-historical perspective to have been inconsistent and revolutionary. The order of creation, in which they placed the state and the vocations, could with a turn of the hand become the deistic order of nature or the atheistic order of reason without any change in its inner structure. The right of the local government to administer the church in the interest of the Reformation could become a right of the state to use the church for its own purposes, and there was no court of appeal. The divine obligation of Zürich or Saxony to shatter the superstructure of the Holy Roman Empire could flip over — especially after the Thirty Years' War had discredited confessionalism as a moral imperative — and appear as the absolute *raison d'etat*. It was, therefore, precisely the attempt of the Reformers to maintain the medieval ideal and to lay claim on the autonomous dynamics of state and profession that led to the secularization that defines the modern period. Fully to accept the Constantinian synthesis is to explode it. The Reformers created modern secularism; not, as the liberalism of two generations ago boasted, intentionally, by glorifying the individual, but unintentionally, through the inner contradictions of their conservatism.

The Constantinian approach has thereby shown itself to be incapable, not accidentally but constitutionally, of making visible Christ's lordship over church and world. The attempt to reverse the New Testament relationship of church and world, making faith invisible and the Christianization of the world a historic achievement with the institutional forms, was undertaken in good faith but has backfired, having had the sole effect of raising the autonomy of unbelief to a higher power. Islam, Marxism, secular Humanism, and Fascism — in short, all the major adversaries of the Christian faith in the Occident and the strongest adversaries in the Orient as well — are not nature- or culture-religions but bastard faiths, all of them the progeny of Christianity's infidelity, the spiritual miscegenation involved in trying to make a culture-religion out of faith in Jesus Christ. As religious adversaries in our day, these hybrid faiths are more formidable than any of the pagan alternatives faced by Paul, by Francis Xavier, or by Livingstone. Those who have refused to learn from the New Testament must now learn from history; the church's responsibility to and for the world is first and always to be the church. The short-circuited means used to "Christianize" "responsibly" the world in some easier way than by the gospel have had the effect of dechristianizing the Occident and demonizing paganism.

What then should be the path of the church in our time? We must first of all confess — if we believe it — that the meaning of history lies not in the acquisition and defense of the culture and the freedoms of the West, not in the aggrandizement of material comforts and political sovereignty, but in the calling together "for God saints from every tribe and language and people and nation," a "people of his own who are zealous for good deeds." The basic theological issue is not between right and left, not between Bultmann and Barth, not between the sacramental and the prophetic emphases, nor between the Hebraic and

Greek mentalities, but between those for whom the church is a reality and those for whom it is the institutional reaction of the good and bad conscience, of the insights, the self-encouragement — in short, of the religion of a society.

If with the apostles we confess the Holy Spirit and the church, we must further recognize that unbelief also incarnates itself. The "world" must return in our theology to the place that God's patience has given it in history. The "world" is neither all nature nor all humanity nor all "culture"; it is *structured unbelief*, rebellion taking with it a fragment of what should have been the Order of the Kingdom. It is not just an "attitude," as is supposed by the shallow interiorization of attempts to locate "worldliness" in the mind alone. Nor is it to be shallowly exteriorized and equated with certain cataloged, forbidden, leisure-time occupations. There are acts and institutions that are by their nature — and not solely by an accident of context or motivation — denials of faith in Christ.

The problem is also wrongly located when H. Richard Niebuhr sets up over against Christ a quantity named "culture," which one may then attempt to relate to Christ in a number of possible ways. In spite of the effectiveness of this scheme as a tool for classification and teaching, in spite of the erudition and sympathetic understanding with which Niebuhr deals with the various possibilities, and in spite of the literary qualities which have won the book *Christ and Culture* its broad circulation, it must be recognized that his fundamental Christ/culture polarity, and typology of possible ethical standards which he builds upon it, are at bottom unfair to history and unfruitful for ethics. The reason for this is the assumption that culture "as such," i.e., as distinct from Christ, is a tangible reality patient of being related consistently to "Christ" in one of the five typical ways: "Christ against culture," "the Christ of culture," "Christ above culture," "Christ and culture in paradox," or "Christ the Transformer of Culture." This is to attribute to the world that intrinsic ontological dignity that neither the New Testament nor history allows it to claim. We must affirm the reality of the world but not by ascribing to it the right to the place it usurps.

The awareness of the visible reality of the world leads to two scandalous conclusions. The first is that Christian ethics is for Christians. Since Augustine this has been denied; the first criterion for an ethical ideal for the laity is its generalizability. From Kant's rigorous formulation of this criterion to the lay application in questions like, "What would happen if we were all pacifists like you?" the presupposition is universal that the right will have to apply as a simple performable possibility for a whole society. Thus the choice is between demanding of everyone a level of obedience and selflessness that only faith and forgiveness make meaningful (the "puritan" alternative) and lowering the requirements for everyone to the level where faith and forgiveness will not be needed (the medieval alternative). This dilemma is *not* part of the historical situation; it is an artificial construction springing from a failure to recognize the reality of the world.

The second scandalous conclusion is that there may well be certain functions in a given society which that society in its unbelief considers necessary, and which the unbelief renders necessary, in which Christians will not be called to participate. This was self-evident in the early Christian view of the state; that it had to be rejected later becomes less and less self-evident the longer we live and learn.

This view of the church commends itself exegetically and theologically. Contrary to the opposing view, it refuses to accept pragmatic grounds for deciding how Christians should relate themselves to the world. And yet after saying this we observe that this biblical approach is in fact the most effective. The moral renewal of England in the eighteenth century was the fruit not of the Anglican establishment but of the Wesleyan revival. The Christianization of Germanic Europe in the Middle Ages was not achieved by the "state church" structure, with an incompetent priest in every village and an incontinent Christian on every throne, but by the orders, with the voluntaristic base, the demanding discipline, the mobility, and the selectivity as to tasks that characterize the "free-church" pattern. What moral tone there is in today's Germany is due not to the state-allied church and the church-allied political parties but to the bootleg *Brüderschaften* of the Barmen Confession.

This makes it clear that the current vogue of the phrase "responsible society" in ecumenical circles is a most irresponsible use of terms. Even if we let pass the intentional ambiguity that makes society both the subject and the object of the responsibility, and the further confusion caused by the hypostatising of "society," there remains a fundamental misdefinition, furthered by a misreading of socio-ethical history. It continues to work with the Constantinian formulation of the problem, as if the alternatives were "responsibility" and "withdrawal." The body of thought being disseminated under this slogan is a translation into modern terms of the two ancient axioms: that the most effective way for the church to be responsible for society is for it to lose its visible specificity while leavening the lump; and that each vocation bears in itself adequately knowable inherent norms. Thus we are invited to repeat the mistake of the Reformation, and that just as the time when the younger churches, themselves in an essentially pre-Constantinian position, need to be helped to think in other terms than those of the *corpus christianum* framework that has already dechristianized Europe.

Christ's victory over the world is to be dated not A.D. 311 or 312 but A.D. 29 or 30. That church will partake most truly of his triumph that follows him most faithfully in that warfare whose weapons are not carnal but mighty. The church will be most effective where it abandons effectiveness and intelligence for the foolish weakness of the cross in which are the wisdom and the power of God. The church will be most deeply and lastingly responsible for those in the valley of the shadow if it is the city set on the hill. The true church is the *free* church.

How then do we face deconstantinization? If we meet it as just another turn of the inscrutable screw of providence, just one more chance to state the Constantinian position in new terms, then the judgment that has already begun will sweep us along in the collapse of the culture for which we boast that we are responsible. But if we have an ear to hear what the Spirit says to the churches, if we let ourselves be led out of the inferiority complex that the theologies of the Reformation have thus far imposed on free church thought, if we discover as brethren in a common cause the catacomb churches of East Germany and the *Brüderschaften* of West Germany, if we puncture the "American dream" and discover that even in the land of the God-trusting post office and the Bible-believing chaplaincy we are in the same essentially missionary situation, the same minority status as the church in Sri Lanka or Colombia; if we believe that the free church, and not the "free world," is the primary bearer of God's banner, the fullness of the One who fills all in all, if we face deconstantinization not as just another dirty trick of destiny but as the overdue providential unveiling of a pernicious error; then it may be given to us, even in the twentieth century, to be the church. For what more could we ask?

A People in the World

"A People in the World" was originally prepared for the Conference on the Concept of the Believers' Church held at Louisville, Kentucky, in 1967, and was subsequently published under the title of "A People in the World: Theological Interpretation" in the volume *The Concept of the Believers' Church*, ed. James Leo Garrett (Scottdale, Penn.: Herald Press, 1969), 250–83. The editor's summary of the response to Yoder's presentation by Dr. C. Emanuel Carlson, at that time the executive director of the Baptist Joint Committee on Public Affairs, Washington, D.C., which was included in the publication of the proceedings of the Louisville Conference, has been deleted from the following version of Yoder's essay. Other changes, including supplementary notes and stylistic changes, have been made, but the substance of the argument remains much the same as Yoder delivered it twenty-five years ago.

In his prefatory comments, Yoder indicated that he would be resorting to the use of typology for the sake of discussion. The triangular typology of "theocrat," "spiritualist," and "believers' church" that Yoder presents, following the analyses of Troeltsch and Littell, focuses on the "locus of historical meaning" within ecclesial patterns of association. Some elements of the typology bear a rough resemblance to arguments found in Yoder's "Ecumenical Perspectives" essays in *The Original Revolution* (see below pp. 143–218), particularly the essay "Let the Church Be the Church." While Yoder is not unaware of the possibility of distortion, he frankly states that there is no way to proceed in clarifying the uniqueness of the believers' church ecclesiology without using (at least some) of the language that others have used to caricature the communions that lay claim to what might be

65

called the "Anabaptist Vision," to borrow a phrase coined by Harold Bender. Yoder cautions: "Whatever we say must be distinguished from what someone else has already said, using the same words, but meaning something else." At the same time, Yoder goes on to articulate the distinctiveness of the believers' church model of the church from both hermeneutical and ecclesiological angles.

Yoder persuasively calls attention to the ecclesiological implications of recognizing the distinctiveness of the *visible* embodiment of God's people in the world. "The work of God is the calling of a people, whether in the Old Covenant or the New. The church is then not simply the bearer of the message of reconciliation. . . . Nor is the church simply the result of a message. . . . That men and women are called together to a new social wholeness is itself the work of God, which gives meaning to history, from which both personal conversion . . . and missionary instrumentalities are derived." After offering several samples of New Testament texts that would appear to presuppose the kind of visible community that he is describing, Yoder concludes: "In every direction we might follow in exposition, *the distinctness of the church of believers is prerequisite to the meaningfulness of the gospel message.*" Although in the remainder of the essay Yoder draws on various traditional rubrics — including the traditional "notae ecclesiae," Menno Simons' contribution to the discussion of the "marks of the church," and twentieth-century ecumenical contributions of Visser 't Hooft, Neill, et al., the latter discussions can be seen as a careful elaboration of the ecclesiological vision of the believers' church outlined in the passages quoted above. In the process of explicating this model of the church, Yoder discusses the centrality of such practices as fraternal admonition for the embodiment of the discerning community in the congregation and beyond.

A People in the World

We may situate the task before us by taking stock of the rehabilitation that Anabaptism, as one specimen of the believers' church, has undergone at the hands of the writers of history in the last half century. Beginning with Troeltsch, the opinion has become increasingly widespread that the Anabaptists were, without knowing it, and prematurely, "the wave of the future." What they called for by way of separation of church and state and voluntary expression in matters of religion has now been widely accepted.[1] They have proved their point. Just as the magisterial Reformation was the particular form of Protestantism that dominated northern Europe from 1555 to the age of Enlightenment, so sectarian Protestantism is the official form of North American religion, so much so that even the Lutheran and Anglican denominations must be structured and supported as voluntary associations.

We could take this to mean that, since their point has been made, their followers and descendants should lay this issue aside and go on to more important matters. Why keep on belaboring an issue everyone has already accepted? Such a way of arguing from the cultural acceptance of certain free church positions might be appropriate for some matters of detail, such as the rejection of religious persecution and the Crusade. But as the point of departure for a fundamental understanding of the mission of the believers' church, such an approach would be wrong in more ways than one.

First of all, such an assessment of the tapering off of the uniqueness of the believers' church is questionable in method. It fixes upon a negative, corrective, formal difference between the sixteenth-century believers' church and the magisterial tradition. For the Anabaptists and all who have followed in their train, however, the rejection of the church-state tie has not been an issue debated in its own right but a reflection of or a deduction from their concept of the nature of Christian discipleship and community. Instead of finding the uniqueness of the believers' church defined at that central point from which it was possible, *even* in the sixteenth century, to *derive* the concept of religious liberty, such an approach as I have been describing fixes on the derivative concept itself.

Second, this approach is wrong in the incongruity of the measures it uses. To say that the Anabaptist position on church and state has "triumphed" is to say that it has become the dominant social form of a given society. Its prescriptions with regard to the withdrawal of the state from matters of religion have been translated into legal form in some countries. The course of the mainstream of history reflects the acceptance of the sectarians' complaint. But all of these ways of stating the

---

1. This estimate is distilled in Roland H. Bainton's characterization: "an amazingly clear-cut and heroic anticipation of what with us has come to be axiomatic." "The Anabaptist Contribution to History" in Guy F. Hershberger, ed., *The Recovery of the Anabaptist Vision: A Sixtieth Anniversary Tribute to Harold S. Bender* (Scottdale, Penn.: Herald Press, 1957): 318.

"success" or the "progress" of the free church social critique presuppose precisely what the Anabaptists and their spiritual relatives denied, namely, that the course of history and the structures of society are the most significant measures of whether people are doing the will of God. As far as these first free churchmen were concerned, the rightness of their position had no necessary connection to whether it would succeed, in one generation or in twenty,[2] in being adopted by a whole society.

One conclusion that nevertheless does follow from the widespread acceptance in our society of some elements of the free church critique is that, since our society thinks it has accepted that critique, we cannot restate it without encountering a misunderstanding. "What more do you want?" the interlocutor asks. "You have your separation from the state and your liberty of conscience. Did we not agree about all the other essentials?"

If thus we are to seek to unfold from its own heart the vision of the community of believers, we cannot do so simply, without encountering distortion and misunderstanding for all the terms that we shall need to use have been preempted and all the issues have been crystallized. Whatever we say must be distinguished from what someone else has already said, using the same words but meaning something else. If then we are to break through to a renewed focusing of the real issues, we must run the risk of speaking with types and caricatures, recognizing the dangers of distortion, trusting that the point to which our conversation has come will enable this simplified approach to be used without profound injustice.

The Classical Options

Let us take for a moment the terrain of the sixteenth-century Swiss and South German Reformation as the source of our typology. The same

2. What Bainton has said very pointedly about the Anabaptists would be as true of any other believers' church group; namely, that the positions they took were not so calculated as to contribute effectively to social progressor democratization, even if such developments may have been the long-range implication of their witness. "Let it now be said that the worth of their endeavor is not to be judged in the light of their contribution to history. They took their stand in the light of eternity regardless of what might or might not happen in history. They did not fall into the error of those who treat the way of the cross as if it were a weapon; . . . the cross is not a strategy. It is a witness before God, no matter whether there may or may not be any historical consequences" (ibid., 325).

demonstration could be derived elsewhere as well; it seems that the same possibilities spring forth in every age.

In the development of the Reformation under the shadow of Huldrych Zwingli, to the theological left and the geographical southwest of the Lutheran Reformation, three different streams of spiritual vitality may be usefully distinguished.[3] Despite the presence of borderline figures, the types are very clearly distinguishable. They are not three different positions along one clear continuum, with one of them mediating between the other two; each goes off in another direction. They can best be described with a triangular image.

At one corner of the triangle, claiming to carry to its logical conclusion the Reformation principle of the restoration of original conclusion Christianity, is Anabaptism, as best exemplified in Michael Sattler and Pilgram Marpeck. Anabaptism is now long recognized as a major landmark, though not the first nor the last, in the history of our concept of the believers' church. Their appeal, over against Zwingli himself, was to the same text that he himself had in January 1523 used with such great effect against Johannes Faber: "Any plant that is not of my heavenly Father's planting will be rooted up" (Matt. 15:13).[4]

At another corner of the triangle, claiming to carry to its logical extreme the dismantling of externals and the search for the true inward-

3. This classification is sliced along a different axis from that proposed by George H. Williams in his introduction to *Spiritual and Anabaptist Writers*, The Library of Christian Classics, vol. 25 (Philadelphia: Westminster Press, 1957): 28–35. Williams identifies three kinds of Anabaptists and three kinds of Spiritualists, with the magisterial Reformation not included on the chart. To relate this typology of that to Williams, it could be said that we are here dealing with a transversal section of his repertory: evangelical spiritualism, evangelical Anabaptism, and evangelical magisterialism.

4. The form that this concern for restoration took in the sixteenth century was *sola scriptura;* the differences of degree all the way from Anglicanism through Lutheranism and Zwinglianism to Anabaptism were differences as to how much authority Scripture was to have over against Christian tradition. Yet we should take care not to misinterpret the appeal to Scripture through the categories of a later Protestant scholasticism. Anabaptists coupled their appeal to Scripture with an accent on the "Inner Word," analogous to the later Quaker concept of "Christ's coming to teach his people today." Thus the issue is the authority of Christ versus the authority of humans, not the Christ of Scripture versus the present Christ. The simplest way Zwingli put this point was his use of Matthew 15:13; "Every planting not planted by my heavenly Father shall be uprooted." This was the main argument in Zurich's January 1523 Disputation against Johannes Faber. Cf. my *Die Gespräche swischen Täufern und Reformatoren*, Karlsrahe Schneider, 1962, p. 17; and *Balthasar Hubmaier: Theologian of Anabaptism* (Scottdale, Penn.: Herald Press, 1989): 184.

ness of faith alone, we find the so-called "Spiritualizers," best represented by Caspar Schwenckfeld. Their appeal was to the kind of argument Zwingli had employed in his tract of 1522, "Clarity and Certainty of the Word of God,"[5] namely, true inwardness and a religious certainty neither supported nor diluted by outward marks.

In the third corner we find those who carry to its ultimate implementation the logic of theocratic humanism that Zwingli had borrowed from Erasmus, whereby the word of God, as spoken by the "prophet" to the whole society, brings about the renewing of that society according to the will of God. This is the path that Zwingli himself took beginning in 1523, in which he was followed by the Reformed churches along the crescent from Calvin's Geneva through Heidelberg and the Netherlands to Edinburgh.

Each of these parties saw itself standing in a one-dimensional polarity with regard to the other two. From the perspective of Zwingli and Calvin, the Spiritualizers and the Anabaptists were alike in their wrongheaded divisiveness and their undermining Christian government. They shared the error of Martin Luther in his rejection of the theocratic vision and his relegation of government to a realm outside the gospel.

From the perspective of Caspar Schwenckfeld, the Anabaptists and the magisterial Reformation alike were too concerned with outward forms. Both of them had, like Luther, failed to carry to its consistent conclusion the logic of their withdrawal from the Roman Church with all its ceremonies.

From the perspective of Pilgram Marpeck,[6] the Spiritualizers and Zwingli were very similar. Both of them denied the ultimate importance of proper church order. Schwenckfeld, because only spiritual reality matters, made no issue of outwardly challenging the established forms of Christendom and, therefore, suffered no severe persecution as did the Anabaptists. Zwingli, with almost the same arguments, could conclude that, since the true church is invisible, therefore the church that we organize cannot be the true church anyway. Thus nothing stands in the way of our organizing it as we please, or more precisely, as good

5. See text in *Zwingli and Bullinger*, trans. and ed. G. W. Bromiley, The Library of Christian Classics, vol. 24 (Philadelphia: Westminster Press, 1953): 59–95.

6. Pilgram Marpeck was the most prolific south German Anabaptist leader of the 1530s. Against Caspar von Schwenckfeld he argued that the church must be visible, and against the Reformed State churches he argued that it must be free. Cf. William Klassen and Walter Klaassen, eds., *The Writings of Pilgram Marpeck* (Scottdale, Penn.: Herald Press, 1978).

public order demands. Since faith is invisible, it was equally appropriate for Zwingli to baptize all infants and for Schwenckfeld to attach no importance at all to baptism. Since the Lord's Supper is a simple external ceremony, it is equally possible to teach (Zwingli) that its meaning is that of "signifying" a message distinct from the symbol itself or (Schwenckfeld) to abandon it. Thus both Schwenckfeld and Zwingli, in the name of a deeper spirituality, withstood the Anabaptists' call to bring into being a visible congregation of committed believers.

As normal as it was for each of these three parties to see the other two merging in their rejection of its own favorite concern, we do well, following the guidance of Ernst Troeltsch (as reiterated pointedly by Franklin H. Littell in a landmark article)[7] to see the triangular character of this division. It is important to identify this as exemplified in a bygone context because we in our day suffer the same temptation to see our problems in polarities rather than triangles.

With careful discernment we would probably find the same pattern recurring in every critical period of renewal, whether it be the Bohemian Brethren between Utraquists and the solitary Peter Chelcicky, or Alexander Mack between the radical and the churchly Pietists, or George Fox between Cromwell and the Ranters. In drawing from this patterned history a consistent descriptive typology, let us settle arbitrarily on a terminology whose use may accompany us in our contemporary and systematic argument. Within the Reformation to the left of Luther, as within free churchdom ever since then, let us recognize and label these three distinct types of stance, each with its own coherence.

Let us characterize as "theocratic" that vision of the renewal of the church that hopes to reform society at large with one blow.[8] Whether the church and state as administrative agencies be merged, as with Bullinger or Erastus, or be quite distinct as with Calvin and the Scots, is a matter quite subordinate to the common Christian takeover of all society for the greater glory of God, which is common to both polities.

For the theocrat, the locus of historical meaning is the movement of the whole society. Better that the young and the dissenters do the

7. Franklin H. Littell, "Church and Sect (With Special Reference to Germany)," *The Ecumenical Review* VI (April 1954): 262–76.

8. If one were free to use labels without regard for the emotional coloring of words, this type should have been called "puritan," and it would not be unfair to history so to label it. Since, however, in our culture this label has strong value-laden overtones, positive for some and negative for others, I have chosen another label. Nonetheless a few scattered references to Puritanism as a historical phenomenon representing this stance have had to be retained.

will of God grudgingly than not at all. Since there is power in every society, it will best be exercised by the Christian, be his calling farmer or statesman, banker or industrialist. The preacher or prophet must not seek to govern the state or the economy — that would be to relapse into clericalism — but it shall be governed by men who in their Christian calling do what God demands as the preacher has interpreted it to them.

Second, let us label as "spiritualist" the reaction, in the footsteps of Schwenckfeld, that moves the locus of meaning from society to the spirit.[9] Spiritualism does not, indeed, withdraw from all forms. It remains in the frame of the theocratic society to which it reacts. Like Schwenckfeld, by giving no specific social form to its dissent, it leaves the established church in place. Like Spener preaching to princely households or Francke building schools, it contributes readily to the social structures whose spiritual inadequacy it at the same time points up. But all of this outward form, it insists, is vanity, unless the deep inward reality can be found.

Our third type, the believers' church, stands not merely between the other two but over against both of them. With spiritualism it castigates the coldness and the formalism of official theocratic churchdom, but it corrects that formalism not by seeking to have no forms at all, nor by taking refuge in para-churchly forms, but rather by developing those forms that are according to Scripture and that are expressive of the character of the disciples' fellowship.

With the theocratic vision, it rejects the individualism and the elite self-consciousness of the spiritualist. But the social form that it proposes as an alternative to individualism is not the undifferentiated baptized mass of the reformed *corpus christianum* but the covenanted fellowship enjoyed with others who have pledged themselves to following the same Lord.

I wrote at the outset that I would attempt to catalyze our conversation by bringing into the arena a blunt typology. Now I may say more precisely that it helps to bring a triangular typology into what had seemed like a bipolar debate. I shall claim that the church is called to move beyond the oscillation between the theocratic and the spiritualist patterns, not to a compromise between the two or to a synthesis

---

9. Here the historically fitting name would be "Pietist," but this is an even more feeling-laden term. Much of what has been historically labeled "Pietist" has been at the same time very much in the believers' church format, especially the Brethren and Methodist origins. Much of what is currently condemned as "pietist" by one stream of ecumenical thinkers is not congruent with historical Pietism at all.

claiming like Hegel to "assume" them both, but to what is genuinely a third option.

The Message Is the Medium

Few assumptions have been more widely shared in Protestant thought than the identification of the messages of Paul and Luther with the promise of a new hope for the individual in his subjectivity. Luther in his rejection of the cultural religion of the Middle Ages, following Paul in his rejection of cultural Pharisaism, raised as his banner the *pro me* of the forgiven sinner. That God is gracious *to me* is the good news that Zinzendorf, Wesley, Kierkegaard, and today both Rudolf Bultmann and Billy Graham (in their very different ways) have derived from Luther and have labored to keep unclouded by any effort to derive from it (or to base upon it) a social program or any other human work. To safeguard the pure gratuitousness of grace, any binding correlation with human goals or achievements must be studiously kept in second place.

This assumption — to put it crudely, that Paul was a Lutheran — is now being dismantled under the impact of the exegetical theology of this century. Not only does biblical theology in general discover a fuller meaning to the dimension of *peoplehood* in all the working of God throughout the Bible story; not only does one find in Jesus' proclamation of the coming of the Kingdom in the Gospel accounts a dimension of genuine social creativity and in the calling of the twelve the nucleus of a new community. Today such scholars as Markus Barth and Hans-Werner Bartsch are finding as well even in the writings of Paul, yea even in Galatians and Romans, a hitherto unnoticed dimension of community extending even into the meaning of such words as *justification*.[10]

Since Protestantism from Luther to Bultmann has so broadly as-

10. Hans-Werner Bartsch, "Die historische Situation des Romerbriefes," *Communio Viatorum* VIII (Winter 1965): 199–208; Markus Barth, "Jews and Gentiles: The Social Character of Justification in Paul," *Journal of Ecumenical Studies* V (Spring 1968): 241–67. The conclusions of these are all the more striking in that they arise out of the critical-exegetical expertise of the Continental university style of theology with no hidden apologetic-sectarian agenda. Barth's earlier *Acquittal by Resurrection* (New York: Holt, Rinehart and Winston, 1964), also "mixes" faith and sociology in a way that creatively disgruntles the puritists. I have described the further progress of this corrective tendency in pp. 217ff. of my *Politics of Jesus* (Grand Rapids: Eerdmans, 1972).

sumed such a correlation between "Gospel" and subjective awareness of guilt and forgiveness, one cannot emphasize too strongly how significant is this exegetical breakthrough. The work of God is the calling of a people, whether in the Old Covenant or the New. The church is then not simply the bearer of the message of reconciliation, in the way a newspaper or a telephone company can bear any message with which it is entrusted. Nor is the church simply the result of a message, as an alumni association is the product of a school or the crowd in the theater is the product of the reputation of the film. That men and women are called together to a new social wholeness is itself the work of God, which gives meaning to history, from which both personal conversion (whereby individuals are called into this meaning) and missionary instrumentalities are derived.

The centrality of the church in God's purposes is stated in a figurative way in the first vision of the Apocalypse, where the question of the meaning of history is represented to the seer in the form of a sealed scroll. When it is announced that the Lamb that was slain is worthy to open the seals and unroll the meaning of history, the *new song*" in which all the heavenly creatures join proclaims that the meaning of the sacrifice of the Lamb is that he has "purchased" "for God" a priestly kingdom out of "every tribe and language and people and nation" (5:9f.).

Almost the same language is used in the sermonic context of 1 Peter 2, where the phrase "priestly kingdom" finds its counterpart, "royal priesthood," in addition to three other parallel collective nouns describing the church as a people claimed by God. Here "having received mercy" and "being a people," after having been "not a people," are synonymous.

The same statement is made more systematically in Ephesians. Here the apostle claims to have been given understanding of a mystery hidden not only through the ages but also to the other apostles, which has been revealed first of all in his ministry and then in his understanding of that ministry. The creation of one new humanity by breaking down the wall between the two kinds of people of whom the world is made, Jews and Gentiles, is not simply the result of reconciliation of individuals with God, nor is it an ad hoc organization established to support the propagation of the knowledge of individual reconciliation. This creation of the one new humanity is itself the purpose that God had in all ages, is itself the "mystery," the gospel now to be proclaimed.

In every direction we might follow in exposition, *the distinctness of the church of believers is prerequisite to the meaningfulness of the gospel message.* If what is called "the church" is the religious establishment of a total society, then the announcement that God has created human community is redundant, for the religiously sanctioned community is identical with the given order. The identification of the church with a given society denies the miracle of the new humanity in two ways: on the one hand by blessing the existing social unity and structure that is a part of the fallen order rather than a new miracle, and on the other hand by closing its fellowship to those of the outside or the enemy class or tribe or people or nation. If any concept of meaningful mission is to remain in this context, it must be transmuted to the realm of subjectivity, calling a few individuals to a depth of "authenticity" that separates them from their brethren.

Pragmatically it is self-evident that there can be no procedure of proclamation without a community, distinct from the rest of society, to do the proclaiming. Pragmatically it is just as clear that there can be no evangelistic call addressed to a person inviting him or her to enter into a new kind of fellowship and learning, if there is not such a body of persons, again distinct from the totality of society, to whom to come and from whom to learn. But this congruence between the free visible existence of the believers' church and the possibility of valid missionary proclamation is not a merely pragmatic or instrumental one. It is founded deeply in the nature of the gospel itself. If it is not the case that there are in a given place people of various characters and origins who have been brought together in Jesus Christ, then there is not in that place the new humanity and in that place the gospel is not true. If, on the other hand, this miracle of new creation has occurred, then all the verbalizations and interpretations whereby this body communicates to the world around it are simply explications of the fact of its presence.

Tools for the Study of the Church: The *Notae Missionis*

The classical instrument for the interpretation of the mission and nature of the church is the concept of a shorter or longer list of "marks" that are the minimum standards that enable one to recognize the existence of a particular church. "The church is wherever the Word of God is properly preached and the sacraments properly administered." From this definition of classical Protestantism we may appropriately begin our analysis.

The shortcoming of this two-point statement is not merely its petitionary character. Obviously, the entire meaning of these two criteria is utterly dependent upon what "properly" is taken to mean. Conceivably one could pour all of any theology into these two phrases. This observation does not demonstrate that they are either right or wrong but only that they were not coined with the intent that they should serve usefully as principles of discrimination in ecumenical conversation. They were not really meant as "marks" in the sense that they could be used objectively by some third party to determine whether in any case of conflict a given entity calling itself "church" really is one.

But a more fundamental flaw in this statement of criteria is that the point of relevance in their application is not the church but its superstructure. The place you would go to ascertain whether the word of God is properly preached in a given church is the preacher or conceivably the doctrinal statement by which that ecclesiastical body is governed. The place you go to see whether the sacraments are being properly administered is again the officiant. The concentration of your attention might be upon his or her way of proceeding or it might focus upon his or her understanding of the meaning of the sacrament. But in either case it does not focus upon the congregation.

Now certainly it is taken for granted in this Protestant formulation that there will be a congregation present. As a matter of fact, since all of the Reformation statements were produced by state churches, we can be sure that the total community is assumed to be present under pain of punishment by the state. Yet the presence of the community is not part of the definition. How many persons are present, in what attitude they are listening, what they understand, how they respond to what they have heard, to what they commit themselves, how they relate to one another, and with what orientation they return to the week's activities is not part of the touchstone definition of the church. We thus have criteria that apply to recognizing the legitimacy of a magisterial superstructure but not to identifying a Christian community.

The churches of the Reformed tradition were attempting to remedy this gap when they added a third criterion, namely, "proper discipline." This is again a petitionary definition that could be expanded to include much more, but in the Reformation setting it applied primarily to the synod pattern of government, the fourfold ministry, and some kind of moral control over the behavior of members. It is clearly just as petitionary as the other two.

It is thus highly significant when today pioneering thinking about the nature and the mission of the church begins with statements of its task that look quite different from the classical Reformation marks. In his book, *The Pressure of Our Common Calling*,[11] Willem A. Visser 't Hooft identifies three functions of the church: namely witness (*martyria*), service (*diakonia*), and communion or fellowship (*koinonia*). To some extent these labels could be interpreted as overlapping with the older ones. "Fellowship" might include proper use of the sacrament of the Lord's Supper; "witness" would have something to do with proper preaching of the word. Yet, each of these functions is clearly more than that. It is characteristic of all three that they reach out into two dimensions quite different from the earlier description.

First of all, the three functions of witness, fellowship, and service all have to do with the Christian church *as a community* of people. They ask about the relationships and the behavior of the Christian community. It would not be possible to measure whether these requirements have been met by looking only at the functioning of the preacher or at the doctrinal stance of the church hierarchy. They test, or describe, the *congregation*.

Second, these descriptions of the function of the church are characterized by the relationship in which the church stands to *the world*. Ministry and witness demand the world beyond for the function to be meaningful. Even "fellowship" implies a relation, in a sense a negative one, in that by definition one's "fellow" is not every other human being but one with whom one has entered into a particular relationship that does not include all others. These marks test, or describe, a *mission*.

Similar in substance, although different in detail, is the proposal of Stephen Neill in his book, *The Unfinished Task*.[12] Bishop Neill suggests that to the traditional Reformation marks there should be added three more: "fire on earth" (missionary vitality), suffering, and the mobility of the pilgrim. Again these are descriptions of the total Christian fellowship in the midst of the world and not of a leadership body.

What these two senior statesmen of the modern ecumenical movement are saying was said in the sixteenth century by Menno Simons. To the two standard Lutheran marks (which he, of course, would have defined quite differently in detail from Luther), Menno added four more: holy living, brotherly love, unreserved testimony, and suffering.[13]

We could attempt to exposit the arguments in favor of including

11. (London: SCM Press Ltd., 1959), esp. p. 28.

12. (London: Edinburgh House Press, Lutterworth Press, 1957): 19f.

13. "Reply to Gellius Faber," *The Complete Writings of Menno Simons, c. 1496–1561,* trans. Leonard Verduin and ed. John Christian Wenger (Scottdale, Penn.: Herald Press, 1956): 739–44. I proposed a list of five defining functions in my "Sacrament as Social Ethics," *Theology Today,* April 1990. Ross T. Bender in *The People of God* reproduces on p. 143 a chart with eight definitional functions.

these added dimensions in a normative description of the church. But since the testimony of Visser 't Hooft and Neill demonstrates abundantly the currency of this kind of thinking, an expository argument should not be necessary here. We shall, therefore, limit our concern to two other comments by way of expositing their continuing contemporary relevance.

First, by way of introduction, let us note the interrelation of the two dimensions that we have observed to be common to these new marks. They have to do with the congregation rather than solely the preacher; and they see the church in relationship to the world rather than describing ecclesial existence "by definition" or "as such." How do these two dimensions relate to one another?

It would be possible to add either one of these dimensions to the standard Lutheran criteria. Martin Luther himself, for instance, thought seriously of the possibility of creating a committed Christian community, to which he testified in the oft-quoted preface to his "German Mass" of 1526. It would have been desirable, he said, that in addition to a continuing use of the Latin liturgy and to the introduction of the high Lutheran German language liturgy there might have been in the third place new corporate expressions in visible congregations.[14] Pietism later sought to fill this gap by creating circles of believers. Yet, without the dimension of outward mission, this type of gathering around common pious experiences is immediately threatened with stagnation and becomes little more than communal introspection.

On the other hand, it is also possible to add to magisterial Protestantism the element of propagation. Some early visions of missionary responsibility, especially as sometimes linked to the early commercial colonial corporations of Britain and the Netherlands, could assume it to be quite adequate to think of the missionary task as adequately discharged by propagating right preaching and right sacramental practice in other parts of the globe; but in the absence of the creation of a genuine indigenous community this turns out to be pure paternalism and makes the alienating elements of sacramentalism and clericalism all the more distasteful by the alien form in which they are exported into another society.

Thus peoplehood and mission, fellowship and witness, are not two desiderata, each capable of existing or of being missed independently of one another; each is the condition of the genuineness of the other.

14. Cf. Luther's vision of 1525 as discussed in John H. Yoder, "Martin Luther's Forgotten Vision," *The Other Side*, April 1977.

Second, and at greater length, after having accepted on the word of Visser 't Hooft, Neill, and Menno that the marks of mission and of community are indispensable, I must proceed to interpret how and why it is the stance of the believers' church, rather than of the spiritualist or theocratic traditions, that most adequately meets these criteria. Menno's outline will be as good as any other scaffold.

Nota 1. Holy Living

For it is God's will that by doing right you should silence the ignorance of the foolish. (1 Pet. 2:15)

The late Harold S. Bender, dean of the in-group historians of Anabaptism, gathered into one article[15] many descriptions of the striking quality of life that even according to the testimony of their adversaries was typical of the sixteenth-century Anabaptists. Certainly the same testimony could be duplicated from the history of the other believers' churches. This is not to suggest that the believers' church tradition is alone in its ethical concern. As a matter of fact the epithets "puritan" and "pietist" currently used to identify those other traditions,[16] have had their greatest (and their most pejorative) currency as descriptive of particular ethical styles. Pietism designates for many a regimen of abstinences from personal gratification, and Puritanism a pattern of social control, both of them predominantly expressed in negative form. In none of these three traditions is there lurking any of that acquiescence in the lower level of the masses' moral performance of which Lutheranism and Anglicanism are accused, nor any of the antinomianism of the enthusiasts. Yet the ethical concern in the three settings is not of the same nature.

With regard to the substance of ethics, spiritualism and theocracy, i.e., Pietism and Puritanism are more alike than different, for the concentration on personal authenticity and on social control is not contradictory but complementary. The person who is truly regenerated and who, therefore, is humble and unselfish will certainly make the best statesman. Or to say it the other way around: the person who governs most needs the illumination and the counsel and admonition of the

---

15. " 'Walking in the Resurrection': The Anabaptist Doctrine of Regeneration and Discipleship," *Mennonite Quarterly Review* XXXV (April 1961): 96–110.

16. Cf. footnotes 7 and 8.

gospel. So the typical context of moral decision is that of the ruler: How shall all society be managed? What are the evils and how may they be eliminated? What is the will of God and how may we assure its being done? What shape should our society have? The samples of decision making dealt with in the ethics text are those persons in "responsible positions": in government, in business leadership.[17] The test eases and the paradigms are not drawn, as so often in the New Testament ethic, from the underside of social relationships: the wife, the child, the slave, the subject. And what the father or the ruler or the banker is to do is not derived from either the words or the example of Jesus, but from what any honest and reasonable person in that same position would do. The imperatives are defined by the situation (or, as an older system said it, "the station"), in which the responsible person finds himself or herself and not by the positive word of the covenant God. Thus from John Calvin to Harvey Cox those who have seen the total social order as the locus of the doing of the will of God have differed only in their language from those others, from Philip Spener to Norman Vincent Peale and Howard Pew, who place their trust in the personal integrity of those in high places.[18]

The alternative to all of this is the biblical demand that holiness is the separateness of a called *people* and the distinctiveness of their social existence. The need is not, as some current popularizers would suggest, for most Christians to get out of the church and into the world. They have been in the world all the time. The trouble is that they have been *of* the world, too. The need is for what they do in the world to be different because they are Christian; to be a reflection not merely of their restored self-confidence nor of their power to set the course of society but of the social novelty of the covenant of grace. Instead of doing, each in his or her own station or office, whatever a reasonable person would do in the same place according to the order of creation;

17. When testing ethical generalizations for their applicability, the standard paradigmatic question (regarding war, for instance) is not "What should a Vietnamese peasant do?" nor "What should a teenage Christian draftee do?" but rather "What should Dean Rusk do?"

18. We cannot here go into detail in the analysis of the logical structure of the ethics of the vocation, to demonstrate how the coincidence of spiritualist and theocratic ethics is explained by the natural law character of their ethical standards. It must suffice to suggest here that there is a very logical connection between the absence of a visible committed community in sociology and the impossibility in epistemology of deriving an acceptable ethic from the positive moral teaching of the Bible.

the need is for what they do there to be judged and renewed by the difference it makes[19] that Christ, and not mammon or mars, is their Lord.

So much for the formal concern for the inner coherence of Gospel ethics: the believers' church is a presupposition of biblical ethics. But now how is that community that is marked by holy living peculiarly the missionary community? First of all, in that the moral nonconformity of Christians is an indispensable dimension of their visibility. If the church is visible in that these people keep their promises, love their enemies, enjoy their neighbors, and tell the truth, as others do not, this may communicate to the world something of the reconciling, i.e., the community-creating, love of God. If, on the other hand, those who call Christ "Lord, Lord" do whatever the situation calls for just as do their neighbors, then what is communicated about their "religion" will probably be that just like the other cultures they have preachers and Sunday gatherings and prescribed ceremonies. The visibility of the witness, and thereby the concept of what it means to hear and accept it, is then misplaced.

Second, ethics is mission in the sense currently and properly being pointed to by the advocates of the "new worldliness." Civil rights advocacy or responsible concern for peace in Vietnam or for food in Mississippi or India can in given circumstances be not only prerequisite for the credibility of preaching but actually themselves the necessary proclamatory action. Likewise, when the more ordinary social structures are asked to determine the "shape of the mission," it is only meaningful for Christians in a business or a factory to gather as a "missionary task force" if there is some available definition of what difference their faith makes in their behavior there.[20]

19. A few decades' observation of the perennial debate on this point suggests that "specific" would be better than "distinctive" or "different." To be "specific" is to belong to one's species, to befit one's kind. That will not always involve being different, although the cases where it "makes a difference" will be the decisive ones.

20. From the believers' church perspective one is at a loss to understand the juxtaposition of two emphases that constantly recur in the "mainstream" traditions:

(a) When speaking on the general topic of social involvement and Christian vocation, our magisterial brethren argue the importance of "taking responsibility for" the course of events in politics, the economy, the university, etc. Often one has the impression that "taking responsibility" means "taking charge" and that it is being understood within the framework of Christendom's assumptions. Over against the spiritualist's unconcern for the mundane, this concern for the course of events is valid, though it is theocratic in

Nota 2. Brotherly and Sisterly Love

Now the whole group of those who believed were of one
heart and soul. (Acts 4:32*a*)

Menno's second mark of the true church is "brotherly love." With Visser
't Hooft's *koinonia,* this moves the locus of definition from the administration of the sacrament to the meaning of the sacrament. As we
suggested before, the loving community was likewise a part of the
vision of Martin Luther. Yet, contrary to the changes that he felt he was
fully authorized to make in the external forms of the magisterial church,
Luther felt it improper to seek actively to form at his own initiative a
group with this quality of relationships, without the prior presence of
the people required to form it, for fear of its becoming a clique.

As Luther thus recognized, this is the point where voluntaryism
makes all the difference. You can make people come to church, but you
cannot make them love one another. The criterion of unfeigned love is,
therefore, the index of the voluntary character of the fellowship.

Menno has the reputation, which at least some of his colleagues and
successors did something to earn for their movement, of practicing
discipline with an unloving and unbending rigor. Yet significantly, the
ban or "discipline" is not, for him, as with Calvin, part of the definition
of the church. Fraternal love is. Here we have a pointer to the structural
difference between church discipline, even when it extends to the point

---

its unspoken trust that control over how things turn out is always desirable
or usually possible.

(b) When, however, one turns to the narrower theme of the ethical standards
that should guide the Christian in this realm of vocational responsibility for
society, the same thinkers will argue strongly against a specifically Christian
ethic. They reject pacifism, for instance, while admitting that it is the position
of Jesus and the apostles, because one's social ethics must be drawn from the
order of nature. They reject the ideals of poverty and chastity, any kind of
withdrawal, any kind of non-generalizable ethic, fearing monasticism, legalism, and the like.

Now it is possible to see, if Christian ethics were concerned as specifically
different from non-Christian ethics, why Christians would have a duty to bring their
contribution to bear on society; for in that case they would be doing something that
no one else can. If, however, one argues at the same time that there is no difference
in substance between the standards Christians apply and those that intelligent,
honorable non-Christians can perceive and attain, it is not self-evident that much
remains of the case for involvement.

of excommunication, within the voluntary church tradition and the very different meaning that such discipline could have in state church systems like those of Geneva, the Netherlands, Scotland, and New England. It is the concern to "win the brother or sister" (Matt. 18:15) that stands behind the discipline of the believers' church, not a desire to inflict suffering, or teach a lesson, or protect the reputation or the standards of the church.[21]

It is by no means far-fetched to suggest that this very quality of aggressive concern for reconciling the brother or sister is a dimension of mission most regrettably lacking in modern Christendom. In the framework of puritan theocracy, with the coercive character of its social sanctions, the effect of "love" in later years was appropriately to soften the pressures and punishments. But when the congregation's "binding and loosing" is the implementation of the commonly covenanted commitment to a manner of life dictated by grace, then to leave the brother alone in his sin is not love at all but irresponsibility. Like the child who misbehaves because it is a sure way to get parental attention, my brother's or sister's sin may testify more to his or her solitude than to either his carnality or his freedom.

Now that in the secular city the given solidarities of the clan and the village cannot be counted on to provide willy-nilly a place where everyone can belong, one may well rejoice in the new freedom that urban anonymity gives us to choose our own associates; but then the question of salvation is posed all the more acutely. Can I find that loving community, for the sake of the finding of which it was good to be freed? If not, then in the words with which Jesus described just this fate, "the last state of that person is worse than the first" (Matt. 12:45*c*).

Nota 3. Witness

> For in this city, in fact, both Herod and Pontius Pilate, with the Gentiles and the peoples of Israel, gathered together against your holy servant Jesus, whom you anointed, to do whatever your hand and your plan had predestined to take place. And now, Lord, look at their threats, and grant to your servants to speak your word with all boldness. . . . (Acts 4:27–29)

21. An outline for study of the discerning and forgiving functions of the community is included as an appendix to this volume. See "Binding and Loosing," pp. 323–58.

The third of the distinctive marks of the church according to Menno is "that the name, will, word, and ordinance of Christ are constantly confessed in the face of all cruelty, tyranny, tumult, fire, sword, and violence of the world, and sustained unto the end." Just as Menno had previously sharpened the definition of the "right use of the sacraments" by insisting that they are not to be administered undiscriminatingly to the impenitent, so here the accent in the definition of witness as a mark of the church is not simply on the holding forth of a message but on the readiness to do so in the face of hostility from the world. Thus the initial and the derived meanings of the word *martyria* are linked. This is, as we have noted, one of the points where the marks of the mission as stated by Visser 't Hooft and Neill would strikingly coincide with those of Menno.

As has been increasingly demonstrated by historical studies, beginning in 1952 with one chapter of *The Anabaptist View of the Church* by Franklin H. Littell[22] and building up to the massive Heidelberg dissertation[23] of Wolfgang Schäufele dealing with the missionary consciousness and activity of the Anabaptists (1966), the concept of a missionary witness is structurally incompatible with the sociological and political posture of the established church, since all of the subjects in a given country are already within that church and in any other *regio* everyone by the same token is the responsibility of some other *religio*. By the same token, only the believers' church is structurally committed to and dependent upon a witness addressed to those who are not its members-dependent, that is, both for its own survival and for the accomplishment of its task.

It is noteworthy that in Menno's interpretation of this faithful witness the accent does not fall upon the subjective response of the hearers. Whether many will hear and be converted, or any, does not enter the discussion of this mark. Thus the debate that has been raging for two centuries about whether the subjective conversion of individuals is the core of the definition of missionary witness is not the central issue. What is central is that the witness be proclaimed without compromise in the face of opposition.

We find in this statement the clear reflection of a particular polemi-

22. *The Anabaptist View of the Church* (Boston: Starr King, 1958). Reissued as *The Origins of Sectarian Protestantism* (New York: Macmillan, 1964).
23. *Das missionarische Bewusstsein und Wirken der Täufer,* "Beiträge zur Geschichte und Lehre der Reformierten Kirche," vol. 21 (Neukirchen: Verlag des Erziehungsvereins, 1966), cf. my own "Reformation and Missions" in *Occasional Bulletin from The Missionary Research Library* 22 (June): 1–9.

cal theme of the sixteenth century. Beginning in the early 1520s, a debate was simmering in both Lutheran and Zwinglian quarters about the concept of *Schonung,* the indulgence or caution or forbearance with which the reformer takes account of the limited understanding of his faithful.[24] In order not to shock the flock with too radical a reformation message, the true preacher of the Word, although convinced that the judgment of Scripture must reject radically much of the inherited Catholic system of piety, will be careful, some argued, to criticize and dismantle only one point at a time and to move only as fast as his constituency can follow.

This is another point at which the theocratic and the spiritualist streams could agree. Zwingli and Luther argued in favor of *Schonung* in order to bring all of society along; for the greatest danger would be to jeopardize the religious unity of the Christian people. Schwenckfeld, on the other hand, was equally committed to *Schonung,* leaving untouched the traditional ceremonies, because it is not worth the trouble to change them and because the very act of centering one's attention on changing them attributes to external forms more attention than they merit. For Zwingli, then, the concept of "witness" is limited to the issue of the authority of the preacher and his wisdom in properly establishing the dosage of novelty that his listeners can tolerate at any one time. For Schwenckfeld "witness" is an expression of concern for the conversion and the inward vitality and authenticity of the life of the individual.

In both cases "forbearance" had the effect of guaranteeing that the impact of the witness on the social order would not be revolutionary nor lead to suffering. Thus the whole problem of the strategy of "reformation" versus "restitution" was encapsuled in the issue of "forbearance," and in that in turn was enclosed the difference between witness and pedagogy as keynotes of the definition of mission. Is the faithfulness with which the church has discharged its mission to be measured by how well it "brings along" the crowds or the authorities? Or the children of the faithful? Or by the unbending conformity of its testimony to the character and person of him to whom it points?

Thus the issue that recent debate on evangelism has stumbled over does not become central. By concern for "who says what to whom" a hopeless polarity has been set up in the interpretation of "lay witness." For the spiritualist it means buttonholing people about their souls; to the theocrat it means speaking to relevant issues from a Christian perspective. For Menno it is both, but neither is the unique focus; for the

24. Cf. *Balthasar Hubmaier* (note 4 above) pp. 46 and 390.

crucial issue is not that there must be one particular idea content but that the witness must avoid his or her testimony's being diluted or distorted by what people want to hear.

As we shall see later in the more polemical section of this study, exactly the same debate is still with us. On the one hand there are those for whom the focus of concern in the faithful witness of the church is the subjective authenticity of the conversion with which the listener manifestly responds. The locus of the meaning of the act of witness is therefore in the listener. Then we shall, of course, expect the convert in turn to become a witness and also, secondarily, to change the surrounding society by faithfulness in his or her calling. On the other hand, there are those for whom the witness of the church centers on a strategy of directed social change. Witness is needed in order that this change shall be called forth. Wisdom is needed that it may be guided at the pace that is set by the institutional possibilities of the agencies that the church can get to listen: change is itself the objective.

Free church theologians have long been trying to choose between these options, and they thereby fall short of the originality of their own heritage. Menno would have addressed to both the criticism that the "witness" was being diluted by opposition: on the one hand by withdrawing from a direct challenge to the orders of society and on the other by setting goals in terms of what the authorities can reasonably be asked to do.

Nota 4. The Cross

"Servants are not greater than their master." If they persecuted me, they will persecute you. (John 15:20b, c)

Fourth, according to Menno and Stephen Neill, the true missionary congregation is marked by suffering. This suffering, like that of the faithful servant in 1 Peter (2:18ff.; 3:14–18; 4:1, 12–16), is not the result of misbehavior but of conformity with the path of Christ. It is not the resigned acceptance of limitations or injustice in an imperfect world but the meaningful assuming of the cost of nonconformed obedience.

It is no accident that the word "martyr" has the double meaning of testimony and innocent suffering. The suffering of the church is not a passing tight spot after which there can be hope of return to normalcy; it is according to both Scripture and experience the continuing destiny of any faithful Christian community.

86

Here again our threefold typology will be of assistance in clarification. For medieval mysticism, for Thomas Müntzer, and for Zinzendorf the "cross" is an inward experience in which the self struggles with doubt or with pride until it is brought to that brokenness and surrender that permits the mystical vision. The concepts of cross and surrender (*Gelassenheit*) then have basically an inward meaning.

For the theocratic world and for the usage of pastoral care across the ages, to have "a cross to bear" means to live with an incurable illness or a difficult relative or poverty. It designates, in other words, a kind of suffering built into one's own social situation for which one may or may not be partially to blame but which is mostly the simple result of where one finds oneself, not of a particular moral commitment. If in this context there is such a concept as "surrender," it must be simply the acceptance of one's being who and where one is as "where God has placed you."

For the believers' church on the other hand, as for the young Zwingli from whom the Anabaptists learned it, "the cross" is to be understood much more narrowly as that kind of suffering that comes upon one because of loyalty to Jesus and nonconformity to the world. "Surrender" has certainly an inward dimension; but its confirmation will be found in one's joyfully doing, in the world, regardless of cost, the will of God. The New Testament scholar Ethelbert Stauffer, who in his New Testament studies has given special attention to the concept of discipleship and to the conflict between Christ and Caesar, has written an interpretation of the meaning of suffering in Anabaptism,[25] in which the demonstration is clear that suffering is not merely the regrettably unavoidable cost of holding to those positions that merit salvation but is rather a participation in the victory of Christ over the powers of this age. The same could be said, for instance, of Quakerism, whose concept of the Christian mission was summed up in the phrase, "The War of the Lamb."[26]

Now it is possible for anyone to agree with the early free churches (and with Stephen Neill) that readiness to suffer is part of the faithfulness of the church and that suffering may often be characteristic of the experience of the faithful church. But this leaves two questions still

25. "The Anabaptist Theology of Martyrdom," *Mennonite Quarterly Review* XIX (July 1945): 179–214.

26. Hugh Barbour, in his definitive *The Quakers in Puritan England* (New Haven: Yale University Press, 1964), identifies the phrase "War of the Lamb" as the standard early Quaker characterization of their place in the movement of history. See his fourteen citations in the index, p. 267.

open. First of all, is there not some danger of seeking suffering or glorifying it for its own sake? Here the distinction already made over against spiritualistic and theocratic concepts of the cross is helpful. Mysticism and monasticism can glorify suffering for its own sake because it is thought of as a tool in the discipline of the soul. The theocratic vision, on the other hand, can consider it as a not necessary, because incalculable, dimension of Christian faithfulness, arising as Providence permits out of the order of things and less prevalent when Christians do better at governing the world. If, however one sees the cross of the Christian, as the language of the New Testament indicates, to be a reflection of and participation in the character of the saving work of Christ, then one does not seek it, but when it comes neither does one consider it simply as a matter of having been providentially chosen for a hard time.

But in our context the perhaps more difficult question is what this mark of suffering has to do with faithfulness in mission. The simple answer would be to ask what suffering had to do with the mission of Jesus, but such a cryptic response is not enough. Since the free church definition was developed over against the religious establishment, the place to look for this answer is not on the foreign mission field (for there every church is a free church in the first generations) but in the conflicts of the Reformation. The free churches arose out of attempts at reformation in various times and places where other leaders of that reformation process wanted not to stay with the status quo but to move slowly and strategically. The process of reformation, never complete (*ecclesia semper reformanda*), was conceived as a gradual curriculum, in which the authorized teacher would move his total flock progressively from apostasy or paganism into true evangelical faith. For this reason, he argued, one must not say everything at once; one must not be too radical; one must respect the conscience of the weak. Since the time when the argument from the tender conscience of the weak brother or sister was used by Zwingli in favor of maintaining the use of the mass after he had condemned it as theologically wrong, the same debate has been repeated many times at the birth of every free church movement. The "cross" that the gradualist official reformer is unwilling to bear is, therefore, not necessarily outright persecution, death, or exile but simply the tension and rejection, on the part of the mass of the population or the civil authorities, that would need to be faced by someone committed first of all to restructuring the church according to the will of God. Thus willingness to bear the cross means simply the readiness to let the form of the church's obedience to Christ be dictated by Christ rather than by how much the population or the authorities are ready to accept. When stated in this way it is then clear that the readiness of the church to face suffering thus understood is precisely the only way in which it is possible to communicate to that society and to its authorities that it is Christ who is Lord and not they. The preacher who tailors his or her message to what the people will understand is not simply making a practical mistake of "not moving fast enough"; he or she is failing by the very structure of his or her approach to communicate one particular thing, namely, that his or her loyalty to Christ is the sole absolute.

Mission Compromised

For the label "believers' church" to be meaningful, it must be assumed that there is some other kind of church, or more precisely some other concept of the church, not structured upon faith in the same way, with which it stands in tension. To know honestly what it means to affirm that the community of believers is the form of the mission, we therefore must face as well, in loving polemics, the real possibilities of unfaithfulness and the serious claims of other options. How could it happen that the church could become Christendom? Wherein lies the essence of that apostasy whereby what calls itself church, continuing to do great deeds avowedly in the name of the Lord, defeats his purposes instead?

The Roman and Eastern forms of Catholicism, when they speak of one another as "apostate," date that fall from grace with their breach of hierarchical communion with each other. When Magisterial Protestantism sought a date for fall of the church, it was found somewhere after the fifth century, so that the ancient creeds could all be retained. Anabaptism found the root still deeper, at the point of that fusion of church and society of which Constantine was the architect, Eusebius the priest, Augustine the apologete, and the Crusades and Inquisition the culmination. If the reconciliation of all races and peoples is the mission, then the sacralization of one people or, even worse, of one bearer of sovereignty, or the identification of the Kingdom with the movement of one imperial society, is its denial. But now this thesis demands application to the current scene.

Compromise 1. Evangelism

For one major portion of our study we have not the liberty of choosing our own topic. Current debate on the mission of the church in the world has been radically and publicly polarized again in the mid-1960s around contradictory definitions of the meaning of evangelism.

Perhaps the word "contradictory" is too strong for some. There are many for whom the two polar positions seem extreme and who would seek somehow to mediate between them. But the debaters on both sides are right at least in principle; there is no papering over the difference between two ultimately incompatible points of orientation.

On the one hand, symbolized internationally by the July 1966 World Conference on Church and Society in Geneva and in the United States by those parallel concerns for which "the secular city" and "go where the action is" are the slogans, we have the contemporary form of the theocratic program. It finds the locus of meaningfulness in the course of the history of a society or of the world at large and calls upon the church to discern God as the agent of that movement and upon Christians to join God in bringing it about. Now with regard to ethics, the particular standards of moral evaluation for such issues as work and leisure or sexuality will in this context have a quite different outline from what used to be called "puritan." But our typology here is dealing with the question of the locus of the meaning of history, and on this structural level it can hardly be doubted that the vision of the "secular city," which David Little has perceptively called "the social gospel revisited," is today's edition of the Genevan theocratic vision.

On the other hand, in that position, represented internationally by the October 1966 World Congress on Evangelism in Berlin and locally by the presence of Billy Graham at the National Council of Churches General Assembly in December, there is the continuing vitality of that stream of church leadership that sees the locus of all meaning in the stance of the soul. What should matter ultimately to a person is the destiny of one's own soul. In my concern for the welfare of others, the good I seek for them is of the same kind.

Now it does not solve this problem at all to temper one of the extreme positions by adding a few elements of the other. It is possible, for instance, to add to spiritualism a recognition of the serious social concern that will be expressed by the converted person, while still holding a conception of the saving experience that is completely in-dividualistic. Billy Graham does this, even using the term "Social Gospel." On the other hand, it is possible to recognize that only a personally convinced and committed person will be effective as an agent of social change and that every significant social cause is carried by a few firmly committed, "converted" individuals whose devotion and effectiveness can only be explained as unique divine gifts, while still holding that what ultimately matters in God's purpose is the building of better society. But such mitigation of the extremes does not change their opposition.

It is already no easy task, with the debate set up this way, just to describe the current polarization of the meanings old and new of evangelism and revolution, to say nothing of attempting to lead this discussion to a wholesome conclusion. But if instead of seeking to mediate or to assign percentages to these two components of the Christian missionary responsibility, we were to bring to bear our tripartite typology, we might be partly freed from the dilemma. For if it is the predominant purpose of God neither to direct all of world history coercively toward a predetermined end, nor to make individuals whole each by herself or himself, but to constitute a new covenant people responding freely to God's call, then the strong and weak points of the earliest debate fall into a new configuration. The error of spiritualism is not adequately tempered by insisting that saved individuals will get together sometimes or that saved individuals will be socially effective. But neither is it to be corrected by replacing personal change and commitment with the remodeling of the total society. The complement to personal decision is the "new humanity" of covenant community. Preoccupation with making world history come out right or making the secular city be the city of God is not adequately tempered by saying that even the best technopolis would still be imperfect or that there will sill need to be voluntary associations within the coming great society. But neither must concern for the social dimension of the kingdom be replaced by a mere call to a new attitude.

The political novelty that God brings into the world is a community of those who serve instead of ruling, who suffer instead of inflicting suffering, whose fellowship crosses social lines instead of reinforcing them. This new Christian community in which the walls are broken down not by human idealism or democratic legalism but by the work of Christ is not only a vehicle of the gospel or only a fruit of the gospel; it is the good news. It is not merely the agent of mission or the constituency of a mission agency. This is the mission.

Compromise 2. History

It was predictive of this major contemporary debate when in 1961 the Study Commission on the Missionary Task of the Church of the World Council of Churches identified as one of the continuing questions far from being resolved the issue of the relationship between the work of the church and the course of secular history:

> What is the relation between the Course of the Gospel and what is going on in the world? What is God's redemptive purpose in and for world history?

The commission's response to this question was modest and moderate. While solidly affirmative about Christian social responsibility and the partly biblical origins of radical social criticism, the statement maintained a distinction in kind between the church and the wider history, between its faithfulness and its social efficacy, and between its hope and secular messianisms.[27] But this study did not become a landmark, and in the broader stream of "Church and Society" talks the same modesty has not always been evident. So the debate goes on.

This same question comes to the surface in contemporary ecumenical debate on a number of levels, all the way from the attitude to take toward particular power structures within a given local society to the interpretation of the whole course of world history as this reflects the impact of "Christianization" and "secularization." But whatever the breadth of the view, the structure of the thought is the same. In opposition to what it identifies as "pietism," the currently prevalent mode of thought prominent in World Council circles identifies the structures of secular society as the locus of the meaning of mission. On the broadest level this means interpreting the process of secularization itself as an outworking of the desacralization that is the impact of the biblical witness.[28] It is itself the ultimate goal of the witness of the church. In the local context, as has been developed in considerable

27. I am citing here from my own notes from the 1961 meeting. I cannot ascertain whether this particular text was published.

28. The theses of Arend Th. van Leeuwen to this effect have been given wide currency, partly through ecumenical agencies. The publication of the Study Division of the World Council of Churches, *Study Encounter,* treated the theme in its second issue (1965), and van Leeuwen was the featured speaker at the First Assembly of the Division of Overseas Ministries of the National Council of Churches in October 1965.

length in the extended series of studies on the Missionary Structure of the Congregation, the emphasis has constantly been laid upon turning one's attention away from the church and what goes on within in order to discern instead what it is that God, independently of the church if need be, has been doing in the world, namely, in the structures of society and their evolution, so that, having discerned his working, the church can welcome it and join it. Between the two extremes of philosophy of history and techniques of social change, the most typical and journalistically attractive discussion deals with "revolution" as the not clearly defined label for the profound and rapid social change that all agree is needed in most of Asia, Africa, and Latin America if people are to be able to live together in dignity. Since it is needed, this revolution must be approved of by the church, however it comes; it must be discerned as both inevitable and the will of God.

A careful encounter with this new mood in Christian social ethics under the heading of mission would go far beyond the scope of the present study. Our concern here is only to point out that, in spite of its undeniable originality in detail, such a position is in its structure but another form of the theocratic conception of the mission of the church. It is very aware of the differences, since the old Puritanism labeled as "Christian" the society whose structures it supported, and now these societies are accepted as "secular." Yet, the powers at work and the forces upon which one relies, the evils one identifies and the images one nurtures of how people should live together have the same shape. The old theocracy could baptize the world. Now that the world will no longer let itself be baptized, the church nonetheless claims it in spite of itself as the "latent" church and proclaims its salvation whether it will or not. In earlier centuries the rulers did at least sometimes what they were told to do by preachers, especially within the Zwinglian tradition. Today Christian thinkers claim to discern a revelation of what God is doing in what the powers of this world are doing anyway for their own reasons. The world has "come of age," but we still baptize it as our baby.

Certainly the testing of this new Constantinianism is not furthered by the spiritualistic alternative, which is all that most critics seem able to propose. The spiritualistic critic argues (rightly as far as that goes) that no juggling of the structures of society can do away with the effects of human sinfulness, so that the premises and promises of a new secular optimism are deceptive, in addition to being less than the New Testament gospel, because they bypass the elements of personal rebellion, guilt, and reconciliation. But as we saw before, this critique does not have an alternative social ethic of its own. Then in effect those who criticize the "gospel of the secular revolution" presuppose in its place that they shall continue to give their blessing to the present anti- or pre-revolutionary order, which is sanctified for them by virtue of the fact that some at least of the people who hold office within it are Christians doing their duty in a secular vocation.

Thus in spite of the vast difference in focus and language, the theocratic and spiritualist social ethics are structurally the same. One sanctifies the present or recent order and the other the future order, but both make that total order the framework of social ethics. One sanctifies the coming order because it is what matters the most under the Lordship of Christ; the other leaves things as much as possible as they are because this is not what matters the most spiritually, but the logical outcome is the same. Both derive the substance of their ethics from the "vocation," i.e., from the naturally discernible structures and values built into the social order, present or evolving.

It would be possible to argue on either side of the thesis that, if Christians are to be in servitude to the principalities and powers, it at least is better that it be the powers of the future than those of the past. But from the context of the covenant community the argument should rather be that such servitude, whether past or future, is part of what we have been freed from by the work of Christ and the gift of his Spirit.

The context of the covenant community represents a radical alternative to both the theocratic and the spiritualist views of historical movement, first of all, because the community is a *discerning* community. The promise of the presence of the Holy Spirit is clearly correlated in the New Testament with the need for the church prophetically to discern right and wrong in the events of the age. Not all visible events are God at work, not all "action" is divine, not every spirit is of Christ (1 Cor. 12:3; 1 John 4:1). We cannot "go where the action is" until we know *which* action should be blessed and joined and which should be denounced. Precisely because a community of faith is distinct from the wider society not only in membership but also in decision-making structures and values, it can be the agent of responsible moral discernment.

The church is qualified to be such an agent of discernment, secondly, because it is committed not simply to doing "good," whatever that may be and wherever it may be found, but because it has in its allegiance to Jesus Christ criteria of good and evil that are significantly different from those that prevail in even the most respectable segments of the larger society. However much it makes sense to modern Western thought, the ethic of vocation that tells each Christian simply to do what is "called for" by the inherent and unambiguous standards of his "situation" or "station" or "office" finds no support in the New Testament. After a long stretch of time when, under the impact of Albert Schweitzer, the study of New Testament ethical thought was paralyzed by the idea that the irrationally radical ethic of Jesus was conditioned upon his mistaken expectation of the end of history, more careful study is now beginning to rediscover a consistent pattern of ethical thought in the several strands of the New Testament literature. This is not an "interim ethic" in the sense that its logic depends upon the expectation of an early end of the world. It is derived not from any such calculations but simply from Christology.

The difference between this New Testament ethic and that of our age is most clearly demonstrated by what Jesus says about serving and ruling. "'The kings of the Gentiles lord it over them; and those in authority over them are called benefactors. But not so with you . . .'" (Luke 22:25–26a; cf. Matt. 20:25). In modern parlance, "public service" has become the standard euphemism for the exercise of power, thus fulfilling in the name of the "Christian calling" what Jesus ironically said about pagan rulers, namely, that they glorify the exercise of power over people as being "benefaction." Now Jesus and the New Testament writers following him do not reject rulership because the world is coming to an early end, nor because it is ethically impure (when measured, as Reinhold Niebuhr would measure it, by the standards of absolute selflessness), nor because the people who exercise it are always evil brutes. They do not say that the world can get along without such powers; but neither do they suggest that if by conquest or by elections we put Christians in all those positions they would do a much better job. They simply say that it was the mission of the Son of Man to serve and not to rule and that his disciples will follow him in the same path. If there is to be any solid critique of the contemporary wave of enthusiasm for religiously glorified revolution, it must not be in the name of religiously glorified conservatism nor of social unconcern or neutrality or withdrawal but rather an expression of an ethic of social involvement as servants derived from the man Jesus, whose messianity and lordship we affirm and of whom we confess (whether the "action" to this effect be visible or not) that his way of servanthood shall triumph.

Thus what is questionable about the "gospel of revolution" as currently being propagated by the popularizers is not that it is too revolutionary but rather that it is just a new edition of the same old pattern of seeking in the name of God to make history come out right instead of seeking in the train of Christ only to be servant.

95

Compromise 3. The Congregation

It is characteristic of policy statements within the study processes of the World Council of Churches that the centrality of the local congregation is always affirmed. In one classical statement, the paper on "A Responsible Society" with which the veteran ecumenical statesman J. H. Oldham launched a slogan that was to find a wide echo, the development began with such an affirmation:

> The church is concerned with the primary task of re-creating a true social life in two ways. In the first place, its greatest contribution to the renewal of society is through the fulfillment of its primary functions of preaching the Word and through its life as a worshipping community.[29]

It was only after this statement of priorities that the argument then moved on in a very significant sequence to the work ethic of the individual, then to the morality of decisions in small groups, and last to discussing the form of the political order.

As a series of further study conferences and programs circled the globe between Amsterdam and Evanston, applying the concept of responsible society especially to the strategy of the churches in areas of rapid social change, every conference and every document continued to reaffirm his preamble (Bangkok 1949, Lucknow 1952, Evanston 1954, India 1960). But as far as the actual subject matter of study was concerned, the sequence very rapidly became the reverse. The discussion turned first on a picture of what the total social order should be, then on the decision making of power groups and leadership groups within a society, only third on individual ethical responsibility in the vocation, and then the place of congregational life was left for last.

At New Delhi, 1961, the concern for the congregation was refocused, partly because of the emphasis laid by the Faith and Order Commission on the thesis that the unity we seek is not so much an organizational change on the national or world level but rather the possibility for "all in each place" to be united in fellowship and in mission. There then began the series of studies on the "Missionary Structure of the Congregation" that ran through the 1960s. The course of this study may be summarized roughly as follows:

---

29. *The Church and the Disorder of Society*, vol. 3: *Man's Disorder and God's Design* (New York: Harper and Brothers, 1948): 127.

A. One begins with the starting assumption that the parish structure, which has obtained in European Christianity and its cultural extensions where colonization has planted "Christian culture," was appropriate and at least in principle adequate then as an expression of the responsibility of the church to and for and in a stable society prior to the Industrial Revolution.

B. The changes that have taken place in social organizations and communication through the revolutionary cultural developments and movements of peoples in the last century and one-half make it clear that the residential parish is no longer the cultural home or *oikos* of the living of people in our age. If then the Christian congregation is to discharge the responsibility that hitherto has taken the shape of the residentials parish, it must learn to adapt itself to the new shape of the life of modern society. This, a consensus of the writers in this stream of study processes would seem to be saying, will call for breaking up the traditional concept of "congregational life" along two different lines.

C. The first line of bifurcation is the definition of that shape which society provides to the church and to which the church shall adapt itself.

(1) There is, first of all, the actual matrix of the basic life experiences that replace the residential neighborhood with a group of people gathering around a particular function. For the children and their teachers this is the school; for the wage earners it is the factory or the office; for the housewives it is the shopping center; for students, the university where "congregating" should occur. These are, therefore, the *oikoi* in which new task forces should gather, each taking, for that segment of society, a kind of "parish" defined functionally rather than spatially, the same type of function that the church in the old days tried to take for the neighborhood. These will be groups much smaller and less rigidly organized than the traditional congregations.

(2) But it will also be necessary to move to groups much larger than the ordinary congregation. Modern men and women with their media of communication and transportation feel "at home" in a total urban area. The "world" with which men and women are familiar is that which is within a traveling distance of a few hours from their homes and in which, if they have lived there a

few years, they can feel that they know their way around and recognize the major landmarks and the leading personages. There will, therefore, have to be some kind of organization on this level, that of the metropolitan complex or the "human zone." As Hans J. Margull summarizes it, "Man's life formerly lived in his small parish is now being lived in a large and specific region, and it came to us to affirm that nothing less than such a region ought to be seen as a parish."[30] In a somewhat comparable way, Stephen C. Rose in his vision of *The Grass Roots Church*[31] suggests a regional pattern that might bring forth congregations many times as large as the present ones.

D. The other line of bifurcation distinguishes not size or scale but functions. While the terminology varies and the lines are variously drawn between them, the distinction is usually in some way drawn between those functions that have traditionally defined the inner life of the church and those that express its mission. One may speak of the "instituted means of grace" as continuing to be administered by the traditional residential parish and then of the "prudential means of grace" as the forms of missionary creativity.[32] Or the distinction may run between education and ministry or between "chaplaincy" and "abandonment." Wherever Christians gather, the meeting may be spoken of as in some sense a congregation, but out of respect for the momentum of history or for some genuine function served by the historic structures, these two patterns shall be retained side by side, and the gatherings that seek to discern and to implement God's will for a given social need shall be distinct from those that affirm God's saving work in the past in the language of Scripture and liturgy and proclamation.

Our purpose here cannot be to carry on a substantial conversation with this stream of study and popular writing. It must suffice to indicate at which points this line of thought makes assumptions that cannot be taken for granted from the perspective of the believers' church tradition, so that it comes to conclusions that are less than convincing.

30. *Concept*, "Papers from the Department on Studies in Evangelism of the World Council of Churches," Fascicle XII (December 1966): 11.

31. (New York: Holt, Rinehart and Winston, 1966), esp. chs. 5, 6.

32. This distinction made by John Wesley, *Works*, VIII, 322–24, is reinterpreted by Colin W. Williams, *Where in the World? Changing Forms of the Church's Witness* (London: Epworth Press, 1965): 61–64.

The first of these assumptions is the one that underwent no examination in this study process, namely, that *until* the industrial revolution the parish pattern was quite proper, whereby a given area was assumed to be the responsibility of one given pastor by virtue of the baptism of all members of that community, whereby moral tutelage was exercised by the church organization with the backing of government, and whereby the pastor was named to that place by the church hierarchy. All of these aspects of the historic parish pattern, of which the geographical limitation of areas of responsibilities is simply the mechanical outworking, have been challenged for centuries by the believers' church tradition. In fact the first formal reproach addressed to the Anabaptists in 1525 by Huldrych Zwingli was that they interfered with the standard geographically limited parish authorities by migrating and itinerating without governmental authorization. Fox and Wesley were subject to the same reproach. So the believers' church has been since its origins a group of people who have not been brought together by geographical contiguity but rather who were drawn together, often from considerable distances, even before the industrial revolution, by a common commitment. For this heritage, where the church is thought of as the people gathering from many quarters rather than as the agency ministering to an area, the greater flexibility of modern urban society ought to facilitate rather than undermine the expression of its unity. You *can* do it in the city. It is becoming increasingly more difficult for any particular segment of population to feel itself a parish, i.e., the self-evident field of ministry of a given church office or officer; but it is becoming from generation to generation easier for those who want to gather on a voluntary basis with others of common commitment to do so.

Since from this perspective the parish pattern was questionable in the first place, it can hardly be the most constructive way of meeting the modern world to accept and then update the parish assumptions. What was really wrong with the parish was the most wrong not when it became obsolete but when it worked the best, namely, when there was no challenging of the proprietary claim that the local parson had over the allegiance and the beliefs of the people of his village by virtue of his having been named by the local lord.

The "missionary structure" study process has in one way repeated the pattern of the "responsible society" studies. The movement of study topics has been decidedly away from serious attention to what Hans-Jochen Margull calls "the normal local congregation." Of course, without having discussed together what is considered "normal" and by whom, we cannot know how serious such an omission was. But both those who like and those who question the actual substance of the rapidly expanding treatment of social and political ethics in the name of "mission" recognize that here are issues having to do with the functioning of existing congregations that have not been seriously dealt with. The conviction of the believers' church tradition would need to raise serious question about the segregation of three different strands of church life that results from this development. On the one hand there is the picture of the mass of membership in the mammoth congregations of Stephen Rose's "human zone," most of whom are not expected to take any active part in the life of the visible community beyond attending the services of liturgy and receiving the sacraments, because their "mission" is in their daily life. On the other hand, there are the task force groups gathered around specific missionary interests but segregated by these interests along lines of occupation, class, capability, and interest. Then third, somewhere between these two types of groups and serving to relate them to one another, but subject to neither, there would be the professional staff responsible for institutional continuity, the use of facilities, specialized services like counseling and education that could be provided only by "the church" (as administration, not as membership). This staff would be organized on the level of the mammoth congregation or the "human zone."

It is the conviction of the believers' church tradition that all of these necessary functions would need to be more integrally related to one another than such a trichotomy would dictate. The face-to-face encounter of the small group wrestling with a given task is vitiated if separated from the liturgical celebration and proclamation of the miracle of reconciliation. The service of the "magisterial" leadership of the congregation is vitiated if it is carried on independently of the government of a visible body in which those special ministries find their legitimacy and their only effective control. The massive celebrations of proclamation and liturgy are vitiated if most of those who attend are not at some other point called to account for a deep personal participation in the disciplined exchange of fraternal concern. Since the "missionary structure study" was not established to be a conversation with the believers' church tradition, this comment is not a final evaluation but rather a statement of continuing agenda. The alternative we would suggest would not be to depreciate any of these severally defined and designated functions, but to recognize as most important not that they be seen as separate functions but rather the means of their coordination. Or to put the matter in terms of the slogan, instead of the "missionary structure of the congregation" we would have asked to see more about the congregational structure of the mission.

Envoy

If space permitted, we should argue further the link between the liberty of the believers' church, as it used to need to be affirmed over against the *Volkskirche*, and ecumenical concern today as it is in turn dictated by and strengthened by mission, constituting itself a dimension of mission. How evangelism, mission, and unity are interlaced cannot be adequately rehearsed here. Nor need it be repeated that only a church free from the promise to sanctify a given society can conceive its mission as universal. We could argue further that the congregationalism of the believers' church provides an alternative definition of "the unity we seek," more real than the spiritualist "spiritual unity" of like-minded believers and yet more realistic than the theocratic vision of a nation-wide merger of polity structures. We could demonstrate from history how much of the original momentum of the modern ecumenical movement came from the way the "mainstream" church structures were bypassed by voluntaryistic groupings like the Evangelical Alliance and the Student Volunteer Movement. But we have already come to the point where the parallelism in the structure of the argument from one issue to the next has begun to confirm the inner coherence of the believers' church stance, and further exposition would have diminishing returns.

Let us then simply conclude by reiterating with reference to mission the thesis stated in the conference prospectus. That in the believers' church heritage there exists "an apprehension of the nature of . . . the church which is specific" we have sought to demonstrate by contrasting it with those views that locate mission in the heart or in the total course of history. That this apprehension, beyond being specific, is also "coherent, a theologically valid option and a needed contribution in ecumenical debate" we have sought to display by observing how uniformly relevant it is to issues currently being debated less satisfactorily in the terms dictated by other traditions. Should the conference body deem the demonstration unconvincing, I would remain certain that the flaw has been in the argument and not in the thesis.

Why Ecclesiology Is Social Ethics: Gospel Ethics Versus the Wider Wisdom

"Why Ecclesiology Is Social Ethics: Gospel Ethics Versus the Wider Wisdom" originated as the first of the "Stone Lectures" given at Princeton University in January 1980. A slightly revised version of these materials was given as the "Morgan Lectures" at Fuller Theological Seminary a few weeks later. Later that same year Yoder used some of this material in a series of lectures given at Loyola University in New Orleans. In 1984, James William McClendon, Jr., conducted a graduate seminar in which Yoder's Stone lectures were the focus of discussion. McClendon's unpublished "report" on Yoder's Stone and Morgan lectures and his comments in Vol. I of his *Systematic Theology: Ethics* attracted the interest of a few graduate students in theology and ethics during the mid-1980s, who in turn raised questions with Yoder about this body of unpublished material. Several of the major themes originally explored in the Stone Lectures have been developed by Yoder over the past decade in such articles as "Sacrament as Social Process" in *Theology Today* (April 1991) and the recently published *Body Politics: Five Practices of the Christian Community before the Watching World* (Discipleship Resources, 1993). However, the first essay has not heretofore been circulated beyond a small circle of scholars familiar with Yoder's work. It is published here, with revisions, for the first time.

This article centers on a set of issues raised in a discussion of "The Order of the Community" in Karl Barth's *Church Dogmatics* IV/2 (719–26), where the notion of "True Church Law" is discussed in the context of the doctrine of the Holy Spirit, in relation to Barth's earlier essay on "Christian Community and Civil Community." In part, of course, Yoder used Barth's work in this lecture because of the strong Reformed heritage of both

Princeton Seminary and Fuller Seminary. However, it should also be noted that there are substantive reasons for taking Barth's work as a point of departure. As Yoder points out, Barth is the only mainline theologian for millennia to take seriously as a starting point for ethics the fact that the civil community *does not acknowledge,* as the church *does* acknowledge, the lordship of Christ. In this sense, as Yoder argues, Barth can be said to be, in Troeltsch's use of the term, a "sectarian" theologian (for a fuller argument on this point, see Yoder's article "Karl Barth: How His Mind Kept Changing" in *How Karl Barth Changed My Mind,* ed. Donald McKim [Grand Rapids: Eerdmans, 1986]: 166–71). From this observation, Yoder moves on to call attention to the significance of Barth's grounding of social ethics in the confession or non-confession of Jesus Christ, as the only necessary dualism for social ethics.

Accordingly, Yoder's ecclesiological conception in this essay takes shape in relation to several important inferences that he has drawn from Barth's discussion of "The Order of the Community" in the *Church Dogmatics* IV/2. Each of these Barthian insights in turn serves the purpose of unfolding Yoder's thesis that "the access to social ethics should consist in the exemplarity of the church as foretaste/model/herald of the kingdom." The net result of Yoder's exposition of Barth's discussion of "church law" is that he is able to spell out not only *why,* theologically speaking, ecclesiology *is* social ethics but why Christian ethics must be unfolded as part of the explication of the church's embodiment as both a political community and a doxological community. The dialectical interplay of these two related claims, and their implications for how Christians should engage ethical claims derived from what Yoder here calls "the wider wisdom," recalls Yoder's discussion of "messianic ethics" in *The Politics of Jesus* (1972), as well as Yoder's more recent ecclesiological essays in such works as *The Priestly Kingdom*.

Why Ecclesiology Is Social Ethics: Gospel Ethics Versus the Wider Wisdom

To approach "social ethics as gospel" means to state dissatisfaction with the various ways in which Christians, including ethicists themselves, have dichotomized ethics from gospel, or at least social ethics from the

Good News. Second, to approach "social ethics as gospel" identifies some biases in method; an expectation that the New Testament texts, and especially the story they tell, can speak to us in our time; not immediately, yet with a good-news-bearing quality that the necessary disciplines of historical distance and technical analysis need not completely filter out.

To say that the kingdom is at hand, that the new world is on the way, is first of all to anchor our thoughts in the priority of grace. Before we can set out toward the New World, it must have — and by God's goodness it has — come to us. We can only be on our way because of that prior coming. We do not go out to find or to build the kingdom but only to meet it. It is already on the way, and our common confession, our being-social as believers, is the "first fruits" of that promise's being more than a promise, of its being real good news because it has already begun, and of its being social in its essence, not only by implication.

I begin with a gloss on a modern text, a passage from Karl Barth.[1] Like any gloss, this use of a modern classic author is at once respectfully submissive to the intent of the original author and riskily independent of him in the lines of prolongation that it suggests. By no means does what I mean to argue here depend for its claim to credibility upon Karl Barth's having said it well before me. But his having said it may well result from its being true and especially appropriate for our age, when the dynamic of the imperative *semper reformanda* has outrun the deposit of the *ecclesia reformata*.

Barth writes: "True Church law is exemplary law. For all its particularity, it is a pattern for the formation and administration of human law generally, and therefore of the law of other political, economic, cultural and other human societies." He goes on to cite a comment by Erik Wolf: "What might it not mean for the world if Church order and law were not merely spiritual adaptations of worldly constitutions and codes, but genuine and original witnesses to the brotherly fellowship of Jesus Christ!" Then Barth continues his discussion:

> ... In the formation and administration of its law the Christian community, while it is first and decisively responsible to its Lord, assumes also a responsibility on the human level. . . . The Christian Church, as the body of Jesus Christ and therefore the earthly-historical form of His existence, is the provisional representation of the humanity

---

1. *Church Dogmatics* IV/2. English translation (Edinburgh: T & T Clark, 1958): 719ff. The citations are presented in Barth's order. I do not burden the reader by a footnote each time.

sanctified in Him. Jesus Christ did not sanctify Himself for His own sake, but for the sake of humanity. That He did this, and that humanity is therefore sanctified already in Him, is what the Christian Church has to represent to it; to the world which is not yet aware of it. . . .

The exemplary nature of Church law cannot be understood in the sense of a law which has to be imposed upon the world. . . .

But why not in the sense that it has to express the Gospel to the world in the form of its particular law? . . . The decisive contribution which the Christian community can make to the upbuilding and work and maintenance of the civil consists in the witness which it has to give to it and to all human societies in the form of the order of its own upbuilding and constitution. . . . It is itself only a human society moving like all other to His manifestation. But in the form [in] which it exists among them it can and must be to the world of men around it a reminder of the law of the kingdom of God already set up on earth in Jesus Christ, and a promise of its future manifestation. Whether they realize it or not, it can and should show them that there is already on earth an order which is based on that great alteration of the human situation and directed towards its manifestation . . . worldly law, in the form in which they regard it as binding which they believe that they cannot know any other or regard any other as practicable, has already ceased to be the last word and cannot enjoy unlimited authority and force; there are other possibilities, not merely in heaven but on earth, not merely one day but already, than those to which it thinks that it must confine itself . . . if there is to be right and order and peace and freedom on earth even in the defective and provisional forms of the present time, there is needed a recognition and acknowledgment of the law of the One who has reconciled them with God and in whom the sanctification of humanity has already taken place . . . it attests the Gospel of the kingdom of God to all human law, whether it be common or statue law, civil or criminal, the law of property or the law of contract. If the community were to imagine that the reach of the sanctification of humanity accomplished in Jesus Christ were restricted to itself and the ingathering of believers, that it did not have corresponding effects *extra munros ecclesiae*, it would be in flat contradiction to its own confession of its Lord.

. . . its cognitive basis, the lordship of Jesus Christ *ad dexteram Patris omnipotentis*, is the actual basis of all temporal law as well. Is it not to be expected, therefore, that in its forms — however defective these may be . . . there will be at least some analogies or correspondences to ecclesiastical law?

. . . Already the law of the world has been improved, and not without some assistance on the part of the Church. . . . The community must not be vexed that the model which it has to give to the world cannot have more than a corrective influence . . . it cannot and must not be too small a thing for it to give a provisional but real representation of the law. (726)

A number of obvious and more elegant paths suggest themselves for my effort to unroll the thesis that the access to social ethics should consist in the exemplarity of the church as foretaste/model/herald of the kingdom. One could extend and analogize from the classic creedal marks of the church: unity, holiness, catholicity, and apostolicity. One could use as an outline the classic Reformed formulation of the necessary *notae:* the Word, the sacraments, and discipline. Or would it be possible (as I propose to do in a fragmentary way later) to use as a base a selection of specific biblical statements about how the church is to function, i.e., works of the Spirit or ministries to be discharged.

I propose, however, to take a different path to the same goal, namely to be guided by an analysis of a few of those ways in which the originality of this particular Barthian innovation unpacks the critical analysis of the situation of Christendom. There would be many other ways to approach the same critical assignment, but let me seek to enter the chink in the armor of the dominant Western tradition of social ethics at the point Barth has identified.

We could take other paths for characterizing what is most definitional for the notion of "Christendom," but certainly a simple definition is that it speaks of a place and a time where the name of Christ was invoked over a global cultural/social/political phenomenon without regard for whether all the participants in that process were invoking that name as their own confessional identity. If we begin with that simply operational definition, then the insight at the bottom of Barth's programmatic text opens the doors for review.

Aficionados of that particular branch of archaeology devoted to the stratigraphic analysis of the thought of Karl Barth will recognize here an echo of a much earlier statement, his brief text on *Christengemeinde und Bürgergemeinde,* translated into English as "Christian Community and Civil Community" from the early post-war period.[2] There

---

2. The essay "Christian Community and Civil Community" was published in Will Herberg (ed.) *Community, State, and Church* (Garden City, N.J.: Anchor Doubleday, 1960): 149ff.

Barth for the first time identified a structural problem intrinsic to the free church perspective toward which some elements of his thought more than others had been moving since more than a decade before. Two different bases for belonging together in society demand two different ways of speaking to that togetherness from the perspective of faith.

The simplicity of the title of this essay is deceptive. The reader of the English title can be forgiven for assuming that it is made up of one noun and two adjectives. Both "Christian" and "civil" seem to be adjectives describing the substantive "community," the latter representing a well-known sociological concept and the two adjectives being similarly familiar although not quite equivalent in level.

The difference in nuance is worth looking at. In Barth's title the term "Christian" is a plural noun and not an adjective. It defines the confessional status of the people who make up the community. It is not merely a predicate of their being or of their being together. Similarly the other noun is "citizen"; again a definitional qualification of persons, not the description of a quality or a particular segment of life. Thus the most literal rendering would be "Community of Christians and Community of Citizens." Likewise we misunderstand the noun. *Gemeinde* is not the German term ordinarily translated "community," for it has a more concrete set of connotations. By no means is it a specifically religious term. It applies as well to the organization of a village. Yet its predominant usage in the Protestant experience has been to identify the free church or the theological church as over against church as establishment (*Kirche*). Barth is thus speaking of two distinct concrete forms of commonality, one the real togetherness of people who are all Christians and the other the real togetherness of people who are citizens. In neither case is the togetherness a mere voluntary association according to contract theory. In each case the commonality is unavoidable once the quality is defined.

The thrust of Barth's article on the two communities can be misunderstood because it can easily be put in a context different from that of its greatest originality. Any perspective within social ethics will distinguish between the individual and the social on the basis of the difference of the kinds of questions to be dealt with. This is still a commonsense difference. So any perspective can make sense out of distinguishing between the individual and the social levels. But this is not what Karl Barth is talking about.

Any perspective is likely to have some way of distinguishing as well between levels or realms one of which is spiritual or religious or sacral and the other of which is material or worldly or everyday. Different Christian traditions will make this distinction of realms or levels in quite different ways, but almost every tradition finds it an illuminating division.

It thus is possible for many to think that this is what Barth is doing, but it is not.

This the first insight we must underline: *What Barth is distinguishing is not levels or realms in either of those ways but rather two different kinds of political and social identification. Both are social. Both are outward, institutional, "worldly." But the difference is that in one of them the commonality of all the people who form together a "Gemeinde" is that they are Christian: they all confess Jesus as Christ and as Lord, and the members of the other group do not.* In his definition of what he calls the citizen-community, Barth is affirming for the first time in mainstream Protestant theology since Constantine the theological legitimacy of admitting, about a set of social structures, that those who participate in them cannot be presumed to be addressable from the perspective of Christian confession.

Thus Karl Barth is beginning to develop an approach for which the technical term in Anglo-Saxon sociology of religion since Troeltsch is "sectarian." This term, in this usage, has to do not with the narrowness of the "sect's" truth claims, or the pettiness of its cultural self-understanding, nor with the size of the group, but with the quality of the group's recognition that it is not in control of the wider society. When Barth posits it as a theological problem, that the expression of Christian concern for the shape of the wider society must take into account the fact that the participants in that society are not addressable from a perspective of faith in Jesus Christ, that is a profound structural innovation, far more important than the continuing superficial flaws of the way he did it.

So it is right that we should begin at this point. The definition of the gathering of Christians is their confessing Jesus Christ as Lord. The definition of the whole of human society is the absence of that confession, whether through conscious negation or simple ignorance, despite the fact that Christ is ("objectively," "cosmically") Lord for them as well. The duality of church and world is not a slice separating the religious from the profane, nor the ecclesiastical from the civil, nor the spiritual from the material. It is the divide on this side of which there are those who confess Jesus as Lord, who in so doing are both secular and profane, both spiritual and physical, both ecclesiastical and civil, both individual and organized, in their relationships to one another and to others. The difference as to whether Christ is confessed as Lord is a difference on the level of real history and personal choices; not a difference of realm or levels or even dimensions.

This is not the dualist slice between two "planes of reality," which has been so effectively and properly denounced recently by Gustavo Gutierrez as the philosophical defense of political conservatism in the name of the church.[3] It is not the dualism between religious and secular vocations or between ordination and laity, or between Reformed and Anabaptist. Pardon my burdening you with such a long list of ready-to-hand dualisms that are not intended; I have seen too often how their habitual unchallenged use has kept gospel social ethics from being understood.

The originality of Barth's approach is precisely that he makes this difference the difference that matters. This is obviously the result of his beginning emphasis on the place of the Word of God as the principal reorientation of all theology. But only now, in the late 1940s, has he begun so simply, programmatically, to derive the sociology of the community around the Word from the central place of confession.

Using this particular point of entry to initiate our critique of Christendom enables us to see that the most important error of the Christendom vision is not first of all its acceptance of an ethic of power, violence, and the crusade; not first of all its transference of eschatology into the present providence with God working through Constantine and all his successors in civil government, not its appropriation of pagan religiosity that will lead into sacerdotalism and sacramentalism, not its modeling church hierarchy after Roman administration, nor any other specific vice derived from what changed about the nature of the church with the epoch of Constantine. Those were all mistakes, but they were derived from the misdefinition of the place of the people of God in the world. The fundamental wrongness of the vision of Christendom is its illegitimate takeover of the world: its ascription of a Christian loyalty or duty to those who have made no confession and, thereby, its denying to the non-confessing creation the freedom of unbelief that the nonresistance of God in creation gave to a rebellious humanity.

First, then: we can only have gospel social ethics if we let confession and non-confession make a difference. Second, now: we can only be doing gospel social ethics if we are telling the story of Jesus.

3. Gustavo Gutiérrez, *A Theology of Liberation* (Maryknoll, N.Y.: Orbis, 1973): 68ff.

Second: *The principle of coherence of the church's self-understanding is narrative rather than deductive. What it means to be the church is to be spoken of as a cause being implemented and not an ontology being realized. Kingdom rather than gnosis is the key mystery.* This is what Karl Barth meant, in the paragraph of *Church Dogmatics* immediately preceding the one we read, where he spoke of the life of the church as "liturgical." By this Barth clearly did *not* mean a concentration on rites. He meant that because the meaning of Jesus was known within the categories of ordinary historical reality, he must be re-known, re-presented, on through time in a celebratory recounting that ties the particularity of his history to the particularity of ours, without trusting to the "bridge" of some mediating generalizations about the nature of things.

The narrative character of the church thus implies first of all the wholehearted affirmation of its particularity. For some the notion of particularity as problematic is recent, but this scandal has really always been with us. A gospel connected with a particular name and place and time, with Jesus and the Jews and Jerusalem, has always provoked some people to try to reach "beyond" to some other "mainstream" that would somehow be "out there," "common" or "public," more fundamental or more central or more objective or more general. It is not easy to argue on what grounds that "mainstream out there" should be preferable to the particularity of Jesus since any argument tending to prove that point would be circular. Neither is it very clear exactly where that mainstream is located, since any definition of where it flows and what it means would again be particular. Nonetheless from the very beginning the faith has been subject to the challenge of those who seek to incorporate it within the somehow more trustworthy or less precarious framework of some wider wisdom. Sometimes the technicians of ethics use the formal term "natural theology" or "theology of being" to designate that leaning.

Already in the apostolic age of Christendom there was the Gnostic temptation, what H. Richard Niebuhr calls the "Christ of Culture," submerging the specificity of Jesus in the obviously more valid humanism of the broader Hellenistic culture and its profounder Gnostic religiosity. The next greater broadening occurred when the fourth century incorporated other nations and cultures as well as religions into the majestic unity of the imperial civilization. The medieval church felt it equally fitting to borrow and baptize the classical wisdom of antiquity as it was rediscovered a little later thanks to the Arabs, incorporating Christianity with the overarching, or should we say underlying, structure of natural reason. In early modern times the challenge was put again by the classical question of Lessing[4] and equally classically answered by the majestic synthesis of Hegel.

At each recurrent phase it was obvious that Christianity could be included without remainder in the wider wisdom. Each time, that domestication of the biblical witness meant relegating to unimportance the specificity of the Jewishness and the ethic of Jesus. By no means was Jewishness all that was lost, nor ethics; but ethics is my current concern.

In our century the challenge has been restated by the encounter with non-Western cultures, not only in the sense that particularity and provincialism become more embarrassing as the world looks bigger, but also because of the clear counter-thrust of the inclusive and non-contradictory logics of eastern religious philosophies. Twenty years ago in his "Stone Lectures" Hendrik Kraemer described the dialogue within which we stand as essentially the encounter between Hebraic and Hindu logics, with many of the (morphological) Hindus coming from the West.

This drive to disavow particularity, however explainable in terms of the embarrassment of needing to dismantle triumphalism and to disavow provincialism, does become a new and powerful kind of unbelief, sectarian and missionary in its own way. But it would be a mistake to take the arguments that pretend to be corrective for the real causes. The stronger drive, I am convinced, in the thrust against particularity is much older and more natural concern to shun the risk of particular allegiance itself, especially to avoid the specified risk of having that allegiance bound to the crucified Jesus and the cost of following his way. Seen from this perspective, today's dismantling of specificity in the interest of wider catholicity looks more like a continuation of the Christendom ethos that went before than like a correction for it.

Since the collapse of Western self-confidence and the growth of awareness of alternate social monuments, we have the question of amateur comparative religion: "Can you really condemn a Hindu or Buddhist who believes differently and leads a better life than you?"

---

4. Lessing stated his question as follows: "Accidental truths of history can never become the proof of necessary truths of reason. . . . That . . . is the ugly, broad ditch which I cannot get across, however often and however earnestly I have tried to make the leap. If anyone can help me over it, let him do it, I beg him." Gotthold Ephraim Lessing, *Lessing's Theological Writings*, trans. Henry Chadwick, Library of Modern Religious Thought (Stanford University Press): 53, 55.

Since the ascendancy of physical science models for understanding not only the phenomena of physics and chemistry, but also for projecting new methods into the interpretation of society and culture, we have the challenge of the closed universe. And then there is the question of the amateur Darwinian: Can you demonstrate that people programmed to act this way will on the average be succeeded by more viable progeny? The parallel risk of the methodologies of skeptical historiography put the post-Rankean question: "Can you assure us that it really happened just that way, by demonstrating that none of the people who told us about the teachings and the resurrection of Jesus had any vested interest in our believing it?"

Without denying in any way that every one of these counter-visions is worthy of some response and merits some degree of respect, all I mean to be saying by this fleeting allusion to them all is that there is something peculiarly questionable going on when it seems so evident to so many of our contemporaries that these critical questions cut the ground from under Christian allegiance more than from any of the other alternatives, or that they undercut the applicability of the ethical guidance of Jesus more than the other kinds of ethic competing for our loyalty, or that they justify other kinds of hope that are perhaps more humanistic or more immanentistic than ours. Whether admitting it or not, those who with this rejoinder assume or claim that it is in a special way the particularity or the particular content of Christian loyalty that these newer currents undercut are being just as particular and just as missionary as is the believer in Jesus. To undertake with more care and detail proper apologetic encounters with some of these modes of modern relativization would be worthwhile for its own sake, but not for now. My reason for noticing them, and for noticing the particularistic and missionary quality of their claims to be more generally valid, has only two implications that we can take the time to develop now.

The broadest response is that I should state, without being able in any deep way to prove it, my suspicion that the real attractiveness of each of these rejoinders is that they provide respectable grounds to relativize the real claims of Christ. The skeptic who in the face of missionary Christianity says, "Yes, but what about all those good Hindus who lead decent lives and don't believe that Jesus is the only one?" is not really expecting to become a good Hindu or even to be friends with good Hindus. Certainly this skeptic does not plan to get involved at all in the problems of differentiating between good Hindus and bad Hindus but only to back away from the call of Jesus, who has always admitted that if we entrust our life to him and his cause, we will never be proven right until beyond the end of this story and cannot count on being positively reinforced along all of the way. What is thus stated in the form of a general rejection of all particularity in favor of a vision of universal validity is, when more deeply seen, more particular and more negative; namely, a specific pattern of avoidance of the particular claims of Christian loyalty in its continuing risk and uncertainty.

The other side of my response to this observation is to affirm that when we speak with Barth of the Christian community as a liturgical or celebrating community we are accepting, willingly rather than grudgingly, as an affirmation rather than as a limitation, our rootedness in the particularity of Judaism and Jesus. To say that social ethics is the life of a believing community says that despite the possible or imaginable projections of something that *might* be "universally" valid, these people are willing to live within the limits of the story of their faith and even to celebrate that faith in a form that holds its meaning open for others to join. We would need to return in another context to the notion of mission proclamation as a theme in its own right. What was important to touch briefly here is that the confessing community is unembarrassed about the fact that its confession is not ultimately subject to irresistible verification (or falsification) from outside its own system. The quality of confirmation or validation that the faith community does claim is the internal coherence of the several elements of confession and experience among themselves and their reciprocal confirmation among the several members of the body.

The stated intent of the advocacy of the "wider wisdom" in each of these many cases — in ways which of course differ enormously in dimensions of detail we cannot here be precise about — is to bring together a more valid and solid total truth system less subject to arbitrariness and petty provincialism. Breadth and tolerance are the stated goals. Yet, it has been noticed occasionally, also by Hendrik Kraemer, that there is a peculiar negative focus when this inclusivism arises specifically in a Christian or post-Christian cultural context. It is singularly less tolerant for an empathetic understanding of Christianity than for the other options. What is true already with regard to the general systemic encounter, of which Kraemer was speaking, is true perhaps even more bluntly when we move to the narrower terrain of social ethics. Here it becomes the most clear that the "wider wisdom" serves as a corrective for or a buffer against the critical impact of the specificity of the call of Jesus, and usually as a defense of the dominant social system and its value assumptions. Depending on the particular tradition, this wider wisdom may be called the orders of creation, as in magisterial Protestantism, guiding an ethic of the "station" or the "vocation," from Luther and Calvin to Brunner and Bonhoeffer and Dooyewerde. It can be spoken of by H. Richard Niebuhr sometimes very vaguely as "culture" and somewhat more precisely as the ethical concerns of the Father and the Spirit that need to be called upon to correct for an overly Christological centering of ethics, which, taken alone, would be too radical. Catholicism would call it "nature" and "reason." It would be utterly unfair to suggest that all of these forms of what I have been calling "the wider wisdom" are the same: but they do have the commonality, in the experience of the social ethics of Christendom, that all are effectively appealed to in order to relativize the impact of Jesus.

The alternative to particularity can manifest itself in a great variety of forms. There is a strange symmetry just now in debates about the truth content that it is the business of Christian mission to proclaim. On the one hand, there is the proposal that since the meaning of salvation must certainly, somehow, relate to where people are in their lostness, and since the salvation that God is bringing must somehow be for the real world, one way to know what salvation should look like would be to go to ask people what it is that they need. From an earlier slogan like "making human life more human" through to the material circulated under the heading "Salvation Today" as background material for the 1973 Bangkok study conference of the Division of World Mission and Evangelism of the World Council of Churches, the guideline was that people themselves must know what would be the "salvation" they long for.

Another major stream of definition coming from the world to meet the gospel has been the product of a wave of creative use of cultural anthropology to illuminate the communication patterns of missionaries, especially as they relate to primal peoples and cultures. One can draw from study of such cultures the anthropological constants of how a civilization handles a change of gods; how it is that a challenge to old loyalties can be processed in authentic social change. Sometimes this analytical process is called "contextualization," when its concentration is upon the process of translating the message into the frame of the host culture. Sometimes basically the same logic is labeled "functional equivalence" when the definition comes from the other end, finding what it is in the host culture that is ready to be grasped as the handle on conversion.

My concern for missions makes me take both of these movements seriously. My concern for theological accountability leads me to prepare a few questions to address to both. It is a fluke of institutional politics that the sets of agencies and thinkers carrying these two major streams of missionary thought consider themselves adversaries, one calling itself "ecumenical" and the other "evangelical," even though as far as I can see there is a significant methodological commonality in that neither one makes the particularity of the Abraham-Jesus story determinative in dictating what the method of the witness must be.

But does this warning against the wider wisdom not condemn us to provincialism? This could well be the case, if the particular content of what we find in our particular history, or the ways we celebrate in our continuing liturgical narration, were themselves esoteric or provincial. For now let it be said in shorthand that there are two important safeguards against that danger. One is that this particular celebrating community is missionary. It is defined not by race, nor by geographic isolation, but only by the story itself. That is a story that by its very nature must be shared, and which invites into its celebration all who hear it. Second, this particular particularity is safeguarded against destructive narrowness by the content of its ethic: it forbids itself either to impose its identity or desires on others coercively or to withhold it from any as a privilege. The content of the ethic of this community includes at its heart its affirmation of the dignity of the outside and the adversary in such a way that while the dangers of arbitrary narrowness can never be totally banned, they can at least be warded off. The inner presupposition of particularity is election. By that term here I mean not what later individually concerned Protestant theology has made of it, namely the basis for projections about who knows they will get to heaven, but the original meaning in our narrative, namely that the story God has chosen to have us tell is the story of some people more than others, of Abraham and Jesus.

Primal religion assumes the total known community as the bearer of the meaning of sacral history: whether it be the whole village, the tribe, the kingdom, or even the empire. The sacralization of life in primal cultures binds and unifies along every axis of possible differentiation. The crown and the cult reinforce one another. The agricultural is not separated from the military, the government from the land; the regime is not distinguishable from the people nor any of the people from other people. With the call of Abraham that changes. A part of the whole creation is separated from the whole on the ground not of its intrinsic qualities but by the peculiarly selective wisdom of a distinctively identifiable God: if all the world is to be blessed, it will be *through* the distinctive response of this man and his seed to their particular call.

The transition from early Christianity to Christendom amounted to a reversion from the Jewish and early Christian specificity of call and identity back into the pagan pattern of multi-dimensional inclusiveness. The critique of Christendom will therefore need, as every renewal movement has done, to restate the question: "Who is a child of Abraham?" This is what Barth's new *Ansatz* does by defining the community not in terms of its members' being, but by virtue of their response to the Word.

Being clear about this critique means first of all that Christian ethics is for Christians. The specific types of behavior called for by Jesus would be at best hardly possible, more likely not credible or even conceivable, apart from the particular resources normally related to that call:

a. a personal and public awareness of who Jesus was and what he did and said;

b. personal and public response to that call, normally expressed by the confession of baptism and maintained through processes of community involvement;

c. whatever definition or redefinition of personal identity one holds to be identified by the work of regeneration (and, in some traditions, of sanctification);

d. whatever processes of illumination one understands under "the guidance of the Holy Spirit";

e. whatever subjective and objective resources one understands under the heading of "mutual consolation of the brothers and sisters";

f. whatever educative resources a community may provide by way of catechesis and training in a lifestyle of discipleship.

It will be important for Christians to explain their ethical stance to nonbelievers. In most societies it will be important to find modes of common discourse to enable clear conversation with one's neighbors about how to get along together. A free church stance, because it is critical in principle of the Christendom heritage, is most aware of these needs, but they are not our first concern here. We must first recognize that it is inappropriate to filter and tailor the claims of the Christian calling through the estimation made for "Everyman" (whether this be done by the "person in the street" on his or her own or some teacher or translator) as to what may reasonably be expected of ordinary people. In this connection discipleship is often spoken of as "heroic" or as expressive of a "unique vocation," as sacrificial or risky in ways that cannot be asked of most people.

Medieval moral theology was quite honest about this. One distinguished the "advice" or "counsels" derived from the Gospels, binding only upon those who voluntarily chose to confess it to be so, from the "precepts" or mandates that church and government have the right to make binding upon everyone. Thus a moral dualism, not between Christians and non-Christians, or between belief and unbelief, but between two different kinds of Christians, was given legitimacy within the church. Shunting the gospel call off into the special track of "vocation" for those who have special strengths or sensitivity (and, in many cases, fewer and less demanding duties out in the real world) is the standard defense of Christendom against the "call to come out and die" of gospel ethics. It moves ethical dualism from the line between belief and unbelief to the line between two kinds of believers.

So the moral reasoning of Christendom has taken several interlocking steps. First, in order not to be provincial or sectarian, one has said that Christian ethics must be for everyone. The church must not duck the responsibility to take on the moral chaperoning of the whole culture and all its weaker members. In order then to make the ethics that one calls "Christian" accessible to ordinary people, the condescension must follow that asks of moderately motivated people only a moderate level of devotion. Then, in order not to have utterly forsaken the starting point in the biblical tradition, one must create a new "religious" status for the minority whom we are still glad to have among us as reminders of what the call in some ideal sense still really ought to be.

It belonged to the primal pattern that the privileged actor of history was the emperor. From Abraham to Tertullian this was no longer the case. Even in the age of the Israelite state, the place of the king in the doing of God's will through his people was ambivalent. There were other movers in that history: judges and priests and prophets and the elders in the gate.

But with Constantine, as interpreted by his biographer Eusebius in the most glowing terms, it has come to pass that the emperor is God's chosen instrument. The break-up of Christendom into separate nations had to change this on the superficial level: now within each nation we believe that it is our nation and its regime that has that meaning. The formal institutional disestablishment in some Western nations in recent centuries has not changed it either. As Presbyterian historian John E. Smylie said in a *Theology Today* editorial in 1963, the typical American Christian still believes that this nation, especially acting through its civil order, is the primordial vehicle of the meaningful historical process. That is why it was so important to disavow what we were doing in

Vietnam as unworthy of us. Even when we have deep debates within the family and change or even depose our presidents, we still look toward the rest of the world from an identity that assumes deep national commonality. Even social movers as profoundly critical and as cosmopolitan in total vision as Mohandas Gandhi and Martin Luther King, Jr., still saw the nation as the social unity to whose best identity one should appeal and whose integrity one hoped to see redeemed.

If our task at this point were merely to work for greater maturity and sobriety in the use of insights from the social sciences, we would need already on that modest level to accentuate the importance of denationalizing our sense of the shape of human community and disentangling our sense of history from the regime as the central definition of what a nation is. There are larger unities like the continent or the hemisphere or the "third world." There are smaller unities that are defined geographically but have no political sovereignty. There are other unities not described geographically like the Indians of East Asia, the Chinese of southern Asia, refugees from Armenia, or (prototypically) the Jews. There are world communities held together by profession or by the arts or by sports.

But my task is not really to plead for a more mature social science. It is to get our elbows free to perceive, as gospel and not as embarrassment, the fact that biblically the meaning of history is carried first of all, and on behalf of all others, by the believing community. This theme is so fundamental in the biblical witness, and since Constantine so scandalous for many of us, that it must be a major theme within this essay.

In order to ward off the most obvious criticisms usually provoked by that claim, let me protect it against the most obviously and easy misinterpretations. It does not mean in-group pride, nor does it mean quietism, nor does it mean clerical theocracy.

Let it not be thought that to affirm that the confessing community is the beginning of a new social history is a way of setting aside the wider society and either its moral challenges or its power structures. That caricature is widely represented in our time, both by those who affirm the "priority of the spiritual" in that way and by those who argue against them. That mutual agreement in caricature is so widespread that I do need to name it and rebut it head-on.

When I follow the apostles in speaking of the confessing community as first fruits of the world to come, I am speaking neither of clericalism, whereby the institutional church claims a privileged handle on the social decision process, nor of quietism, whereby the fellowship patterns of the believing community are interested only in their own integrity or intensity. The great variety of Christian traditions in high church and low that have drawn a church/world dichotomy that way have not done it with the ethic I am talking about. Whether clericalism or quietism has been the style, in both cases the effective social ethic has been drawn from elsewhere than the New Testament: from political pragmatism, or from a theology of the natural orders, or from the models of Old Testament theocracy, or from the inspiration of a crusade. With all the differences among these types just named, they have in common the fact that the distinctiveness of the church as body over against the world does not call for an ethic derived from Jesus and does make the church as body an end unto itself.

Something structurally different is going on when the priority of the believing community is seen not as lordship but as servanthood, not as privilege but as pointer, not as achievement but as promise.

The second distortion is just as understandable. To say that the first service of the church to the world is to be that part of the world that is already entered upon its fulfillment may seem like withdrawal from concern or involvement beyond the church's membership. This conclusion has been drawn far too often, but when it has been drawn it has not been on the basis of this theological understanding. The sense in which this calling to be first of all the believing community is primary is not a chronological sequence whereby one task must be achieved before there is leisure to turn to the other. The church's being the church is primordial rather in the sense of orientation. In order to be whatever I want to be with all of my time wherever I am I must first be who I am in myself. The priority of authentic identity does not postpone for some later time its implications for worldly living but produces them immediately. We speak of a priority or primordiality in terms of identity and not of sequence.

It is thus a caricature and not what we are talking about when the response is made, "We should be working at righteousness in the world rather than trying first of all to tidy up the purity of the church." The Christian is always engaged in both. The questions that matter are not which to be engaged in, or which to do first, but how each of them is defined and how the definitions of both are related to each other. For those who wish to assert the primordiality or autonomy of the duties of implementing justice in the world, what we need to question is not their stating that those duties are duties but their assumption, hidden behind the caricature quoted above, that the way to do it is to be guided by standards of justice other than those of the incarnation.

119

Another necessary general observation about the implications of the narrative quality of the church's identity has to do with the task of the theologian in that "liturgical" body. Usually the task of the theologian tends to center upon clarifying how it is that the thought patterns of the church — and now that we are speaking of ethics we mean the thought patterns relating to decisions and values — are derived from a limited number of first principles. The more insightfully the theologian does this job, and the more properly consistent is the particular church, the better (this account assumes) is the coherence of the system, and the more visible is the way it unfolds from the minimal number of starting definitions.

A lively example of this set of assumptions is the current discussion about the sense in which Karl Barth's systematic theology correlated with his radical political commitment.[5] The new thesis is an excellent sample of what I have called the overvaluing of first principles. One particular intellectual move, one specific reorientation of the Hegelian logic of how Spirit works in history, as first discernible in one socialist speech of the younger Barth, made radical politics self-evident. Once translated into theology with the help of an exercise in the interpretation of Anselm, it also established the main lines of an entire dogmatic system. Thus everything that really mattered in the theology of Karl Barth was decided by the early 1930s, before either the writing of the *Church Dogmatics* or the church struggle had got well underway. In a similar sense, others explain all of Martin Luther from one flash of insight in 1516 and all of Reinhold Niebuhr from one lesson learned in the unionization struggles of the auto industry.

Far be it from me to deny that there can be such seed thoughts and formative experiences. But if they are important, it is precisely because they feed into continuing organic development and determine the ongoing story by contributing formatively to more decisions made later in the face of more (and usually more complex) challenges. The task of the theologian is not to impose upon continuing development the deductively ineluctable determinations of his seed idea, after the model of an inertial guidance system whereby a missile knows, when it leaves the silo in Nebraska, which Russian city is to be destroyed. Theology should rather minister to a community-at-large, living through history as if it had not been lived through or thought of

---

5. See, for example, the essays in *Karl Barth and Radical Politics*, ed. George Hunsinger (Philadelphia: Westminster Press, 1976), especially the essay by Friedrich-Wilhelm Marquardt on "Socialism in the Theology of Karl Barth," 47–76.

before,[6] in concern for faithfulness that cannot be taken for granted. Its role would be not to discern in what shape to impose first principles but rather to defend the community against the danger that the precipitate identification with slogans or uncritical bondage to the implications of unexamined language should prevent a creative response to the next confessional context.

Another aspect of the peculiarity of the way of doing theology I advocate here is its subservience to particular issues and needs, which may make it a luxury to find time for elegance and roundedness. I do not present that as an excuse for the inelegance and the disjointedness of these lectures; yet the vision of the *ecclesia viatorum* does account properly for a permanently fragmentary quality in what needs to be done by the ministry of teaching. One set of functions in teaching involves the restatement of warrants for what we already have been doing without knowing exactly why. It, therefore, will seem unoriginal. At other points, the duty is to concentrate on casting light on certain breaking points or certain breakthroughs along the path. Starting from scratch with a general system and unfolding it with balance and completeness will be a rare privilege. The theologian is always "on the way" because his or her first duty is always to a present crisis of disobedience or opportunity.

Our third lesson in response to Barth: *The story of the life of the church is constantly redefined in the encounter of principle and place, of identity and situation.*

Some among us will remember that seven or eight fads ago we were being told that something called "the situation" was an independent and almost adequate source of ethical guidance. Tracing that challenge, it seemed that some others were expected to have to deny this by arguing that something else instead of the situation has that adequacy and clarity, whether that something be called "law" or "principle." Even in strict logic, that debate between principle and context was never serious. I am speaking here of the socio-logic of the believing community in which the impossibility of such a disjunction is even more obvious. Social ethics is always in the situation, always choosing among situationally defined options, always unfolding an identity inherited from the community's previous story. The guarantee that the

6. I have reviewed the importance of reading history with a grid of freedom rather than fatalism in my essay "The Burden and the Discipline of Evangelical Revisionism" in Louise Hawkley and James C. Juhnke, eds., *Nonviolent America* (North Newton, Kans.: Bethel College, 1993): 21–37.

two dimensions can meet with integrity is what the New Testament calls the Holy Spirit: not a reasoning process but a mode of God's own working. That this is what the Holy Spirit does is stated programmatically in John 14–16, illustrated anecdotally throughout the book of Acts, and projected procedurally in 1 Corinthians 14.

What was really wrong with what called itself "situation ethics" a generation ago was not that it expected some moral guidance in the situation. Nor was it the expectation that, in the process of situational guidance, inherited principles would be helpful but would not in themselves dictate all the details of the available answers. What was wrong was the assumption that the *way* the situation works to provide the decision is located individually, usually in a temporally punctual decision made all at once,[7] and that the assurance behind it was a quality more of intuition than of explanation and dialogue. The narrative quality of the church's doing ethics provides both that the decision shall always be in the situation and that the moment of decision shall never be isolated but rather finds itself oriented and, in fact, driven along by the momentum of the memories of the communal story.

We must thus reject the strong occasionalism that ultimately abandons ethical accountability to intuition; but we properly want to affirm a weak occasionalism, which insists on the insufficiency of all our memory, and on the limits to the number of decisional constants which can be carried into one context from others, so that it is very clear that the ongoing discernment of the church must be seen as God's own work and not simply our replicating or transposing what God did before.

The decision reported in Acts 15 seems to be recounted by Luke, as much as a model for how to make decisions as out of interest in the subject matter of the decision itself. In the face of an issue that could not possibly have been resolved a priori by a word from Jesus, or by an interpretation of the *halakah*, the conclusion that is reached by completely finite and human process of open dialogue, arguing from experience as well as from Scripture, is then confessed as the ongoing work of God. "It seemed good to the Holy Spirit as well as to us" carries all the flexibility and up-to-dateness that any situation ethics can want,

---

7. Some use the term "decisionism" to designate this methodological tilt, or "quandarism" to label the predilection for illustrating general issues in principle by concentration on hard cases. I prefer the term "punctualism" because the metaphor of the "point" says well that one is denying length (the past and future dimensions of decision), breadth (the communal dimension), and depth (the "spiritual" or metaphysical).

yet with none of the impulsiveness or the making of bad law with hard cases that so marked and marred the "situation ethics" debate of the 1960s and 1970s.

Fourth: *The life of the church's character is* doxological. *Not only does the church proclaim God as worthy, as sovereign, but also as victor. God is not simply the one who by nature possesses or merits praise:* God is also the one who is, and has always been, in the process of leading us along in the train of Christ's triumphal procession (Col. 1:14–15).

Earlier when discussing the "scandal of particularity," I referred to the "wider wisdom" with which we are tempted to make Jesus' rewards less precarious and his call less threatening. Now I must return to that theme by observing that when this phenomenon relates to social ethics there is a specific body of alternative wisdom marked by the fact that it not only comes from somewhere else than Jesus but also, necessarily, tells us to do something other than what Jesus tells his disciples to do. Jesus tells us to love our enemies, including holding their lives sacred. The orders of creation, known through the specific locations of some of us in civil responsibility, tell us that for the sake of our love for the life of some nearer neighbor we might need to destroy the enemy neighbor. Jesus tells us to share our bread and our money: those of us who have the particular calling of entrepreneur or of banker should do just the opposite, because there is a structure in the order of things that declares certain spheres to be independent of the pertinence of those instructions from Jesus. One would hardly admit that those other values have the status of idols, since it is claimed that God, as the creator who set things up before Jesus, or the Spirit who keeps on leading since then, has provided them. Still the effect is to relativize the theme that Christ is victor. Partly it says that "victory" is not yet accomplished since we still need to haggle with "realism" to determine how much obedience we can get away with.

We must thus deny any claim to glory or authority made on behalf of alternative value definitions, even if they be affirmed as complementary to God's will or part of it. When I say doxology, that means not only that the glory of God is verbally recognized but that it is celebrated. The word points not simply to an awareness or a conviction but to a spirituality and the cultivation of a distinctive consciousness. To celebrate, and to celebrate repeatedly in memory of Jesus, the glory of God as righteous and as sovereign means to cultivate explicitly an alternative consciousness, to maintain a sense of reality running against the stream of the unquestioningly accepted commonplaces of the age.

In other times and places, other accepted commonplaces would need to be combated: but for our present subject matter it will have to suffice to concentrate on what for the past two generations has called itself "realism," a kind of creeping utilitarianism that does not quite avow the systematic narrowness of the utilitarian philosophical tradition but operates largely within its limits. It is assumed that we all share a common knowledge of what is possible and what is not, of what makes things happen, so that we know what kinds of power need to be applied at what points in the global social system to make events come out for the best. For some critics, this "realism" is to be challenged because it implicitly denies transcendence by accepting social science analyses, which themselves assume the world to be a closed system. For other critics the shortcoming of "realism" is its failure to let both the analysis and the prescription be illuminated more normatively by revealed value standards. Both of these criticisms have some value, but for now it suffices to identify one internal limit of this kind of approach, namely its failure to be fully realistic, because it posits a degree of both actual analysis and ability to predict, to say nothing of ability to control, which are not, in fact, present in any important social conflict.

This is not simply a matter of ignorance due to the bluntness of our present tools of observation, analysis, and prediction, which could be done away with with greater refinement. It is rather an intrinsic limitation of the very nature of our self-understanding as social animals, like Heisenbergian uncertainty in the realm of small scale physics. We can never know with precision everything about a system that we ourselves are interfering with in the very process of trying to know about it; even more is this the case to the extent to which our trying to know about it includes trying to take charge of it. By definition, a social system is one in which there are numerous actors, various awarenesses, and various goals, with each actor knowing that the others are acting on the basis of their several conflicting awarenesses and interests. The one thing that is mathematically positive is that the system will not move in the particular way we wish or predict it should. This is what Reinhold Niebuhr wrote about under the heading "the irony of history,"[8] what Herbert Butterfield calls "imponderables."[9] Hendrik

8. Reinhold Niebuhr, *The Irony of American History* (New York: Scribner, 1952). Routinely national policies advocated as righteous turn out to be selfish. Actions taken with a view to good consequences produce bad ones.
9. Herbert Butterfield, *Christianity and History* (London: Bell, 1950). There is no chapter on "imponderables"; it is his code for the ways in which reality is more complicated than our tools of interpretation.

Kraemer in his "Stone Lectures"[10] quoted from Wilhelm Wundt the label of "heterogony of ends" to describe the way in which our choice of means sets its own ends, or the way the ends we set transform themselves in the course of our seeking to reach them. This is the least ideological of the reasons that lead political practitioners from Mohandas Gandhi to George Kennan to say that an ethic of means is the only globally responsible way to be honest with our stated ends. The kind of calculus that will sacrifice the legitimacy of immediate, manageable means for the greater value of projected ends that it hopes to produce is itself a denial of the limits of the human condition, however attractive that trade-off may seem in a given situation. The limits of our ability to trade means for ends is not thus a mere limitation in the accuracy of our present measurements but rather an intrinsic quality of all genuinely social decisions. If our only concern were "realism," the accent would belong on modesty. If our concern is doxology, then that modesty becomes confession.

Authentic Exemplarity

There are some inadequacies in what Barth, in his initial experimentation with the concept of analogy, was ready to do next. He used the notion of analogy, especially in the booklet on the two communities but also in the *Church Dogmatics* IV/2 (719ff.), with a certain exploratory whimsicality. It will fall to us to ask more clearly how analogy should and should not work.

Sometimes in Barth's examples the comparison was to the church as body: but other times it was to the nature of God about whom the church speaks (e.g., at the point where there was reference to the civil authority using violence), sometimes to major doctrinal emphases and sometimes to less central descriptions of the church's work. If we are to take seriously the notion of the mission of the church as constituting the backbone of social ethics, it will need to be disciplined more firmly. The concern that what we say about the church be cognate with what we say to the world should be worked out somewhat more regularly.

But the church is not only an analogy, which would be to place its function only on the level of communication. The church is also "first

10. Hendrik Kraemer's *World Cultures and World Religions: The Coming Dialogue* (Philadelphia: Westminster, 1960) grew out of "Stone Lectures" presented at Princeton in March 1958.

fruits": i.e., it is or is to be in itself the beginning of what is to come. This means both that the church's presence constitutes a part of the promise that more is to come (what is meant by the biblical word "earnest"); but also that its quality and direction have begun to be manifest. The church does communicate to the world what God plans to do, because it shows that God is beginning to do it.

Our angle of entry into the issue would seem to indicate that the latter (knowing *what* God is doing) is prior because it was our question. But certainly the former (*that* God is doing it) is prior. The fact that God is already doing in the world what God plans ultimately to do is certainly prior both in sequential logic and importance to the use we might make of that fact as a source of information and language to provide self-conscious guidance to our sharing in the outgoing process.

The church is also pilot project, and podium, pedagogical base and sometime power base. In none of these ways does it really depend on the church's presence or its day-to-day faithfulness whether, or when, the new world, to which the church witnesses and from which its being is derived, shall actually come upon us in power. Part of the grace from which the church lives is the grace of its not needing to be responsible for that. But the church is responsible for the congruence between its ministry and that new world that is the church's way, because it is on the way.[11]

11. The general title of the "Stone Lectures" series on the place of the church in social ethics was "New World on the Way."

To Serve Our God and
to Rule the World

"To Serve Our God and to Rule the World" originated in John H. Yoder's presidential address to the Annual Meeting of the Society of Christian Ethics at Duke University in January 1988. The text that is reprinted here is the same as the text originally published in *The Annual for the Society of Christian Ethics 1988* (Georgetown Univ. Press, 1988): 3–14.

In this essay, Yoder is addressing the professional guild of Christian ethics in the American context. For this reason, various references in the text and the footnotes refer to articles by Society of Christian Ethics members. Some references to Methodism also are made to take into account the denomination with which Duke University is affiliated. The doxological vision of history that Yoder explicates in this address involves a positive appreciation of the role of apocalyptic literature in Christian Scripture, a genre that some contemporary Christian ethicists shun. While Yoder does not presume that "apocalyptic discourse" is the only language to be used within the community of faith, neither does he think that it can simply be excluded from moral discourse of communities of faith whose life together is normed by the Rule of the Lamb of God. Thus, alluding to Matthew 15:13, Yoder reminds the members of the Society of Christian Ethics that "we are the scribes, agents of communal memory, selecting from a too-full treasury what just happens to fit the next question."

Here also, the ways in which Yoder's work as a historical theologian informs his approach to the task of Christian social ethics are clearly in view. As he states in the second section of the address, "To see history doxologically is to be empowered and obligated to discern, down through the centuries, which historical developments can be welcomed as progress

127

in the light of the Rule of the Lamb and which as setbacks." Yoder's steadfast refusal to approach the ethical task as an "autonomous discipline" once again highlights both the ecclesiological grounding of Christian ethics and the importance of the canon of Christian Scripture, which provides the basis for ecumenical ethical reflection in relation to the lordship of Jesus Christ. In this address, Yoder situates the discipline of Christian ethics within the biblical cosmology depicted in the Apocalypse of John (5:7–14), the passage that frames Yoder's address. As such, this essay highlights the rich way in which Yoder's approach to Christian ethics is informed by Scripture and reminds the reader of his essays in *The Politics of Jesus* (1972) and the biblical meditations in *He Came Preaching Peace* (1985).

To Serve Our God and to Rule the World

The Lamb came forward to take the scroll
from the right hand of the One sitting on the throne.
When he took it the four animals prostrated themselves and
with them the twenty-four elders.
Each one of them was holding a harp and a golden bowl of
incense — the prayers of the saints.

They sang a new hymn:
"You are worthy to take the scroll and to break its seals
because you were sacrificed and with your blood you bought
for God
people of every tribe and tongue, people and nation,
and made them a priestly royal lineage
to serve our God and to rule the world."

(Apocalypse 5:7–10)

To see history doxologically, in the metaphor of this cultic vision, is to describe the cosmos in terms dictated by the knowledge that a once slaughtered Lamb is now living. If, in the jargon developed by our guild's methodological navel-gazing in recent decades, you call your kind of moral reasoning "teleological" then that glory should be your *telos.* If you reason from principle, that is why the principles are binding.[1] If with others you prefer the language of "vision" or "virtue," "character" or "community," it is this doxological practice which should prescribe the content with which those formal terms need to be filled.

Eight years ago in our annual meeting we devoted a plenary session to "liturgy and ethics." Paul Ramsey opened it by setting in triune parallel the disciplines of ethics, of liturgics, and of dogmatics.[2] I here take for granted such a triune parallelism, or multidimensional unity, of which ethics is only one component. Yet doxology, as I here take it to be a mark of faith, is more than liturgy. It is a way of seeing; a grasp of which end is up, which way is forward. For that reason I here shall speak first of the cosmic story as the apostolic seer saw it, and only derivatively of an ethic which we might distill out of it.

That is my first point, and an obvious one: ethics, in the technical sense of our discipline, which analyzes the conditions of validation of dispositions, decisions, and actions, is not an autonomous discipline. It always is and always properly should be in the service of some cosmic commitment or other. There is no nonsectarian "scratch" to start from, beneath or beyond particular identities, no neutral common ground which some sort of search for "foundations" could lay bare. To disengage the structure of the subjacent cosmology must therefore be prior to describing the conceptual mechanics of the moral discourse itself.

There is therefore no one right place for ethics "as such" to begin. It is insufficient to own that ethics is a subdiscipline of ecclesiology or of anthropology or of social science (as it is academically). More important is that all of the intellectual disciplines of critical articulation and reconstruction are embedded in a larger life process. The choir in the heavenly vision sings that that "larger process" is praise, and that it rules the world.

I. To see history doxologically demands and enables that we appropriate especially/specifically those modes of witness which explode the limits that our own systems impose on our capacity to be illuminated and led. Apocalypse is only one of many modes of discourse in

---

1. My doubts about the value of deep disjunctions between ethical modes are stated in my *Priestly Kingdom* (Notre Dame: University of Notre Dame Press, 1984): 113ff.

2. Paul Ramsey, "Liturgy and Ethics," *Journal of Religious Ethics* 7, no. 2 (1979): 139–71.

the believing community. We should not prefer it; we should use them all. Yet it is one of those with which we have the most trouble, and for that reason it may have more to teach us. It is undeniably one of the modes of discourse in which the praise of God as world ruler was couched in the first century, not just by happenstance. It is the one in which the hymn with which I began is embedded.

Scripture scholars have been busied since Albert Schweitzer, but especially since Ernst Käsemann,[3] with the hermeneutic challenge posed to us all by this unmodern component of our heritage. Among systematic theologians Jürgen Moltmann once projected a *Theology of Hope.* Some of those who consider the paradigm of "liberation" most helpful have claimed to be fusing the dialogical promise of socialism with the virtue of hope.[4] Few liberation ethicists, however, would claim either that the way they argue is particularly compatible with the canonical texts of an apocalyptic genre or that it is very important to them for it to be so. But at least all of the above-mentioned thinkers, with whatever degree of success, whatever degree of consistency, are working at the challenge of making some sense of the apocalyptic component of our canonical heritage. In our guild the effort to retrieve apocalypse is less widely evident.[5] The reasons for that are obvious; doxology does not easily fit our grid. That is just one of the reasons we need it. Apocalypse as such is not my theme on this occasion: I allude to it first in order to move past it. Yet we do have to begin with it: it is the language of the text in which the seer spoke of "ruling the world."

To see history doxologically meant for John's addressees that their primordial role within the geopolitics of the *Pax Romana* was neither to usurp the throne of Nero or Vespasian, Domitian or Trajan, nor to pastor Caesar prophetically, but to persevere in celebrating the Lamb's lordship and in building the community shaped by that celebration. They were participating in God's rule over the cosmos, whatever else they were or were not allowed by the civil powers to do. That it was not given them to exercise those other more blatantly "powerful" roles —

3. "Apocalyptic was the mother of all Christian theology. . . ." Ernst Käsemann, "The Beginnings of Christian Theology" (original 1960), *New Testament Questions of Today* (London/Philadelphia: SCM/Fortress, 1969): 102.

4. Jürgen Moltmann presented at the SCE session in Kansas City, 1968, a lecture titled "Freedom in Christian and Marxist Perspective." In substance, this lecture was similar to "The Revolution of Freedom: Christians and Marxists Struggle for Freedom," *Religion, Revolution, and the Future* (New York: Scribner, 1969): 63–82.

5. The only exception I find in the SCE record is "Millennial Ethics and the Holy Community" read by Theodore W. Olson in 1978.

130

whether assassinating Trajan or becoming his chaplain — was not for them either a renunciation or a deprivation. They considered themselves to be participating in ruling the world primordially in the human practices of doxological celebration — perhaps in Ephesus? — of which John's vision of the Heavenly Throne Hall is the projection. Some would take John's vision to mean "if we keep the faith through these tough times, in a century or two the tides will turn and we can dominate the Empire then the way Domitian does today." Others would think it meant: "if we keep the faith, the world as we know it will very soon be brought to a catastrophic end, and a new nonhistorical state of things will be set up, with us on top." Some would favor this latter interpretation because they are themselves enthusiasts, believing themselves to be on the brink of the final saving catastrophe, as its beneficiaries. Others would ascribe that meaning to John's vision in order to discredit it, since, after all, that catastrophic victory did not happen.

What then did the vision mean? "Neither of the above," we must respond. Each of those restatements is incompatible with the hymnic text. The line about "serving our God [the priestly role] and ruling the world [the royal one]" is found in the second strophe sung in the Heavenly Hall, the one concerned with the present age. The hymn of verse 4:11 was about the past, the praise of creation. The strophe of 5:12ff. is about the future universal consummation, when all the creatures chime in. Our strophe, the "new song" elicited by the work of the Lamb, describes the seer's present, the same age in which people of every tribe and tongue are being called into a new community. It is not about a future, either organic and therefore distant, or imminent and therefore catastrophic. It has to be taken as a statement about their own time, the late first or early second century, and about what they were then involved in doing. What then *could* it mean? What could it mean *then*?

Some readers of the New Testament think the early Christians were all poor. Another set say that not all of them were. But no one thinks that taken all together they were socially significant. How then could they think — even in ecstatic flights of worship that they were involved in governing the world? That seems odd to us because we forget that what we take metaphorically they took realistically, that is to say, doxologically. For them, to say "Jesus Christ is *kyrios*" was a statement neither about their subjective psychic disposition (as pietism would say) nor about their sectarian belief system (as scholasticism would assume) but about the cosmos, the way the world really is. "Sitting at the right hand of the Father," the eighth article of the Apostles' Creed, designated a role of cosmic viceroy, invisibly in charge of history, sovereign over the principalities and powers. That royal rule of Jesus at the Right Hand is the "service to God and rule over the world" in which they confessed themselves to be participants.

It is quite possible to "demythologize" the affirmation that by participating doxologically in the ascension and kingly rule of the slaughtered but living Lamb the early believers were helping to rule the world. One can translate or transpose that language into the form of a statement understandable to moderns, about how that doxological form of life tends to contribute indirectly but efficaciously to the course of public events. Such a translation would unfold the power of consciousness-raising, of delegitimizing tyranny, of unmasking the powers with the truth. To pursue that would, however, be to dwell upon, to objectify, and to analyze the strangeness to us of the apocalyptic mode — and that is not my concern here.

II. To see history doxologically is to be empowered and obligated to discern, down through the centuries, which historical developments can be welcomed as progress in the light of the Rule of the Lamb and which as setbacks. Not all historical movement is forward. Thus to "discern the signs of the times" is not the same as ascribing to God the course of events as such. Such ascription would be fatalism. That does need to be said, since both socialist and capitalist schemes of progress, to say nothing of the wilder fascist and nationalist claims, do pretend to be able to read a moral lesson off of the surface of history as such. Nor does it mean that we should welcome specific political victories as providential signals, as did Eusebius in heralding Constantine's power as the beginning of the millennium. That would be triumphalism, even if the victors can for the moment convince themselves that (for them) it is liberation. Nor can it be the same as simply defending the biological and anthropological givenness of a society as it stands, which some have called the order of nature or of creation. That would be patriarchalism. In most historical cases it has meant one form or another of *apartheid*.

For there to be accountable discernment of the meaning of particular events within history there must be criteria, themselves part of history yet discernible within it, whereby to discriminate between the setbacks and the steps forward. To that end we have to know, and we do know, as did John's readers, that the slain lamb before the Throne in the Heavenly Hall was not just one more personage tacked onto the libretto of the vision of Isaiah, but stood for Jesus the crucified Jew. His mother, bearing the name of the songstress of the battle of the Reed Sea, Moses' sister, gave him the name of Moses' successor, as the angel said she should, because he would liberate his people. He was crucified because although his very presence threatened the bearers of power, he waged his holy war nonviolently. He was crucified because as herald of the messianic age he articulated the fulfilling of the law in such a way that love of neighbor is transmuted into love of enemy. The image of a slaughtered Lamb is no empty cipher; it is the code reference, utterly transparent to John's addressees, to the simple narrative substance of the work and the words — not the words without the work nor the work without the words — of that particular Palestinian populist, in all of his Jewishness and all of his patience.

III. To see history doxologically is to appropriate as did Jesus the full and patent ambivalence of the Jewish experience with the usability of majesty, whether Canaanite kingdoms or Mesopotamian empires, as instruments of Divine rule. That ambivalence had been building up slowly as the Hebrew canon grew. The early accounts of the wars of JHWH were utterly uncritical of Israelite ethnocentrism and also devoid of political realism. Jotham's fable in Judges 9 makes kingship the least useful of a community's resources. The olive tree, the fig tree, and the vine all had something better to do, but the bramble bush was glad to reign over the trees. JHWH's word to Samuel (1 Sam. 8) interprets the transition from the line of ad hoc charismatic judges to standard Canaanite kingship to mean that the Israelites are rejecting not only the ad hoc authority system of the generations of the judges, and not only Samuel's person, but also God's own rule. The norm for kings stated in Deut. 17 condemns by contrast any king but Josiah; there shall be no accumulation of horses, or of women, or of gold and silver, and daily Torah study is commanded. Yet as long as the royal house of Judah stood, the royal ideology could claim equal status in the same histories and in the psalms beside the prophetic one.

In the early sixth century, however, things began to be sorted out. The age of Jeremiah, and his message, precipitated the definition of diaspora as not merely a chastisement but also a calling. To "seek the peace of that city where JHWH has sent you"[6] meant for Jewry all the way from Jeremiah to Rosenzweig and Bucer the acceptance of a non-sovereign, non-territorial self definition. Efforts to restore the royal ideology, from the Maccabees to Bar Kochba, all failed. Devoted efforts to maintain a Jewish residential presence in the land were pursued over the centuries, yet the cultural and economic center of Jewry continued

6. Jeremiah 29:7; cf. my article "Exodus and Exile," *Cross Currents* 23 (Fall 1973): 279–309.

to be Babylonia. The viability of the Palestinian settlements from Bar Kochba to Hertzl was conditioned on renouncing temporal sovereignty. The rabbis, some as early as Johanan ben Zakkai and all of them after 135, read that history as God's having ratified his word to Jeremiah.

In this respect there was then nothing original about the political stance of Jesus in the Gospels, or of John or his addressees in the Apocalypse. The difference did not lie in the Christians' low view of the importance of what kings can do, nor did it lie in their picture of the form of their own life under the powers. In those respects they were indistinguishable from the other Jews. They differed at two other points, naturally: the incorporation of Gentiles into that life, which is not our present point, and the incorporation of the principalities and powers under the jurisdiction of the Lamb's Kingship,[7] which is. The world which is not in their own hands — and over which the kings of this world have precious little control either — is (for John and his readers) not out of control. It is being ruled, i.e., it is in the process of being brought under control, by the Lamb.

The most concrete practical import of this low view of kingship is not emigration, which would after all leave the world to the pagan king. What most ought to be done had been described by Jeremiah in the terms of ordinary cultural creativity: "build houses, settle down, plant gardens, take wives and have sons and daughters, choose wives for your sons and seek husbands for your daughters, work for the good of the country. . . ." The oracle shared by Micah and Isaiah had said it, too, in cultural terms: what will enable reforging swords into plowshares and studying peace instead of war will be "oracles" and "judgments" sent out to the nations not from the Davidic throne but from the miraculously restored Temple. The minority status of Jews since Jeremiah, far from accepting enclosure within the ghetto, could with integrity express itself in important though non-sovereign participation in pagan power structures, as with Esther or Daniel. The very same legends recounted *at once* the radical refusal of the Jewish hero to have anything to do with the gentile regime's idolatrous ways and the recognition of the true God by gentiles who asked the Jews to provide leadership *on their own terms*. There needed to be no tradeoff of a certain amount of faithfulness for a certain amount of effectiveness. These were the non-utopian visions and the success stories of the canon of the early

7. Cf. Hendrik Berkhof, *Christ and the Powers,* trans. John Yoder (Scottdale, Penn.: Herald Press, 1962), and Walter Wink, *Naming the Powers* (Philadelphia: Fortress Press, 1984).

Christians no less than of the other Jews. To "rule the world" in fellowship with the living Lamb will sometimes mean humbly building a grassroots culture, with Jeremiah. Sometimes (as with Joseph and Daniel) it will mean helping the pagan king solve one problem at a time. Sometimes (again as with Daniel and his friends) it will mean disobeying the King's imperative of idolatry, refusing to be bamboozled by the claims made for the Emperor's new robe or his fiery furnace.

IV. To practice seeing history doxologically is to learn to claim for the Gospel its share of credit for the democratizing thrusts which have created in North Atlantic societies more space for political dialogue than ever or anywhere before. The institutional success of democracy with its full vision of civil liberties was enormously aided by the acids of enlightenment, but that is not where it began.[8] Philip of Hesse was surnamed "the Magnanimous" partly because he resisted the pressures of Melanchthon and Luther toward the execution of religious dissenters and sent Martin Bucer into the Marburg prison to negotiate with the so-called "Anabaptists" instead of executing them. In the midst of the Netherlands' revolt against Spain in the 1570s, William of Orange became the first modern European monarch to provide documentary guarantees of religious liberty, and he did so because the *doopsgezind* had prepared the way for the Calvinists with their blood. William of Orange, III, who put an end to sixty years' political turmoil in Britain by accepting the invitation to join a nonviolent *coup*, initiated with a Bill of Rights a century older than our own an unprecedented story of political stability; he accomplished this by sharing more powers with Parliament and giving more freedoms to dissenters. Roughly contemporary with that "glorious revolution" the Quaker William Penn was founding a colony with a statutory commitment to religious liberty, democracy, and the rights of Indians. Before him, a century before the Enlightenment and two and a half before Max Weber and Ernst

8. Max Stackhouse, in a 1986 lecture on "Piety, Polity, and Policy" (in Carl H. Esbeck, ed., *Religious Beliefs, Human Rights and the Moral Foundation of Western Democracy* [University of Missouri-Columbia]: 13–26), has restated the claim that Western notions of freedom are rooted in religion rather than in Enlightenment secularism. Roland Bainton, in "The Anabaptist Contribution to History" (in Guy F. Hershberger, ed., *The Recovery of the Anabaptist Vision* [Scottdale, Penn.: Herald Press, 1957]: 317–26), distinguishes appropriately between those who first hold an idea and those who first institutionalize it. I agree with Stackhouse that the Enlightenment cannot take all the credit for vesting the right of religious liberty, but I doubt the utility of either/or formulation of such a question on the idea level. My interest here is rather in the social bearers of the pressure to relativize political demands for religious uniformity.

Troeltsch, Roger Williams gave the lie to the legend that people without armies or people called "sectarian" by their persecutors cannot shape society.

Tolstoy was wrong: there is no reason to let the Tsarist Holy Synod count as prototype of the institutional church, so that the only place for faith is outside it. There is no reason to let Tsarist authoritarianism count as prototype of the civil order, so that the only place for the Kingdom of God is outside it.[9]

V. To discern our moral setting doxologically is to learn to derive behavior from Good News, not from the concern for justification. Scripture scholars have been seeing and saying for some time that the so-called "beatitudes" or *makarisms* in the Sermon on the Mount are not statements of impossible moral rigorism but of Gospel. When Jesus says, "*makarioi*, blessed are they who . . . ," that adjective does not mean "virtuous" or "meritorious"; it means, rather, "fortunate, well-off, privileged." In colloquial American: "good for them!" The ascription of blessedness is inseparable from the proclamation of the Kingdom's imminence. Some people are meek: "good for them!" for the Kingdom is breaking in, and the earth is their legacy. Some people hunger for justice: "good for them!" for the Kingdom is on the way, and they shall be sated. That action is right which fits the shape of the Kingdom to come. Moral validation is derived from the imminent Kingdom which Jesus announces, not from the righteous state of affairs our action promises to bring about. Moral being and behaving are primordially proclamation or celebration. Only derivatively are they debatable positions in value theory or efficacy. That is why the prologue to the Sermon ends by saying that people watching the kingdom-like behavior of Jesus' hearers will "give the praise to your Father in Heaven."

VI. To see history doxologically is to see the present in its liturgical setting. This week is the second of Epiphany, when we remember the sages from the East. Their arrival disquieted Herod to the point of provoking a massacre and the flight to Egypt. This signals at the very outset of Matthew's account that the very local story he is about to tell has when it begins (and not only by implication) a foundational significance for the rest of the world. In our discernment the magi can stand

9. H. Richard Niebuhr, *Christ and Culture* (New York: Harper and Brothers, 1951), is representative of those who make Leo Tolstoy representative of a principled withdrawal from all social responsibility. This is not fully fair to Tolstoy; more important is that Tolstoy's elite purism is not representative of the experience of radical reformation nonviolence.

for the outsiders of every age, whom we should count on to join in celebrating the insurrectional potential of the Bethlehem event. The way to get from Bethlehem to Chaldea or to Rome need not be to filter out or to bargain away, to dilute or to transmute, the particular Jewishness of Jesus with something else claiming to be less particular and thereby more "reasonable" or "natural" or "public." What it takes to make particular experience generally accessible is not a conceptual question, to be resolved by definitional moves in the realm of language. It is a question of empirical history, resolved by real contacts between communities. It suffices that the magi should have been brought to see, and the historical fact, read doxologically, is that they have come.

VII. To see history doxologically is to own the Lamb's victory in one's own time. Yesterday Martin Luther King, Jr., one of the victims who in our century have enabled us to keep talking about the power of meekness, would have been fifty-nine. The power of his vulnerability taught us again something about the weakness of Caesar. The provisions of the United States Constitution and its amendments and the solemn oaths of office of generations of White officeholders had been powerless, for ninety years after emancipation, to keep the promise of letting Blacks into the civil community. It took the principled non-cooperation of America's Black minority to enable elite powerbearers, whether the shrewd pragmatist Johnson or the more programmatic Kennedys before him, to make small steps toward being honest with the American dream. It took the churches of the underdogs to move the churches and the synagogues of the comfortable — and then only some of them — to support the most modest steps toward the most elementary public morality in matters of race.

Tolstoy was right: progress in history is borne by the underdogs.[10] It was not the strong but the weak, not the persons exercising the responsible power of office but those excluded, who could and did take decisive steps to save America's face and to enable such movement forward as we have seen.

VIII. To read history doxologically means that the criterion most apt for validating a disposition, a decision, an action, is not the predictable success before it but the resurrection behind it, not manipulation

10. ". . . if there is in history a movement towards the elimination of ego, it is thanks only to those men who have . . . endured evil and not resisted it by violence. Progress towards the welfare of mankind is made not by the persecutors but by the persecuted." Leo N. Tolstoy, *What I Believe*, Oxford Classics, No. 229 (Oxford: Oxford University Press, 1951): 352.

but praise. Hope is not a reflex rebounding from defeat but a reflection of theophany.

Yet those analyses of moral methodology are wrong which assume that a moral stance derived from a transcendent commitment would foreclose consequential reasoning. By no means. What is inadequate about the teleological calculation of likely success is not that it cares about the future and about the human values at stake. Rather, teleological reasoning proves inadequate when the reasoner presumes to read the future as a closed system, as if only one person, the ethical subject in question, were making a decisive choice. It proves inadequate when the "human values at stake" are so defined as to exclude those of one's enemies. It operates deceptively when the ethicist presumes to know so much about the starting position of the universe and about all the mechanisms at work that the right choice is thought to be derived by a reductive quasi-mechanical utility calculus. Then the error is not in thinking teleologically but in being naively or manipulatively determinist.

IX. But King's death was almost twenty years ago; Gandhi's, forty. Can we attend as well to what died more recently? Nineteen eighty-seven was a year of losses. South Africa and the West Bank are both qualitatively worse off than a year ago. So are the Philippines, Nicaragua, and Ethiopia. Shall we ascribe some meaning to the death of the self-confidence of Wall Street or of the Reagan regime? When *Newsweek* tells us that "greed has gone out of style," is that ground for praise? Is it ground for praise when national economic policies based upon greed succeed in a decade in making us a colony of Japan? When public knowledge of private misbehavior breaks the career of a politician and an evangelist? When a new virus makes sexual freedom and drug use more costly? Or when we find out how soon over-farming the land makes it infertile? The reading might be different if today we were in Japan or Germany, nations who learned about losses when we were victors; but for this culture, the new medium-range challenge of reading the signs of our times may well be that we parse more honestly the lessons of defeat.

To see the course of human experience doxologically is not *Schadenfreude,* rejoicing that somebody got what they had coming. Since Eden God is busy protecting people from what they have coming. God's glory transcends human confusion but neither needs it nor rejoices in it. When Dietrich Bonhoeffer warned us against "methodism[11] what he

11. Bonhoeffer used the term "methodism" twice in his prison letter of June 8, 1944 (*Widerstand und Ergebung* [München: Kaiser Muchen, 1951]: 217 and 221;

meant was not the denominational loyalty of our host school here at Durham. He meant our tendency to rejoice in people's humiliation in the belief that such pain should further their salvation since God exalts the humble. That is not doxology. Nor is trend-watching (which some uncritically call "discerning the signs of the times") the way to be serious about history. A doxological commitment should free us from the self-contradictory but still widely practiced worldliness of those who, when the trends go against their tastes, decry them, yet when the trends go "the right way" claim them as validation. The doxological integrity of our contextual discernment will be greater if our first response to change is something like what Karl Barth called "doing theology as if nothing had happened."[12]

I began with a hymn: why not end with one? But since this is a professional society and since our banquet has been eucharistic only in a most uncanonical sense, I turn first to a job description. It is not we who rule the church or who set the conditions of the meaningfulness of moral discourse. It is not we who set the terms of sense-making. Our task is more modest. The agent of moral discernment in the doxological community is not a theologian, a bishop, or a pollster, but the Holy Spirit, discerned as the unity of the entire body.

The life blood of that body is language. When the ability of human blood to carry its freight is threatened by an antigen, the type B lymphocytes produce antibodies to fit that specific invader. The lymphocytes' function has no independent merit. While the body is healthy, they are not needed. There is no use for the antibodies before the antigen invades, although their traces stay in the system after the disease is over. Our guild's vocation is vigilance against the abuse of the words or of the logic of the discerning community. We are neither the umpires nor the examiners, the bishops nor the catechists, the evangelists nor the moderators. We are the immune system of the language flow that keeps the body going. Or we are the scribes, agents of communal memory, selecting from a too-full treasury what just happens to fit the

---

Letters and Papers from Prison: The Enlarged Edition [London: SCM, 1967]: 326 and 329); the second time, it is in quotation marks, signaling his recognition that he is using the term in some special way. In that second use, "methodism" is a code for "the attack by Christian apologetic on the adulthood of the world." In his last letter, July 28 (*Widerstand und Ergebung*, 254; *Letters and Papers*, 374), it is qualified as "unhealthy" and as depriving "suffering of its element of contingency as a divine ordinance."

12. Karl Barth, *Theologische Existenz heute!* (München: Kaiser Verlag, 1933): 3.

next question. Or we are the ecumenical runners, carrying from one world to another the word of what has been suffered, learned, celebrated, confessed elsewhere.

To do theology, the proverb said, is to be careful about one's words in the fear of God. To do moral theology doxologically is to watch our language in the light of JHWH's mighty works. The "mighty works" I have alluded to are those celebrated under the rubrics of epiphany and of ascension. The rest of the celebratory cycle would belong as well in a full review: passion, resurrection, pentecost, even midsummer and Halloween.

That Jesus is Lord is not something Christian ethicists have to determine, to validate, or to define. Whether it is true does not depend either on our works or on our faith. It is what we celebrate, as we participate in his priestly role and kingly rule by watching our words. That is our share, modest but irreplaceable, in the public — yea the cosmic — victory that is already assured.

> Then I heard all the living things in creation,
> everything that lives in the air and on the ground
> and under the ground and in the sea, crying:
> "To the one who is sitting on the throne
> and to the Lamb be all praise, honor, glory and power for ever,"
>
> And the four Animals said: "AMEN"
>
> (Apocalypse 5:13–14)

140

II. Ecumenical Perspectives

Peace Without Eschatology?

The essay "Peace Without Eschatology?" originated in a paper presented to a theological study conference at Heerenwegen, Zeist (The Netherlands), in May 1954. Subsequently, it was reproduced as a pamphlet (with foreword by Franz Hildebrandt) in the *Concern* reprint series (1961). Footnotes were added in 1970, and the essay was subsequently published by Herald Press as chapter three in *The Original Revolution: Essays in Christian Pacifism* (1971, 1977) under the title "If Christ Is Truly Lord." Except for additional minor stylistic changes and the restoration of the original title and the final section, "Peace with Eschatology," this text is reprinted here substantially in the form that it appeared in *The Original Revolution*.

With the events of World War II as a backdrop, Yoder makes reference to people (Dulles, Molotov) and events (V-E Day) that would have been familiar to his readers in the early days of the "Cold War" between the United States and the Soviet Union. Here again, we see Yoder in conversation with a variety of groups and themes that were current in the 1950s and 1960s. As the essay makes clear, it was written in the context of ecumenical conversations that emanated from the Evanston Conference of the World Council of Churches. Yoder is also drawing upon recent developments in New Testament scholarship that had placed the question of eschatology front and center in the interpretation of the canon of Christian Scripture.

Although the name Reinhold Niebuhr does not appear until near the end of this essay, Niebuhr's writings are clearly in view. Here Yoder can be seen working with some of the same issues that he addressed in "Reinhold Niebuhr and Christian Pacifism," *Mennonite Quarterly Review* 29 (April

1955): 101–17. Using words that summarize well the argument of that earlier essay, Yoder argues here against the kind of "Christian realism" (without naming it as such) espoused by Niebuhr et al. "[T]his view, based on a realistic analysis of the old aeon, knows nothing of the new. It is not specifically Christian, and would fit into any honest system of social morality. If Christ had never become incarnate, died, risen, ascended to heaven, and sent His Spirit, this view would be just as possible, though its particularly clear and objective expression may result partly from certain Christian insights." In contrast to Niebuhr, Yoder argues that "only a clearly eschatological viewpoint permits a valid critique of the present historical situation and the choice of action which can be effective."

Implicitly as well as explicitly, Yoder takes up the challenge laid down by Niebuhr in such essays as "Why the Christian Church Is Not Pacifist"; thus Yoder argues that "every member of the body of Christ is called to absolute nonresistance in discipleship and to abandonment of all loyalties that counter that obedience, including the desire to be effective immediately or to make oneself responsible for civil justice." In his argument, Yoder identifies the ecclesiological implications of taking seriously the eschatological perspective of the New Testament writings, and in the process he articulates the theological basis of a specifically Christian pacifism. In sum, this essay is one of Yoder's most carefully wrought responses to "responsibility ethics" argumentation prior to the publication of *The Politics of Jesus* (1972, rev. 1994) and *Nevertheless* (1971, rev. 1992).

Peace Without Eschatology?

Christian thought is learning to give increasing attention to the importance of the Christian hope for the Christian life. Christian thought in the decades prior to the Second World War was strongly influenced by thinkers and preachers who hoped for "the brotherhood of man" just around the corner and who, therefore, thought they had no time to waste on eschatology. The very word frightened them; it seemed to suggest weird speculations and wild-eyed fanatics out of touch with the world's real needs. And yet for all their down-to-earth social concern and their avoidance of date-setting, these optimists and believers in man also had an eschatology. Their simple confidence that they could be sure of the meaning of life was in itself a doctrine of what is ultimate — i.e., an eschatology — though a questionable one, being in part unconscious and not directly based on Christian foundations.

The plan of the World Council of Churches to set the Christian hope in the center of its theological deliberations at Evanston[1] is a recognition that history and human endeavor can be understood only in terms of God's plan. There is no significance to human effort and, strictly speaking, no history unless life can be seen in terms of ultimate goals. The *eschaton,* the "Last Thing," the End-Event, imparts to life a meaningfulness that it would not otherwise have.

A singularly apt example of the eschatological mode of thought is the use of the term "peace" to designate the position of the conscientious objector or of the "Historic Peace Churches." "Peace" is not an accurate description of what has generally happened to nonresistant Christians throughout history, nor of the way the conscientious objector is treated in most countries today. Nor does Christian pacifism guarantee a warless world. "Peace" describes the pacifist's hope, the goal in the light of which Christians act, the character of Christian actions, the ultimate divine certainty that lets the Christian position make sense; it does not describe the external appearance or the observable results of Christian behavior. This is what we mean by eschatology: a hope that, defying present frustration, defines a present position in terms of the yet unseen goal that gives it meaning. Our task here is to examine the relation between the present position and the goal, between pacifism and "peace," in the basis of the biblical eschatology.

We must first of all distinguish between *eschatology* — whose concern as we have defined it is the meaning of the *eschaton* for present history — and *apocalyptics* — the effort to obtain precise information as to the date and shape of things to come. In marked contrast to the apocryphal literature of the time, the Bible is far more interested in eschatology than in apocalyptics; even when an apocalyptic type of literature occurs, its preoccupation is not with prediction for the sake of prediction but rather with the meaning that the future has for the *present.* It would be inaccurate to maintain that an apocalyptic interest is foreign to New Testament Christianity, but we may nevertheless carry on our present study without asking the questions that the apocalypses answer.

---

1. The Second General Assembly of the World Council of Churches, planned for summer 1954 in Evanston, Illinois, under the topic, "Christ, the Hope of the World," set the theme of the Heerenwegen conference.

Recent New Testament study has devoted itself to lifting out of the records of the life of the first churches the content of the *kerygma*, the central message of the apostolic preachers. The message is no timeless theological statement; it is from beginning to end eschatological, a declaration about events and their place in the unfolding of God's purpose. It would be a rewarding study to analyze the various stages of salvation history — the backward look to David and the prophets of old, the recital of the works of Christ, his passion and resurrection, the forward look to his coming in preparation for which all humanity must repent[2] — for each stage has a particular significance for ethics. We must, however, limit our present study to the meaning of our present age, which extends from the resurrection to the final coming. In this framework we shall seek the answer to two questions: how shall we understand attempts to build "peace without eschatology," i.e., to build a strategy for Christians in society upon a wrong understanding of eschatology? and how does a biblical eschatology clarify the place and meaning of Christian pacifism? The biblical emphases presupposed here are generally accepted by contemporary theologians of all schools of thought.

Peace with Eschatology: Nonresistance and the Aeons

The New Testament sees our present age — the age of the church, extending from Pentecost to the Parousia — as a period of the overlapping of two aeons. These aeons are not distinct periods of time, for they exist simultaneously. They differ rather in nature or in direction; one points backward to human history outside of (before) Christ; the other points forward to the fullness of the kingdom of God, of which it is a foretaste. Each aeon has a social manifestation: the former in the "world," the latter in the church or the body of Christ. The new aeon came into history in a decisive way with the incarnation and the entire work of Christ. Christ had been awaited eagerly by Judaism for centuries; but when he came he was rejected, for the new aeon he revealed was not what people wanted. Jesus' contemporaries were awaiting a

---

2. This particular list of major affirmations is that of C. H. Dodd, in his *The Apostolic Preaching and Its Developments* (Willet, Clark and Company, 1937), esp. pp. 9–15. Under Dodd's impact the word *kerygma* became standard jargon in theology, sometimes meaning this brand of central narrative outline, and sometimes a far broader notion of "proclaiming" as a communication style.

new age, a bringing to fulfillment of God's plan; but they expected it to confirm and to vindicate their national hopes, prides, and solidarities. Thus Christ's claims and kingdom were to them scandalous.

The new aeon involves a radical break with the old; Christ also was forced to break with the Jewish national community to be faithful to his mission. The gospel he brought, even though expressed in terms borrowed from the realm of government (kingdom) and involving definite consequences for the social order, proclaimed the institution of a new kind of life, not of a new government. All through his ministry, from the temptation in the desert to the last minute in Gethsemane, violent means were offered him from all sides as short cuts to the accomplishment of his purposes, and he refused to use them. He struck at the very institution of human justice with his "Who made me a judge over you?" and even into the intimacy of the family circle with his "not peace but a sword!" Students of the Bible have in the past given inadequate attention to this aspect of Jesus' attitude; for our present problem it is of utmost significance to be aware that human community (as it exists under the sign of the old aeon) was far from being Jesus' central concern.[3]

Jesus' interest was in people; the reason for his low esteem for the political order was his high, loving esteem for concrete people as the object of his concern. Christ is *agape;* self-giving, nonresistant love. At the cross this nonresistance, including the refusal to use political means of self-defense, found its ultimate revelation in the uncomplaining and forgiving death of the innocent at the hands of the guilty. This death reveals how God deals with evil; here is the only valid starting point for Christian pacifism or nonresistance. The cross is the extreme demonstration that *agape* seeks neither effectiveness nor justice and is willing to suffer any loss or seeming defeat for the sake of obedience.

But the cross is not defeat. Christ's obedience unto death was crowned by the miracle of the resurrection and the exaltation at the right hand of God.

3. This paragraph uses words like "government" and "political" to designate the structures of the human community "under the sign of the old aeon," which was the predominant usage in theological conversation at that time. The rest of this book is committed to a more contemporary and helpful usage, in which the work and will of Christ should be spoken of as "political" in the most proper sense of this term, i.e., as having to do with the *polis,* the common life of human beings. While the writer strongly prefers his contemporary usage, the difference between what is said in the rest of the book by accepting the characterization "political" and what is said in the above (1954) passage by rejecting the word differ only semantically.

> Bearing the human likeness,
> revealed in human shape,
> he humbled himself, and in obedience
> accepted even death — death on a cross.
> Therefore God raised him to the heights
> and bestowed on him the name above all names. . . .
>
> Philippians 2:8–10

Effectiveness and success had been sacrificed for the sake of love, but this sacrifice was turned by God into a victory that vindicated to the utmost the apparent impotence of love. The same life of the new aeon that was revealed in Christ is also the possession of the church, since Pentecost answered the Old Testament's longings for a "pouring out of the Spirit on all flesh"[4] and a "law written in the heart."[5] The Holy Spirit is the "down payment" on the coming glory, and the new life of the resurrection is the path of the Christian now. But before the resurrection there was the cross, and Christians must follow their Master in suffering for the sake of love.

Nonresistance is thus not a matter of legalism but of discipleship, not "thou shalt not" but "as he is, so are we in this world" (1 John 4:17), and it is especially in relation to evil that discipleship is meaningful. Every strand of New Testament literature testifies to a direct relationship between the way Christ suffered on the cross and the way the Christian, as disciple, is called to suffer in the face of evil (Matt. 10:38; Mark 10:38f.; 8:34f.; Luke 14:27). Solidarity with Christ ("discipleship") must often be in tension with the wider human solidarity (John 15:20; 2 Cor. 1:5; 4:10; Phil. 1:29; 2:5–8; 3:10; Col. 1:24f.; Heb. 12:1–4; 1 Pet. 2:21f.; Rev. 12:11).[6]

It is not going too far to affirm that the new thing revealed in Christ was this attitude to the old aeon, including force and self-defense. The cross was not in itself a new revelation; Isaiah 53 foresaw already the path that the Servant of YHWH would have to tread. Nor was the resurrection essentially new; God's victory over evil had been affirmed, by definition one might say, from the beginning. Nor was the selection of a faithful remnant a new idea. What was centrally new about Christ

---

4. Peter's sermon at Pentecost, Acts 2:17, interprets Pentecost as the fulfillment of Joel 2:28.

5. Hebrews 8:8–12 characterizes the new covenant as the fulfillment of this promise from Jeremiah 31:33.

6. Compare my fuller treatment of the theme of sharing in the suffering of Christ in *The Politics of Jesus,* Chap. VIII.

was that these ideas became incarnate. But superficially the greatest novelty and the occasion of stumbling was his willingness to sacrifice in the interest of nonresistant love, all other forms of human solidarity, including the legitimate national interests of the chosen people. Abraham had been told that in his seed all the nations would be blessed, and most of his descendants had understood this promise as the vindication of their nationalism. Jesus revealed that the contrary was the case: the universality of God's kingdom contradicts rather than confirms all particular solidarities and can be reached only by first forsaking the old aeon (Luke 18:28–30).

In the Old Testament the prophets had mostly been lonely men, cut off from their people by their loyalty to God (which was, in the deepest sense, their real loyalty to their people, even though the people condemned them as troublemakers). Then in the New Testament the body of Christ came into being, a new people in the prophets' line, succeeding Israel as the people of the promise.[7] Nationalism and pragmatism are both rejected in the life of the people of the new aeon, whose only purpose is love in the way of the cross and in the power of the resurrection.

Christ is not only the Head of the church; he is at the same time Lord of history, reigning at the right hand of God over the principalities and powers. The old aeon, representative of human history under the mark of sin, has also been brought under the reign of Christ (which is not identical with the consummate kingdom of God, 1 Cor. 15:24). The characteristic of the reign of Christ is that evil, without being blotted out, is channelized by God, in spite of itself, to serve God's purposes. Vengeance itself, the most characteristic manifestation of evil, instead of creating chaos as is its nature, is harnessed through the state in such a way as to preserve order and give room for the growth and work of the church. Vengeance is not thereby redeemed or made good; it is nonetheless rendered subservient to God's purposes, as an anticipation of the promised ultimate defeat of sin.

This lordship over history had already been claimed for YHWH in the Old Testament. Isaiah 10 exemplifies God's use of the state's vengefulness to administer judgment, but without approving of the

---

7. The phrase "succeeding Israel" should not be understood as attributing to the N.T. writers the anti-Semitism of the second Christian century. The disobedience of Israel was a constantly recurring theme of the Hebrew prophets. The testimony of the apostles is not that Israel is displaced but rather that Israel is restored or rediscovered in a new form that takes Gentiles into the covenant.

vengefulness, and without exempting the "scourge of his wrath" from judgment in its turn. When the New Testament attributes this lordship over history and the powers to Christ, it means that the essential change that has taken place is not within the realm of the old aeon, vengeance and the state, where there is really no change; it is rather that the new aeon revealed in Christ takes primacy over the old, explains the meaning of the old, and will finally vanquish the old. The state did not change with the coming of Christ; what changed was the coming of the new aeon that proclaimed doom for the old one.

Romans 13 and the parallel passages in 1 Timothy 2 and 1 Peter 2 give us the criteria for judging to what extent a state's activities (since the state incarnates this semi-subdued evil) are subject to Christ's reign. If the use of force is such as to protect the innocent and punish the evildoers, to preserve peace so that "all might come to the knowledge of the truth," then that state may be considered as fitting within God's plan, as to that extent subject to the reign of Christ. This positive evaluation cannot apply to a given state in all that it does, but at best in one case at a time, each time it chooses the best alternative rather than adding evil to evil. It is, however, possible, and even frequent, for a state to abandon this function, to deny any sort of submission to a moral order higher than itself, and in so doing to punish the innocent and reward the guilty. That state is what we find in Revelation 13, best described as demonic. Pilate condemning Jesus, not daring to be honest with his own recognition of Jesus' innocence, shows the weak form of this disobedience; the strong form is sufficiently well-known in our day to need no further description.

Cullmann describes the subjugation of the old aeon in terms of "D-Day" and "V-Day." D-Day, the successful invasion of the continent of Europe by the Allied forces, was the decisive stroke that determined the end of World War II. Yet the war was not over. Between the decisive stroke and the final surrender (V-Day) there was a period in which the Axis powers were fighting a losing battle and the Allies were relatively sure of final triumph. This corresponds to the age of the church. Evil is potentially subdued, and its submission is already a reality in the reign of Christ, but the final triumph of God is yet to come.

The consummation will mean the fulfillment of the new aeon and the collapse of the old. The "world" in the sense of creation becomes after purgation identical with the new aeon, after having been the hostage of the old. It is in the light of this promised fulfillment that life in the new aeon, which seems so ineffective now, is nevertheless meaningful and right.

The consummation is first of all the vindication of the way of the cross. When John weeps in despair because there is no one to break the seals of the scroll in which is revealed the meaning of history, his joy comes from the cry that the Lamb that was slain is worthy to take the scroll and open its seals (first vision, Rev. 5), for the Lamb has ransomed people of every nation to make them a kingdom of servants of God who shall reign on earth. The ultimate meaning of history is to be found in the work of the church. (This relationship of Christ's suffering to his triumph is also stated in Philippians 2; the centrality of the church in history in Titus 2 and 1 Peter 2.) The victory of the Lamb through his death seals the victory of the church. The church's suffering, like the Master's suffering, is the measure of the church's obedience to the self-giving love of God. Nonresistance is right, in the deepest sense, not because it works, but because it anticipates the triumph of the Lamb that was slain.

The apparent complicity with evil that the nonresistant position involves has always been a stumbling block to nonpacifists. Here we must point out that this attitude, leaving evil free to be evil, leaving sinners free to separate themselves from God and sin against humanity, is part of the nature of *agape* itself, as revealed already in creation. If the cutting phrase of Peguy, *"complice, c'est pire que coupable,"* were true, then God must needs be the guilty one for making his creatures free and again for letting his innocent Son be killed. The modern tendency to equate involvement with guilt should have to apply par excellence, if it were valid at all, to the implication of the all-powerful God in the sin of his creatures. God's love for us begins right at the point where God permits sin against himself and against others, without crushing the rebel under his/her own rebellion. The word for this is divine *patience,* not complicity.

But this gracious divine patience is not the complete answer to evil. We have seen that evil is already brought into check by the reign of Christ; the consummation of this reign is the defeat of every enemy by the exclusion of evil. Just as the doctrine of creation affirms that God made us free and the doctrine of redemption says this freedom of sin was what led agape to the cross, so also the doctrine of hell lets sin free, finally and irrevocably, to choose separation from God. Only by respecting this freedom to the bitter end can love give meaning to history. Any universalism that would seek, in the intention of magnifying redemption, to deny to the unrepentant sinner the liberty to refuse God's grace would in reality deny that human choice has any real meaning at all. With judgment and hell the old aeon comes to its end (by being left to itself) and the fate of the disobedient is exclusion from the new heaven and new earth, the consummation of the new society begun in Christ.

It is abundantly clear in the New Testament, as all exegetes agree, that this final triumph over evil is not brought about by any human or political means. The agent in judgment is not the church, for the church suffers nonresistantly. (Note the themes of patience and endurance in Revelation 6:9–11; 13:10; 14:12.) Nor is the agent the state, as it is for the judgments of God within history; for in fact the king or the state, refusing ever more demonically Christ's dominion, becomes God's major enemy (Antichrist). God's agent is his own miraculous Word, the sword coming from the mouth of the King of kings and Lord of lords who is astride the white horse (Rev. 19). Just as has been the case ever since the patriarchs and most notably at Christ's cross, the task of obedience is to obey, and the responsibility for bringing about victory is God's alone, God's means beyond human calculation. God's intervention, not human progress, is the vindication of human obedience. The Christian's responsibility for defeating evil is to resist the temptation to meet it on its own terms. To crush the evil adversary is to be vanquished by him because it means accepting his standards.

The term "interim ethics" has often been used to describe the ethics of the New Testament. Customarily (according to the line of thought derived from Albert Schweitzer) this term means that Christ and the New Testament writers were led by their expectancy of an early end of time to an irresponsible attitude to ethics in society. This analysis springs from the attempt to judge on the basis of the old aeon. The New Testament view is rather: "Were you not raised to life with Christ? Then aspire to the realm above" (Col. 3:1). It means being longsighted, not shortsighted; it means trusting God to triumph through the cross. Faith is just this attitude (as the examples of Heb. 11:1–12:4 show), the willingness to accept the apparently ineffective path of obedience, trusting in God for the results. Faith, even in Hebrews 11:1f., does not mean doctrinal acquiescence to unproved affirmations, but the same trust in God that Christ initiated and perfected in itself (12:3). Again, the example is the cross, which was right in itself even though its rightness (in terms of ultimate effect) was not yet apparent.

Peace Without Eschatology: The Constantinian Heresy

We have seen that the eschatological situation — in which nonresistance is meaningful and in which the state has its place — is one of tension between two aeons, tension that will be resolved by the triumph of the new in the fullness of the kingdom of God. The attitude that seeks peace without eschatology is that which would identify church and world, or fuse the two aeons in the present age without the act of God whereby evil is removed from the scene. This means a confusion between the providential purpose of the state, that of achieving a "tolerable balance of egoisms" (an expression borrowed with gratitude from Reinhold Niebuhr) and the redemptive purpose of the church, the rejection of egoism in the commitment to discipleship. This confusion leads to the paganization of the church and the demonization of the state.

The common understanding of religion in the ancient Middle East was that of the tribal deity; a god whose significance was not ethical but ceremonial. God's purpose was not to tell his people how to live but to support their tribal unity and guarantee their prosperity through the observance of the proper cultic rites. This pagan attitude came to light in Israel as well in the form of the false prophets, whose significance in Old Testament times we often underestimate. Whereas the true prophets of the Lord proclaimed YHWH's ethical requirements, judgment, and call to repentance, the false prophets were supported by the state in return for their support of the state's projects. Rather than define ethical demands of God, they committed God to the approval of the king's own plans. Jeremiah summed up their service as being to proclaim "peace" when there is no peace, i.e., proclaiming prosperity without judgment, peace without eschatology. This position was far from pacifism. "Shalom," "peace" as the false prophets preached it, referred not to the absence of war but to the blessing of God on national aims, including wars for national interest (Jer. 6:13–15; 8:7–14). The false prophets, making God to be a handyman rather than a judge, thus inaugurated the line of those who seek to sanctify nationalism with the name of God. This line goes on into the Maccabees and to the various parties of Jesus' time who attempted to unite faith and nationalism in various ways — the Sadducees by collaboration, the Zealots by rebellion. Jesus, in close contact with the Zealots' movement, consistently refused their intention to wage war for national independence.[8]

The classic expression of this attitude in the Christian epoch is known as Constantinianism; the term refers to the conception of Chris-

---

8. Oscar Cullmann, *The State in the New Testament* (New York: Scribners, 1956). Compare my later broadening of the theme of the Zealot temptation in my *The Politics of Jesus* (Grand Rapids: Eerdmans, 1972, rev. 1994).

tianity that took shape in the century between the Edict of Milan and the City of God. The central nature of this change, which Constantine himself did not invent nor force upon the church, is not a matter of doctrine nor of polity; it is the identification of church and world in the mutual approval and support exchanged by Constantine and the bishops. The church is no longer the obedient suffering line of the true prophets; it has a vested interest in the present order of things and uses the cultic means at its disposal to legitimize that order. The church does not preach ethics, judgment, repentance, separation from the world; it dispenses sacraments and holds society together. Christian ethics no longer means the study of what God wants of us; since all of society is Christian (by definition, i.e., by baptism), Christian ethics must be workable for all of society. Instead of seeking sanctification, ethics becomes concerned with the persistent power of sin and the calculation of the lesser evil; at the best it produces puritanism, and at the worst simple opportunism.

It is not at all surprising that Augustine, for whom the Constantinian church was a matter of course, should have held that the Roman church was the millennium. Thus the next step in the union of church and world was the conscious abandon of eschatology. This is logical because God's goal, the conquest of the world by the church, had been reached (via the conquest of the church by the world). By no means did Augustine underestimate the reality of sin; but he seriously overestimated the adequacy of the available institutional and sacramental means for overcoming it.

This reasoning goes one step further. If the kingdom is in the process of realization through the present order, then the state is not merely a means of reconciling competing egoisms in the interest of order; it can be an agent of God's defeat of evil and may initiate disorder. The Crusades are the classic case. Rather than preserving peace, which 1 Timothy 2 asserts is the purpose of kings, the Holy Roman Empire wages war for the faith and against the heathen. Thus the function of judgment, which the New Testament eschatology leaves to God, becomes also the prerogative of the state, with the church's consent, if not urging.

Herbert Butterfield, in his study *Christianity, Diplomacy, and War* demonstrates that the periods of relative stability and cultural advance have been those where wars were limited to pragmatic local adjustments between conflicting interests (in which case they could be somehow compared to the police function and considered as subject to the reign of Christ). Likewise, the least social progress has come when nations, in a Constantinian attitude, have felt obligated by honor to fight for a "cause." The Thirty Years' War and the ideological wars of our century are good examples. In these cases the use of force, by claiming to be a positive good rather than an evil subdued by Christ, becomes demonic and disrupts the stability of society more than it serves it. No longer subject to the restraint of Christ, the state, blessed by the church, becomes plaintiff, judge, jury, and executioner; and the rightness of the cause justifies any methods, even the suppression or extermination of the enemy. Thus even the New Testament doctrine of hell finds its place in Constantinianism; the purpose of exterminating, rather than subduing, evil is shifted from the endtime to the present. Standing not far from the brink of a world crusade to end all crusades, we do well to remember that the Constantinian and crusader's mentality is, far from being a way to serve Christ's kingdom, a sure road to demonizing the state by denying the limits to its authority and failing to submit its claims to a higher moral instance.

Constantinianism was at least consistent with its starting point; it knew only one society, that of the Roman empire, and sought to Christianize it. But today nations are numerous, and each nation claims for itself the authority from God to represent the cause of history. The origin of this kind of nationalism is also to be found in the example of Constantine. For Constantine, in replacing Christ's universal reign by the universal empire, shut out the barbarians. This seemed quite normal, since they were not Christian;[9] but in reality it gave the church's sanction to the divided state of the human community and opened the door to the concept that one nation or people or government can represent God's cause in opposition to other peoples who, being evil, need to be brought into submission. When the Germanic tribes replaced the Empire they applied this sense of divine mission to their tribal interests, despite all the efforts of the medieval church toward maintaining peace. Once admitted in principle, this attitude could later bless nationalism just as consistently as it had blessed imperialism. The universality of Christ's reign is replaced by the particularism of a specific state's intentions.

This goes even further. Once it is admitted that a particular group egoism is the bearer of the meaning of history, so that the nation's or the group's cause is endorsed by God, the divisiveness thus authorized does not stop with nationalism. Just as the medieval unity of Europe broke down into autonomous kingdoms each claiming God's sanction,

9. Or so it was assumed; in fact some of the Goths were Christian.

so also each nation now tends to break down into classes and parties, each of them again sure of divine approval or its secular equivalent. Once a "cause" justifies a crusade or national independence, it may just as well justify a revolution, a cold war threatening to grow hot, or the toppling of a cabinet to suit a particular party's interest. All these phenomena, from the Bolshevik Revolution to John Foster Dulles, are examples of one basic attitude. They suppose that it is justified in the interest of a "cause" for a particular group, whose devotion to that cause is a special mission from God, to rend the fabric of human solidarity, poisoning the future and introducing a rupture that is the precise opposite of the "peace" that it is the duty of the state under the lordship of Christ to insure.

If, with the New Testament, we understand the unity of the church as a universal bond of faith, we can understand that the real sectarianism, in the biblical sense of unchristian divisiveness, was the formation of churches bound to the state and identified with the nation. And on the other hand, some so-called "sects," notably the sixteenth-century Anabaptists, the seventeenth-century Quakers, the eighteenth-century Moravians, and the nineteenth-century Open Brethren, were by their freedom from such ties, by their mobility and their missionary concern, by their preference of simple biblical piety and obedient faith to creedal orthodoxy, the veritable proponents of ecumenical Christianity. On the other hand, the revolution of Münster (1534–35), with which uninformed historians still blacken the Anabaptist name, was not consistent Anabaptism; it was a reversion to the same heresy accepted by Lutherans and Catholics alike — the belief that political means can be used against God's enemies to oblige an entire society to do God's will. It is for this reason that the nonresistant Anabaptists denounced the Münsterites even before the conversion of Menno. Münster attempted, just as did Constantine, to take into human hands the work that will be done by the Word of God at the end of the age — the final victory of the church and defeat of evil.

One of the startling manifestations of modern particularized Constantinianism is the parallelism between the opposing groups, each of which claims to be right. In our day the examples are as patent as they were in the Thirty Years' War. Both Dulles and Molotov were convinced that no coexistence of two opposing systems was possible; each was willing not only to wage war but even to destroy all culture rather than let the enemy exist. Each was sure that the other was the aggressor and that any injustices or inconsistencies on one's own side (like the police methods in the people's democracies or the West's support of Rhee,

Tito, Franco, French colonialism) were only rendered necessary by the enemy's aggressiveness and espionage. Each was convinced that history is on the side of his system and that the opposing system is the incarnation of evil. Each was willing to have the people's morale upheld by the churches; neither was willing to stand under God's judgment and neither felt the need to repent. Each felt obliged to take God's plan into his own hands and guaranteed the triumph of the good by means of the available economic, political, and if need be military weapons. Each sought peace by the use of force in the name of God without accepting God's judgment, without abandoning group egoism, without trusting God to turn obedience into triumph by divine means. In short, both were right where Israel was in the time of Micaiah, and both were amply served by churches faithful to the tradition of the four hundred prophets of 1 Kings 22. "Attack," they answered, "the Lord will deliver it into your hands" (v. 7). Peace without eschatology has become war without limit; thus is fulfilled the warning of the Lord, "Satan cannot be cast out by Beelzebub."

Eschatology and the Peace Witness

Having seen how the crusader's thesis that the end justifies the means is finally self-defeating, and that the Constantinian heresy ultimately reverts to a purely pagan view of God as a tribal deity, we must return to the New Testament eschatology for a new start. We shall ask not only what is required of Christians (for on this level the imperative of non-resistance is clear) but also whether any guidance may be found in the realm of social strategy and the prophetic witness to the state. Certain aspects of a biblical, eschatological, nonresistant Christian view of history may be sketched here.

First of all, we must admit that only a clearly eschatological view-point permits a valid critique of the present historical situation and the choice of action that can be effective. Noneschatological analysis of history is unprotected against the dangers of subjectivism and opportunism, and finishes by letting the sinful present situation be its own norm. History, from Abraham to Marx, demonstrates that significant action, for good or for evil, is accomplished by those whose present action is illuminated by an eschatological hope. There are some kinds of apocalypticism that may favor a do-nothing attitude to social evil; this is precisely what is unchristian and unbiblical about some kinds of apocalypticism. But Schweitzer's thesis, generally accepted by liberal

157

theologians, that the eschatological expectancy of the early church led to ethical irresponsibility, is simply wrong, exegetically and historically.

Within pacifist circles there is urgent need to clear up a serious ambiguity in the understanding of our peace witness. This ambiguity contributed to the weakness of the optimistic political pacifism of the Kellogg-Briand era, and was really a Constantinian attitude, as it felt that true peace was about to be achieved in our time by unrepentant states. Once again the hope was for peace without eschatology.

Restoring our peace witness to its valid eschatological setting, we find it to have three distinct elements. One is addressed to Christians: "Let the church be the church!" As *Peace Is the Will of God*[10] attempts to do it, we must proclaim to every Christian that pacifism is not the prophetic vocation of a few individuals but that every member of the body of Christ is called to absolute nonresistance in discipleship and to abandonment of all loyalties that counter that obedience, including the desire to be effective immediately or to make oneself responsible for civil justice. This is the call of the Epistle to the Hebrews — a call to faith and sanctification. Eschatology adds nothing to the content of this appeal; but the knowledge that the way of the Lamb is what will finally conquer demonstrates that the appeal, for all its scandal, is not nonsense.

Second, there is the call to the individual, including the statesman, to be reconciled with God. This is evangelism in the strict contemporary sense and is a part of the peace witness. Any social-minded concern that does not have this appeal to personal commitment at its heart is either utopian or a polite form of demagoguery. But we must still face the problem with which we began. What is our witness to the states-man, who is not in the church and has no intention to be converted? Here only the eschatological perspective can provide an answer, whereas the "realisms" that agree with Constantine finish by giving him a free hand. We must return to the first Christian confession of faith, *Christos kyrios*, Christ is Lord. The reign of Christ means for the state the obligation to serve God by encouraging the good and restrain-ing evil, i.e., to serve peace, to preserve the social cohesion in which

10. The Heerenwegen conference at which this paper was first presented was immediately followed by a working session of the Continuation Committee of the Historic Peace Churches and the International Fellowship of Reconciliation, which completed the editorial work for the text, "Peace Is the Will of God," which was then jointly submitted by them to the World Council of Churches just prior to the Evanston assembly. "Peace Is the Will of God" is again available as appendix to the newer *Declaration on Peace* (Scottdale, Penn.: Herald Press, 1991).

the leaven of the gospel can build the church, and also render the old aeon more tolerable.

Butterfield, not a pacifist but an honest historian, applies this sort of viewpoint to the question of war. He concludes that the Constantinian war, i.e., the crusade whose presupposition is the impossibility of coexistence and whose aim is unconditional surrender, is not only bad Christianity but also bad politics. He concludes with a qualified approval of what he calls "limited war," i.e., war that is the equivalent of a local police action, aiming not at annihilation but at a readjustment of tensions within the framework of an international order whose existence is not called into question. His thesis is that this sort of balance-of-power diplomacy that one associates with the Victorian age is the most realistic. In virtue of its recognition that it is not the kingdom of God, it is able to preserve a proximate justice that permits the silent growth of what Butterfield calls the "imponderables," those attitudes and convictions, not always rational or conscious, that are the real preservatives of peace. These factors of cohesion — ideals of brotherhood, of honesty, of social justice, or the abundant life — are the byproducts of the Christian witness and the Christian home and have leavening effect even on non-Christians and non-Christian society. It would even be possible to speak of a limited doctrine of progress within this context. As long as the state does not interfere, either through fascism or through violence that destroys the tissue of society, these byproducts of Christianity do make the world, even the old aeon, immensely more tolerable. Yet, they make men and women ultimately no better in the sight of God and no better administrators of the talents entrusted them.

The function of the state is likened by Butterfield to the task of the architect in building a cathedral. The force of gravity, like human egoism, is not in itself a constructive force. Yet, if art and science combine to shape and place properly each stone, the result is a unity of balanced tensions, combining to give an impression not of gravity but of lightness and buoyancy. This sort of delicate balance of essentially destructive forces is what the political apparatus is called to maintain under the lordship of Christ, for the sake not of the cathedral but of the service going on within it.

Thus the church's prophetic witness to the state rests on firmly fixed criteria; any act of the state may be tested according to them and God's estimation pronounced with all proper humility. The good are to be protected, the evildoers are to be restrained, and the fabric of society is to be preserved, both from revolution and from war. Thus, to be precise, the church can condemn methods of warfare that are indiscriminate in their victims and goals of warfare that go further than the localized readjustment of a tension. These things are wrong for the state, not only for the Christian.[11] On the other hand, a police action within a society or under the United Nations cannot on the same basis be condemned on principle; the question is whether the safeguards are there to insure that it become nothing more. In practice, these principles would condemn all modern war, not on the basis of perfectionist discipleship ethics, but on the realistic basis of what the state is for.

Two comments must be appended here. First of all, the kind of objectivity that makes it possible to see the task of the state in this light is really possible only for Christians. For only the Christian (and not many Christians at that) can combine forgiveness (not holding the sins of others against them) with repentance (the willingness to see one's own sin). The pagan sees all the sin on the "other side" and the proclamation of repentance is, therefore, the only liberation from selfishness and the only basis of objectivity.[12] Second, the message of the prophets always took a negative form. In spite of all the ammunition that the social gospel theology took from the Old Testament prophets, those prophets do not propose a detailed plan for the administration of society. This is necessary in the nature of the case, for the state is not an ideal order, ideally definable; it is a pragmatic, tolerable balance of egoisms and can become more or less tolerable. To define the point of infinite tolerability would be to define the kingdom; it cannot be done in terms of the present situation. Thus the prophet, or the prophetic church, speaks first of all God's condemnation of concrete injustices; if those injustices are corrected, new ones may be tackled. Progress in tolerability may be achieved, as the democracies of Switzerland, England, and the Netherlands show us; but only in limited degree and in specific areas, and the means of progressing is not by defining utopias but by denouncing particular evils and inventing particular remedies.

---

11. This conception has been further spelled out in my booklet *The Christian Witness to the State* (Newton, Kans.: Faith and Life Press, 1964).

12. The term "Christian" in this text refers to a normative stance and state of mind. It is not claimed that people calling themselves "Christian" live up to this description or even that most of them would want to. Likewise "pagan" points not to particular adherents of other religions but to the stance of unbelief or idolatry from which the Christian confesses that he or she has been called. For further description of the idea of a Christian vision of the historical process cf. Andre Trocme, *The Politics of Repentance* (Fellowship, 1953), and Herbert Butterfield, *Christianity, Diplomacy, and War* (Abingdon-Cokesbury, 1953), especially the chapter, "Human Nature and Human Capability," pp. 41ff.

On the larger perspective the forces of disintegration are advancing as rapidly as the church. We need not be embarrassed when politicians ask us what they should do; our first answer is that they are already not doing the best that they know, and they should first stop the injustices they are now committing and implement the ideals they now proclaim.

Constantine and Responsibility

The relation of this entire development to an understanding of nonresistant Christian pacifism is obvious. It is just as clear that the New Testament, by its ethics as well as by its eschatology, rejects most kinds of nationalism, militarism, and vengeance for the Christian and calls Christians to return good for evil. Any attempt to draw from Scriptures an approval of war in principle, on the basis of what John the Baptist said to soldiers, what Jesus said before Gethsemane, what Samuel said to Saul, or of Jesus' use of a whip when he cleansed the temple, is condemned to failure.

We must, however, give greater respect to the one serious argument that remains to justify participation in war. This argument has not always been clearly distinguished from the untenable exegetical points just mentioned; but it has another foundation, and in its purest form it admits that nonresistance is God's will for the Christian, and that war is evil. In spite of this concession it is held that in a social situation where third parties are involved nonresistance is not the full response to the problem of evil. The Christian as an individual should turn the other cheek; but in society Christians have a responsibility for the protection of their good neighbors against their bad neighbors — in short, what we have seen to be the police function of the state. This is not to say that the good neighbors are wholly good or the bad wholly bad; but in the conflict in question, one neighbor's egoism coincides more closely with order and justice than the other's. It is, therefore, the Christian's duty, through the functions of the state, to contribute to the maintenance of order and justice in this way. Even war as an extreme case may be justified when the alternative would be permitting passively the extension of tyranny, which is worse than war.

We must recognize the sincerity and the consistency of this viewpoint and the honest realism that its proponents demonstrate when they do not claim to be angels or to have a divine mission to go crusading. This view of the function of the state is the only true and reliable one and coincides with the biblical view of the police function of the state under the lordship first of YHWH, then of Christ. That is precisely our objection to it; this view, based on a realistic analysis of the old aeon, knows nothing of the new. It is not specifically Christian and would fit into any honest system of social morality. If Christ had never become incarnate, died, risen, ascended to heaven, and sent his Spirit, this view would be just as possible, though its particularly clear and objective expression may result partly from certain Christian insights.

The contemporary slogan that expresses this prevalent attitude to war and other questions of a social nature, especially in contemporary ecumenical and neo-orthodox or "chastened-liberal" circles, is the term "responsibility." This term is extremely dangerous, not because of what it says, but because of its begging the question and its ambiguity. The question that matters is not whether this Christian has a responsibility for the social order, it is what that responsibility is. Those who use this slogan, however, proceed from the affirmation that we are responsible to the conclusion (contained in *their* definition of responsibility) that it must be expressed in a specific way, including the ultimate possibility of war.[13] The error here is not in affirming that there is a real Christian responsibility to and for the social order; it is rather in the (generally unexamined and unavowed) presuppositions that result in that responsibility's being defined from within the given order alone rather than from the gospel as it infringes upon the situation. Thus the sinful situation itself becomes the norm, and there can be no such thing as Christian ethics derived in the light of revelation.

We have seen that there is a real responsibility of the Christian to the social order but that, to be accurate, it must distinguish between the objects of its witness. Thus we find the basic error of the "responsible" position to be its Constantinian point of departure. This starting point leads first of all to confusion as to the *agent* of Christian ethics. Since the distinction between church and world is largely lost, the "responsible" church will try to preach a kind of ethics that will work for non-Christians as well as Christians. Or, better said, since everyone in such a society may consider themselves Christian, the church will teach ethics not for those who possess the power of the Holy Spirit and an enabling hope but for those whose Christianity is

13. The precise argumentative meaning that the word "responsible" has come to have in Protestant political ethical discussion is further analyzed in a later chapter, "Christ, the Light of the World," esp. p. 142.

conformity. This excludes at the outset any possibility of putting Christian ethics in its true light and concludes by making consistent Christianity the "prophetic calling" of a few, who may be useful if only they don't claim to be right. But the most serious criticism of this definition of social concern is its preference of the old aeon to the new and the identification of the church's mission and the meaning of history with the function of the state in organizing sinful society. This preference is so deeply anchored and so unquestioned that it seems scandalously irresponsible of the "sectarians" to dare to question it. This is why the American churches as a whole are embarrassed to be asked to talk of eschatology. Yet, it is clear in the New Testament that the meaning of history is not what the state will achieve in the way of a progressively more tolerable ordering of society but what the church achieves through evangelism and through the leavening process. This "messianic self-consciousness" on the part of the church looks most offensive to the proponents of a modern world view, but it is what we find in the Bible. The claim is frequent that by not taking over themselves the police function in society Christians would abandon this function to evil people or to the "demonic." Again, this apparently logical argument is neither quite biblical nor quite realistic: (a) because the police function would be abandoned not to the demonic but to the reign of Christ; (b) because through the "leavening" process, Christianized morality seeps into the non-Christian mind through example and through the education of children who do not themselves choose radical Christianity, with the result that the whole moral tone of non-Christian society is changed for the better and there are honorable and honest people available to run the government before the church is numerically strong enough for "responsibility" to be a meaningful concept. (A case in point: Quakerism, Methodism, and the revivals along the American frontier did more to give a moral tone to Anglo-Saxon democratic traditions than did Anglican and Puritan politicking — once again, leavening works better than policing); (c) because the prophetic function of the church, properly interpreted, is more effective against injustice than getting mixed in the partisan political process oneself; (d) because there always exists the potential corrective power of other egoisms (Assyria in Isa. 10) to keep any abuse from going too far.

It is within the scope of this "responsibility" mentality that the argument of the "lesser evil" is formulated. While it shows commendable honesty in refusing to claim that violence and war are good, it betrays still more logical confusion in the use of the terms. Generally neither the agent, the nature of evil, the criteria for comparing evils, nor the relation of means to ends is clearly defined, much less biblically derived.

Leaving aside several valid criticisms at this point, let us give the "lesser evil" argument its most defensible form. The contention is that out of love for my Neighbor A I should protect him when Neighbor B attacks him, for if I did not I should share the guilt for the attack. Being guilty of defensive violence against Neighbor B is less evil than being passively guilty of permitting offensive violence against Neighbor A for one of two reasons: either because Neighbor B is the aggressor or because Neighbor A is my friend or relative or fellow citizen for whom I have more responsibility than for Neighbor B.

The nonresistant answer here cannot help being scandalous and pushing the scandal of the cross to the end. If the cross defines agape, it denies:

a. that "one's own" family, friends, compatriots, are more to be loved than the enemy,[14]
b. that the life of the aggressor is worth less than that of the attacked;
c. that the responsibility to prevent evil (policing Neighbor B) is an expression of love (it is love in the sense of a benevolent sentiment but not of *agape* as defined by the cross) when it involves the death of the aggressor,
d. that letting evil happen is as blameworthy as committing it.

These four denials are implicit in the positive development of this essay. To develop them further here would be repetition. That these denials appear scandalous to our neighbors demonstrates simply how thoroughly the Western Christian mind-set has been Constantinianized, i.e., influenced by pagan and pre-Christian ideas of particular human solidarities as ethical absolutes.

When this argument is phrased in terms of the war question, its customary formulation is the claim that tyranny is worse than war. Apart from the confusion of agents (tyranny is the tyrant's fault, war would be ours), this raises seriously the question of ends and means.

---

14. The preference for the enemy over the friend as an object of the Christian's moral responsibility is explicitly stated in Matthew 5 and Luke 6. It is founded in the nature of the love of God, who favors his enemies in loving rebellious men and seeking their restoration. I have exposited Barth's position in the pamphlet *The Pacifism of Karl Barth* (Church Peace Mission, Herald Press, 1964) and at greater length in *Karl Barth and the Problem of War* (Abingdon-Cokesbury, 1970).

For "absolutist" ethics ends and means are inseparable and there can be no legitimate calculation of predictable success. For "lesser evil" ethics, however, the comparison of results is paramount and, once mystical arguments about fighting to the death against all odds are rejected (on the lesser-evil basis), it is hard to demonstrate that the national autonomy, even with the cultural values it protects, would be a greater loss than what would be destroyed in an atomic-bacterial-chemical war and in the totalitarization even of the "free" nations that war now involves. Since no one but Gandhi has tried submission to tyranny, the comparison is hard to make; but the nations that in World War II resisted Hitler the most violently did not necessarily suffer the least thereby. For the Christian disciple, it is clear from Jesus' attitude to the Roman occupation forces and his rejection of the Zealots' aims and methods, as well as from the first centuries of Christian history, that war is not preferable to tyranny; i.e., that the intention of liberating one's people from despotic rule does not authorize the use of unloving methods. In fact the claim that God is especially interested in any people's political autonomy or that God has charged any one modern nation with a particular mission that makes its survival a good *in ipso* is precisely what is pagan about modern particularized Constantinianism. Personal survival is for the Christian not an end in itself; how much less national survival.

A second objection to the "lesser-evil" argument is the incapacity of the human agent to calculate the results of his or her actions in such a way as to measure hypothetical evils one against another, especially to measure the evil he or she would commit against the evil he or she would prevent. The very decision to base one's ethical decisions on one's own calculations is in itself already the sacrifice of ethics to opportunism. Such calculations are highly uncertain, due to the limits of human knowledge and to the distortion of objective truth by human pride. To shift our critique to the Christian plane: the way in which God works in history has often been such as to confound the predictions of the pious and the faithful, especially those who tied their predictions about God's working too closely to their national welfare. The most significant contributions to history have in the past often been made not by the social strategists, who from a position of power sought to steer toward the lesser predictable evil, but by the "sectarians" whose eschatological consciousness made it sensible for them to act in apparently irresponsible ways. The most effective way to contribute to the preservation of society in the old aeon is to live in the new.

A third objection, which should be of basic significance to the "responsible" school even though notice is seldom taken of it, is that the effect of the "lesser evil" argument in historical reality is the opposite of its intent. Consistently applied, this argument would condemn most wars and most causes for war and would permit a war only as a very last resort, subject to strictly defined limitations; yet, the actual effect of this argument upon the church's witness is to authorize at least the war for which the nation is just now preparing, since at least *this* war (one claims) is a very last resort. Whereas in intent this position should hold wars within bounds and would condemn at any rate the wars now being waged and being prepared, its effect on those who hear theologians speaking thus is to make war or the threat of war a first resort. Whereas in consistent application the "lesser-evil" argument would lead in our day to a pragmatic (though not absolutist) pacifism and to the advocacy of nonviolent means of resistance, in reality it authorizes the church to accept the domination of modern society by militarism without effective dissent.

This writer was present in 1950–51 in the University of Basel when Karl Barth dealt with war and related questions in the lectures that were to become volume III/4 of his *Church Dogmatics.* For most of an hour his argument was categorical, condemning practically all the concrete causes for which wars have been and may be fought. The students became more and more uneasy, especially when he said that pacifism is "almost infinitely right." Then came the dialectical twist, with the idea of a divine vocation of self-defense assigned to a particular nation and a war that Switzerland might fight was declared — hypothetically — admissible. First there was a general release of tension in a mood of "didn't think he'd make it," then applause. What is significant here is the difference between what Barth said and what the students understood. Even though a consistent application of Karl Barth's teaching would condemn all wars except those fought to defend the independence of small Christian republics, and even though Barth himself now takes a position categorically opposed to nuclear weapons, calling himself in fact "practically pacifist,"[15] every half-informed Christian thinks Karl Barth is not opposed to war. Similarly, Reinhold Niebuhr's justification of American military preparedness is used by the Luce thinking of some American patriots to justify a far more intransigent militarism

---

15. Karl Barth, *Church Dogmatics* IV/2 (Edinburgh: T & T Clark, 1958): 550. The original German makes the point even more clearly against the interpretation his position is popularly given: *Die Kirchliche Dogmatik,* IV/2 (Zurich: Evangelischer Verlag, 1955): 622.

than Niebuhr himself could justify. This tendency of theologians' statements to be misinterpreted is also part of "political reality." Even the most clairvoyant and realistic analysis of the modern theologian is thus powerless against the momentum of the Constantinian compromise. Once the nation is authorized exceptionally to be the agent of God's wrath, the heritage of paganism makes quick work of generalizing that authorization into a divine rubber stamp.

Peace With Eschatology

See what love the Father has given us,
    that we should be called children of god;
    and so we are.
    The reason why the world does not know us
    is that it did not know him.
Beloved, we are God's children now;
    it is not yet clear what we shall be,
    but we know that when he appears
    we shall be like him
    for we shall see him as he is.
Everyone who thus hopes in him
    purifies himself as he is pure.

1 John 3

Let the Church Be the Church

"Let the Church Be the Church" originated in a lecture presented to the Episcopal Pacifist Fellowship at Seabury House, Greenwich, Connecticut, in August 1964. Previously published in *The Witness,* April 22, 1965, pp. 10ff., this essay appears here with a few stylistic changes in substantially the same form that it appeared in *The Original Revolution* in the section on Ecumenical Perspectives.

Here Yoder is in conversation with ecumenical themes, particularly the slogan "Let the Church Be the Church," which of course provided the title for this essay. Accordingly, Yoder draws upon and critically interacts with the various proposals for ecumenical unity ranging from the writings of the veteran ecumenist Willem Visser 't Hooft to the rubrics of the World Council of Churches.

Yoder also addresses issues that are particularly prevalent in the American context, where national identity often distorts ecclesial reality to the extent that America becomes for its citizens "a substitute church." It is in this context of nationalism that the issue of "Constantinianism" is raised again in this essay. Yoder's thesis here is stated succinctly: *"God's pattern of Incarnation is that of Abraham, and not of Constantine."* The argument unfolds in relation to the images of the "chaplain" and the "puritan," each of which in overlapping ways suggest the ways American Christians habitually have blessed existing power structures. By calling attention to these "caricatures" of the church's presence in Western culture, and American culture in particular, Yoder exhibits the need to re-envision *what it means* for the church *to be the church* in the world.

Ecclesiological themes sounded earlier in "The Otherness of the Church"

168

essay recur here. Moreover, Yoder can be seen articulating a different approach to both ecumenism and international relations. In contrast to the nation-state-centered form of "internationalism" prevalent in this era, Yoder asserts that "Christian unity is the true internationalism," and he calls upon the church ecumenical to restore that vision of what the church is called to be by re-creating communities of visible unity that at one and the same time call attention to the "otherness" of the church and its *more extensive* and substantial inclusivity in a world divided by nationalism.

Let the Church Be the Church

In the slogan, "Let the church be the church," which has been so sorely overworked in recent times, there is a paradox that is not only grammatical. The form of this call, "become what you are" is true to the New Testament pattern of thought. Often the Apostle Paul, following a ringing proclamation of what it means to be a Christian, to be "in Christ," then continues with an imperative, "let this be true of you." "Did you not die with Christ?" the apostle appeals, "Then put to death those parts of you which belong to the earth" (Col. 2:20; 3:5). After declaring that Christians have been made one (Eph. 2; 3), Paul continues with the appeal to them to act according to this call.

The call to "become what we are" means on the one hand that we are not being asked anything unnatural, anything impossible by definition. The summons is simply to live up to what a Christian — or the church — is when confessing that Christ is Lord.

And yet at the same time this imperative says negatively, "You are not what you claim to be." The church is not, fully and genuinely, all of what it means to be the church; otherwise we should not have to be called on to become that reality that in Christ we are supposed to be. We have been giving our attention to being something other than the church. It is from this lack of clear dedication to our major cause that we need to be called to cease trying to do something else and to become what we are.

What then is the church and what should it be? One source will tell us that it is "one, holy, catholic, and apostolic"; another will tell us that it is to be found "where the sacraments are properly administered

169

and the Word of God is properly preached." Still others would test the moral performance or the intensity of piety that can be seen in individual members. But in our age there is arising with new clarity an understanding that what it means to be the church must be found in a clearer grasp of relation to what is not the church, namely "the world."

For us to say with the current ecumenical fashion that the church is a witnessing body, a serving body, and a body fellowshiping voluntarily and visibly,[1] is to identify it thrice as not being the same thing as the total surrounding society. This definition demands for the church an existence, a structure, a sociology of its own, independent of the other structures of society. It can no longer be simply what "church" has so long meant in Europe, that administrative division of civil government that arranges to have preachers in the pulpits, nor can it be what is so often true in America, one more service club, which, even though it has many members registered, still needs to compete with other loyalties for their time and attention.

One of the stimuli of the rediscovery of the significance of the church as a sociological reality has been the great foreign missionary movement of the past century. Missionaries have needed, if they were to preach outside the West, a different understanding of what is different about being a Christian than was needed in Europe's Middle Ages; for then to be a Christian was not to be different. Other developments have helped, too. Within biblical studies there has been in recent decades a renewed awareness of the uniqueness of Israel's being a covenant people and of the New Testament church's constituting a new kind of social reality. The ecumenical movement has begun to make Christians think of the church in other places around the world as a human reality to which they owe loyalty, warning them that simple identification with a local or national community and its religious authorities is not enough. Even in the "secular sciences" of psychology and sociology there are new developments that can enable us to see the reality of the church as a different kind of community more clearly than before.

In all of our effort to understand our experience we humans are prone to polarize. Christians have traditionally distinguished between the visible church and the invisible church, between the spirit and the body, between the ordained and the laity, between love and justice. We may now come to see that a more useful and a more biblical distinction would be one that does not try to distinguish between realms of reality

1. W. A. Visser 't Hooft, *The Pressure of Our Common Calling* (New York: Doubleday, 1959).

like body and spirit or the visible and the invisible, nor between categories defined by ritual (lay and ordained), or by abstraction (love and justice), but rather between the basic personal postures of men and women, some of whom confess and others of whom do not confess that Jesus Christ is Lord. The distinction between church and the world is not something that God has imposed upon the world by a prior metaphysical definition, nor is it only something that timid or self-righteous Christians have built up around themselves. It is all of that in creation that has taken the freedom not yet to believe.

In recent centuries those denominations whose heritage was that of the European state church have in many places moved significantly to modify or temper the effects of that relationship of mutual subservience between "church" and government. Yet, there remains a far deeper job if we are to contemplate changing the categories of thought so as to deal not only with institutional relations but with the moral and psychological implications of that identification of church and society that stems from the age of Constantine.

The old yardsticks for knowing what constitutes a church used to be called the "marks" (notae) of the church. They pointed almost exclusively to characteristics that could be measured by looking right at the management of the church's liturgy or its business. They had to do with theological affirmations, with the qualification of clergy and the meaning of the sacraments. But today increasingly it is coming to be recognized that the real tests of whether the church is the church calls for measurements to be taken not in the meeting, nor in the administrative structure but at the point of the relation of church and world. The three marks of the church in mission to which Dr. Visser 't Hooft pointed[2] were all defined with reference to its distinct nature as church; not by the identification of the church with the total society but rather in its distinctness from it. The presuppositions of a relevant witness or ministry are a distinctiveness, a "having crossed over"; otherwise there is nothing to offer. Mission, then, is its witness to its distinctiveness, its calling, rather than to the church's own self-confidence.

When we confess that Christ is the light of the world this implies a critical attitude toward other pretended "lights." When we confess that Jesus Christ is Lord, this commits us to a relative independence of other loyalties, which we would otherwise feel it normal to be governed by.[3] Likewise, with reference to the nature of the church it must be said

2. Cf. note 1 above.
3. See below the discussion of "other lights," pp. 186ff.

that the identification of the church with a given society, for which the church-state marriage of the Middle Ages was a sign and a safeguard, is wrong. This is not only because of the ultimate outworking in the religiously sanctioned national selfishness into which such Christians may fall (and have fallen in the history of the West) but even in the prior idea that one given society could be somehow "Christianized" or "sanctified" through the church's possession of such authority in its midst.

It is especially from the Anglican tradition that the rest of us have learned something of the pervasive intellectual power of the idea of Incarnation. It has been a most impressive vision, to say that all human concerns have been divinely sanctioned and hallowed by God's coming among us, taking on our flesh. Gardening and the weather, our work and our family, the total fabric of our society — economics and warfare, have been bathed in the light of God's presence. All of humanity is thus now seen to be good, wholesome, holy. This seems to a non-Episcopalian to be a deceptively incomplete way of saying something that is nonetheless deeply true. When God came into human society God did not approve of and sanction *everything*, in "normal, healthy, human society"; God did not make of *all* human activity, not even of all well-intentioned human activity, a means of grace. There are some loyalties and practices in human community that God rejected when God came among us. When God came among us God was born in a migrant family and not in a palace. Abraham, the father of the faithful, forsook the great civilization of Chaldea to become a nomad; Israel escaped from Egypt.

The pattern of faithfulness is one of genuine obedience in human experience — which we may well call Incarnation; but it is always also a break with the continuities of human civilization and the loyalties of local human societies, which we call Election or Exodus. When we then speak of Incarnation it must not mean God sanctifying our society and our vocations as they are, but rather God's reaching into human reality to say what we must do and what we must leave behind.[4] Not all of life is to be blessed; not all human efforts can be penetrated by the glow of divine indwelling. In a world that is not yet the kingdom of Christ, it is through the initiative of the Incarnation that we can trace the reality of human obedience. Yet, that obedience, at the same time that it is truly human, is also clearly different from the world around us. *God's pattern of Incarnation is that of Abraham and not of Constantine.*

4. The significance and normativeness of the life of Jesus (rather than all human life) is the theme of my *Politics of Jesus*.

Permit me to clarify by caricature. The church in the past has been in this respect most properly represented by the chaplain. Whether in industry, in a university, in the military, or in the feudal prince's court from which the term is derived, the chaplain is called to bless an existing power structure. He or she is given this place by the authority in power; the chaplain is supported by that authority and in turn will put the stamp of divine approval upon what is being done there. The chaplain's social posture is defined by his or her renouncing the liberty ultimately to challenge the selfish purposes of the community which he or she serves and for which he or she prays at proper times. For him or her thus to stand in judgment upon this community would be first of all to condemn his or her own service to it, for the chaplain's own ritual and moral support of that community's doing in the name of religion is itself the strongest claim the community makes to righteousness.

This "chaplaincy" stance in society can work out in one of two ways. If the preacher is a powerful person and the "prince" or general whom the chaplain serves is well-intentioned, the effort may be made to use the power of his or her position and that of the patron to impose upon all of society that vision of morality prescribed by religion. The chaplain has the ear of the prince and will use that power to oblige the people to live the way they should according to his faith. This is the pattern we have come to describe as "puritan," and we all have some idea of what it does to the soul of a community. Those who do keep the rules are proud of it because they can; those who do not wish to keep them or cannot because of the way they are defined, are crushed or driven away. Furthermore, since everyone is to be obliged to keep most of the rules, only those rules can be stated that can be enforced. You can forbid polygamy; you cannot prevent impure thoughts. Puritanism thus concentrates its attack upon the coarse and crude sins that it is possible externally to punish or prevent.

The alternative for the chaplain who does not wish to be "puritan," and who renounces the effort to use his or her position of power as a level to change society, will be to limit himself to calling down sacramentally the blessing of God upon society, sanctioning whatever means society (or rather the prince) needs to keep society (or rather the prince's place in it) afloat. Then the moral standards that he or she preaches will be those that are feasible for everyone. The understanding of God's purposes that guide the chaplain's preaching will be that which is in line with interests, the capacities, and the needs of the employer. The chaplain will say that it is proper, legitimate, to do all of those things that in his society seem to be necessary to preserve its prosperity and its authorities. In other ages this argument went under the heading of "the divine right of kings" or the "just war"; today one speaks of "responsibility."

This being our heritage, most debates about ethics have been between the "puritans" and the "priests." It is between those who say that there are objective, absolute standards that must be forced on everyone and those who say that if we do what we have to do we had better be able to say it is morally right. This debate, although it is constantly being renewed with new vocabulary, is fruitless; for it defines the issues in such a way that a Christian solution is logically excluded. Both the "puritan" and the "priestly" positions are looking for a course of human behavior that is possible, feasible, and accessible to all conditions of women and men; one that will "pay" in terms of survival and efficacy. The demands of ethics must be "possible" so that after having done whatever he or she did (as an effective "puritan" or "priest" doing what is necessary) a person can be confident of being righteous because of what he or she did.

But Christian ethics calls for behavior that is impossible except by the miracles of the Holy Spirit. When we set up the question in such a way that the ethical prescriptions we hope to unfold must be within the realm of possibility, the cards must have been stacked against a Christian answer. This Puritan-priestly debate is furthermore fruitless because it is about form and not substance. It debates whether ethical standards are absolute or not rather than asking what particular standards should be applied. The entire argument about how to be politically relevant can be run through at book length without any specific statements of value preference derived in a demonstrable way from the center of what the New Testament story is about.

If this insoluble controversy between the "puritan" and the "priest" is the natural result of the position of the chaplain, then the solution to the problem cannot be a new set of definitions of terms or a different set of Bible verses to quote. The solution must begin on the level of sociology, restoring the church to that posture in the world that is in accord with its message. It must renounce seeking a new doctrine for the court preacher to preach, which will leave the chaplain in his or her pulpit but make the court preacher either "more effective" or "more flexible" in prescribing a Christian morality for society as a whole, with special consideration for the strategic importance of the person at the top.

The alternative to Constantine was Abraham, father of the faithful. And what was the posture of Abraham? Or of Moses? That of the prophet who was listened to by only a minority. To recognize that the church is a minority is not a statistical but a theological observation. It means our convinced acceptance of the fact that we cannot oblige the world to hold the faith that is the basis of our obedience and, therefore, should not expect of the world that kind of moral performance that would appropriately be the fruit of our faith. *Therefore* our vision of obedience cannot be tested by whether we can ask it of everyone.

By now, in the age of secularism, everyone is ready to recognize that we cannot oblige the world to be Christian. But is the recognition to be grudging or joyful? Some of us grumpily abandon the vision of Christianizing the world by controlling it, because after having been tried for a millennium and a half this vision has broken down. Instead, should we not recognize repentantly that we ought never have wanted to Christianize the world in this way, from the top down, through the prestige of governmental backing and wide social acceptance? Now that the church has become weak may we not recognize with joy that her calling is to be weak? Should we not, by definition and without reluctance, renounce all grasping for the levers of control by which other people think they can govern history?

One of the logical implications of the acceptance of minority status will be that we no longer hold ourselves to be morally or psychologically obligated to tailor our moral standards to the needs of the people who are running the world. The most frequent response to the testimony of Christian pacifists is "What would happen if everybody did this?" Since we are all children of Christendom we think we must answer this; but logically we need not and cannot — because everybody will not.

It was Immanuel Kant who gave the classic statement of this logic by saying, "I have the right to apply to myself only such standards as I could wish would be applied by everyone." As long as this principle is stated hypothetically it may still have some use. But Christian faith is possible only on the grounds of repentance and forgiveness, only within the restoration of human community as a resource for experienced forgiveness and as a source of ethical counsel, only as it grows from a faith that relates to the meaning of God in the person of Christ. Now if by Kant's statement we mean, "I can only ask radical discipleship of myself if I would wish it for everyone," it makes sense. But the question as usually phrased means rather, "What would happen if everyone were a conscientious objector while most people were still not Christian disciples?" This is an eventuality that we have no reason to "fear," for it won't happen. It is most unrealistic to think that such

175

a calculation would ever be the basis for making our decisions. We must make our decisions on the assumption that most of the world is not going this way, for it does not share our faith. Only then will Christian moral thinking be realistic.

Not only do most people not believe; not only are they not asking us for ethical guidance; but we must make our peace with the fact that this will continue in our age to be the norm. I say "norm" not in the sense of desirability or finality: but we shall not be surprised when the stream of history continues to take another course than the one we propose.

Here lies one of the major debates within the Christian pacifist camp. We have all read the interpretations of what happened as civil rights concerns moved in the late 1950s beyond the professional core of Christian pacifists to a larger group of people. Almost unconsciously but almost unavoidably, "The Movement" seemed to be making to millions of black people the promise of a new order that no one would be able to deliver; and then the question became acute whether non-violence is able to produce what it promises when what it promises is such a solution to society's problems as has never been produced before. If nonviolence cannot "deliver," is violence then justified?

New Testament moral thought begins by facing the fact that we live in a world that most of the time does not listen to all that Christians have to say and some of the time will listen to nothing. Recognition of this minority posture calls not for social cynicism or for withdrawal but for a profound intellectual reorientation. Going far beyond the mere statistical awareness that not as many people will show up on Sunday morning as used to, this reorientation will move on to the recognition that probably many of those who do attend are not yet committed to orienting their lives around a profound conviction that Jesus Christ is Lord. Continuing to give them practical counsel about how to live just a little better does little ultimate good either to them or to the world.

Professor James Smiley in his *The Christian Church and National Ethos*[5] details embarrassingly the extent to which America has become for its citizens a substitute church. It is from the nation and not from the church that Americans expect salvation in history. It is not the church but the Federal Bureau of Investigation that people are willing to trust to investigate one another's moral character and to decide who is and is not in the community. Now if our hope is that of the American

5. See *Biblical Realism Challenges the Nation*, Paul Peachey, ed. (Fellowship Publications, 1963): 33ff.; also printed as a pamphlet by the Church Peace Mission, 1963, and in *Theology Today*, October 1963, pp. 313ff.

religion, it will be appropriate for our churches to strengthen the moral conviction of our civilization by having nothing to say but "God bless America." Similarly if our hope were that of Marxism, then we would believe that it is through our party's taking over the reins of society that the meaning of history will find its fulfillment. Then our hope for the world would appropriately include the need to rule the world and make every kind of compromise, concession, and strategic zigzag that is needed for the party to achieve this end.

The Christian community is the only community whose social hope is that we need not rule because Christ is Lord.[6] Such hope then goes on into the substance of social ethics to affirm that because it is from the cross that he reigned, because it is "the Lamb what was slain that is worthy to receive power," therefore our faithfulness and the triumph of God in human history are not linked by the mode of direct cause and effect. We do not sight down the line of our faithfulness to his triumph. We do not say that if we behave thus and so the mechanism of society will bring about this and that effect and the result will be this desirable development or the containing of that particular evil. There is not that kind of mechanically imaged relationship between our obedience and God's fulfillment.[7] Because, therefore, our hope is in Christ, the prophetic originality that the church must represent in the world is not simply that the church has a more sacred cause for the sake of which it can worthily push people around. It is rather that the church has a cause that dispenses it — enjoins it — from pushing people around in unworthy ways. The "otherness of the church," toward the discovery of which Christians in our age are moving on several paths, is, therefore, the test of the clarity of the church's commitment to a servant Lord.

It was such a discovery that a small circle of Christians made under Adolf Hitler, even though their theological education had trained them to think of the church as the church of only the German nation. It is such an awareness to which worldwide Christendom is being forced by the recognition that Christians in India, in Indonesia, in China, or in Japan cannot guide their contribution to their society by the assumption that its survival or its moral character will depend immediately on how effectively they are able to bend or to bless the structures of their society. It is this kind of "disestablishment," not of

6. See the preceding essay "Peace Without Eschatology," in this volume, pp. 143–67.

7. Alternatives to this mechanical model of the efficacy of ethics are discussed below, pp. 203ff.

buildings or bishoprics but of the soul of the church, that is the sole hope of a renewed relevance, whether we be speaking to civil rights or civil marriage, to automation or to war.

We began by noting the paradox of the imperative, "be what you are." Since Constantine, this "something else" that the church has been trying to be instead of "the church," instead of the beginning of a new kind of human relations, has been to be the soul of the existing society. Christians have felt they needed to provide religious resources for the morality of Everyman, and it was largely the accommodations necessary to meet that standard that seemed obviously to legitimize war and violence. It was assumed that if Christians did not take management responsibility for society, there was no one else who could do it and the world would fall apart.

Now we are in an age that often calls itself post-Christian. Christians and the churches recognize that they are not fully in charge. In many places they are not even in the majority. Christians cannot do everything that needs to be done, nor should they need to. The survival of our society is not dependent upon its being controlled by Christians and the effectiveness of government is not dependent upon the willingness of Christians to make all kinds of compromises in order to be able to fill all the necessary offices. They must, therefore, judge what they do and what they leave to others by the standards of what is most specific, what is most clearly in the line of their primary mission.

The failure of the Constantinian vision to produce a reliably Christianized world is not the result of its having been criticized by the radicals or undermined by the sectarians. Constantine and the leaders of his kind of church had control, after all; that was the point of their ethical approach. If then this strategy of being the church identified with the political structure could ever work, if the commitment to be the soul of the total society seeking to save the whole society by baptizing all its infants and counseling its statesmen was ever a viable vision, and could work, it has been given a good try! The end of the Constantinian age comes not because the sectarians argued against it but because of the contradictions within its own self-assertion. It is not an approach that has not been given a chance but one that, given centuries to work with, has defeated itself.[8]

This recognition that the caretaker function of the church in society will no longer work and is not needed does not in itself provide

8. See the earlier essay "The Otherness of the Church," in this volume, pp. 53–64.

an argument for pacifism, although it does undermine the reasons that originally lead to pacifism's being rejected. For the pre-Constantinian church, which was only a church, idolatry and militarism had coincided; being the minority church, rejecting idolatry, and rejecting militarism were all of a piece. What changed in the fourth century was not a new ethical insight about the morality of killing but rather the phenomenon of a Caesar, and a culture, claiming to be Christian, and redefining "Christian" in order to make it fit. Through the breakdown of Christendom, Christians find themselves again in the position of a voluntary minority. For our grasp of the mission of the church, it may now be more possible to admit to the relevance of the testimony of the pre-Constantinian church, predominantly pacifist from New Testament times until after the age of Tertullian. In that age the logic of thinking from a minority stance, in which saving society is not a conceivable imperative, was clear. The Christians' abhorrence of the idolatrous character of the Roman government and the nonresistant ethic of Jesus combined without question to support that early Christian pacifism.

What changed between the third and the fifth centuries was not the teaching of Jesus but the loss of the awareness of minority status, transformed into an attitude of "establishment." If it was this that helped let the church cease to be the church, then the breakdown of the establishment status of Christianity, while not in any way guaranteeing a renewal of the authentic status of the church as body of Christ, might at least open the door to such a renewal. If it was this that helped make the church cease to be pacifist, then the waning of the Constantinian age opens the door to that agenda, too. If the novelty of that phenomenon was what brought the ethic of the Roman state into the church, its withering-away at least reopens the question of the status of that ethic in Christian thought.

This much attention has been given to the psychological disestablishment of the church and its implications for ethics because it seems to be at this point that Western Christendom has been most unfaithful in the past and stands today to gain most by saying yes to the shaking of its foundations. But there are other dimensions of being the church that are up for renewal as well in our age and that relate as well to the renunciation of war.

One fruition of the modern missionary movement was that it reminded people "back home" in Christian Europe that most of the world was not Christian. Just as important was that it dramatized the unity of the globe. It is as much the missionary movement as the commercial and political imperialisms of the same age that created for us today the possibility of seeing our one world as a cultural family. *Christian unity is the true internationalism,* for it posits and proclaims a unification of humankind whose basis is not some as yet unachieved restructuring of political sovereignties but an already achieved transformation of vision and community. That all humanity is one cannot be demonstrated empirically nor can it be brought about by political engineering. That all humanity is one must first be affirmed as a theological proclamation. Only then is the engineering and structuring that are needed to reflect it ever conceivable. It could just as well be said that *Christian internationalism is the true unity* that the servant church must let be restored. The original meaning of the word "ecumenical" had to do with a geographical wholeness. Recent decades have brought into more prominence a secondary meaning having to do with divisions among churches on the ground of faith or order, doctrine or sacrament or church structure. As significant as this latter kind of division may be, it is still the dividedness along national lines which has made Christians ready to kill each other: Lutherans kill Lutherans, and Catholics, Catholics. There is a not fully explicable skewing of vision involved when massive institutions seek to reunify the structures and the creeds of nationally separated churches. Especially within the Western nations such forms proliferate, making not only little or no progress but, in fact, very little effort toward the development of structures of visible unity that can reach across national boundaries, most importantly, those of nations at war.

Christ, the Light of the World

"Christ, the Light of the World" originated in a lecture presented to the Episcopal Pacifist Fellowship at Seabury House, Greenwich, Connecticut, in August 1964. Apart from a few stylistic changes, the text reprinted here is substantially the same as the essay that was published as the second essay in the "Ecumenical Perspectives" section of *The Original Revolution* (1971, 1977).

As with the essay "Let the Church Be the Church," Yoder uses one of the slogans of the modern ecumenical movement to reflect on the moral significance of the Incarnation and its consequences for the life of the Church. Here again, Yoder can be seen reflecting on the historical significance of the struggle of the "Confessing Church" in Germany prior to World War II, particularly insofar as this struggle raised new questions for the ecumenical movement. More significant still is the Christological reflection embedded in the essay: Drawing upon the discussion of biblical theology that developed in the late 1950s and early 1960s, Yoder emphasizes that the significance of the Incarnation is not so much a matter of metaphysics or other kinds of abstract thought; rather the significance of *"the humanity of Jesus is a revelation of the purpose of God for a person who wills to do God's will."* Several of the arguments adumbrated in this essay, such as the "political" significance of the words and deeds of Jesus, would be explored more fully in *The Politics of Jesus* (1972).

Here also, Yoder explores several proposals that seek "other light" than the "light of Christ" on ethical issues. For example, Yoder cites Reinhold Niebuhr's restatement of the just war tradition in relation to the traditional Protestant notion of the "orders of creation." Similarly, Yoder

181

calls into question the ease with which H. Richard Niebuhr distinguishes between the "ethic of the Son" and the "ethic of the Creator," the effect of which is to rule out the discipleship ethic of Jesus. Yoder is not so much concerned with the specifics of each proposal or how they diverge from one another as he is with what they share in common. "All of them make or presuppose a case for placing our faith in some other channel of ethical insight and some other way of behaving than that which is offered us through Jesus as attested by the New Testament."

Christ, the Light of the World

This phrase, the general theme of the Third Assembly of the World Council of Churches at New Delhi in 1961, brought with it a very solid freight of precise meaning.

This was the first General Assembly held outside the Western, once "Christian" world; it met in a nation where people of many faiths seek to understand themselves in the glow of many different lights. The imagery of "light" is understandable in any culture (as other phrases such as "high priest" or "Son of God" might not so easily be); the quality of missionary witness that was thereby represented in New Delhi was not a mere happenstance slogan or "theme." The choice of such a phrase in such a place was a confession, a proclamation.

This concentration upon the claims of Jesus Christ represents a long-term, special emphasis in the history of the World Council. The original statement of the "basis of membership" in the Council did not refer explicitly to the Bible or to the Trinity, nor to any ancient doctrines, but it did make essential a confession of Jesus Christ. Dr. Willem A. Visser 't Hooft, provisional secretary of the World Council of Churches then in process of formation, when invited to characterize the original theological developments of the wartime period in Europe, responded with a series of lectures on *The Kingship of Christ*.[1] Following a long period of mutually getting acquainted with one another, the Faith and Order series of conferences decided at Lund in 1952 that instead of seeking further to negotiate among fixed traditional positions, it should

1. Willem A. Visser 't Hooft, *The Kingship of Christ* (New York, 1948).

182

henceforth proceed, even in the area of church confessions and constitutions, to try to begin afresh with Christ.[2]

But the figure of Christ is crucial not only in the context of unity,
as a more promising basis of common confession than the comparison
of traditional creeds would be, and not only for mission, as one whose
human ministry is explicable and can be communicated to humans in
every culture. Beyond this, the appeal to Christ represents a particular
type of confession of truth, a criterion whereby to evaluate faithfulness
(and unfaithfulness) within the Christian community.

This most significant impact of the appeal to Christ was, therefore,
first of all that of a criterion for judgment within the "Christian" part of
the world. This development was rooted in the impact of Karl Barth,
renewing all the theological disciplines by concentration upon the truth
claim of Christ. Here, too, was rooted theologically the spiritual resistance
of European churches to Hitler, theme of the book just referred to.

Dr. Visser 't Hooft's story of the rediscovery of testimony to the
Kingship of Christ is a resounding truth claim within Christendom. It
centers upon the Confessing Church as it resisted the designs of the
Hitler government. This resistance, feeble but real, centered in the confession of the authority of Jesus over against fixed doctrinal statements
or evolving church structures.[3] The threat to Christians in Germany
was a conformist movement, the "German Christians," who had taken
to an extreme conclusion the traditional Lutheran confession that there
is revelation in the orders of creation and in the course of history. They
pushed this to the point of the claim that "if God has given us a Hitler,
it must be that a Hitler is what we should have." Over against this
temptation arose the appeal of the Confessing Church to the normativeness of Christ, echoing the language of the reformation creeds but
relating them to a new set of issues, which gave to the resistance of the
churches its modest but real character and effectiveness.

The issue to which we are led is one that is technically and traditionally known in the churches as "natural theology": the claim that
there is somehow a given body of truth, whose givenness is self-evident
to reasonable humanity, which gives us guidance of a kind and content

---

2. Oliver Tomkins, ed., *The Third World Conference on Faith and Order* (London:
SCM, 1953): 15–20.

3. Arthur C. Cochrane, *The Churches' Confession Under Hitler* (Philadelphia:
Westminster, 1962), especially p. 256: "We reject the false doctrine, as though there
were areas of our life in which we would not belong to Jesus Christ, but to other
lords."

different from what we might learn from Jesus. Now it happens that it is "truths" of this kind that have to be appealed to in favor of war: the givenness of the nation, the "reasonableness" of the arbitrage of superior power, the "realism" of the criteria of effectiveness and political responsibility, the unacceptability of other alternatives; these are all self-evident truths whose claim is of the "natural" type.

This background comment may have prepared us to make the outright statement of our claim: the issue of war is a crucial and a most typical touchstone. Perhaps it is the most crucial test point for our age, the point where we are asked whether it is ultimately Jesus or some other authority whom we confess as "the light of the world." We have just noted that the claims that need to be made to support an ethical acceptance of war are of the "natural" kind; but this does not lead us to the acceptance of a clear polarity between Christ and "other lights" unless we are clear in what sense Christ as "Light" would point us in another direction. Thus it is most significant that concurrently with the unveiling of the revelation claim of the German Christian movement there also developed a new way of reading the record of the social humanity of Jesus.

One of the major developments in biblical theology in the past generation has been a new awareness of the whole social humanity of Jesus. Previously, liberal and orthodox theologies alike assumed that the relevance of Jesus to ethics was that of a teacher of morality. One could debate only the specific meaning of his teaching: its scope, how the Sermon on the Mount was meant to be taken, and other issues revolving around the didactic sections of his teaching. His cross or his public career was assumed to have no meaning for morals.

Now it is much more widely recognized that Messianity was for Jesus and for his disciples a political claim, and that his human career was politically relevant. This undercuts not only the idea that he was only a teacher but, in addition, the opposite idea, also widely accepted, that his teaching was ethically irrelevant because he was a rustic not involved in problems of social structure. Or because he was an apocalyptic who thought the world would soon end and, therefore, had no perspective for social concern.[4] Jesus must, therefore, be seen not just as a teacher nor just as an actor on the social scene but in the unity of his teaching and his person. His life is a life according to the Sermon on the Mount; the cross is the meaning of his moral teaching.

4. These ways of undercutting the relevance of Jesus are described more fully on pp. 15ff. of my *Politics of Jesus*.

It then follows that *the humanity of Jesus is a revelation of the purpose of God for a person who wills to do God's will.*

The concept of Incarnation, God's assuming human nature, has often made us direct our thought to metaphysics; asking how it can be that the human nature and the divine nature can be present together in one person. Whether this substantial miracle be joyously affirmed, as in the Athanasian tradition, or found unthinkable, as for John A. T. Robinson, it seems agreed by all that metaphysics is the question. But when, in the New Testament, we find the affirmation of the unity of Jesus with the Father, this is not discussed in terms of substance but of will and deed. It is visible in Jesus's perfect *obedience* to the *will* of the Father. It is evident in Jesus that God takes the side of the poor. It is evident in Jesus that when God comes to be King, Jesus rejects the sword and the throne, taking up instead the whip of cords and the cross. The gospel is that God does this for his enemies. Then if this is what God is revealed to be doing, this is by the same token a revealed moral imperative for those who would belong to and obey God.

This deepening of the resources for ethics to be found in the person of Jesus was a very needed corrective to some of the temptations of much recent pacifist tradition. A major handicap of some earlier kinds of pacifism was their concentration upon the teachings of Jesus in abstraction from his life and from the manner of his death. This concentration was not in itself wrong but could easily be misunderstood or become superficial. It could seem that pacifists who were concerned to do what Jesus said were thereby unrealistic about the possibilities really available within history for human obedience and achievement,[5] or that they were puritanical in the nearly superhuman demands they would make on the capacity of humans to be unselfish and accept suffering, or that they were monastic in the concern for moral innocence and willingness to withdraw from the scene of conflict, or that they were linguistically or semantically naive about how it is possible to interpret precisely the full meaning for all times of a written command.

All these pitfalls are real, and to concentrate upon the words of the command does not protect against them. A fuller feel for the revelatory authority of incarnation is a far-reaching corrective at these points. In the life and death of Jesus we find a reality and the possibility

5. Reinhold Niebuhr's simplest negation was always: pacifism considers love to be a simple possibility. Concerning the shortcomings of earlier pacifist positions, see my book *Nevertheless: The Varieties of Religious Pacifism* (Scottdale, Penn.: Herald Press, 1972; revised 1992).

of all that the teachings say. It is possible to live that way if you are also willing to die that way.

In the personal case of Jesus it is made clear that he rejects not only unjust violence but also the use of violence in the most righteous cause. It is no longer possible to misinterpret his teaching as simply a call to vigilance or to sensitivity in excluding the *improper* use of violence; what Jesus was really tempted by was the *proper* use of violence. It was concerning the use of the sword *in legitimate defense* that Jesus said that they who take it will die by it.

So we learn from the rooting of pacifism in the person of Jesus that the traditional tension between law and love or between the ideal and possible is artificial.

The result of this total development has been an end to efforts to find justification for war in the New Testament — in the failure of Jesus to tell a centurion to become a conscientious objector, in the silence of John the Baptist about the immorality of the profession of the soldiers who came to him for baptism, in the cleansing of the temple. Increasingly, sober theological criticism of pacifism renounces argument on that level and begins with the assumption of a nonresistant Jesus.[6] This recognition then lays the foundation for a more clear awareness than had obtained in the early theological tradition, that other standards of ethics must be appealed to over against Jesus' teaching, if war is to be justified at all. Thus, as was the case in the German Church struggle, behind an issue of political ethics there looms an issue of theological authority.

We can perhaps best illuminate this phenomenon of "other lights" by brief reference to the two most current forms it takes in the debate about war.

The ways this pattern of thought is encountered most clearly today are the traditional doctrine of the "just war" and the contemporary argument of Reinhold Niebuhr and his disciples on political "responsibility." Quite different in the details of structure, these two patterns of thought nonetheless have in common one particular assumption.

The doctrine of the "just war" must be dealt with far more respectfully than most pacifists have been willing to do. It takes seriously, as the other available thought patterns do not, that there can be an

---

6. Reinhold Niebuhr makes this clear in his book *An Interpretation of Christian Ethics* (New York: Harper, 1935): 37. This represents great progress over against more traditional Protestant thought.

ethical judgment upon the use of violence in the name of the state. Most Christians, after all, do not make this assumption. They more often sympathize with the Maccabean assumption that the violence of the state is itself sanctified by religious dimensions or with the Machiavellian view that the state is a law unto itself. Wherever any new opening for the moral criticism of the use of violence arises, it is in some way a use of the just war logic and should be welcomed as at least an opening for possible moral judgment.

Our purpose here is not to analyze the just war theory itself[7] but simply to take note that it makes some specific assumptions that, in effect, claim normative authority, i.e., that claim that they ought to be accepted as expressive of the meaning of the will of God.

The "just war" theory grounds its justification of violence in a network of carefully defined, logically appropriate criteria to determine the particular case in which a particular type of violence will be legitimate; the accent of Reinhold Niebuhr is rather upon the imperative of commitment to the use of power for the sake of justice, with less precision (and less conviction that prior logical precision matters) in the definition of particular legitimate cases. But both approaches have in common the fundamental axiom that it is the obligation of the Christian to direct the course of history so that it attains the goals he or she chooses, in more traditional words, "to be lord" over other people and over the social process.

Now in particular cases we could test this sense of obligation to direct history by asking whether I am a good enough person to have the right to claim for myself such an imperative. Or we could ask whether I am wise enough to know in which direction history ought to move. Or whether I am strong enough to make it move in the way I think it should. On all of these dimensions the thought of Reinhold Niebuhr has been very sobering. But the more fundamental point at which to face the question is to recognize that the imperative itself, "Thou shalt make history come out right," is so deeply founded in our culture that we cannot even perceive that it might be in need of verification.

We have just referred to "that other light" in the particular form of the theory of the just war because it is the most thoroughly worked out body of tradition on the subject, and in the person of Reinhold Niebuhr, who is responsible for the most powerful and creative restate-

7. Cf. the restatement of Ralph Potter, *War and Moral Discourse* (Richmond, Va.: John Knox Press, 1969).

ment of it in contemporary language. It can, however, be said in a host of other ways as well.

There is the language of the "orders of creation," widely trusted in Protestant social thought. Here it is said that because God created a world in which there is authority, whose bearers justify their violence by various moral claims, therefore we must take it on God's *creative* authority that God wants us to operate that way. This again is an affirmation that could be tested logically, since the only place we have creation within our view is in a fallen form. But that again is an internal criticism. The positive affirmation is that creation is a channel of revelation whereby we receive an imperative different from that of the work and the words of Jesus Christ. The most articulate formulation of this position in recent Protestant thought has been in the writing of H. Richard Niebuhr, who distinguishes between an ethic of the Son and an ethic of the Father, with God the Father seen as representing the revelatory quality of the created order.[8]

Still another way of defining that "other light" is the claim to immediate revelations by the Holy Spirit. From Montanus in the second century to the "situation ethics" of the mid-1960s, it has been held that if we were to do away with the definite prescriptions of past authority, there would be a clear present authority speaking in our midst, which would give us instructions different from those of the past authority. Once again we would have numerous internal critiques of the "situational" approach. Is everything I think in the situation right? Is there still some meaningful distinction between right and wrong? Can I credit my every idea to the Holy Spirit or are there other spirits too? But again, let us be content to note simply, formally, that this is another way of finding instructions which differ from those of Jesus. Next to the realm of sexual behavior, it is the realm of killing from which the popular writers on "morality in the situation" draw their most striking anecdotes.

In addition to these strands is the attempt to develop an ethic of "self-fulfillment" or a claim of priority for "love," a love whose content is different from that of Jesus' example. What concerns us here is not the differences of these several approaches, which are significant, but what they do that is always the same. All of them make or presuppose

8. H. Richard Niebuhr's "trinitarian" approach is referred to in *Christ and Culture* (New York: Harper & Row, 1951): 81, 114, 131, but spelled out more fully in "The Doctrine of the Trinity and the Unity of the Church," *Theology Today* (Oct. 1946). See also John H. Yoder, "How H. Richard Niebuhr Reasons: A Critique of *Christ and Culture*," in John H. Yoder, Diane M. Yeager, and Glen H. Stassen, *Authentic Transformation: A New Vision of Christ and Culture*, forthcoming from Abingdon Press, 1995.

a case for placing our faith in some other channel of ethical insight and some other way of behaving than is offered us through Jesus as attested by the New Testament. All these approaches thereby justify my trusting myself to have the wisdom to know, for example, when I may properly sacrifice the life of my neighbor to the righteousness of the cause that I represent. All of them thus find in this other *channel* of ethical insight also another *substance* of ethical instruction. Whereas Jesus instructed his disciples to return good for evil, this other light demands or permits returning a certain amount of evil. While Jesus told his disciples that they should expect to be persecuted, this other light indicates that in some grounds under some circumstances we should cause others to suffer. The one perspective with which it is impossible for these approaches to deal openly is the possibility (which is more than a mere possibility in the biblical witness) that the basic problems of human nature might not be that there are bad guys out there. It might be that what is most wrong with me and the world is my own will to power and my own calling upon God to legitimate my self-assertion. Not only is it not recognized that the will to power might be the basic human flaw; it is in fact precisely my will to power, which is, it is claimed, sanctified and authorized by that "other light."

What we have to do with here is then not simply a confusion that makes the gospel message somewhat less categorical or somewhat more humble. It is not a further dimension that makes it somewhat less possible than naive people had thought to "apply directly" Christian insights to social problems. What we have to do with here is fundamentally nothing other than a competitive revelation claim. If I say it is my duty to make history come out right, appealing to the concept of "creation" or of "love driving me to take political responsibility" or to the call of "the situation," in all of these cases I am setting up over against Jesus another imperative and another source of imperatives. It is not simply a supplementary kind of knowledge that speaks to a gap in the teaching of Jesus; it is a contradiction of something he spoke to clearly and centrally. "In the world, kings lord it over their subjects; and those in authority are called their country's 'Benefactors.' Not so with you" (Luke 22:25, 26).

The concept of revelation is not a clear nor a popular one in the 1970s. Yet, whether the recognition be popular or not, every value claim that commends itself to the loyalty of Christians will affirm in some way or another a transcendent authority for what it calls humans to do. We need not in this context have a definition of the sense in which Jesus is "revelation" that will satisfy modern philosophy. All that we need for present purposes is to observe, functionally, that the imperative to make history come out right is being given, by those who will weigh it over against the imperatives of Jesus, a normative authority equal to or practically greater than that which they will accord to him. The very sense of self-evidence that permits the advocates of those "other lights" not to feel any need to justify the truth claims they make is itself all the evidence we need that it has for them that kind of irrational authoritative quality that is traditionally called "revelation."

As it would be worthwhile to demonstrate at greater length, the total body of doctrine of the just war is a kind of begging of the question. It is assumed that a great number of other moral values are solidly known and accepted, so that they can provide a perspective from which to evaluate a given war or the use of a given kind of weapon. It is said, for instance, that war need be waged only by a legitimate authority; but where do we get the definition of legitimacy for political authority? It is said that only such weapons may be used that respect the nature of humans as rational and moral beings; but who is to define just what that nature is and what means of warfare respect it? The evil that is sure to be brought about by war must not be greater than the evil that it seeks to prevent, but how are we to measure the weight of one evil against another? A just war can only be waged when there is a clear offense; but what is an offense? In a host of ways, the total heritage of just war thought turns out to be a majestic construction whereby a case is made, on the grounds of the self-evident values that seem to need no definition, for setting aside the examples and instruction of Jesus with regard to how to treat the enemy. In order thus to function, the other values, as well as the logic whereby they operate in the given case, must have a kind of authority for which the best word is "revelatory." Otherwise they could not be weighed against Jesus.

Once we have ascertained that we have to do with a revelation claim, we are almost at the end of our argument. It is possible to explain quite clearly the claim Jesus made upon the obedience of his disciples to do the will of his Father as he understood it. If someone claims to be a Christian and yet commits him- or herself to other revelatory authorities, then it is, by definition, impossible to debate theologically that option, since it is ultimately the choice of another "light" or another god. This is especially so if they authorize him or her to turn away from specific implications of following Jesus and choose actions that are less costly or more profitable to one's self or to the extended self of one's own society. I could try to argue that other gods are less worthy of obedience than the one whom Christians call "the Father of our Lord

Jesus Christ," or I could argue that it has pleased this One Only God to reveal himself through the life and ministry and teaching of Jesus Christ as through no other medium; I could even try to argue that people who follow other gods do not turn out to be happy. But all such argument would be beside the point once we have ascertained that the basic issue is whether to set up beside the Jesus of the canon and the creeds some other specific sources and contents of ethical obligation.

Since we are discussing this in an ecumenical context it can further be noted that the appeal to Christ alone, though it was favored as the "style" in the World Council from 1948 to 1961,[9] was discovered also to be the most genuinely ecumenical posture. If I say I am committed to the authority of Jesus *plus* a particular church or of Jesus *plus* common sense or of Jesus *plus* my own best insights, or of Jesus *plus* a particular creedal heritage, that very addition of something extra is structurally sectarian. It makes it impossible for me to converse with those who have a different "plus" or who claim to have no "plus" — and thereby refuse to avow their own historicity. If, on the other hand, one claims rigorously that the only normative point of orientation can and must be the Jesus of the New Testament witness, then there is no one in the ecumenical conversation whom this excludes, except those who might choose to exclude themselves by their commitment to a specific hierarchy or a special doctrine.

For Christian pacifists to appeal to Jesus alone is to strengthen their case in conversation with other Christians as over against less worthy kinds of argumentation to which they are often drawn. For the non-pacifist to insist that we must be committed to Jesus plus social responsibility, or Jesus plus the defense of Western liberty, or Jesus plus "the revolution," is to create a new sectarianism that by its commitment to a second value standard renders itself unable to converse further.

9. It may be said that 1961 marked the beginning of a tapering-off of the Christological concentration of World Council thought. Attention began to turn to the "Cosmic Christ" or to "God at work in history" or to "Participation in nation-building" — concerns for which (it was assumed by many) a specifically Christian stance would be unduly narrow.

Christ, the Hope of the World

"Christ, the Hope of the World" originated in two lectures presented in June 1966 to the Facultad Evangelica de Teologia of Buenos Aires, Argentina. Subsequently, these lectures were translated and rewritten for publication as the last essay in the "Ecumenical Perspectives" section of *The Original Revolution* (1971, 1977). The text that appears here is substantially the same as the previous published version except for minor stylistic changes and scholarly additions to the notes.

In the first part of the essay Yoder provides an "anatomy of the Constantinian temptation" that pervades contemporary Christianity, particularly in the West. In the process, Yoder depicts the structure of the various "neo-Constantinianisms" of the Reformation and post-Reformation periods. Yoder argues that these "new phases" or "new kinds of unity between church and world" are ultimately not so different from one another, despite the fact that each refutes the preceding "marriage" of church and world: "Each says that it is right to identify God's cause with a human power structure. . . . They differ only in that the generation before made the wrong choice of which authority to bless. . . ." Nor is this development unique to the North Atlantic nations and societies; Yoder argues that there are comparable forms of Constantinianism in Latin America that stand in judgment of European versions of the Constantinian temptation.

In conjunction with this critique of Constantinianism, Yoder clarifies the kind of peoplehood that the church should embody in its engagement with the principalities and powers, thereby calling the church to fulfill the role ascribed to it by the writer of Ephesians 3:10. As Yoder insists, this proclamation involves taking into account the cosmic destiny of the people of God in relation to the world. Thus, as Yoder also notes, one of the most tragic results of the identification of the empire with the whole world was a distortion of the way the *oikoumene* itself came to be understood in Christianity. Ironically, despite the various attempts to secure the *oikoumene*'s linkage to the world, "catholicity" has been progressively abandoned, not because of the break with the papacy but by virtue of the alliance with various empires since Constantine. There are internal consequences as well for the church in the circumstance; as authentic catholicity is eroded so is the capacity of the church to render moral judgment. In turn, this raises questions about how history itself should be read in light of God's Providence. For those who would have "let the triumph of Christ be their guide" and thereby live in "evangelical nonconformity," history will not be narrated as the exploits of the sword.

Thus, the middle part of Yoder's essay explores the relationship of claiming the Hope that is Christ to the ongoing discernment of the community of faith. Here the referent of the "sign" that must be read is "the presence and the posture" of Christ, not his efficacy. Given that the church is not "in control" of history, Yoder frankly states the implication of this way of relating the "Signified" to its referent: "there will be times when the only thing we can do is to speak and the only word we can speak is the word clothed in a deed, a word that can command attention from no one and that can coerce no one." Yet, it is exactly this disconcerting situation that constitutes the transcendent Hope that, for the Christian, provides the courage to confidently speak in the knowledge that it is "the Lord of history and his Holy Spirit, not our eloquence or artistic creativity, which will make of our sign a message." In the process of recognizing this sign, it may be that certain "idols" will have to be unmasked, and according to Yoder this, too, is the legitimate role of God's people in the world.

Christ, the Hope of the World

Understanding of History

In an earlier study[1] I observed that the equivalent of a "philosophy of history in the light of Christian faith" or perhaps even a "theology of history" is contained within the thinking of the Apostle Paul concerning the "principalities and powers," those structures of the present world order in whose autonomy humankind has become enslaved and to which are to be proclaimed the implications of the lordship of Christ. Then I was describing the implications of this vision of "the powers" for a Christian understanding of power and structure in society. Here I return to another aspect of the same question, asking what this vision enables us to say about the course of history, its direction and meaningfulness.

A Modest View of History

Perhaps the best description of the effect of Christian proclamation on the powers would be to say that it constrains them to be modest. What had been considered an end in itself comes to be seen as a means to promote human welfare. What had been a source of social and cultural stability turns into a part of a process of change. As long as the commitment of the Christian community is clear, the powers that have been "spoiled" can be kept under control.

But it can also happen that instead of accepting the news of their relegation to a modest state, the powers may rebel or reaffirm their idolatrous independence. Hendrik Berkhof speaks thus of the "anger" of the powers: fascism, nihilism, and other forms of secularism. Their vitality in conflict is greater than that of ancient paganism. In response to the message of the meaning given to human life and to history by Christ, they respond with equal energy in a counterclaim. In the face of the challenges put to the church, the key to success in witness and faithfulness will be the church's maintaining its own identity. The church's task is to call the powers to modesty. The church that understands its own identity can thereby be freed from the temptation to

1. "Christ and Power," *The Politics of Jesus*, Chap. IX; cf. H. Berkhof, *Christ and the Powers* (Scottdale, Penn.: Herald Press, 1962).

sanctify the power structures, which should be objects of patience but not honor. And in the other case, when the rebellious powers appear once again with their destructive power, it will be the proclaimed unity of Christians that will enable them to resist faithfully such pressures.

Constantinianism Old and New

Unfortunately this position is not that which was taken by the mainstream of Christian churches for the past two thousand years. Whether Catholic or Protestant, churches generally identified themselves with the power structures of their respective societies instead of seeing their duty as calling these powers to modesty and resisting their recurrent rebellion.

When the cultural unity of Christendom began to disintegrate, it was not because churches had seen clearly the path of biblical fidelity. It happened rather because the unity upon which the church had been leaning began to fall apart of its own weight in the century of the "wars of religion," which ended in 1648. It was really only logically possible to think of church and society as a unity, the Holy Roman Church and the Holy Roman Empire, when each of these bodies had (or convinced itself that it had) worldwide dimensions. Although it was never literally the case, it was at least possible for the Roman Church and the Roman Empire to claim world dimensions. But since 1648 the separated churches were obliged to accept identification with separated specific nation states. This is no longer the unity of the whole church with the whole empire but the unity of a particular provincial or national church with the local government (later we can see a fractioning movement going on even within a given society). Perhaps we should identify this situation as "neo-Constantinianism." It is a new phase of unity or a new kind of unity between church and world. This unity has lost the worldwide character of the epoch of Constantine, yet the fusion of church and society is maintained. We can even say it is tightened, since the wars of religion linked particular churches with particular national governments in a way that had not obtained in the Middle Ages. Now the church is servant, not of humanity at large but of a particular society; not of the entire society but of a particular dominating class.

The next logical step in the same direction was to take place in the century of the political revolutions that swept the Western world from 1776 to 1848. Now there begins to be visible a progressive "secularization"; it is now evident that the identification between church and society can no longer be taken for granted; it is society that is withdrawing from the alliance. This can take place, as it has in North America, in that the formal links between church and government are cut away for political or philosophical reasons. Yet the identification between church and society remains firm in the minds of the people. The United States of America, despite the formal separation, considers itself a Christian nation. The majority of our citizens consider themselves as members of some church; the army, congress, schools, and even football games have chaplaincy services.

In a country like Sweden the secularization process went in another direction. Here the churches continue to enjoy the formal support of government but can no longer count on any important popular support. Different as these two examples are, they have in common nonetheless the fact that they represent the secularization of a Constantinian dream. In both cases it is possible that the church can continue to give its blessing to the nation and that the church and the government, as visible institutions, mutually support one another even though it is widely recognized that it is no longer possible to speak of the mass of society as in any specific sense "Christian." In the United States the military and political loyalty of most church members testifies to the continuing identity despite formal separation; in Scandinavia the church continues to support the national politics and the government continues to pay for the clergy despite the absence of most convinced Christians from the church services. For this stage where the church blesses the society it inhabits (and particularly its own national society) without a formal identification therewith, or without religious rootage in the common people, we might coin the phrase, "neo-neo-Constantinianism." Unity between church and world has been doubly weakened, yet even now the church keeps on linking itself and its vision to its subservience to the state.

But this movement can go still further. In our century there are non-Christian philosophies which have come to power, which are not simply separate from the church but which in fact are explicitly opposed to the religious dimension of the culture that they seek to change. We find the society being led by secularists, perhaps antireligious, at least post-religious, and convinced that all significant human values can be better understood and better attained without religious support. Even in such cases where society seeks to repudiate religion it is possible for the church to keep holding to its former posture, claiming that the process of secularization can best succeed when favored and fostered by the church. Some forms of Protestant thought in the 1960s and the

1970s in East Germany and Czechoslovakia interpreted and understood the "nonreligious interpretation of the biblical message" that had been proposed by Dietrich Bonhoeffer as a way to prepare the path for mutual recognition between Protestant Christianity and communist governments.[2] In the West, similar transposition of the gospel into the terms of nonreligious language has been proposed as the price for bringing the message of the church to the new "world."[3] In the younger nations of the third world, preoccupied with overcoming the restrictive influence of earlier generations, Christians energetically argue their ability and their obligation to make common cause with "secular" governments under which they live, preferring such structured neutrality to any religious preference their nation might otherwise choose. This preoccupation of the church to be allied even with post-religious secularism, as long as this is effective and popular, could perhaps be called "neo-neo-neo-Constantinianism."

This series of alliances between church and world has brought us up to the present. Now that we have gotten the hang of it, it is possible to try to apply it for the future as well. Convinced that the future belongs to some particular cause, that history is assured a move according to the insights of some particular system, it is possible already in the present to take sides with this cause so that we will not be discredited when the old order collapses and the new is victorious. Something of this seems to have taken place in North America with the predictions of how the church will be radically transformed in the age of urbanization. Something of the same character takes place in Latin America when Christians give their a priori approval to the political revolution that they consider imperative and, therefore, imminent. Such advance approval of an order that does not yet exist, tending to be linked with approval of any means to which people resort that hope to achieve it, we would call "neo-neo-neo-neo-Constantinianism."

2. Hanfred Muller, *Von der Kirche zur Welt* (Leipzig, 1961).

3. Also under Bonhoeffer's influence: Paul van Buren, *The Secular Meaning of the Gospel* (New York: Macmillan, 1963), or Harvey Cox, *The Secular City* (New York: Macmillan, 1965). A very widespread theme in ecumenical thought about mission and evangelism in the 1960s and 1970s was that rather than "doing mission" Christians should discuss, join with, and celebrate what "God was doing in the world to make it more human."

Anatomy of the Constantinian Temptation

All of these efforts to defend the cause of the church before the bar of secular analysis have in common the same basic axiom. This is then what is really important; the true meaning of history, the true locus of salvation, is in the cosmos and not in the church. What God is really doing is being done primarily through the framework of society as a whole and not in the Christian community.

Second (for reasons not clearly linked with the former assumption), it is assumed that if we pitch in and help it will be possible as it would not be otherwise to achieve for the world that fullness of salvation that it was already on the way to achieving *by itself*. We will then do well to ally ourselves with the powers that surround us as our way of participating in the creating of a society worthy of humankind.

It would seem that much distinguishes these views one from another; it would appear that neo-Constantinianism is the enemy and finally the executioner of Constantinianism, and on down the line, and in fact they have usually considered themselves as mortal enemies. As a matter of fact, the most fundamental assumption that they make is the one they hold in common. It is because they want to fight for control of the same terrain that they are enemies; not because one can rise to a higher moral level than the preceding one. All of them together agree to limit the validity of the church, of Jesus Christ, and of the New Testament, as sources of moral norms. For them the structure of social development in this world is itself a revelation of what must and should and will take place. In the beginning this "secular revelation" came by way of the power of the emperor of Rome. Today in contemporary secularism this "revelation" is the respect that we have (neo-neo-neo) for the fantastic capacity of our technocratic society to make things work or else the conviction we have (neo-neo-neo-neo) that everything is so bad that revolution is the only meaningful imperative.

This other "truth," the survival or the prosperity or the development or the restructuring of the national unit, has thus become and remained more decisive than the biblical imperatives. In this sense the church is not seen first of all as a gathering of believers nor as a critic of things as they are. The church is rather considered as chaplain to society, providing resources to help people meet specifically spiritual needs.

The other assumption common to all these kinds of Constantinianism is that it is the business of the church to identify with "our side," with the good guys. It was the churches of the West who supported the action of the United Nations in South Korea. It is the churches of the Socialist countries who take for granted the superior moral value of Marxist secular society. It is the churches of the American Bible Belt that sustain popular patriotism. The identification is never with "the other side," unless it be a church trying to serve a community of young rebels by sharing in their systematic rejection of the church of their parents. This, if it is an exception at all, is only one of the kind that proves the rule.

At each state we observe a powerful desire to repudiate the previous "marriage." In the sixteenth century the argument was that it had been wrong for the church to become the ally of the Roman emperor. In order to break this unholy alliance (Martin Luther called it a Babylonian captivity), the church was called to enter a new alliance with national governments. The next step was to say that it had been wrong to identify the church with national governments but it would be right to identify it with a particular segment within society. Or else: it was wrong to identify the church as an organization with the state as an organization; henceforth we should proclaim that the correct Christian form of social organization is one in which the church and state are separate but allied. Next it was argued that it was wrong for the church to become the ally of the liberal humanism of the West; instead it should have an alliance with the Marxist humanist republics of eastern Europe. Thus again and again an alternative new alliance of the church with the world has been proposed as necessary to overcome the bad effects of the previous alliance. What is rejected, in other words, is not the principle of such alliances but rather the recurrent mistaken choice of allies or the mistaken timing of the church's maintaining an alliance that has become antiquated.

Each generation blames the blindness of the church of earlier generations for having accepted identification with an unworthy political cause.[4] This sense of being right, over against the error of others,

---

4. A more refined and relativistic approach would say that each position or alliance was right in its time. If we understand history as moving through a series of phases, each of which is right in its time and becomes wrong when the next phase is due, then it could be claimed that the identification of the church with past power structures was not wrong when it occurred but only when it lasted too long. The church was right to bless imperialism or racism or sexism before the time when it became possible to move beyond that phase. This is not the place to attempt to evaluate what is left of moral reasoning when all questions of right and wrong are thus translated into questions of timing. Certainly there can be ethical discourse in that language too, but it makes more difficult to see how there could ever be a

seems largely to blind each generation to the observation that the fundamental structural error, that of identifying the cause of God with one particular power structure, is not thereby overcome but only transposed into a new key. All these mistakes agree formally, although they disagree about substance. Each says that it is right to identify God's cause with a human power structure and (what is more fundamental) our enemies with God's enemies, so as to give us a good conscience in seeking to destroy or at least to neutralize them. They differ only in that the generation before made the wrong choice of which authority to bless, supporting one from the past rather than one from the future.

It is not enough to say, as we look back over this pattern, that the basic error of identification in principle with a dominant structure has not been overcome. The shortcomings of that identification have as a matter of fact been seriously heightened with each "neo" stage. On each level another fragment of what had made the medieval synthesis, if not biblically and morally correct, at least culturally understandable and in a sense noble, has been sacrificed.

First of all there is the progressive abandonment of the vision of catholicity. Constantine did not *really* rule the entire world. In order to link the church with Rome and Byzantium, he had obviously to write off as enemies the known neighbors to the north, the east, and the south, some of whom were Christian, to say nothing of the rest of the globe that was less known. Nevertheless, we can understand those who felt that the part of the globe that God in Constantine was now controlling was the *oikoumene*, as the Roman empire was already calling itself in gospel times (Luke 2:1). So the identification of the empire with the whole world, although wrong then, was understandable. But as we move from stage to stage, the unity that is affirmed through the identification of the church with its rulers becomes smaller and smaller. It is reduced from the entire Mediterranean world to the Europe of Charlemagne and then to the nation. In our time of partition and regionalism even the nation is too large. When we move on to the last level of fragmentation in the name of God working in history, the bearer of the hope of the future is only a segment of society, the proletariat or, even

---

serious moral mandate to be against the stream in the way that biblical witness seems to call for. Nor does it account for the vigor of moral reproach that is usually addressed by social critics to the friends of the old regime, if actually what separates them from the advocates of the next phase were only a judgment as to timing, since they were (by this analysis) only doing what was right in the earlier phase. In any troubled situation opinions can vary as to whether the older phase is really gone.

more realistically, the "party" or morally elite minority, to which is ascribed the duty to destroy the enemies of God.

Yet this progressive abandonment of catholicity, moving from the *oikoumene* to the privileged party of the bearer of the moral mandate, is not the only loss as the Constantinian stance hangs on from stage to stage of its transmutation. At each level the capacity of the church as a body to be critical of internal injustice shrivels as well. The capacity of the church to be critical in the face of the pretensions and the performance of the bearers of power has both institutional and cognitive dimensions. Whatever else was wrong with the Middle Ages, this wherewithal for critique still existed. The ecclesiastical hierarchy had a power base and a self-understanding that enabled independent moral judgment. An emperor or a prince could really be forced to listen by the ban or interdict. As to the cognitive equipment for resistance, the criteria of the just war theory and other limits on the prerogatives of princes (the rules of chivalry, the peace of God, the civil exemptions of the clergy, the rights of pilgrims, and the like) had a real effect.

Most of this moral independence was swept away in the first shift. The Reformation did away with the institutional autonomy of the church. Renaissance skepticism destroyed the power of the interdict. In the Reformation confessions the theory of the just war became an affirmation, whereas previously it had been a question.[5] Obviously, each further shift, as the church seeks to hang on to a status that is slipping from its hold, and to win back an audience that no longer senses its need for its ministry, increases even further the capacity to be concretely critical. The causes of this are many. Denominational pluralism, which ascribes to the individual his or her choice of churches, completes the destruction of the notion of objective moral authority as borne by an institution. Philosophical pluralism destroys it conceptually, as many of the churches' thinkers become more preoccupied with how to commend her ministries to a skeptical audience than with how to keep her value message significantly distinctive. Least of all can one be critical of a projected future, when a dozen revolutionary and pseudo-revolutionary moral minorities compete with conflicting definitions of the scientifically objective reading of the signs of the times, and none of them is in a position to promise that "come the revolution" they will have either the capacity or the convictions to produce a fundamentally more just regime.

5. Cf. my "The Reception of the Just War Tradition by the Magisterial Reformers," *History of European Ideas* 9, no. 1 (1988): 1–23.

Thus it is a question both of historical effectiveness and of moral faithfulness, not a pitting of one against the other, when one asks whether the principle of the alliance, and not the choice of the partner, was the mistake. At each of these stages the church tried to strengthen its hold on society and its usefulness within society by taking the side of the people or the ideologies currently in power. Then when a given ruler or ideology needed to be rejected the church would take the side of the next triumphant one. Yet, as it has worked out, the succession has not brought progress but rather disillusionment. Should we not, therefore, suggest that the error of the church in earlier days was not that it allied itself with the wrong power, with the outgoing ruler rather than the incoming one, but that it accepted the principle of sanctifying a given social order at all? Should we not rather question the readiness to establish a symbiotic relationship to every social structure rather than questioning only the tactics of having allied itself with the wrong one? Whether the ruler was on the way out instead of on the way in was then no more than a strategic miscalculation within a larger choice that was wrong in principle. Should we not rather call into question the tendency — or shall we call it a temptation — of the church to establish symbiotic relations with every social order rather than be critical only of the tactics of having chosen the wrong partner at the wrong time?

This is the way we can put the question from a logical point of view, granting that it is the desire of the church to obtain a firm position within society in order to have a vigorous impact. Does not experience suggest that in order to do this we would do well to abstain from close alliances with the power structures? But our concern should not be with a simply logical question about pragmatic efficacy. We are supposed to be asking a theological question. Does the gospel give us any indication of how to avoid alliances? Might we not expect to find that the contribution of the Christian church can be more helpful and more efficacious when it maintains its identity distinct from the rebellious powers, even where they seem successful?

It can be argued that this is the lesson of history. The Christian church has been more successful in contributing to the development of society and to human well-being precisely when it has avoided alliances with the dominant political or cultural powers. Why should we not expect it to be the same in coming years if the church is going to make a worthy contribution? We would then not simply look out into the streets for the evident form of "what is happening in the world" in order to unite ourselves with this movement in the claim that "it is God who is doing this." Not everything that is happening is the work of God.

Instead of asking, "What is God doing in the world?" the church should ask, "How can we distinguish, in the midst of all the things that are going on in the world, where and how God is at work?" The answer to this question will not be found by reading on the surface of daily history but by the Spirit-guided understanding of the discerning community. In our age many are profoundly impressed by the needs of the oppressed and tend simply to declare, "revolution is the will of God," feeling that to be a firm statement. But we need to learn to ask a more precise and profound question. "In a world where revolutions of many kinds are popular and probable, what is the shape of the revolutionary servanthood to which the disciples of Christ are called?" Whether it be in ancient or future society, this particular calling is to be not master but servants. Thus what we have to discern for the church is not a new way to establish a much more promising alliance with the most constructive powers that we can see at work in society as much as to discern the shape of the moral independence that is demanded in order to exercise over against these powers the ministry that only the church can exercise, its constant call to sobriety and to respect for human dignity.

Instead of Efficacy

This survey of the successive failures of the varieties of Constantinianism leads us to conclude that our effort to perceive and to manipulate a casual link between our obedience and the results we hope for must be broken. If we claim to justify the actions we take by the effects they promise, we shall be led to pride in the abuse of power in those cases when it seems that we can reach our goals by the means at our disposal. When we insist on the presence of this link the opposite also happens. We are led to resignation and withdrawal in the cases where we fail. In both cases we are drawn away from the faithfulness of service and singleness of a disciple's mind. We are drawn into the twofold pride of thinking that we, more than others, see things as they really are and of claiming the duty and the power to coerce others in order to move history aright. If our faithfulness is to be guided by the kind of man Jesus was, it must cease to be guided by the quest to have dominion over the course of events. We cannot sight down the line of our obedience to the attainment of the ends we seek.

What then is the validity or the relevance of our hope? What then is the reason for our obedience? With what kind of reasoning can we continue to be present actively in a world that we cannot control? If we cannot guarantee that we can produce the ends we seek, what abiding reason do we then have for working at them?

> And what of ourselves? With all these witnesses to faith around us like a cloud, we must throw off every encumbrance, every sin to which we cling, and run with resolution the race for which we are entered, our eyes fixed on Jesus, on whom faith depends from start to finish: Jesus who, for the sake of the joy that lay ahead of him, endured the cross, making light of its disgrace, and has taken his seat at the right hand of the throne of God. Think of him who submitted to such opposition from sinners: that will help you not to lose heart and grow faint. (Heb. 12:1–3)

Why then is it reasonable that we should continue to obey in a world that we do not control? *Because that is the shape of the work of Christ.* The relation between our obedience and the achievement of God's purposes stands in analogy to the hidden lordship of him who was crucified and raised.

It is reasonable because there is the continuing relevance of *the sign.* When Jesus washed the feet of his disciples he made no abiding contribution to the hygiene of Palestine. Nevertheless, this act took a position in the world that has in itself both spiritual and ethical value. Similarly, when Christians devote themselves to the care of the seriously ill, of the mentally retarded, of the unproductive aged, the fruitfulness of this service cannot be measured by any statistical index of economic efficacy. Whether evaluated from the perspective of the individual or the society, the meaning of this deed is what it signifies, the reality for which it is *the sign,* namely, that this man is here to be the servant of his neighbor. His presence and his posture, *not* his productivity, are the referent of the sign. Much of the achievement of the civil rights movement in the United States must be understood by means of this category of symbolic evaluation. A sit-in or march is not instrumental but it is *significant.* Even when no immediate change in the social order can be measured, even when people and organizations have not yet been moved to take a different position, the efficacy of the deed is first of all its efficacy as sign. Since we are not the lord of history there will be times when the only thing we can do is to speak and the only word we can speak is the word clothed in a deed, a word that can command attention from no one and that can coerce no one. But even in this situation the word must be spoken in the deed in confidence that it is the Lord of history and God's Holy Spirit, not our eloquence or artistic creativity, which will make of our sign a message. This is the hope that our efforts seek to proclaim. It would be best if our "demonstrations" and "manifestations" were concerned to demonstrate or manifest something rather than to wield power as instruments of coercion and pressure, obliging an adversary to yield unconvinced.

The relevance of a transcendent hope includes within it *"wonder."* Every explanation of the most important social movements, such as the American civil rights movement or the peace movement, has to give serious attention to the dimension of the unexpected and unprogrammed. A full Christian accounting of history must make much of the inexplicable coincidences — the pious call them providential — at certain decisive points. Often brilliant solutions, heroic resistance, reconciling initiatives turn out not to have been the fruit of strategic programming but to have been "given" by the situation in a way that is a surprise, a revelation, "a marvel before our eyes." The most careful strategists see things knocked out of their hands and find solutions that would not have been evident if they had been able to keep on controlling the situation. This is the way it usually goes with the lordship of the Crucified One. God's power is not a divine rubber stamp whereby history has no choice to accredit our best wishes but rather a treasure in earthen vessels, a force that is made complete in powerlessness.

The relevance of a transcendent ideal is sometimes that of the unmasking of idols. There are times when a society is so totally controlled by an ideology that the greatest need is that someone simply identify a point where he or she can say a clear no in the name of loyalty to a higher authority. We have no right to say that those who refused to enroll in the racist crusade of Adolf Hitler should first have been obligated practically or morally to propose an alternative social strategy before they had the right to refuse. The imperative of the denouncing idolatry is not conditioned by our immediate capacity to bring about an alternate world. Many times the nonconformist or the conscientious objector are the ones who discover new and creative social solutions. But the obligation to refuse conformity is independent of the capacity to project such better solutions.

The relevance of a transcendent hope is sometimes that of a *pioneer.* It has often been argued that Anglo-Saxon democracy is traced after the pattern of the congregational meeting of the evangelical churches. It was the church that in other ages invented the work of the school and the hospital, creating institutional models that much later could be generalized and supported by the wider society, by the state. In our age it has been the service agencies of churches that first developed the concept of voluntary service for young people that is now coming to be adopted by universities and governments in various forms of overseas service and Peace Corps. It was the Christian Committee for Service in Algeria that in the early 1960s first undertook on a very small scale a project of reforestation, beginning a promise to restore to North Africa a part of the agricultural wealth that it possessed before the goats made desert of much of its land. Christians can undertake pilot efforts in education and other types of social service because, differing from public agencies, they can afford the risk of failure.

The relevance of a transcendent hope may sometimes be that of the *spring in the desert*. If, in a desert region, water can be found it is because in some distant and unknown place incalculable quantities of water have sunk into the ground and disappeared. Only because of that infiltration in some distant place, continuing over a long time and developing pressure in a stratum of porous rock, can water be carried under the desert soil. Far away, it can be found as a seemingly miraculous source of sustenance. So it is with deeds of Christian obedience. Lost in the earth, filtering away without being seen or heard, they contribute to the building up of pressure, creating a subterranean reservoir of saving and invigorating power that can be tapped at the point where people are most thirsty. Sociologists may speak of it as the creation of custom, the development of public opinion, or the raising of the general level of capacity for generous conduct. All of these are simply other ways of affirming that the relationship between my obedience and the accomplishment of the purposes of God must include my losing track of my own effectiveness in the great reservoir of the pressure of love.

The relevance of a transcendent hope may be that of *a mirage*. If we are speaking of a mirage and not of a hallucination, then what the voyagers see is real. It is not on the immediate horizon where the voyagers see it, but it is truly there. It has that shape and is really off in that direction. They will not be able to reach that goal as soon as it seems that they ought to, but what they see is of the same shape and quality as the reality of their destiny, and it lies in the same direction. When the multitudes who had supported the civil rights campaign in the United States sang in the streets of "freedomland" as if it were just around the corner, that was a mirage: Even the most effective efforts to do away with racial injustice will still leave for generations the traces of that evil to be compensated for, repaired, and rebuilt. But the effort is nonetheless justified by the vision of that city on a mountain to which God will call all the nations in the last days so that they may learn the law of the Lord and convert their weapons into instruments of culture.

We are not marching to Zion because we think that by our own momentum we can get there. But that is still where we are going. We are marching to Zion because, when God lets down from heaven the new Jerusalem prepared for us, we want to be the kind of people and the kind of community that will not feel strange there.

In such ways there is a link between our obedience and the accomplishments of God's purposes. Yet the link is more cognacy than causation. We see it when we find life by way of the cross, power by means of weakness, wisdom by means of foolishness. We see it when we find wealth by throwing our bread on the waters, when we find brothers and sisters and houses and lands by giving them up, when we save our life by losing it. This is the evangelical norm of social efficacy. The ultimate and the most profound reason to consider Christ — rather than democracy or justice, or equality or liberty — as the hope of the world is not the negative observation, clear enough already, that hopes of this kind generally remain incomplete and disappointing or that they can lead those who trust them to pride or brutality. The fundamental limitation of these hopes is found in the fact that in their search for power and in the urgency with which they seek to guarantee justice they are still not powerful enough. They locate the greatest human need in the wrong place. The Apostle Paul once wrote, "The weapons of our warfare are not carnal but mighty" (RSV: "not worldly but have divine power"). The implicit set of alternatives is striking. We would have expected him to say "not carnal but spiritual," or "not weak but powerful." There is in this unexpected apposition more than a stylistic slip. The opposite of carnal power is real power; worldly power is intrinsically weak. Those for whom Jesus Christ is the hope of the world will for this reason not measure their contemporary social involvement by its efficacy for tomorrow nor by its success in providing work, or freedom, or food or in building new social structures, but by identifying with the Lord in whom they have placed their trust. This is why it is sure to succeed. The certainty of effect is founded not in our capacity to construct a mechanical model of the connection from here to there, to "sight down the line of our obedience" to Christ's triumph; but rather in the confession itself.

Discerning the Patterns of Providence

Thus far we have been thinking about "history" as the realm of social strategy. We now turn to asking as well whether this "messianic" orientation will have particular implications for history as an intellectual discipline, i.e., for historiography, the recounting of events and the discerning of meanings. Can one gain new light upon the relevance of a free church vision of ethics by claiming that it also leads to a new way of interpreting events in the past? Decision in the present is often very much the product of how the past has been recounted to us. If we are then to open up a new future it must be the extension of a rereading of the past. Historiography must be rehabilitated by being taken back from the grasp of the military historians and the chroniclers of battles and dynasties and informed by other criteria to judge a society's sickness or health. Instead of reading history as proof of a theory of political science, i.e., the definition sine qua non of the state as its monopoly of physical coercion, could we study the story with some openness to the hypothesis that genuine power is always correlated with the consent of the governed or legitimized in some other way? Is there such thing as a "peace church historiography"? There was a time when such a question would have been sufficient occasion for horror-struck reaction from the historians' profession; to read history from any point of view, it was held, is biased and unscientific. One must read from no point of view at all or "objectively." Fortunately the very "objectivity" of the historians allowed this misunderstanding to pass. There is no historiography without a viewpoint; the most honest historiography is not that which claims to be value free but rather that which is open about its prejudices and includes in its method a check against their leading it to distort the record.

The following observations, none of them original with the writer, are intended only to make a logical point. Whether the interpretations of the empirical events underlying these analyses are correct is a question I cannot vouch for. The logical appropriateness of the argument being made is not fully dependent upon whether all of the cases are well chosen or adequately proved. The suggestions made here are not meant to constitute a complete and careful political theory nor a doctrine of the state. They are merely exploratory theses calculated to provoke to fresh and careful thinking among those who are willing to let the triumph of Christ be their guide.

The Sword Is Not the Source of Creativity

For obvious reasons, having to do mostly with the ease of observation and the accessibility of the facts, the writers of history have for centuries centered their memories and their reports on the violent side of the story. The personages who have been remembered have been the rulers. The great events whose dates are fixed on the calendar are the wars and the dynastic changes. Even such a collective concern as social justice is dealt with in terms of legislation or taxation. This gives to us and to our school children the impression that history is basically made up of the interrelations of ruling houses and that their problems are solved on the battlefield. It therefore follows, nearly automatically for the minds of many, that if, as Christians, we desire to be useful, it is on the level of political control that we should seek to work. The prerequuisite of usefulness and the primary way of expressing concern for the neighbor is to be politically strong.

We have all read of the public slogan of Kwame Nkrumah, "Seek ye first the political kingdom." Many were shocked by Nkrumah's use of the language of Scripture, for they assumed Jesus to have been talking about some spiritual kingdom. But most serious Christians would agree with Nkrumah that the preeminent way to be helpful to one's neighbors, especially in an age of resurgent nationalism, is to get control of society.

In the writing of history, scholars in the past century have begun to understand that at many points dynastic history is unimportant. Often it is quite different considerations that make society take the course it does. Karl Marx has taught us all — even the anti-communists — that to a great extent the history of our society could better be written as an economic history; the ways in which goods are produced and distributed are socially more important than who is on the throne. Max Weber demonstrated that intellectual or even theological considerations can make a major contribution to the spirit of an age and to political developments. Similarly the geographer can explain to how great a degree events are really dictated by the placement of travel routes, rivers, arable land, and mineral resources.

In a way somewhat comparable to the liberating effect that new perspectives of analysis have brought to the writing of history, might it not be suggested that the conviction of Christ's lordship would also enable us more wholesomely to read the traces of our own past?

For example, it is not true in an unqualified sense that the person on top of the social pile is all-powerful. Such a person is very often the prisoner of the intrigues and "deals" whereby she or he has reached that position and of the consensus she or he is attempting to maintain. Often the bargains he or she needed to make to get into the office are the very reasons why, once firmly established there, he or she is not in the position anymore to help those truly in need — for whose sake he or she first sought to achieve power. Nor is it to be taken for granted, as popular Marxism tended to do, that if the "former system" is intolerable, some new, strong person will surely be able to solve those same problems more successfully. The new prince is not necessarily more humane than the predecessor; the Marxist theory that the state will wither away once the outside sources of injustice have been eliminated has yet to become practice anywhere. It is not certain that Marxists in government authority are more effectively able to govern in the interest of the population than rulers of other convictions.[6]

Conversely, there are other more useful ways to contribute to the course of society than attempting to "rule." If the history of the Middle Ages is carefully read, we shall increasingly discern that such success as there was in "Christianizing" medieval society was obtained less by the power of the princes than by the quiet ministry of the monastic movements, in rebuilding the community from the bottom. Similarly, what we now call modern civilization was created not by governmental fiat but by the research of intellectual (and religious) nonconformists studying the ways of the natural world with the curiosity of the disinterested voluntary searcher. Let us, therefore, learn to write and to read history as the history of peoples, not of nation states; to evaluate a civilization not by the success of its armies but by how it treated the poor and the foreigner, how it tilled the soil.[7]

Human Dignity Is Not Brutality

Not only the history books preach a view of human value according to which physical and political violence is the ultimate test of the value and of personal merit. It is also the case for popular poetry and literature, all the way from the classical tales of the age of chivalry to the modern morality legends of the Western film, the spy story, and the cover story of the successful businessman in *Time* magazine. What these stories impress deeply upon the soul is not simply the picture of a personage but a view of the universe. They tell us we are in a universe

6. The wording in lectures in the 1966 draft left room open for the claims some were then making for Cuba or for Chile, that a genuinely socialist democracy might succeed. Today (1992) the negation could be stronger.

7. Cf. James Juhnke, ed., *Non-Violent America: History through the Eyes of Peace* (North Newton, Kans.: Bethel College, 1993), conference report volume (privately published).

where there are "bad guys" who are utterly beyond redemption. The only satisfactory result of the conflict with them must be that they be banished or crushed. The "bad guys" are not evil because we can know that they have wittingly done evil deeds or expressed malevolent intentions; they are bad by definition, by status, because they belong to the wrong organization or to the wrong race. Then there are the good guys. Goodness, like evil, is not morally based. The good guys lie and kill just like the others; but they are on the right side, they are good because of the cause they represent. This guarantees not only that they have the right to lie and to kill but also that they will always win out in the end.

We have here a picture of the whole moral universe; one that (at least in the United States) has manifestly influenced the national personality and the national style in international affairs, as we can observe in the history of the past few years most abundantly:

a. All conflicts are reducible to black and white moral issues, where one party is wholly wrong, so wrong as to forfeit their right to exist, and the other party right, so right as to be authorized to do almost anything for its cause.
b. Moral issues are not determined from a personal perspective but on the basis of "sides"; people are guilty and worthy of death by virtue of the system or the race to which they belong.
c. For those who are on the wrong side, even their good deeds are a deceptive façade; for those who are on our side, even the most evil deeds are excusable.
d. The "good guys" are sure to be successful in deceit and in physical combat; the story always comes out this way.

This legend paints for youth, those who are most ready to learn, a picture of the nature of the moral universe that is fundamentally false. It is not true, from either the biblical or the historical perspective, that the world is divided into two organizations, two societies, one good and one evil. It is not the case, either factually or on more careful logical or biblical analysis, that the "good guys" are generally triumphant in physical or intellectual conflict. It is not true, from the perspectives either of logic or of the Bible, that every possible means can be considered justifiable if it is used toward an end considered desirable.

At this point, modern critical thinking and faith in Jesus Christ will coincide. They join in their condemnation of the self-justifying vision of conflict and manhood being traced by these legends. If we once dare to challenge the picture, and see it crumble, we then can discover that in fact violence and deceit represent a particular form of moral weakness (the same parallel relationship of violence and deceit that we here observe was striking in the Sermon on the Mount as well).

Secrecy and deceit are forms of slavery. The United States experience of the past few years has demonstrated publicly several times that governmental secret intelligence agencies have been a major source of misinformation. It is Jesus who says that transparency and humility is a test of truth; that it suffices to say yea for yea and nay for nay. Social experience confirms the same point; liars fool themselves first.

Likewise physical or psychic violence is a confession of moral weakness. Those who resort to blows confess they have no better arguments. Violence is weak not only in the motivation and the moral resources that it presupposes but also in its local effects. Violence can keep out the enemy but cannot create a wholesome society. It can aggress but not defend; it can revolt but not build. It can eliminate a specific abuse but cannot bring social health. If a regime established by violence is to survive, this can only be by demonstrating its capacity to increase progressively the areas of freedom and of orderly legal process. The one thing you cannot do with bayonets, as the dictum has it, is to sit on them.

And yet our legend literature, making virtue, personal courage, and success in combat coincide as they do not in real life, sustains a pagan, pre-Christian confusion of manhood with virility.

If You Wish Peace, Prepare for It

A logical extension of confidence in the sword is the ancient maxim. "If you wish peace, prepare for war." The only kind of "peace" of which this could with any truth be said was the kind of imperial control that was once called the "Pax Romana." Once there are several nations, instead of one emperor ruling the world, the effect of the armaments race has generally been to precipitate the very wars its advocates (on both sides) claimed they were going to prevent. The alternative to this self-glorifying identification of "peace" with the predominant power of one's own nation or class is not passive unconcern with the distress of one's fellow human beings, nor is it utopian expectation about the ability to create a warless world. The alternative is the concentration of Christian attention not on the pragmatic predictability of good results promised by recourse to coercion but on the creative construction of loving, nonviolent ways to undermine unjust institutions and to build healthy ones.

War Is Not a Way to Save a Culture

The native Indians of North America, when threatened by European invasion, fought back militarily. Even though they had some technical advantages in their knowledge of military methods adapted to the terrain, and even though they were able to play the French and British colonizers off against one another, the Native Americans of North America were defeated. Their few surviving heirs have been demoralized, their culture has been degraded, their society caved into a rural ghetto.

In contrast to this, the native of what we now call Latin America, facing invaders who were no more gentlemanly, did not fight back in the same way. The Iberian invaders were generally able to sweep over the entire continent, spreading themselves thinner because they met less opposition, even from the highly organized societies of Mexico and Peru. As a result of the inability or unreadiness of the Indians to defend themselves militarily, their population and many of their cultural values have survived to become part of contemporary Central and South American civilization. From the point of view of the European settlers, permitting the Indianization of Catholic religion was a dubious form of Christianization; but our question from the Indian side is whether war is a way to preserve one's cultural values. The corruption of Catholicism in Latin America by the absorption of elements of the pagan Indian heritage is a proof of the cultural wisdom of letting the invader enter and "roll over the top" of one's society instead of fighting him to the death. The fundamental assumption made in all of our society is that, although war is regrettable, almost infinitely so, it would be still worse to see our civilization destroyed. War, therefore, becomes ultimately necessary for the sake of civilization that, it is held, only war can preserve. This is, however, not a statement about moral logic; it is a prediction about the course of political history. Is it actually the case that war is the best way to preserve a society? Is it the case that national sovereignty is the best way to encourage cultural growth?

As long as the Roman Empire was strong enough to repulse by massive military means the invaders from the north, this military effort not only became increasingly ineffective but it also corrupted and impoverished the internal life of the Roman Empire. But once the central

Roman authorities were no longer in a position to defend their borders, wave after wave of Goths and Franks were permitted first to infiltrate into the northern provinces and then to roll over all of western Europe, "conquering" so much territory and spreading themselves and their royal families so thin to administer the entire area that the population over which they moved, and in fact most of the social and cultural institutions of that population, were able to survive intact under their sovereignty, thus laying the foundation for the emergence of a new society out of the "dark ages." It was thanks to the weakness of the government of the Roman Empire at the right time that the cultural strength of the Gallo-Roman (and partly Christianized) heritage was able to sprout again from the roots, as could not happen in those places where there was a brutal battle for every foot of ground and where populations and institutions were destroyed or transplanted.[8]

A third example is suggested in a book by the great historian Arnold Toynbee on *The World and the West*.[9] Turkey and Russia are examples of nations that, threatened by the cultural and military power of western Europe, attempted to respond in kind. They sent their brightest young men to France or to Prussia to study in military academies and bring back a knowledge of military institutions and techniques. It was assumed this preparation would permit them to beat the western Europeans in their own game. But when these young men came back to Russia and to Turkey, the social fermentation that they brought about was such as to disorient their peoples psychologically and culturally; the Western military spirit had introduced a cultural "foreign body" that these nations were never able fully to assimilate except at the cost of recurrent revolution and disavowal of their own earlier history.

India, on the contrary, made no effort to define and defend its identity in Western terms. The bright young men who went off to school in London studied not military science but law and philosophy. They led India in a process of cultural development and much less violent movement toward political independence. This movement was as effective as the efforts of Turkey and Russia to defend their national identity and did so with much less inner emotional upheaval. India is still Indian.

---

8. Roland Bainton notes that when Augustine was arguing the necessity of a just war against the Goths, a more open immigration policy would have been wiser. "An army might not have been needed to cope with invasions had good faith and sagacity prevailed." *Christian Attitudes to War and Peace* (Nashville: Abingdon, 1960): 99f.

9. *The World and the West* (Oxford University Press, 1953).

These examples may be challenged by the historian. I would not claim that they are more than samples of a mode of thought that, with care and imagination, will discern in concrete cases the relevance of the truth that it is the Crucified One who is reigning at the right hand of God, so that ultimately violence will condemn itself.

Social Creativity Is a Minority Function

We have always been taught to understand the nature of power in society so as to expect that the way to get useful things done is to find a place at the command posts of the state. We have suggested already that the people in power are not so free or so strong as they assume, that they are prisoners of the friends and the promises they made in order to get into office. But an even more basic observation is that they are not at the place in society where the greatest contribution can be made. The creativity of the "pilot project" or of the critic is more significant for a social change than is the coercive power that generalizes a new idea. Those who are at the "top" of society are occupied largely with the routine tasks of keeping in position and keeping balance in society. The dominant group in any society is the one that provides its judges and lawyers, teachers and prelates — their effort is largely committed to keeping things as they are. This busyness of rulers with routine gives an exceptional leverage to the creative minority, sometimes because it can tip the scales between two power blocs and sometimes because it can pioneer a new idea. In every rapidly changing society a disproportionate share of leadership is carried by cultural, racial, and religious minorities.

What is said here about the cultural strength of the numerical and social minority could just as well be said with regard to *political* strength. The freedom of the Christian, or of the church, from needing to invest his or her best effort or the effort of the Christian community, in obtaining the capacity to coerce others, and exercising and holding on to this power, is precisely the key to the creativity of the unique Christian mission in society. The rejection of violence appears to be social withdrawal if we assume that violence is the key to all that happens in society. But the logic shifts if we recognize that the number of locks that can be opened with the key of violence is very limited. The renunciation of coercive violence is the prerequisite of a genuinely creative social responsibility and to the exercise of those kinds of social power that are less self-defeating.

By way of conclusion, let us look clearly at what such examples do and do not mean. It might be argued — and is argued by some pacifists — that nonviolent techniques are available or can be found soon that would be successful in defending anything worth defending in any society. Then the feasibility of these techniques and the promise of efficacity is presented as an argument within the prudential frame of reference, i.e., within the acceptance of the idea that the morality of our action is to be measured by its calculable effects in bringing about the possible resulting social situation. What "works" is still what is right: violence never works.

Such an argument, actually basing the rejection of violence on the promise of a better way or proving the relevance of pacifism on the ground of the lessons of history would place in the prudential type of reasoning and the historical type of analysis much greater faith than I can do. I proffer these specimens with a much more modest intent:

1. To support my testimony that the efficacity of violence has not been demonstrated: the prudential frame of ethical reasoning is not conclusive.
2. To demonstrate to the person committed to such a type of reasoning that even within that framework he or she cannot solidly demonstrate the usability of militarism as a way to save a society.
3. As a testimony that, while disagreeing with a person who reasons thus, I do not make fun of or disrespect his or her concerns.
4. As a way to testify to a person with a value commitment other than my own that my confessing stance has a relevance to the decisions he or she makes in the "political" situations used as examples above.

For all these reasons it is not wasted time to ask whether societies larger than the church or even total national or ethnic cultural unities might best retain their unity by disconnecting it from the defense of a nation state. This does not mean, however, that I am morally committed to defending all nation states or any particular nation state at the cost of my Christian commitment to the life of the neighbor, the enemy. To take up the challenge of demonstrating that the way to save the Roman culture was for the Roman Empire to be destroyed as a sovereign political entity is not to take the preservation of the Roman culture as my own criterion for ethical decision.

Evangelical Nonconformity

When then Jesus said to his disciples, "In the world, kings lord it over their subjects. . . . Not so with you," he was not beckoning his followers to a legalistic withdrawal from society out of concern for moral purity. Rather, his call was to an active missionary presence within society, a source of healing and creativity because it would take the pattern of his own suffering servanthood.

Jesus thereby unmasks the pretension to use violence for the good as being a form of hypocrisy: these rulers call themselves "benefactors," but they are not servants. Those who would claim to have the right to use violence, and especially legal violence, against another place themselves outside of the scope of Jesus' mode of servanthood. This is not so much because they sin against the letter of the law from the Old Testament or the New but because they claim (with a pride intrinsic to their position) to have the right — whether on the basis of official status, of superior insight, or of their moral qualities — to determine in a definitive way the destiny of others. The older language in which the theme of "conformity to this world" was stated in Bible times had to do with "idols," with those unworthy objects of devotion to whom humans in their blindness sacrificed. Thus it is quite fitting to describe the use of violence as the outworking of an idolatry. If I take the life of another, I am saying that I am devoted to another value, one other than the neighbor himself, and other than Jesus Christ himself, to which I sacrifice my neighbor. I have thereby made of a given nation, social philosophy, or party my idol. To it I am ready to sacrifice not only something of my own but also the lives of my fellow human beings for whom Christ gave his life.

In the deep nonconformity of mind to which the gospel calls us, we cannot accept the analysis according to which one kind of action (suffering servanthood) is right from the point of view of revelation but some other pattern is equally right from the practical perspective. This ultimately denies the lordship of Christ and shuts him up in the monastery or the heart. There is clearly a double standard in the world, but it is not between discipleship and common sense; it is between obedience and rebellion.

In the world there will continue to be "wars and rumors of wars," and, yet, our Lord Christ is not thereby shut out of that world. He is able to overrule even its brutality so as to "make the wrath of men to praise him." The call to those who know him as Lord and who confess him as such is not to follow the fallen world in the kind of self-concern

217

that he must overrule but to follow him in the self-giving way of love by which all the nations will one day be judged.

When John the seer of the Apocalypse wept at the news that no one could break the seals and open the scroll to reveal the meaning of history, the angelic gospel was that the Lamb that was slain is worthy and able to open and to reveal. To him blessing and honor and glory and power is given eternally. This is the gospel view of history.

"It is not ourselves that we proclaim; we proclaim Christ Jesus as Lord, and ourselves as your servants, for Jesus' sake." This, and no dreamer's confidence in the inborn goodness of humanity or the omnipotence of technical organization, enables our patience, our defeat, our confidence.

"We are never abandoned to our fate. . . . Wherever we go we carry death with us in our body, the death that Jesus died, that in this body also life may reveal itself, the life that Jesus lives" (2 Cor. 4:9, 10).

III. Ecumenical Responses

The Nature of the Unity We Seek: A Historic Free Church View

"The Nature of the Unity We Seek: A Historic Free Church View" originally was published in *Religion in Life* 26/2 (Spring 1957): 215–22, as part of a symposium on "The Nature of the Unity We Seek." The publications were correlated with a Faith and Order Commission study conference held at Oberlin, Ohio, that summer. At the time it was written, Yoder was completing his doctoral studies at the University of Basel, Switzerland. Subsequently, this essay was reprinted in *Christian Unity in North America*, ed. J. Robert Nelson (St. Louis: Bethany Press, 1958), pp. 89ff. The text of the article is reprinted here without substantial change.

As one of Yoder's earliest assessments of the ecumenical movement, this article provides a précis of the kind of arguments that would recur throughout Yoder's ecumenical responses over the course of the next thirty-five years. In this particular instance, Yoder can be seen carefully articulating a different orientation to the ecumenical task than those that would have been current at the time such as Albert Outler's *The Christian Tradition and the Unity We Seek* (1957). In part, the different orientation arises out of a different conception of *the kind of conversation* that should be engaged in ecumenical relations. As Yoder argues, "True conversation exists only where there is movement toward agreement, motivated by appeal to an authority recognized by both parties. If there is not such movement, talking about the differences only serves to harden them."

Yoder's articulation of the historic free church view of Christian unity centered on the confession of faith in Christ as it arises out of the local gathering of Christians. "If the locus of our given unity is Jesus Christ, it would seem that the only feasible solution to the problem of authority would be to declare inadmissible the attribution of authoritative character to any particular historical development and to recognize, as the only legitimate judge *Christ himself* as he is made known through Scripture to the congregation of those who seek to know him and his will."

Yoder also emphasizes the importance of a *supranational* orientation to ecumenical relations as opposed to the kind of ecumenism that presupposes national frameworks within and beyond denominational alliances. This latter point leads Yoder to comment on the progressive exclusion of pacifist perspectives from the ecumenical movement in the middle years of the twentieth century. For Yoder's chronology of "Forty Years of Ecumenical Theological Dialogue Efforts on Justice and Peace Issues by the Fellowship of Reconciliation and 'The Historic Peace Churches'" see Appendix C of *A Declaration on Peace: In God's People the World's Renewal Has Begun* (Scottdale, Penn.: Herald Press, 1991). Here also, Yoder raises the question of the disciplined character of the church, an ecclesiological issue that he would continue to raise over the next four decades of his involvement with various levels of ecumenical conversation.

As Yoder's discussion in this article makes clear, the question of ethical pluralism not only has an impact on the way individuals in the church understand themselves as Christians, it also affects the very way in which congregations embody the *oikoumene*. In light of the developments within mainstream Protestantism over the past three decades, Yoder's criticisms of the "merger" or "common-denominator" approach to Christian unity can be seen to have been accurate insofar as the various church unions of the 1960s and 1970s have come to be seen as not touching some of the very real *sociological* differences that continue to divide Christians in the United States. Further, as Yoder pointed out thirty-five years ago, these mainstream approaches to ecumenicity actually may have had the effect of cutting off these mergered churches from the sources of renewal that were needed to make them thrive.

The Nature of the Unity We Seek: A Historic Free Church View

That the unity we seek should be an expression of the unity we have has become a commonplace in recent ecumenical thinking. But assent to the proposition that Christian unity is a given reality, and not something to be created, has not yet modified the shape of efforts toward a visible expression of that given fact in church order and church life. The discussion of Christian unity in the past has leapt to two questions: "Do we want federation, fusion, or intercommunion?" and "What shall we do together?" with a rapidity that assumed that all the basic questions were settled. To what extent this short circuit has truly furthered the cause it is not up to us to decide; but we can ask at least that henceforth the relation between schemes of union and the givenness of unity be kept clearer.

The Unity We Seek Is Conversation

If I admit the givenness of unity between my interlocutor, whose good faith in confessing the name of Christ I have no grounds to question, and myself, I thereby lay upon myself, as upon her or him, the imperative of conversation at those points where, in life and doctrine, our given unity is hidden by disagreement. I am released from this obligation only when we have come to agreement or when my interlocutor refuses further to converse.

Superficially, the ecumenical discussions of the past half-century have produced one good effect. Christian bodies have become acquainted with one another, have learned to appreciate the sincerity with which strongly variant positions may be held, and have sought to see the good in others' points of view. Yet, as has been learned in recent years, that is not conversation. It is information, and indispensable as such; but it is in itself not conversation because it does not lead toward agreement but, in fact, to crystallizing fundamental differences. True conversation exists only where there is movement toward agreement, motivated by appeal to an authority recognized by both parties. If there is not such movement, talking about the differences only serves to harden them.

The formal requirement for conversation is thus two-sided. (1) Objectively, there must be a mutually recognized authority to which both parties have recourse for ultimate proof, just as physicists have an objective point of reference in their measurements of mass and movement and historians in their documentary sources; and (2) subjectively, there must be the willingness to move, to change positions, when the proof has been brought. When we say that Christian unity is given, that means that the objective requirement has been met, whether we accept it or not.

The tact with which ecumenical conversation has hitherto gone about the process of getting acquainted without asking anyone to move, and the peculiar character of American denominationalism, in which many organizational divisions do not correspond to any real differences of principle, have obscured the cruciality of *the problem of authority* with which true conversation must begin. It has not been asked clearly wherein that common authority resides before which every party to the conversation was willing to be judged.

For Roman Catholicism the solution is the easiest. The court of appeal is an institution, available in history, with an authorized spokesman. The objective requirement, that there be a definable point of reference, is met admirably. No one can disagree (except with regard to a few awkward moments in the Middle Ages) about who is pope. At the same time the subjective requirement for conversation is rendered unattainable by definition. Since the Roman Catholic Church is its own final authority, it is inconceivable, at least in principle, that it converse with anyone.

What is less generally recognized is that, speaking formally, American liberal and post-liberal Protestantism is little different from Rome. Like Rome, it presupposes as undebatable a centuries-long doctrinal and institutional evolution that is not open to question from outside itself. The only difference is that this evolution has gone down another track for four or five centuries. Instead of the Counter-Reformation, Papal Infallibility, and the Assumption of Mary, its dogma is drawn from the Renaissance, the Reformation, the Enlightenment, idealism, the scientific worldview, and (most recent acquisition) a revived Judeo-Christian doctrine of sin. In the institutional realm, Greco-Roman ideals of equity and due process of law and Occidental ideals of democracy are not subject to criticism. Built as it is on layer upon layer of ideological affluvium that it dares not submit to too close a scrutiny, this theological position is just as incapable of talking across the fence as is Rome. The only formal difference is that it is more difficult to identify its pope; but the consensus of what the most popular teachers in the largest divinity schools were teaching twenty years ago serves the same purpose. The affirmations of the Bible and of classical orthodoxy can be accepted by American liberal Protestantism only if redefined into terms of psychology and social ethics that are meaningful to modern "man." The recent rehabilitation of a doctrine of sin by certain segments of this thought-world comes neither from the Bible nor from classical orthodoxy but from the observation by modern "man" of how much trouble "he" has getting along with "himself."

The rest of Christendom generally differs from Rome and from liberalism simply by choosing some other point along the time scale of doctrinal and institutional evolution to which to tie their ability to converse. Anglo-Catholicism and Eastern Orthodoxy would part with Rome at varying dates, depending upon how much "catholicity" they want to conserve. Reformation Protestantism chose to revert to the level of about A.D. 500, thus avoiding popery and the mass *but* maintaining the state church, the accepted doctrinal formulations concerning the Trinity and the natures of Christ, and the persecution of heretics. The Nestorians would back up a little farther yet, and so on and on. . . .

If the locus of our given unity is Jesus Christ, it would seem that the only feasible solution to the problem of authority would be to declare inadmissible the attribution of authoritative character to any particular historical development and to recognize, as the only legitimate judge *Christ himself* as he is made known through Scripture to the congregation of those who seek to know him and his will. This would not necessarily mean that all evolution would ipso facto be condemned, nor would it commit us to an infantile literalism in the use of Scripture; but there would have to be the mutual abandon of any attempt to have recourse to any particular evolution as a canon of interpretation. Neither what the modern mind can accept, nor what the medieval mind could accept, nor what one of the Councils of Constantinople could accept, would have the right to stand above, or beside, or even authoritatively under Christ and Scripture.

This is the position held by the free church tradition; by the Swiss and Hutterian Brethren and the Doopsgezinde of the sixteenth century, by the Congregationalists, Baptists, and Quakers later in England, by most of the churches born and reared on the American frontier in the eighteenth and nineteenth centuries. It has spoken less than its share in ecumenical discussion in recent years. This is partly because its lack of interest in doctrinal and institutional fixation gives it no hallowed monuments, no revered creedal statements or unbroken successions to show the other churches; but also, and more significantly, because many of these groups have failed to make their position articulate or have, in seeking to do so, affiliated themselves either with Protestant Orthodoxy or with American Liberalism and unwittingly betrayed the simple New Testament faith they stood for in the effort to defend it.

In view of the fact that the Faith and Order movement in its early days was largely borne by Anglicanism, and Life and Work by liberal Protestantism, both of them committed a priori to concepts of authority that have no intention of being content with the New Testament, a serious hearing for the free church viewpoint could hardly have been expected. On the other hand, the roots of the ecumenical movement in Christian youth work, which in its nondenominational and voluntary character is a kind of free church, in missions and in evangelism (if John R. Mott was, through the Christian youth and missionary movements, the grandfather of the ecumenical movement, D. L. Moody was its great-grandfather) enabled a serious hearing for the free church view. Missionaries found it easier to tell a Brahman or a Bushman about Christ than to ask him to jump on the escalator of Occidental cultural and ecclesiastical development at some arbitrary point half or two-thirds of the way up.

The Unity We Seek Is Supranational

The efforts of the Constantinian and post-Constantinian state church were unsuccessful in maintaining unity; one after another the Donatists, the Arians, and the Nestorians, all of them incidentally more missionary than Constantine's church, had to be splintered off. But at least the scope within which institutional peace was sought was most of the known world. The Reformation put an end to that. Convinced that separation from Rome was unavoidable, the Reformers appealed to their local princes and city-states to guarantee their survival. The result of this appeal to the state, on a local basis, to back up the breach with Roman Catholicism, has created division ever since. One can even doubt that the difference between Luther and the Swiss Reformers would have led in the end to the formation of two separate Lutheran and Reformed traditions if it had not been for the sanctioning of that difference by local political loyalties. And even beyond this separation into two major streams, the state church system led to the creation of other groups that either refused it for reasons of principle (the free churches) or were driven out of it because it could not find room for a new moving of the Spirit (Methodism, the Moravians).

It goes without saying that a church whose catechism, liturgy, and church order are determined by a state is singularly handicapped in ecumenical conversation. Even if its representatives are convinced of the wrongness of their church's position, they are generally incapable of doing anything about it.

But even more offensive is the outworking of the political a priori in the field of ethics, even in churches not institutionally bound to the state. It would be hard to find a more flagrant implicit denial of the givenness of Christian unity than the churches' unhesitating consent to nationalism in its demonic military form. No doctrine of Christian unity has yet explained why it should be more serious for Christians to disagree about the relative merits of episcopal, synodical, or congregational polity than for them to accept, under formal protest but with no real intention to object effectively, to prepare for, and to carry out if necessary, mass killing of other Christians at the call of their respective governments. (This is not to imply that the mass killing of heathen would be more desirable; but it is a disobedience in the field of missions rather than in the field of ecumenics).

This observation does not necessarily drive one to pacifism. It does mean, however, that to take seriously the fact of Christian unity as given would revolutionize the positions of those Christians who argue the necessity of war, as a last resort, for the defense of order. None of the arguments that justify morally the participation of Christians in war can justify their participation *on both sides* of a war. Ecumenical bodies have never accepted pacifism as the only Christian position; but even such apologies for war as just, or as unjust but necessary, as were recognized at Oxford, Amsterdam, and Evanston, cannot possibly provide grounds for accepting a situation in which Christians neutralize one another's efforts toward justice by fighting on both sides.

If Christians in the Allied nations were right in accepting war because the defeat of Hitler was necessary for the defense of order, then for the same reason all Christians in Germany should have been conscientious objectors. Unless it be admitted that Christian unity goes at least that far, so that even state churches would admit the obligation to look the possibility of mass selective conscientious objection in the face and define the conditions under which the refusal of war would be just, as they have for centuries been defining the conditions under which war is just — it will not only be hard for some of the rest of us to be much impressed by the recurrent advocacy of necessary compromise, of force as the basis of order, and of war as a form of police action. It will be still harder to believe what the advocates of such measures say about their unity in Christ with their brothers and sisters who, because they were born under another flag, are now their victims.

The Unity We Seek Is a Discipline

It is a part of the heritage of the Reformation that, although considered essential, Christian behavior is nonetheless treated as subordinate to

Christian teaching and worship. This explains the predominance of discussion of sacraments and doctrine in the first generation of ecumenical effort. Even more characteristic is the fact that, as ecumenical bodies do begin to open certain fields of ethical study, unity in ethical commitment is not the expressed aim. *That* it is important to be politically responsible is strongly emphasized; *how* it is important to execute that responsibility is much less clear. In most places the result is that Christians conscientiously vote on both sides of most issues, making their decisions for reasons only remotely theological, canceling one another out and making an ethical farce of the spiritual unity they confess. Many will in fact argue strongly in favor of this "pluralistic" system, on the grounds that to unite on any political option, as if a moral problem were involved, would be clericalism. That Christian medical workers should all express their faith through their profession would be agreed ardently by all; but if one were to ask that all Christian doctors unite in a certain attitude toward abortion, socialized medicine, or telling patients the whole truth, the response would be that such a request smacks of encyclicals.

This kind of ethical pluralism, finding its norms in a secularized concept of responsible lay vocation, will not ultimately either unite Christians or make an impact on the world. It begins by assuming that the Christian layperson's final ethical choice will be made, not in any particular normative relation to the center of Christian unity, God's revelation in Christ, but rather on the basis of accepted social and axiological structures. The Christian layperson according to this view will do what he or she does better, more honestly and more humbly than if he or she were not a Christian; but what he or she does will be what any other equally intelligent person would have done in the same situation.

The thought world of the New Testament was entirely different. Unity in ethical commitment was for the apostolic church no less central than unity in faith and worship. Christian behavior was not the lowest common denominator of a fully baptized society but a kind of life strikingly, offensively different from the rest of the world; it dared to claim that Christ himself was its norm and to believe in the active enabling presence of the Holy Spirit.

With Christ as the criterion of obedience and the Spirit as Guarantor of the possibility of discipleship, the Church cannot but be a disciplined fellowship of those who confess that, if there be one faith, one body, one hope, there must also be one obedience; that God's will may be known in the church and commitment to its application expected of the church's members.

This New Testament view of the Church as a unity of ethical commitment might not require believers' baptism; it would at least require bringing a degree of order into the host of mutually contradictory reasons brought forth for baptizing indiscriminately the children of anyone on a church roll, as well as of maintaining on the rolls people who, in awareness of what it would mean, demonstrate no intention of making their ethical decisions in the light of the gospel and in the fellowship of the brethren.

The Unity We Seek Is Not a Common Denominator

Considerable harm has been done to the ecumenical cause by the oversimplification that assumes that if only the major Protestant bodies could get together the problem would be solved. Some religious journalists judge every denominational convention by two criteria: how well the denomination is digesting its past merger and how rapidly it is moving toward the next one.

There is one truth in this oversimplification. It is true, as this view assumes, that most American Protestant denominations have no raison d'être. They no longer, as denominations, stand for any distinctive principles significant enough to justify separate existence. What this attitude does not see is that, when the separate existence of two denominations is not justifiable, then their merged existence, which remains just as clearly a separate existence with reference to the rest of Christendom, and preserves still fewer distinctive values than before, is little better. *If* organizational unity on this basis *were* the real problem, the movement toward merger in the One Great (American) (Protestant) Church with a melting-pot polity and a theology chosen by the majority would have to go much faster to make any sense. Some such mergers may nevertheless be useful; but their utility is on the level of business administration and not on the level of ecclesiology.

One reason that such mergers are no solution is that, within most denominations, merged or not, there exist differences of greater import, with reference to the authority both of Scripture and of the denominations' own traditions, than those with which the merger deals. But more serious is the fact that the common-denominator approach, be it in merger or in interchurch agencies, by channeling into one stream all the institutional inertias and by catering to the urge for centralization, which is more a quirk of the Occidental mind than an ecclesiological necessity, cuts itself off from the united church's two sources of vitality.

Not only does it tend to estrange the better organized and increasingly self-sufficient "leadership" from the local congregations that were the living cell of the church; it further isolates itself from the broadening and deepening effects of conversation across the whole spectrum of Christian convictions, since the concentration on middle ground (or what seems in American Protestantism to be such) loses touch progressively with precisely those groups that are convinced deeply of something or other, which do have a raison d'être, because their distinctive beliefs legitimately motivate distinct existence as long as they are believed and as long as schemes of unity would require their abandon. The convinced Episcopalians and the convinced Congregationalists, the Historic Peace Churches, the nondenominational fundamentalist missions, the Assemblies of God, the convinced theological conservatives and the convinced liberals, the Anglican, Eastern, and Roman Catholics — some of them groups with an irreplaceable heritage, others of them among the fastest-growing churches of our time — must be deliberately left out of the discussion if the locus of unity is to be the attainable consensus. What threatens us at the end of this path is a sort of latter-day *Volkskirche*, a religious projection of the good and bad conscience of the American middle class, open to everybody because it stands for nothing.

The given unity of Christians in Christ will be given as we accept it in faith; in faith that dares take the brother and the sister seriously to the point of grappling with them in true conversation, in faith that will love and serve fellow-believers across every border to the point of subordinating (Jesus said "hating") other loyalties; in faith that will be ethically responsible for them to the point of demanding of fellow-believers the same full obedience we demand of ourselves. To accept less, to believe less, than that *this* is the unity that because it is a promise is a command as well, would be to deny the Lord.

The Free Church Ecumenical Style

"The Free Church Ecumenical Style" was first published as part of a symposium on Christian unity in the journal, *Quaker Religious Thought* 10/1 (Summer 1968): 29–38. In keeping with the purpose of this journal, Yoder is primarily if not exclusively addressing readers from the Historic Peace Church and/or free church traditions, particularly the Society of Friends or Quakers, as several of his examples suggest. The text of the article is substantially the same as the original publication, with only a few stylistic changes having been introduced.

As in some of his earlier essays on ecumenism, Yoder argues against the mainstream conception of ecumenical dialogue, but here he offers an additional set of reasons for rejecting the "merger" approach to Christian unity. Namely, mergers between various ecumenical Protestant groups typically do not deal with the real divisions that are found in the churches. "The real divisions in the churches are between rich and poor, between liberal and conservative, between races, between east and west. These divisions go down through the middle of existing denominations and are the separations that really would demand reconciling initiative."

Like Yoder's earlier essay "The Nature of the Unity We Seek: A Historic Free Church View," it articulates an alternative approach to ecumenical relations. But Yoder is also careful to articulate this alternative in such a way that it is distinguishable from various inadequate forms of "spiritualist" critiques of mainstream ecumenism, some of which had proved tempting to churches in the free church tradition. Here also, Yoder calls attention to the Conference on the Concept of the Believers' Church held at Louisville, Kentucky, in June 1967, and the kind of consensus about the *local* character of ecumenical conversation that issued from that conference; he illustrates this notion with reference to the Quaker practice of the yearly meeting.

Then Yoder proceeds to discuss several subtopics that arise out of this alternative "style" of ecumenism: the question of the meaning of church membership in relation to mission, the meaning of apostasy, the meaning of scriptural authority, and the question of the relationship of church and society. This kind of ecclesiological clarification is necessary for another reason, because Yoder is calling upon the free churches to "return" to the task of ecumenism out of a sense of mission and hope. *Mission* because the modern ecumenical movement drew its early leadership and energy not so much from the mainstream Protestant churches but from the free church tradition. *Hope* because the free church tradition believes that every meeting — even where only "two or three are gathered" — is a meeting for worship in the presence of the Spirit.

The Free Church Ecumenical Style

The thesis of this essay is easy to state but difficult to exposit. It is that the position of the believers' church or the free church[1] is not simply a doctrinal stance that certain denominations may represent in the ecumenical free-for-all of American pluralism: the genius of the free church calls rather for a unique form of ecumenical expression as well. We are called not simply to put different content in containers of the same sizes and shapes but to insist that a unique substance calls for a unique form.

The organized mainstream of contemporary ecumenical expression is a fitting outworking of the magisterial conception of the church.[2] Here the church is conceived of as a structure for the administration of preaching and the sacrament (to use old labels) or for the implementation of common goals (to use American business-like language): in short,

1. Quibbles about nomenclature need not occupy us here. I would like Lewis Benson's choice, "Disciples' Church," if it hadn't been preempted by a denomination.
2. We owe the currency of the label "magisterial" to George H. Williams: it most aptly characterizes the concentration upon the church as a structure of both administrative and doctrinal government.

"the church" is a structure of government. If Christians are divided, it is that their structures of government are divided with each local congregation bearing allegiance to one such structure of government.

In this context of mainstream ecumenism it is taken for granted that the nature of the unity we seek among denominations is analogous to the nature of the unity that we think we already have within a given denomination. Then the unity of Christians is a unity of church government. It can be sought in the short run by the construction of councils of churches, but the only ultimate solution will be a merged or unified organ of church government.

If we were to take a full inventory of the limitations of this approach, there would be numerous practical shortcomings to cite. One is that the vision of unification thus propagated is usually constructed in national units, so that instead of denominational divisions transcending national borders there would be unified national churches divided from one another by their acceptance of political boundaries. This is not merely a practical shortcoming.

On the more strictly practical level, there is the fact that — at least in the Western world — the unification of church governments tends inevitably to the construction of enormous and thereby inefficient bureaucracy, whereby the upper levels of government are almost completely insulated by an increasing number of intermediate levels of representation and delegation from the people they are supposed to be serving.[3]

But the serious limitations of the magisterial structure of ecumenical relations are more specifically theological. A most visible one is the fact that such unification does not deal with the real divisions that separate Christians today. The separation between Methodists and Presbyterians today is not of theological importance, so that to unify Methodists and Presbyterians under a common government, although an enormous bureaucratic achievement, would not overcome any seri-

---

3. Dr. Keith Bridston, himself a well-informed veteran of ecumenical agency administration, stated this danger most pointedly in an article in the *Christian Century* (March 11, 1964): 330f.

Bridston is a representative of numerous Friends and veterans of the conciliar organizations who are beginning to draw back from the process of curialization that they see happening in the Councils. No one who has numerous personal friends, as I do, within ecumenical agency staff can attribute this development of bureaucratic heaviness to selfishness or empire building on the part of the executives. It is, rather, the practically inevitable result of assuming that a council of churches is a council of denominational administrations.

ous theological tensions. The real divisions in the churches are between rich and poor, between liberal and conservative, between races, between east and west. These divisions go down through the middle of existing denominations and are the separations that really would demand reconciling initiative. Even on the denominational level, those denominational differences are not dealt with that matter the most. It is the mainstream denominations in the middle that get together, leaving the fundamentalists on one side, the Unitarians on another, and the Eastern Orthodox on another even more isolated than before.

Another fundamental limitation of the strategy of merger is that, when taken alone, it fails to deal with the problem that created division in the first place, namely that not every position is reconcilable with the Christian claim of truth in Jesus Christ. There has been division in the past because there has been unfaithfulness. As long as one is in a hurry to forget old debates but unable to resolve new ones, one cannot claim to have overcome division at the roots.

Another Style?

The clearest and most current criticism of the magisterial approach to church unity is the spiritualistic critique. It attacks both the existing divided forms and the preoccupation with unifying them as ultimately irrelevant.

The old form of this critique is expressed by conservative evangelicals who argue that "spiritual unity" is primary, so that the concern for organizational relations is a diversion from what matters most. They strongly reject the World Council of Churches' appeal to John 17:21, "that they may all be one . . . so that the world may believe that you have sent me." The unity of Jesus and the Father, which is here made the model for the desirable unity of Christians, is not an organizational matter, they argue, but a spiritual reality.

There is a modern "post-ecumenical" equivalent of this critique that is increasingly being expressed by many advocates of what they call "secular theology": why should one bother to patch together the pieces of a sinking ship? Old church structures are so far from the real issues that neither their division nor their reunion matters much.

Neither the old nor the new form of the spiritualistic critique will suffice. For one thing, those who express such a criticism do not take full responsibility for the fact that even they continue to operate with some kind of structure that is not merely spiritual. The same evangelicals who argue against a new outward structure because it is not "spiritual unity" still place great weight on the existing separate unities for which they speak. The major spokesmen of the "secular" idea that denominational machinery is becoming increasingly irrelevant, to the point that spending much time on merging it is also an effort ill directed, are mostly themselves denominational or conciliar bureaucrats. Thus, in spite of their critical statements to the contrary, these spiritualists are still not discovering a significantly different style.

Many Brethren, Friends, Mennonites, Disciples, Congregationalists, and Baptists have been drawn into one or the other position indicated above; but in the essence of their heritage there would lie the resources for the development of a quite different strategy. In its extreme doctrinaire "landmark" form, the congregationalism that they have in common denies any church reality except in a given location. But in its more sober and rational form, this kind of congregational emphasis proposes an entire new mode of unity. It was stated thus in the findings committee report of the Conference on the Concept of the Believers' Church, at Louisville, June 1967:

> The centrality of the congregation dictates a specific believers' church style of ecumenical relations. This is not the spiritualized concept of a purely invisible unity. Nor need it be denied that councils, boards, conventions, associations, and synods may have any ecclesiological significance. The import that congregationalism has for these other agencies means rather that their authority is that of the "congregational" character, procedures, and unity of conviction which is given them as they meet. They cannot authoritatively bind over local congregations which meet more frequently, whose members know one another better, and whose responsibilities are for the total life of their members.[4]

Of all the believers' church traditions, it is Quakerism that has at least potentially seen the most clearly at this point, as it has testified by using the name "meeting" as the designation for the governing and decision-making process on every level. The difference between the monthly, quarterly, and yearly meetings is not that one is a meeting or a congregation and the others are not. Nor is it that one is a local congregation and the others are not. When a yearly meeting meets it is also local.

---

4. The full text of the findings committee report can be found in the appendix to James Leo Garrett, ed., *The Concept of the Believers' Church* (Scottdale, Penn.: Herald Press, 1969): 318f.

The instrumental difference is that the varying degrees of frequency of meeting permit varying degrees of continuity and depth of acquaintanceship. There is no reason that ecumenical get-togethers gathered on other bases than the present "denominations" could not also have this quality of being "meetings" in the measure of openness, truthfulness, and bindingness to which their experience entitles them. Thus instead of the doctrinaire statement that the geographically localized congregation is the *exclusive* reality, there is here a sober affirmation of the *priority* of the group that meets with frequency and continuity of membership and discipline. The local congregation is not, as with the chain stores, a local branch of a distant administration: it is rather like an independent grocery store, the client of a great number of producers and suppliers.

This view gives more, not less, weight to ecumenical gatherings. The "high" views of ordered churchdom can legitimate the worship of a General Assembly or a study conference only by stretching the rules, for its rules do not foresee ad hoc "churches"; thoroughgoing congregationalism fulfills its hopes and definities whenever and wherever it sees "church" happen.

Other Themes

If the believers' churches were to participate seriously in ecumenical conversation this would have to mean not simply that to the questions already being asked they would give somewhat different answers but that they would begin asking a different set of questions as well.

The Meaning of Membership

It is striking that the past debates about Faith and Order have concentrated on different definitions of the proper doctrinal stance and constitution of *denominations* without asking with anything like the same degree of thoroughness what makes an individual a *member* of such churches. Membership itself, if dealt with at all, is spoken of in terms of the sacramental validity of the baptism and not the reality of the faith of the one baptized.

Since the magisterial denominations are constituted by infant baptism, this is not surprising; but seldom is it recognized to what degree the tone of the conversation would need to change if this issue were to become a matter of responsible debate. For only this position challenges

236

individuals and rejects a priori the assumption that everyone relating to a Christian agency is, therefore, to be accepted as a fellow Christian. Only the believers' church needs to discuss the church status of the individual. For their own good, many who consider themselves to be Christians must be asked on what basis that claim rests and whether that basis is a ground for Christian unity.

There must be study of the meaning of *membership as related to mission*. The life of the Jerusalem church included "adding to the church daily those who were being saved." Now it is quite appropriate to call into question many of the methods whereby increased membership has been made a goal or a tool of mission. The believers' churches will have no quarrel with reinterpreting the "mission of the church," if this phrase is meant in its etymological sense as "that for which the church is sent," so as to include many functions that are carried out simply for the sake of the need of a neighbor or the glory of God, in which the accumulation of new members is not part of the motivation. But this must not be permitted to hide from view, or even to move away from the center of one's preoccupations, the function of inviting and welcoming additional people into the community of faith. One looks in vain, in the materials produced by the recent ecumenical studies on the "missionary structure of the congregation," for a treatment of the meaning of baptism in the missionary congregation; this simply symbolizes the larger question to which we are pointing here.

There needs to be a study of the meaning of *apostasy*. In the biblical vision there is not merely a juxtaposition of two circles, the church and the world, with the world representing that which is not yet the church. There is also, undeniably present as far as the biblical witness is concerned, a counterfaith and counter-community, that which is no longer the people of God. The New Testament is clear that some of those who claim to be in the church are not only ill-informed but actually false brethren or even false leaders. Now in the past none of the churches have hesitated to use the label "apostate" to refer in some cases to one another. Practically every serious division in the history of the church has come because one party of the conflict, if not both, came to the conviction that the other was apostate; yet one does not find serious theological debate in ecumenical contexts about the proper meaning of apostasy. Does this mean that there is no such concept? Or only that ecumenical statesmen do not yet trust one another far enough to deal with it in an open way? Modern manners keep us from using the words; but can theological responsibility permit us to avoid dealing with the reality? Has there ever been a process of study or deliberation to declare that the concept is not useful or that there is no reality to which it points?

The Meaning of Scriptural Authority

Every denominational tradition, seeking in one way or another to appeal to the authority of Scripture, does so through the filtering lenses of its separate tradition. Sometimes this tradition is an openly avowed post-canonical accumulation of binding commitments; at other times it rests upon a choice of a favorite portion within Scripture, as it is traditional for Lutherans to value the writings of Paul above those of Matthew and James, which they willingly leave to Catholics. It may be written or unwritten; it may or may not be called "dogma"; it may be conceived as changing or fixed. It may be a large body of biblical substance such as George Fox presupposed when he spoke of "Christ come to teach his people himself"; it may be the meager humanism some modern Quakers understand under the same label. It may cling to the text of Scripture or it may claim in the name of Christ himself to rise above Scripture. All these traditions have in common is (a) that they interpret the Christian heritage by a canon other than Scripture, and (b) that they thereby separate themselves from those with another history, another canon.

In the face of this profusion of hermeneutical enclaves, the claim of the believers' churches to have "no other creed but the Bible" is naive and false if understood as bypassing the total hermeneutic task. But if it means a commitment to a constant recourse to the entire testimony of the New Testament, rejecting the concentration upon any one "canon within the canon," and rejecting as well the choice of any one normative post-canonical development, then this appeal to Scripture alone and all of Scripture is the most ecumenical position possible. It is thus only the "restitutionist" claim, appealing to all of Scripture over the heads of all particular traditions, that can retain the normativeness of the Incarnation over all of our efforts to reflect it. What restitutionists deny is not that there is development but that any one development in a selective direction, away from the rest of the church and away from the fullness of biblical witness, can have authority over against the totality of that deposit.[5]

---

5. This is the main point I sought to make in my article "The Nature of the Unity We Seek: A Historical Free Church View," in this volume, pp. 221–30.

Church and Society

The widespread current debates carried on under this title are pre-occupied to find the relation between two realms, between the religious and the secular, or perhaps between two messages or two functions of the church. The free churches, if they understand their unique contribution, will not simply say that both missions and service are necessary or that the gospel has a social image and a secular impact. Rather than seeking to mediate between the religionists and the activists, they will suggest that there is a third position that includes the valid claims of both the other two and yet rises beyond them by virtue of a new variable: namely, this is the distinction between the believing community and other communities, between the covenanting community as a secular social reality and the other secular social realities in the midst of which it lives.[6]

An Awareness of History

Even though the official ecumenical movement has since the formation of the National and World Councils of Churches (1948–49) been the business of the church governments that formed the councils, it is clear that the spiritual initiative and the momentum behind this movement came largely from the pietistic and free church creativity of the nineteenth-century evangelical movement and not from the vision or motivation of the mainstream bureaucracy itself. The International Missionary Council owed its drive to the student movements that arose out of the ministry of Dwight L. Moody and his disciple, John R. Mott. The Life and Work movement reflects the social concern into which was poured the evangelical vitality of the German Baptist evangelist Rauschenbsch and the French "social Christian" Tommy Fallot. The student movement and the early social gospel movements were in their form and their motivation voluntary associations of committed believers. They were not arms of state church administration, nor councils of

---

6. In one sense the matter could be spoken of in terms of debating tactics. The Anglican thinks succession matters but cannot expect his interlocutor to take it on the Anglican's authority; the Lutheran quotes his church father and the Augsburg Confession, but the others are not bound to agree. It is only the biblicist who can enter the ecumenical arena without leaving some of his authorities behind. But the real significance of this "advantage" is not tactical but theological. It is the particularity of the Incarnation that gives this privilege to the total canonical witness.

churches, nor were they accredited by properly preaching and distributing sacraments according to traditional standards.

If then the free churches were to return to ecumenical conversation with a sense of mission and a spirit of hope, they might find themselves in lodgings not of their own conception but not on alien ground: our fathers were here.[7]

Another Spirit

It is not yet enough to say as we have that the believers' church has asked for a different form of Christian unity consonant with the priority of the congregation. We must also be committed to the promise of another tone of voice, another mentality in the search.

The believers' churches are committed to the discovery of a unity that is *personal*. One does not so much encounter another tradition as encounter a brother or sister. Ecumenical experience in every tradition testifies to this fact: but the free church is committed to it as an axiom. Although the division of the church expresses itself in divided governments and separate traditions, division when it happens is a personal relationship between leaders, prophets, bishops . . . and if there is to be reunion it must likewise be between brothers and sisters.

Decision making and thereby unity in the believers' church must *begin at the point of offense*. If one seeks wholesome human relations there are certain questions one will not raise; if one seeks to develop a "good atmosphere," or a good negotiating base, coming at problems from a distance, one will avoid the touchy issues of the past betrayals. But the life of the free church begins with fraternal address, with the discipline of responsibility for the reconciling of the estranged brother or sister. There is then about the search for unity an element of repentance and openness, rather than negotiation from fixed positions or representation of entrenched constituencies.

Every meeting of the church is a meeting for worship. Worship is not a ceremonial procedure that would be invalid if not carried through with the right motions or by a properly consecrated priest, but neither is it ever really absent where there is any spiritual communion. The

7. That the free church stance is intrinsically the most ready for conversation in every direction and the most free of commitment to the older structures of division I attempted to indicate in my pamphlet, *The Ecumenical Movement and the Faithful Church* (Scottdale, Penn.: Herald Press, 1958): 33ff.

immense preoccupation of the conciliar movement with inter-communion as a problem of the mutual relationships of church governments is meaningless from the free church perspective: yet, the alternative is not to make nothing of worship but rather to move trustingly into the reality of communion whenever one gathers in the name of Christ.[8] Common worship as defined by the high catholic traditions is possible only as the result of hierarchical unification: common worship understood as the fulfillment of the promise of the presence of the Spirit wherever two or three gather in the name of Christ is possible whenever we will it.

8. A massive study process on "The Missionary Structure of the Congregation" under the World Council of Churches auspices in the last quinquennium has worked creatively in many areas relating to new patterns of involvement in society but has said strikingly little about "the congregation": many original things were said about the mission of the church, some of which may stand up to serious testing and experimentation — but little was said of the structure of the congregation itself. The new structures that were studied were structures of instruction or administration or service in the world, not new ways of congregating.

The Disavowal of Constantine:
An Alternative Perspective
on Interfaith Dialogue

"The Disavowal of Constantine: An Alternative Perspective on Interfaith Dialogue" originated in a lecture presented on 19 February 1976 at the Ecumenical Institute for Advanced Theological Studies at Tantur/Jerusalem. Subsequently, it was published in the *Tantur Yearbook 1975/76*. The text of the essay is substantially the same version except for minor stylistic changes.

As Yoder conceives his task in this essay, he is an interpreter of the free church perspective of how interfaith dialogue should proceed. Accordingly, his purpose in the context of the theological discussions of this particular ecumenical institute in the Middle East is "to ask what difference it makes or would make for interfaith dialogue, if instead of seeing every 'religion' as represented by its most powerful 'establishment,' the disavowal of the establishment of religion were restored as part of a specifically Christian witness." Yoder's answer to that question takes the form of explaining how the process of dialogue might take shape, in contrast with other proposals — "anonymous Christianity" etc. — being discussed by some mainstream Protestant and Catholic ecumenists, particularly Yves Congar and Karl Rahner, in the 1970s.

An important feature of Yoder's argument in this context is his assumption that there is no one shape or structure in which the "disavowal" of Constantinianism is enacted. As he candidly states: "By the nature of the case it is not possible to establish, either speculatively or from historical samples, a consistent anti-Constantinian model. The prophetic denunciation of paganization must always be missionary and ad hoc; it will be in language as local and as timely as the abuses it critiques." This point is notable not only for clarifying the "fragmentary" way in which Yoder thinks of himself as proceeding in this particular essay, but also because it clarifies the challenge of constituting the "anti-Constantinian" or free church challenge to various versions of Christendom. It is at this juncture in his argument that Yoder's stress on the necessity of "community repentance" may pose the most striking ecclesiological challenge to the mainstream Protestant and Catholic claim of the "indefectibility" of the church, which Yoder here attributes to the establishment of the church under Constantine and his successors.

In the process, Yoder effectively describes his vision of the "alternative" approach to interfaith dialogue pursued by the Radical Protestant stream of history. "What is different about Radical Protestantism is the claim that this is enough: that we need no apologetic prestructure, no metaphysical infrastructure, no social victory, no conciliar definitions to be able to move along." In other words: "Mission and dialogue are not alternatives: each is valid only within the other, properly understood." Yoder also calls for maintaining the logical distinction between "ecumenical" and "interfaith" conversations even as he acknowledges that the phenomenon of Constantinianism has clouded this distinction in practice. The alternative model of dialogue that he advocates begins with repentance — the disavowal of particular historical constructions of Christianity in the name of cultural and ideological forms of dominance. ". . . [T]here is no alternative but painstakingly, feebly, repentantly, patiently, locally, to disentangle that Jesus from the Christ of Byzantium and of Torquemada. The Disavowal of Constantine is then not a distraction but the condition of the historical seriousness of the confession that it is Jesus Christ who is Lord."

The Disavowal of Constantine: An Alternative Perspective on Interfaith Dialogue

In its grand outlines, the opening up of the idea — and in a first faltering way of the practice — of "interfaith dialogue" has made some quite traditional assumptions about the social base from which each of the major interlocutors speaks.

The positions needing to enter into conversation, it is assumed, are the "mainstream" forms of each "world religion," and the interpreters thereof are their respective theological elites. It naturally follows that the record of the last two generations, in which pioneers have found their own way across interreligious boundaries, and that of the last decade or so with its explosion both of modest interreligious meetings and of academic writings (at least by Christians) are heavily weighted on the side of Catholicism as representative of Christianity, meeting most typically "Hinduism" as representative of "Eastern religions."

This way of centering the encounter upon the statistical "middle" or the evolutionary "top" of each tradition cannot be surprising. It follows naturally that priority issues will be defined in terms representative of the respective traditions. In the Catholic Christian case, this has dictated a particular set of priority questions needing internal redefinition. Thus Catholics discuss among themselves the possible salvation of people outside the church, the possible truth content of other religions as *religious systems,* or the equivalence of spiritualities. In these areas prodigious effort has been invested in showing how millennium-old traditions, which (at least in normal, institutional circumstances) had seemed to make truth or salvation or valid spirituality the exclusive priority of the Christian, under the normative guidance of the Western Catholic hierarchy, not only are no longer binding, but in fact never did properly mean what they were popularly taken to be saying. Thus room is made for respecting other faiths by a redefinition of one's own stance that claims not to be a real change.[1]

This internal agenda of redefinition, which has an obvious priority when measured by the attention it receives in meetings and publications, will occupy us again in a moment. But first it should be clarified that my primary task in this study is not to add one voice to that chorus. The "alternative perspective" that I have been assigned to interpret is not simply a different slant on the classical set of questions but rather a different approach to what the questions are. For the three themes noted — a truth system, a personal spirituality molded by a teaching elite, and an institutional claim — are themselves characteristic of that particular modulation of Christianity that in a previous lecture I identified as "the post-Constantinian establishment." Since the present lecture, in addition to belonging to the Tantur series, "Aspects of Interfaith Dialogue," was also part of another lecture

---

1. Roman Catholic authors are referred to predominantly because they have been most prolific and were represented within the Tantur lecture series. This is not to suggest that "mainstream" Protestant positions would be very different.

series on "Radical Protestantism" as an alternative perspective on the church's history,[2] it will be useful to summarize here what is meant by "the disavowal of Constantine."

The Roman emperor who began to tolerate, then supported, then administered, then finally joined the church, soon became and has remained until our time the symbol of a sweeping shift in the nature of the empirical church and its relation to the world. Constantine neither initiated that shift nor concluded it, and our present interest is not in the extent to which he knew what he was doing.[3] The shift is what matters. That it took place, was far-reaching, and changed much of the concrete social meaning of Christianity, all historians agree. What they differ about is whether it was a great victory, a great moral defeat, or something more ambivalent.

The tradition I have been invited to represent[4] holds that the redefinition was highly ambivalent when it began and amounted to a moral defeat for the cause of Christ when it had worked itself out.

If, as the New Testament indicates, extending certain phases of the Old, God calls his people to a prophetically critical relationship to structures of power and oppression, then the alliance between Rome-as-Empire and Church-as-Hierarchy, which the fourth and fifth centuries gradually consolidated, is not merely a possible tactical error but a structured denial of the gospel.

If, as Jesus called for it and the apostles practiced it, voluntariness is a constitutive aspect of a valid relation to Christ as Lord and to the church as community, then the shift in the fourth and fifth centuries made the gospel call into its opposite. Theodosius made it a civil offense not to be a Christian. Within a century after Constantine, Augustine was calling for it to be a civil offense to be the wrong kind of Chris-

2. The other series, "The Jewish Jesus and Radical Protestantism," had been initiated 12 February 1976 with an historical survey, "The Restitution of the Church: An Alternative Perspective on Christian History."

3. We shall let the phrase "know what he was doing" stand for a large number of problems historians pose. Was Constantine sincere or was he only using Christianity as a political tool? What did Christianity mean to him? Why did he postpone his baptism? Why did he convene and control the Council of Nicea? Did he see himself as the savior of the church, i.e., as an eschatological sign? Are these questions that can fruitfully be posed?

4. Here the label "Radical Protestantism" has been used, indicating a position that arose within the Protestant Reformation but went farther than the Anglican, Lutheran, and Reformed movements. See note 10 for other characterizations and notes 11 and 15 for further specification.

tian.[5] The meaning of the decision to confess Christ was thereby not simply warped or fogged over but structurally reversed, i.e., denied.

With these basic shifts came many others that, while not necessarily all radically to be rejected in every way and in all circumstances,[6] meant at the least an imbalance and with time could lead to new depths of unfaithfulness.

One of these was a newly affirmative attitude to pagan religiosity, reversing the critical-prophetic stance that had held firm from Moses to the second century, and which rabbinic Judaism continued to represent.[7] The doors were open to the "baptizing" of pagan cults like the creation of Christmas or the early medieval cult of the dead, pagan salvation concepts like those that later provoked the Protestant Reformation, pagan Gnosis systems diverting attention from the Christian way to the pursuit of enlightenment, pagan attitudes toward pomp and power like those that provoked the formation of monasticism in the age of Constantine, and, beginning especially in the eleventh century, a widespread movement of *"pauperes Christi,"* culminating in the twelfth with Francis of Assisi.

I refer specifically to the age of Francis because it is with his analog and contemporary, Peter Waldo or Pierre Vaudès, that Western proto-Protestantism begins.[8] Instead of fitting into the status of an authorized order and thereby agreeing to let the rest of the church go on down the road, the Waldensians — not necessarily because their founder knew what he was doing[9] but because he had got them started reading the

---

5. Henceforth Caesar will not simply support Christianity: he will support orthodoxy and will, therefore, have to have a voice in defining what orthodoxy is.

6. This disclaimer is needed because some historians caricature the "Radicals" as being systematically anti-historical and always only negative.

7. The term "pagan" as used here is inadequate. We shall return to the problem of defining it. The parallel to Judaism is not coincidental; part of the radical reformation's character is a different relationship to the Jewish heritage of Christianity.

8. It is important that the "radical reformation" option begins earlier than the "mainstream Reformation" of the sixteenth century. It was not dependent for its possibility, as the later Reformations were, on state support. Popular historians within the radical reformation movements have, in fact, pushed the history farther back, claiming a kind of succession of faithful underground communities all the way back to the pre-Constantinian church. Cf. J. Yoder, "Anabaptism and History," in H. J. Goertz (ed.), *Umstrittenes Täufertum* (Göttingen: Vandenhoeck & Ruprecht, 1975): 244ff. This essay was also reprinted in *The Priestly Kingdom*, 123–34.

9. It would seem that Vaudès died trusting that he and his "poor preachers" were good Catholics, approved by the pope, and only misunderstood by some inadequately informed bishops.

Gospels — became the first post- and anti-Constantinian "free church," thereby beginning the line of resistance that later surfaced as what we here call "Radical Protestantism" within the Reformations of the fifteenth and sixteenth centuries and still later in Baptists, Quakers, Brethren, and Disciples.[10]

My task here, as an interpreter of this critical stream of Protestant history, is to ask what difference it makes or would make for interfaith dialogue, if instead of seeing every "religion" as represented by its most powerful "establishment," the disavowal of the establishment of religion were restored as part of a specifically Christian witness.

Without seeking completeness, a few of the recurrent accents of the anti-Constantinian critique should be noted:

- its concern for the particular, historical, and therefore Jewish quality and substance of New Testament faith in Jesus;[11]
- its holistic inclusion of communal and cultural dimensions of "way of life" within the faith (decision-making patterns, e.g., or economics) as religious issues, rather than making them peripheral behind the priority of spirituality or dogma;[12]
- its insistence on the voluntariness of membership in the visible church, usually expressed in the baptism of persons old enough to confess responsibly their own faith;[13]
- its rejection of the support, defense, and control of the church by the civil rulers;
- its relativizing of the hierarchical dimensions of the church in favor of maximum freedom and wholeness in the local congregational fellowship.[14]

---

10. The best historical overview is offered by Donald Durnbaugh, *The Believers' Church* (New York: Macmillan, 1968; reprinted, Scottdale, Penn.: Herald Press, 1985).

11. This "Jewishness" (cf. above note 7) may be discerned in:
- the opposition of radical monotheism to superstition and idolatry,
- missionary vigor derived from the conviction that a new messianic age is dawning,
- courage to stand as a minority in a hostile environment, i.e., the destruction of the religious homogeneity of culture
- rejection of violence, based upon trust in God's protection.

12. This, too, is of course Jewish.

13. James Leo Garrett, ed., *The Concept of the Believers' Church* (Scottdale, Penn.: Herald Press, 1970). The label "believers' church" was coined by Max Weber.

14. Again a Jewish characteristic. The juridical authority of the local synagogue is defined by the presence of a *minyan* or quorum of ten. No authorization or legitimation is needed from elsewhere.

Behind these more evident, formal distinctives lie a specific view of the place of Scripture in the church, a specific eschatology, specific views on certain ethical issues, a specific approach to sacraments, ministry, and on down the line.[15] Each of these further elements would also have something more to say concerning the content, and some of them concerning the form, of communication with people of other faiths. But that would take us too far. We must henceforth limit ourselves to the distinctive view of the relation of church and society and the impact of that "disavowal of Constantine" on our perspective in interfaith dialogue. The demonstration will need to be a series of selected specimens rather than a full system.

Disengaging Religiousness from the Gospel

For a millennium and a half, European Christians have been identifying faith in Jesus Christ, for themselves and for others whom they meet, with an all-encompassing set of ideas and practices largely of Greek, Roman, and Germanic origin. This is "Christendom" as a total religious-cultural package, in many ways marked more by those other religious cultures than by the Bible. I previously described this established religion as marked by an institutional claim, a dogmatic system, and a personal experiential model of appropriation. Now I should add that all of this is done in a form that, though it takes itself for the whole world (*oikoumene*), is a very specific Mediterranean-plus-Germanic cultural and geographical location. This is the form in which both Catholic and Protestant expansion after Vasco da Gama will tell the Americas, Africa, and Asia what the word "Christian" means. This is also the form in which "Christian" is defined by non-Westerners in the backlash of anticolonialism and in the renascence of other faiths.

In the contemporary situation of post-colonial contestation, often

15. To the characterization of the "Radical" tradition the 12 February lecture had added:
  • communal economics
  • reconciling discipline
  • nonclerical ministry
  • consensual decision making
  • noncoerciveness or pacifism.
The third lecture in the series, 26 February, developed this last theme more fully under the title, "The Way of the Cross: An Alternative Perspective on Social Ethics."

sweeping "Christianity" with all the rest in the rejection of empire, there are several ways we might go. We may continue to defend the classical claims of Christendom in the classic way. Or we may recant piecemeal by redefining here and there the elements that the contestation reveals are the most offensive to others, while keeping our feet firmly in the Christendom history. This is what it seems to me most of the literature does. Or we could say that we now see that the earlier critics were right, that the entire Constantinian experience was at certain points substantially wrong and that, therefore, the claims of Mediterranean-European religiosity are not what we should be defending or even redefining.

Now when I call for judgment in the face of the uncritical adoption of pagan religiosity, and for the a posteriori use of this criterion as an instrument of repentance, several misunderstandings are easy to fall into. I am not questioning *popular* piety or lay theology in favor of a more elite or "spiritual" experience. I am not preferring the verbal and discursive forms to the physical or artistic. I am not, as H. Richard Niebuhr suggests in his caricature of what he calls the "Christ against culture" social strategy,[16] opposing the adoption by Christians of the language, the arts, the education, or the urbanity of the societies into which they move. All these things, Judaism before Jesus and Jewish-based Christianity before the apologetes had affirmed and used. What the radicals reject is the *uncritical* importation of value-laden substance that is anti-Biblical or pagan,[17] i.e., not only in origin or language *different from* but in content *counter to* the understandings of God, of human community and morality, or of nature inherited by the apostolic church from its Hebrew antecedents. Nor does the identification of paganization as a specific temptation into which the Constantinian church fell mean that the "safe alternative" could be jelled once for all in some successful "non-pagan" form needing henceforth only to be preserved. This would be the temptation of Nehemiah, or of the Mishnah, and of numerous Protestant sects. The prophetic struggle with pagan cults and cultures cannot be resolved by the formal appeasement

16. H. Richard Niebuhr, *Christ and Culture* (New York: Harper, 1940).

17. The difficulty of defining "paganism" has already been noted. Here the usage is pejorative, referring to idolatry, polytheism, superstition, depersonalizing fertility cult, and the glorification of virility and violence. This is not to deny another strand of meaning. *Paganus* (like its equivalents "heathen," "barbarian," "gentile") may refer to the fact that persons outside the biblical stream of history may have quite valid moral and religious understandings and achievements. Jews have traditionally referred to this possibility in terms of the Noachic covenant, Catholics as "conscience" or "general revelation."

of accepting the ghetto, any more than by the spiritual appeasement of a pluralism without challenge.

Fuller analysis of what went wrong would separate three levels:

a. Enculturation: the fact that in any culture, language and other forms will be adopted and adapted. This is indispensable.
b. "Paganization" in the sense denounced here.
c. The sanctioning of the paganized synthesis by the power of money and the sword.

Adaptation (a) would not be wrong and would be no barrier to interfaith dialogue if it were not mixed with the other two. Even paganization (b) would be subject to ongoing critique and correction if it were not solidified by establishment (c). Yet paganization (b) and establishment (c) cannot ultimately be thus separated since the notion of the sacral king or chieftain is itself a pagan concept of great power.

A Stance of Repentance

By the nature of the case it is not possible to establish, either speculatively or from historical samples, a consistent anti-Constantinian model. The prophetic denunciation of paganization must always be missionary and ad hoc; it will be in language as local and as timely as the abuses it critiques. I must, therefore, proceed in a fragmentary way to suggest the positive counterparts of the disavowal of Constantine.

First of all: disavowal itself, the very act of confessing one's fallibility and of confessing God's mercy in confrontation with concrete specimens of unfaithfulness on one's own part, is a constitutive element of valid personal piety. In Hebrew tradition specific public celebrations of repentance and recommitment such as those linked with Joshua or Ezra became landmarks. Community repentance is called for in the New Testament epistles. Yet somehow since Constantine it was decided that the church must be indefectible. It might change the whole tone of interfaith encounter if instead of saying, "We still think we are right, but you may be right, too," or, "Yes, that is a wrong idea, but that is not what we really meant," Christians were to receive the grace to say, "We were wrong. The picture you have been given of Jesus by the Empire, by the Crusades, by struggles over the holy sites, and by wars in the name of the 'Christian West' is not only something to forget but something to forgive. We are not merely outgrowing it, as if it had been acceptable at the time: we disavow it and repent of it. It was wrong even when it seemed to us to be going well. We want our repentance to be not mere remorse but a new mind issuing in a new way — *metanoia.*"

Of course, there are dangers here as well. It is too easy for me to repent of the Inquisition or the Crusades. Open self-criticism may be an inverted kind of pride. But it is still more easy to let the affirmation of a new up-to-date openness avoid the agony of taking responsibility for the past, naming the errors and correcting them. It is far easier — but also less conducive to dialogue — to explain newness as reformulation in new terms, as adaptation to change in the environment, or as clarification of what was always intended, than as confession of fallibility.

There is one evident objection to introducing into interfaith conversation our repentance for the sins of Christendom. One can argue that Christians should handle their self-criticism and internal controversies at home, not bring them to the interreligious conference table. Superficial as this objection is, it may serve to clarify:

a. The "outsiders" already know about our inner clashes and our bad record: our not mentioning it will not hide anything.
b. It is a specific element of the Christian message that there is a remedy for a bad record. If the element of repentance is not acted out in interfaith contact, we are not sharing the whole gospel witness.
c. The thought of a common front at the conference table is itself a part of the mentality we are debating. If the impact of prophetic challenge is to call for a decision that is not predetermined, and where alternative answers to the challenge are not equally valid, then the ongoing debate within the people of God is part of its interfaith credibility.

I do not know, when a movement of revival or renewal takes place within Buddhism or Islam, what its shape is and what authority it claims. I do not know whether in other faith communities the appeal of reformers is to the founder's intent that has since been betrayed or to some other kind of validation. But at least for Christians, the continuing pertinence of the historical memory of Jesus, via the New Testament, as a lever for continuing critique, is part of the message itself. The capacity for, or in fact the demand for, self-critique is part of what must be shared with people of other faiths and ideologies.

An Alternative History

Repentance, it has been said sufficiently, is not mere remorse but an alternative consciousness issuing in alternative behavior. If the dominant Western religiousness is to be challenged, what is the content of the critique?

Non-biblical religion is not wrong just because another *name* than that of the Lord JHWH is used. It must be shown how that name designates another reality: another view of humanity or God, morality or nature. To test these possible other views, the *critique* of religion as a cultural phenomenon may properly become part of the debate. The critique of Marx, who saw in religion a cover for oppression; the critique of Karl Barth, who saw there humanity's pretension to a capacity to save itself; the critique of Bonhoeffer, who saw it exploiting human weakness rather than affirming human dignity; the critiques of many who argue that "God-language" has no real referent in the experience of Western culture: these critiques and yet others *might* be on the side of the prophets. The denunciation of apostasy need not use religious language. Or it might, like the examples of Barth and Bonhoeffer, use the language of one particular theology.

Especially weighty is the stream of critical thought represented by Hendrik Kraemer, who was assigned by the International Missionary Council (IMC) after its Jerusalem conference of 1928 to articulate *The Christian Message in a Non-Christian World.*[18] An affirmative counterpart of these critiques is the development in recent years of a movement proposing to speak of salvation in terms of "liberation." Thus far "liberation" is more a rallying cry than a mature, accountable vocabulary. It can lead to a new Constantinian temptation. Nonetheless, we should be grateful to this movement for its reminding us in yet another idiom that not all religion is good. The kind of "religion" that some recent theologies of dialogue seek to make room for, under such labels as "anonymous Christianity," are very similar to the kind of religion that the theologies of liberation want to disavow in favor of a social, economic, even political definition of what salvation should mean. Even

18. Since we have referred to the International Missionary Council, one of the precursor organizations of the World Council of Churches, it may be noted that the way in which at the 1975 Nairobi Assembly the problem of syncretism, as it had been posed by WCC patriarchs Visser 't Hooft and Kraemer, was named and skirted but not effectively struggled with, constituted as a reminder of unfinished business. Conversation was not helped by the issue's becoming a symbol of European intellectual paternalism.

though both themes belong in the context of dismantling the colonial heritage, we have yet to face the challenge of linking the two critiques.

When around 1900 the Student Volunteer Movement laid the foundations for the modern conciliar ecumenism, it was thought that Westernization, technology, and secularization were the allies of Christian mission, breaking down the bastions of ignorance behind which paganism had to hide. By 1928 when the IMC met in Jerusalem, the thought was stronger that all the religions might do well to band together against secularism.[19] Half a century and a dozen reassessments of "the secular" later, it is no use to try once again to define secularity or secularism; but at least the confusion gives us occasion to insist that we must not assume as a base line the majestically unified religiousness of the medieval European *Weltanschauung*. It is thus to be welcomed that the World Council of Churches has added "and Ideologies" to the purview of its office in interfaith dialogue. Christians have no intrinsic reason to prefer ancient interlocutors to new ones. If Marx, or Freud, or Darwin, or Adam Smith becomes the father of a believing community, those believers, too, are potential partners in dialogue.

The affirmative alternative underlying the critique of paganization is the concreteness of the visible community created by the renewed message. The alternative to hierarchical definition is local definition. The alternative to ritual, dogma, and *Weltanschauung* as preferred content for dialogue is the language of the normal gathering for worship and business. The alternative to a once-for-all Mishnah is a continuing process of gathering and binding deliberation in the power of the Holy Spirit. Matthew's Jesus picked up Old Testament legal language to tell his disciples that "where two or three witnesses concur," he himself was validly working in their midst. That gatheredness of the community is the point where the old language and the new challenges meet, where distinctiveness and commonality are tested, where kerygma and dialogue coincide, where renewed appeal to the biblical Jesus and renewed openness to tomorrow's world are not two things but one.

One office of the World Council of Churches once promoted a very broad study of "the missionary structure of the congregation." Radical Protestantism asks to see the congregational structure of the

19. The same alternatives remain alive in more recent literature. J. Daniélou, *L'Oraison, Problème Politique* (Paris: Fayard), argues that in a world under the threat of atheism Christians should make common cause with anyone who "defends the substance of the sacred" (101). Claude J. Geffre in "The Tension between Desacralization and Spirituality" (*Concilium* IX/2 [Nov. 1966]: 57ff.) does not agree that a shared sense of the sacred justifies siding with idolatry.

mission. The alternative to a book about dialogue is not a better book but a way of conversing. The alternative to an elite dialogue carried on by gurus and professors is not to change elites but to discover the theologianhood of all believers. The alternative to speculation about "anonymous Christians" is becoming locally explicit about Jesus. The alternative to abstract treatment of the tension between the particular and the universal is not a steadily deepening redefinition of terms,[20] or a retraction into the undefinable, but the particular experience of confessing Jesus as Christ here and now. There are few who would deny all this, as far as affirming these easy phrases goes. What is different about Radical Protestantism is the claim that this is enough: that we need no apologetic prestructure, no metaphysical infrastructure, no social victory, no conciliar definitions to be able to move along.[21]

Open Frontiers

Just as all Genevans are Calvinist, all Danes Lutheran, and all Irish Catholic — it seemed, a very short time ago — so we must assume all Burmese are Buddhist, all Tunisians Muslim, and all Greeks Orthodox. If then colonialist models of mission with their alliance of cultural power and superiority claims are to be overcome, the alternative seemed — to some, then — to be to announce the end of missionary intervention, leaving everyone in the national cultural mold where he or she was born and was happy.

It is only fitting, if we reject the decision by Constantine and Charlemagne that every European must be Christian, and the sixteenth-seventeenth-century updating of the same, *cuius regio, eius religio,* that we are then also free to see the boxes on the other side as open. Not all who were born into a society under Buddhist or Animist or Muslim social control have made that faith their own in such a way that to

---

20. In wide reaches of recent literature, the "particular" and the "universal" are assumed to be in tension with one another, so that more of one must mean by definition less of the other. "Universal" becomes nearly synonymous with "valid" or "acceptable," and "particular" with "provincial" or "narrow." If such broad abstractions are usable at all, an assumption that still needs debate, it is clear that they must not be so defined a priori as to beg the important questions. Biblically, the particular and the universal are not alternatives.

21. The point is not that apologetics, metaphysics, or social success are undesirable or even indifferent but only that for the radical reformation tradition they have not the same definitional importance as in other systems.

present another option would be to do them violence. It is the application of Constantinian logic, and not necessarily a defense of human dignity, to posit that all Africans were "happy" in their tribal religion until the missionaries came, every Tunisian satisfied with Islam, . . . any more than every European is Christian. To say nothing of the fact that today, even if the religious missionaries were to stay away, the emissaries of Gulf Oil, Nestlé, Panasonic, Hollywood, and Peking would in any case destroy the simple givenness of inherited faith for everyone.

Open Hearts

But the openness of the encounter does not stop there. To say that "nominal" adherents of an inherited faith should not be shut in, by the accident of birth, within a "faith" they have never made their own deeply, yet never have been offered an alternative to accepting superficially, does not yet suffice to render the openness with which Jesus in Luke 14:25ff. sought to foster the genuineness of choice. We are all "nominal" adherents. No one's faith is final in this life. It may be the Islamicist Kenneth Cragg who for our time has made most poignant the insight that I have only really understood another faith if I begin to feel I could be at home in it, if its tug at me questions my own prior (Christian) allegiance anew. Likewise, I am only validly expositing my own faith if I can imagine my interlocutor's coming to share it. Perhaps the *word* mission has been rendered unusable in some contexts by abuse, but respect for the genuineness of dialogue demands *in both directions* that there be no disavowal in principle of my witness becoming an open option for the other. Mission and dialogue are not alternatives: each is valid only within the other, properly understood.[22]

But I did say I would be ready to replace the word "mission" in present company as having been made unacceptable by its colonial history (or, in Jewish experience, by its European history). Perhaps the

22. A very important and very generous statement of this principle is that of Dean Shemaryahu Talmon: "Anybody who willingly enters into a dialogue with people of different conceptions and persuasions, at least in theory takes the risk of having his own ideas influenced or radically changed as a result of the exchange of views. However, the dialogue situation by definition imposes upon us the obligation to make our voices heard . . . so as to curb any attempts at exploiting the situation . . ." (p. 17 in "Interfaith Dialogue in Israel, Retrospect and Prospect," pp. 9ff in the *Proceedings* of the symposium by the same name held 16 May 1973, published in the Autumn 1973 special supplement to *Immanuel*).

best substitute term, less spoiled because it is from another language realm, is "heralding" or *kerygma*. The *keryx* or herald announces an event. The event is announced as true, of course, and in fact as very important for the hearers, especially for those who have not heard it before. If it were not true the herald would not be raising his or her voice. Yet, no one is forced to believe. What the herald reports is not permanent, timeless, logical insights but contingent, particular events. If those events are true, and if others join the herald to carry the word along, they will with time develop a doctrinal system, to help distinguish between more and less adequate ways of proclaiming; but that system, those formulae, will not become what they proclaim.

The truth claim of the herald or witness must remain thus noncoercive if it is to be valid. You never *have to* believe it. For that there are two reasons. First, because the message concerns a contingent, particular event within the challengeable relativity of historical reporting. It will always be possible to believe that the Exodus and Sinai, or the Resurrection and Ascension did not happen but were imagined later, or were misreported. Secondly, you do not have to believe it because the herald has no clout. He or she cannot bring it about that if you refuse to believe you must be destroyed or demoted. In fact, it is the herald who is vulnerable, not a full citizen. It is not only that he or she is weak and cannot coerce assent. What makes the herald renounce coercion is not doubt or being unsettled by the tug of older views. The herald believes in accepting weakness, because the message is about a Suffering Servant whose meekness it is that brings justice to the nations.

Thus defined, the kerygmatic truth claim stands in no tension with a posture of dialogue that affirms fully the dignity of the interlocutor, including his or her culture and conviction. But it can only be distinguished from the colonial or Crusader truth claim if the herald's double vulnerability is clearly perceived and willingly affirmed.

We have thus been able to locate the mandate and the safeguards for interfaith dialogue at a different point from the "mainstream" discussion. Not the truth content or validity of the ideas or experiences of another religion as system or performance, but the uncoercible dignity of the interlocutor as person and one's solidarity (civil, social, economic) with him or her as neighbor is what must (and can) be defined first.

In a previous Tantur lecture Yves Congar helpfully distinguished between two ways to be affirmative about other faiths.[23] One, relatively

23. "Les Religions Non Bibliques Sont-elles des Médiations de Salut?" *Annales* 1972–73, pp. 77ff.

recent, associated with Rahner and Schlette, affirms the legitimacy of other religious systems as ways of salvation, for peoples outside the visible church. Since this affirmation is based on intra-Christian reasoning, it is not dependent on the empirically definable content of the other religions, on what morality they teach, or on how sincerely they are practiced.

The other path, more deeply rooted in earlier Catholic thought, which Congar prefers, affirms the dignity not of the systems as such but of the persons for whom they are ways of appropriating grace. That the nonevangelized can be saved has long been affirmed by Catholics, with reference to "conscience" as a kind of revelation, often with appeal to the "pagan saints" of the Old Testament.

The position advocated here would share Congar's accent on the person but would go farther than he in its concern for the *particular* interlocutor in his or her particular religio-cultural context. This sensitivity would refrain from ascribing to him or her (even though the ascription be benevolent) a desire for, or an experience of, salvation whose merit is that it is (in our terms) analogous to the Christian's.

I may conclude this section with a provocative oversimplification. Centuries ago it was self-evident to every Christian in Europe that Christian truth was universal truth. Other races and religions were known to exist, to the south and east; but they were no challenge to this confidence. When the technology was ready, this triumphal confidence circled the globe. Now, however, the other races and religions have found ways to talk back.

There are *grosso modo* two ways Christians may respond. We can take as a norm the sense of consensus, the unchallenged confidence of that bygone age. In the search for a new consensus we can then jettison the particular, the local, the Jewish, the specific biblical content. Jesus then matters less and agreement more. Universality will be sought at the price of specificity. Dialogue will mean the uncovering of commonality. One will speak of common denominators, of anthropological constants, of several paths up the same mountain.

But there is another way. It would be possible to say that the error in the age of triumphalism was not that it was tied to Jesus but that it denied him, precisely in its power and its disrespect for the neighbor. Then the corrective would be not to search for a new consensus but to critique the old one. Its error was not that it propagated Christianity around the world but that what it propagated was not Christian enough. Then the adjustment to Christendom's loss of élan and credibility is not to talk less about Jesus and more about religion but the contrary.

One corrective today, one approach to dialogue, approves of Christendom's vision of an all-englobing unchallenged truth system and apologizes for the narrowness of its continuing confession of Jesus. The other would renew the critical impact of the confession of Jesus but must then apologize — yet repent is the better word — for triumphalism, as well as for Mediterranean and Germanic tribalism, and abandon the assumption that a criterion of the true faith will be that it can sweep everyone in. One corrective relativizes Jesus, seeking dialogue by stripping off distinctiveness. The other radicalizes the particular relevance of Jesus, enabling dialogue through the content of the message:

- the love of the adversary,
- the dignity of the lowly,
- repentance,
- servanthood,
- the renunciation of coercion.

One corrects for the error of provincialism by embracing variety: the other corrects for the sin of pride by repenting. Only experience can tell when and where either one of these stances will enable a genuine interfaith meeting.

The Clouded Frontier

Logically we should distinguish between two quite separate levels of interfaith conversation. One, called "ecumenical" in the earlier, narrow sense, takes place among Christians, assuming at least a minimal common commitment to Jesus Christ and the Scriptures. The other, best called "interfaith," occurs where there are other things in common but not the name of Jesus.[24] This distinction must be maintained over against the tendency in some contexts to consider Jesus as one of many variables, all more or less negotiable, along a long scale of differences of degree that separate the religions.[25]

24. Two other intermediate borderlines obviously group Judaism and Christianity, or the three Abrahamic faiths, as categorically distinct from all the others. These groupings share to a degree the kind of problem being discussed in connection with the name of Jesus.

25. What was said before about syncretism and the heritage of Hendrik Kraemer is again relevant, but the question reaches farther than that. There are those

Yet, at the same time I must concede that, precisely because of the Constantinian phenomenon, that theologically firm line has become unclear.

a. The Stranger as Heretic

One of the major initiatives of Constantine, while yet unbaptized, was to convene the Council of Nicea, to deal among other things with the Arian controversy. He not only called the meeting but also intervened in its proceedings, including the formulation of its key conclusions. The linkage of those conclusions with the emperor had the effect with time of reinforcing the linkage of Arianism with the peoples outside the empire to the north. Later imperial-ecumenical councils relegated Nestorianism to Persia and Monophysitism to Abyssinia, thus identifying the concepts of "heretic" and "barbarian," and turning over the expansion of Christianity for a millennium to the heterodox.

b. Jesus as European

A friend of ours in Algiers was once told by a neighbor, "Jesus is French, and we are Arabs." He was quite right, in his own experience. The only "Jesus" he had any reason to know about was the tribal deity of the French colonists. If he had had more historical sense, it would have been little better. If he had remembered the sixteenth century, Jesus would have been Spanish, for it was then that a Spanish fleet, whose admiral was a cardinal, had taken over the Algerian coast, including the massacre of ten thousand in the port city of Oran. What does it do to the usability of the name of Jesus, as distinguishing between the smaller ecumenical circle and the universal one, when for a whole culture that name is defined not by the apostles but by the crusaders?

c. The Follower without the Name

Once some who affirm the name deny or pervert its historic content, the door is also open for others, if they want to affirm the content, to

---

who could substitute another "name," i.e., other historical particulars, for that of Jesus but without proceeding syncretistically.

do it without the name. We may take the person of Gandhi as symbol of the problem. Deriving his ethical communal message from Jesus as interpreted by Tolstoy, Gandhi refused to call himself Christian. Yet, this refusal occurred in a context where "Christian" meant empire, white ethnocentrism if not outright racism, and the conceptual definition of Jesus' uniqueness in medieval Mediterranean terms. Gandhi's relation to Jesus was far different from the wide but relativizing tolerance of a Ramakrishna, letting Jesus into the pantheon beside all the others. It was also quite another thing than the "anonymous Christianity" of someone who without having a name for it responds to life as a whole in ways that have roughly the same human shape as Christian faith. Nor is it like some recent searches for a parallel spirituality transcending equally all separate histories. Gandhi created a new way of life, as genuinely Indian as the churches Paul planted were genuinely Jewish-Hellenistic, yet also genuinely the product of the message of Jesus, as read through Tolstoy and footnoted by Ruskin and Thoreau. Gandhi appropriated Indian language and even Indian scriptures to express this new thing, but with that language he said — and especially *did* — things that had not been said or done before with that language, and which were not acceptable to the established interpreters of Hinduism at the time. He did not reiterate Hindu thought: he reconceived Indian language.

Was Gandhi then a "hidden" or "anonymous Christian"? Since Constantine, it would be no compliment to Gandhi to ask the question that way. But the question is whether he was following Jesus, and if so, which Jesus?

A Battle Already Won?

Some might agree that the stance sketched here is pertinent but not that it is an alternative to the approaches of others. Do we not all know that Constantine is dead? Granting that religious liberty was once a peculiar contribution of the "Radical Reformation," and that for centuries other churches affirmed with conviction that church and state, mission and colonization should be partners, with evil results for interfaith relations, is that time not past? Does not everyone agree to disavow Constantine? Need we review bygones?

It is true that many Western Christians of all confessions have conceded as a fact that the axioms of Christendom no longer obtain, or that Christians are now in a "Diaspora situation." Yet to make this concession in the face of Enlightenment and political pluralism is far less than to appropriate it theologically and still less than having had the theological tools to denounce the error of establishment when it was dominant. Being willing to relinquish power when one has lost it anyway and to affirm the rights of dissent after the United Nations has done so is mature and sober but not as prophetic as it would have been to call for religious liberty and disestablishment when they were not in style. If then we wish to test the theological claims of an alternative global perspective, it is fitting to distinguish between those traditions that disavowed Constantine and the others who can adjust to his passing.

But the deepest need for making the disavowal explicit lies outside the Christian interconfessional debate. There are in the Middle East hosts of Arabs for whom Christianity is still most deeply understood through the memory of the Crusades. There are Jews here whose fundamental memory of Christianity is the pogrom or the Holocaust. Others of longer memory think back to Spain where an "act of faith" used to mean an execution. We do not disavow Constantine because we enjoy concern with either our guilt or our innocence, and still less out of denominational self-righteousness, but because all that we ultimately have to contribute in interfaith dialogue is our capacity to get out of the way so that instead of, or beyond, us or our ancestors, us or our language systems, us or our strengths or weaknesses, the people we converse with might see Jesus.

It is that simple: but that is not simple. It will not happen without repentance. If we mean the Jesus of history, the Jewish Jesus of the New Testament, then even here in the land of his birth — to say nothing of Benares or Peking or Timbuctoo — there is no alternative but painstakingly, feebly, repentantly, patiently, locally, to disentangle that Jesus from the Christ of Byzantium and of Torquemada. The disavowal of Constantine is then not a distraction but the condition of the historical seriousness of the confession that it is Jesus Christ who is Lord.

Another "Free Church" Perspective on Baptist Ecumenism

"Another 'Free Church' Perspective on Baptist Ecumenism" was originally published in the *Journal of Ecumenical Studies* 17 (Spring 1980): 149–59, as part of a symposium on the contribution of Baptist Christians to ecumenism in both the North American and world contexts. The text of the article appears here without substantial revision and with only a few stylistic changes.

Unlike other articles in this section that articulate the "free church" perspective of mainstream ecumenical proposals such as the "Lima Text," this article provides an assessment of a particular ecclesial grouping that is itself closely identified with the "free church" stance. Therefore, this article provides an interesting example of the way the "free church" model can serve as a kind of criterion for the internal self-criticism of an ecclesial community that is — as Yoder observes — "the largest body able to testify for the 'free church' stance." Yoder reminds readers that the Baptist conception of religious liberty is something more than "freedom of assembly"; it includes claims about human rights and is, therefore, a political and not simply an individual claim. Similarly, it involves disengagement from the full range of "structures of unbelief" as embodied in a "saving faith" that presupposes a never-ending conversation with Scripture.

Here again, Yoder's initial discussion of various conceptions of the "free church" helpfully distinguishes between sociological definitions and those conceptions that are normative, while highlighting the fact that the "believers' church" conception that he employs in his essay provides both descriptive precision and theological normativity. With this clarification in place, Yoder proceeds to discuss the ecumenical and ecclesiological significance of the two "marks" for which Baptists are best-known: the practice of voluntary membership and freedom from the state. Ecclesiologically speaking, these two marks have important implications for the ways in which baptism and discipline are practiced. Where the moral accountability of the individual does not lead to moral solidarity in the life of the church, Baptists and/or "free church" groups have raised questions about the adequacy of discipleship. This set of issues, in turn, brings up the question of infant baptism, an issue that Yoder notes has not been "debated in depth in Faith and Order circles, nor one on which those with the strongest opposing views have been well heard." Because of this, those Baptists who have wanted to discuss this question have had to constitute their own forums for ecumenical discussion such as the Conferences of the Concept of the Believers' Church.

At the particular juncture in which he was writing, Yoder urged Baptists to proceed ecumenically not on the basis of structural conceptions but on the basis of congregationalism, understood as "an affirmation instead of a demurrer, and a whole new universe of ecumenical agenda would open up, in which precisely the 'free churches' should be most at their ease." Similarly, given the changing sociological conditions in North Atlantic societies, Yoder foresees opportunities for reengaging the questions of personal discipleship. "The time will soon be ripe for a restatement of what is and is not meant by the individuality of personal saving faith. . . . Those correctives will have to purge us from the past too-close linkage of conversionist preaching with post-enlightenment individualist anthropology." Finally, he argues that given the apparent collapse of some approaches to ecumenism, there is a "largely unmet challenge opening before all the free churches in tomorrow's ecumenical realignments, in which Baptists stand as prototype for us others as well." But he also warns: "What matters . . . is not how Baptists have been doing but what they have to say."

Another "Free Church" Perspective on Baptist Ecumenism

More than might be the case for the United Methodist or the Roman Catholic articles in this symposium, it will contribute to the substance of the later exposition that I clarify what is meant here by "free church perspective." The term "free church" carries a host of varied objective definitions and subjective feeling tones. In Great Britain the free churches are everything but the national church, so the Presbyterians, who are established in Scotland, are "free" in England (as the Anglicans are "free" in Scotland). The definition is formal and non-evaluative. The other extreme would be represented by the writing of Franklin H. Littell for whom the term represents a particular vision of renewal for all churches, a vision that even the "radical reformation" groups he has helped to interpret do not fully live up to. Here I shall take the term to mean roughly the same as the more operational "believers' church."[1] It combines a formal description (voluntary adult membership, institutional independence of the civil authorities) with the normative claim that those differentiae not only are meaningful, in order to identify a certain set of religious movements, but are also important, biblically warranted testimonies worthy of the attention of other Christian bodies. "Freedom" in this sense is not only a descriptive trait but also a theological value. Behind those formal ways in which it has been tested or stated in the past lie deeper concerns regarding the faithfulness of the individual and the Body, their mission and their renewal.

In another context it might be necessary to argue that these characteristic positions are truly Baptist positions. In yet other connections one would need to argue that they are theologically true, on biblical or other grounds. My assignment here warrants that they be simply stipulated, so that I can ask Baptists how they themselves are perceived to be incarnating and advocating them in the ecumenical arena. I here

1. The term "radical reformation," given currency by George H. Williams, is most apt in describing genetic origins, where several patterns of reformation contrast, but is less fitting to describe contrasting options as they live on within pluralism or in more peaceable times, to say nothing of the cheapening of the label "radical" in our time. Max Weber's term "believers' church" is the most sociologically descriptive and involves less evaluative bias, but it still must seem very unfair to Lutherans and Orthodox who believe that infants are believers. In the context of this article the editors' preference for "free church" shall be respected, but with the caveat that I hold its most usable meaning to be narrower than in the older British usage. The landmark (in a non-Baptist sense) of the emergent self-awareness of the free-church family on the ecumenical scene is James Leo Garrett, Jr., ed., *The Concept of the Believers' Church* (Scottdale, Penn.: Herald Press, 1969), as well as the historical survey in Donald Durnbaugh, *The Believers' Church* (New York: Macmillan, 1968). For our purposes, the vision is represented best by the Disciples, Church of the Brethren, Quaker, Baptist, and Mennonite families. Later groups (Pentecostal, Bible churches, Plymouth Brethren) represent it as well but with a less-defined historical sense.

align a few typical theses, which could also be formulated quite differently while making the same point, without seeking to argue them. The claim is that "free church" identity (of which Baptist identity is a prototype) represents a specific, coherent focusing of the call to Christian faithfulness, which merits its own authentic voice in the ecumenical arena. Voluntary membership and freedom from the state are not mere folkloric peculiarities or local cultural adaptations; they are symbolic of and touchstones for a distinctive vision of the Christian church, its mission, its message, and its renewal.

Both of these marks correlate with an accent on the missionary; a Baptist church must be in mission. A state-bound church may send out missionaries, but it comes less naturally to do so. It need not do so in order to live up to its self-definition.

Both of these marks correlate with the church's readiness and capacity to live in a hostile culture, like that of the early Christian centuries or the Soviet Union today. The pedobaptist and state-bound traditions assume a generally friendly world.[2]

Both marks correlate with the expectation that membership in the church includes moral accountability for the individual and, therefore, enables moral solidarity for the group. Balthasar Hubmaier, the earliest great renewer of the theology of the baptism of believers, did not predicate the adult celebration of baptism upon a particular kind of subjective conversion experience or doctrinal affirmation but rather upon the candidate's readiness to enter wittingly and willingly into a covenant of mutual accountability defined by the "binding and loosing" of Matthew 18:15ff.[3] This commitment was what demanded that the confession be informed and adult. In the absence of the constraints and securities of synod or state supervision, it enables the local congregation to have solidarity without legalism and pastoral responsibility without clericalism.

Both marks correlate with the call for religious liberty as a mark of good government. Although it is first of all a claim about what

---

2. It may seem anachronistic to identify the issue of church/state relations in an age (and in a country) where all the churches are (politically) free and none "established." It is nonetheless important, not only because of other parts of the world where establishment still obtains, but more so because there is a great difference between accepting disestablishment and demanding it, and (still more important) because we have not finished our own spiritual disestablishment as it faces the challenges of nationalism, ethnocentrism, and militarism.

3. H. Wayne Pipkin and John H. Yoder, eds., *Balthasar Hubmaier: Theologian of Anabaptism* (Scottdale, Penn.: Herald Press, 1989): 373ff.

constitutes valid faith, "freedom" points also to good government as that which respects and safeguards the liberties of confession and of assembly.

These marks correlate as well — though perhaps not so narrowly as to be easily exposited in a brief paragraph — with the congregationalist vision for the renewal of the church. As over against other renewal visions, the free church vision is not satisfied with a renewal only of inwardness (mysticism) or of especially committed groups that let the rest of the body go its own way (monasticism); rather, it projects a visible, debatable, verifiable, attainable local shape (including the risks of Landmarkist or Campbellite oversimplification of the search for the "New Testament Pattern").[4] As contrasted both with an uncritical trust in the automatic forward movement of the whole Christian story and with naive primitivism, it sees renewed recourse to Scripture as the constantly relevant critical norm, yet without needing to insist on only one doctrine of scriptural inspiration and authority. Freedom for both of these foci is heightened by the priority given the local gathering, as the principal (though not exclusive) place to encounter "the church" in its authenticity and accountability.

Thus, by a "free church perspective" is meant the conviction that this understanding of what the Christian church ought to be, which correlates significantly with what Baptists have been trying to be, is an important slant from which to ask what Baptists actually represent ecumenically.

The more seriously we take this point of orientation, however, the more complex becomes our task from here on. The initial place to observe "Baptist ecumenical views and practices" would properly have to be each of hundreds of thousands of local churches: how they cooperate, how they converse and share with other Christians, and how the free church specificity described above is communicated and interlocked with the Christian commonalities not discussed here. Being neither journalist nor sociologist, I must confess the impossibility of handling my assignment from that end. Thus I must accept the limits of a less verifiable impressionistic reading. But to have noted that we "should really" start there where we cannot is still important. That awareness defines the base line from which we are wandering when

4. The "landmark" movement is the minority movement among Southern Baptists that claimed that *only* the loyal gathering should be called "church." Alexander Campbell was the most visible leader who promoted the same focus among the Churches of Christ.

we now move to the "mainline" definition of the ecumenical arena and agenda. This "normally" means interchurch dialogue on the level of church governments (already an unmanageable concept for Baptists): national and world councils of churches, bilateral conversations of world confessional families, and the parallel, less-institutionalized running conversations for which theological literature and seminary education are the vehicles. We must ask what Baptists have to say in this arena and how they say it, yet we have to note first that it is in some formal ways an alien arena.[5]

One obvious limitation will be that when the problems of "faith and order" that divide Christians are seen to be located between those large bodies that we call denominations or confessional fellowships or "communions," then the instruments we shall have recourse to, both to express the unity we have and to process the diversities that persist, will be constructed in accordance with those models. Thus we will have councils of churches, and the word "churches" in that usage will refer to institutions of a particular kind. Except in cases of very narrowly localized collaboration, the term "churches" will *not* mean parish congregations, nor will it refer to concrete visible gatherings of people who see each other regularly for worship and other kinds of sharing. It will rather refer to wider bodies spoken for by representative leaders. Thus it is unavoidably the case that those with a prior definition of the church as *local*, visible fellowship will have difficulty finding room to act out their convictions within the conciliar movements. They are always meeting in a context defined on someone else's terms.

What is true about "order" in the ordinary ecumenical meaning of church organization beyond the congregational level is just as true of "faith" in its specialized meaning as pointing to doctrinal safeguards and summaries (creeds, confessions). A sizable group of Christians, including many in free churches, have consistently rejected those developments in church history that have given normative status to any extra-canonical or post-canonical formulations. Some have naively argued as if one could avoid having such formulations at all. Others have

---

5. The ecumenical conversation can never be sorted out so as to think of one party in the conversation as only giving or only receiving. Any description of what Baptists do receive or what one might hope that they would receive from others would, however, overlap substantially with the other contributions to this symposium. My primary focus shall, therefore, be on the fact that Baptists are, within the institutional world of interchurch conversation both in North America and on the world scale, the largest body able to testify for the "free church" stance. See also my "A Non-Baptist View of Southern Baptists," *Review and Expositor* (Spring): 219ff.

more soberly argued that there will be many statements of faith but that it is wrong to let any one of them become a final tool to define heresy or to replace the entire body of Scripture as the rule of faith. Sometimes this anti-creedal thrust has been operative in the direction of theological pluralism or liberalism, as perhaps would be admitted within the Society of Friends in Great Britain, or the Doopsgezinde (Dutch Mennonites), or in the French Protestant Federation. All of these groups addressed specific protests to the World Council of Churches in connection with its formulation of a new "basis" that tends to be appealed to as a creed even though it has no ancient documentary credentials. More often, however, the anti-creedal thrust has been expressed by free churches with a bias that was sometimes anti-intellectual, and sometimes anti-institutional, which thereby seemed culturally conservative. The experience of ecumenical conversation in the "mainstream" agencies of our century confirms the difficulty of obtaining a hearing for that kind of concern, without its being written off as obscurantist or undisciplined.

Similar to the above sticky points of "faith" and "order" is the matter of membership. The Faith and Order movement asks about what it takes to be validly recognizable as "church" by asking questions directed to the leadership: Is the priest validly ordained? Is the preaching faithful to the gospel? Is the definition of what is taking place in the Eucharist such that we can recognize that eucharistic celebration as valid? This way of putting the question makes it difficult to handle a different set of questions, namely those having to do not with the officiants and other clerics but with the church considered as the whole membership. Those of us who say that membership in the Christian community should be based upon a mature and conscious commitment in response to having heard the Christian message and that such a commitment can never be made for one person by another are not simply expressing a skeptical view with regard to the theory and practice of baptism in majority churches. We are also asking whether the "members" in those churches have ever accountably asked to be called Christians. Therefore, we are not sure that they should be called Christians. This skepticism may be expressed in very ecumenically gentle ways, whereby one will try to make adjustments to alternative grounds on which people who were not baptized upon confession of faith can nonetheless be given the benefit of the doubt — when the quality of their involvement in the life of the church, or a ceremony of confirmation, or an experience of conversion will have made up for what was lacking in the baptismal practice. Or, at the other extreme, the skepticism may be applied very vigorously, actually to exclude from any recognition as Christians anyone who has not been baptized in just the right way. The difference between these two styles is enormous in terms of etiquette, but the underlying substantial issue is the same.

In ecumenical dialogue we meet people who have not all, as we have, publicly asked to be counted as believers in a congregational celebration of confession and baptism. This does not raise unmanageable questions about the people we meet at those meetings, but when they further argue (as their creeds commit some of them to do) that properly the church should be made of many people baptized as infants with no such confession, that raises questions for us about whether those other churches are churches, questions that are at least as fundamental as questions about creeds and ordination.

What has just been said about baptism applies even more openly on the strictly formal level with regard to polity. If your Presbyterianism says that a national synod or assembly best defines what you believe the church should be, then that synod or assembly may properly join the National or World Council of Churches. If you believe the church to be incarnated in its bishops, it is the house of bishops as juridical entity that the council recognizes as such. But if your theology says with conviction that the basic meaning of "church" must be local, if you are (as I am not) a radically consistent Campbellite or Southern Baptist, there is no way in which what you believe to be your "church" in the theological/spiritual sense can be recognized by a national or world council. Only a large, nationwide body need apply.

It would be pointless to reprimand the mainstream ecumenical bodies for making mainstream[6] assumptions about the unity we have and the unity we seek. I ask only that we be explicitly cognizant of the interlocking of form and substance so as to recognize when the very

---

6. Even more difficult than choosing "free church" for the group in which Baptists belong is finding a common label for all the other Christians. Within the sixteenth-century context, George H. Williams coined the label, "magisterial Reformation," pointing to the prominence of the theologian (magister) and of the government (magistrate). My choice of "mainstream" is likewise double-edged. On one level it grants that a first difference is quantitative. There are more people in those other churches, partly because their membership policies are inclusivist, and partly because — not being as recently or as radically the product of renewal — they have had longer to grow. Secondly, "mainstream" points to the fact that, to some degree at least (the Reformed less than the Anglicans, and the Methodists still less), such groups make of their continuity, their openness to all, their middle-of-the-roadness, even their worldliness, a positive virtue and accreditation, over against particularity and apartness that are seen as intrinsically schismatic.

terrain where we meet our fellow Christians is sloped according to assumptions we must challenge. Each of the topics to which I now return exemplifies this in another way.

Infant Baptism

The time is ripe for a restatement of the case against infant baptism. Biblical scholars within the pedobaptist churches are challenging their tradition on biblical grounds. Pastoral and systematic theologians, especially in "post-Christendom" Europe, are doing so on missiological, catechetical, and pastoral grounds.[7] Worldwide missionary concern increasingly restores evangelization, rather than holding one's own children, as the prototypical way to build the church. Since Ernst Troeltsch, analysts of the social situation of the churches have predicted that only the acceptance of a "sectarian" style of high-commitment membership will keep any community alive in an increasingly disestablished future. Yet, we of the free churches are reticent to make our point as strongly as critics from within the other churches do.

For this we do have some modest excuses. We are honestly aware of the limits of our own practice; we know how often baptisms in our churches do not represent adult commitment or moral covenant — how incomplete is our theology of the child, how manipulative our evangelism. We are aware that some of the simple biblicism and the simple views of religious experience used before to refute pedobaptism are not conclusive, without observing that the classical arguments to advocate it have fared even less well in the face of critical theology. We may look at this fact judgmentally as a failure of nerve or of identity on the part of anti-pedobaptists, or more approvingly as an exercise of chivalrous restraint in the avoidance of self-righteousness. In any case it must be reported that the issue of infant baptism is not one that has been debated in depth in Faith and Order circles nor one on which those with the strongest opposing views have been well heard.

There are understandable reasons for this. One is the simple absence from membership in the World Council of Churches and related agencies of the largest bodies that are anti-pedobaptist. Southern Baptists, Pentecostals of many kinds; and the great number of the small and non-denominational primitivist groups (Christian churches, Plym-

---

7. Cf. my "Adjusting to the Changing Shape of the Debate on Infant Baptism" in A. Lambo, ed., *Oecumennisme* (Amsterdam: ADS, 1989): 201–14.

outh Brethren, Bible churches, etc.) did not come into question as potential member churches of the W.C.C. or other conciliar agencies for reasons largely quite distinct from the issue of the propriety of baptizing infants. It cannot be our purpose here to evaluate the polemic evaluations on both sides of that non-affiliation, which call one party "inclusivist" and "modernist" and the other "fundamentalist" and "sectarian." In any case it means that a great number of voices on the anti-pedobaptist side of this conversation are simply absent from it.

Another difference is in the matter of debating etiquette. Within the councils the major advocates of the Catholic traditions regarding episcopacy and sacraments are the Eastern Orthodox communions, who of course proceed with full confidence of the rightness of their position. The major anti-pedobaptist groups in the North Atlantic world, once the others have been excluded on the grounds mentioned above, are polite proponents of Anglo-Saxon pluralism and the denominational understanding of what constitutes a genteel way to deal with differences. The American Baptists and the Disciples, each having divided from more radical kindred communions in the South — partly on the grounds of this more genteel style — are not accustomed to making denominational distinctiveness an issue when it is not indispensable. This pluralistic etiquette was developed in the Anglo-Saxon Protestant polity to deal with formal differences that are without profound moral meaning, such as the varieties of visions about inter-parish connections (bishops, conventions, etc.) or refined debates about the exact meaning or the efficacy of sacraments or the way in which symbolic meaning can be described. The ethos of mutual interdenominational respect, which was set up for those matters, is then carried over to the question of whether infants should be baptized, even though this has a far more profound constitutive role in what we mean by "church." It would be unfair to say that representatives of Baptists and Disciples and Brethren churches in the World Council of Churches and in Faith and Order ever muted the distinctive witness of their communions in order not to make trouble. But it can be said that occasions have not been sought and structures have not been created to give this issue a major hearing.

A case history may be illustrative. Professor Johannes A. Oosterbaan of the Netherlands was for years one of the major representatives of the Doopgezinde of the Netherlands in ecumenical encounters within the Netherlands National Council, the World Council of Churches, and the Mennonite world communion. The conviction of the Doopgezinde regarding adult baptism is very important in its specific quality because it is not based on particular modern understanding of the subjective conversion experience and being born again, as are views of many revivalistic North American anti-pedobaptists. It is rather (as now held) the expression of a post-enlightenment concern for personal, moral, and religious maturity. This permits the Doopgezinde communion to resist the temptations that are so strong in North America to lower the age of baptism to a point where part of the anti-pedobaptist argument has been sold out by baptizing five-year-olds or eight-year-olds in Baptist, Mennonite, or Brethren churches.

At the 1961 Third Assembly of the World Council of Churches, Oosterbaan was representing his denomination, a charter member church. Within the working papers of that assembly there was a draft document on the subject of baptism that clearly was the product of a dominant pedobaptist conception, without evidence that care had been taken to find formulations that anti-pedobaptists could also accept. Seeking, late in the drafting process, to mobilize support for an effort to bring this consideration to the attention of the drafters, Oosterbaan found that those people whom he was able to contact from Baptist, Brethren, and Disciples churches were not interested in supporting him in "making an issue." We must set aside any effort to estimate from this distance to what extent that reticence was based on considerations of timing and etiquette. In any case, he returned home with the conviction that the various churches that practice believer's baptism are not thinking together about how important that particular ecclesiological concern is and how to commend it to the other Christian communions. He thus began a very personal effort to mobilize understanding for the importance of the issue and to try to give it the shape of some kind of interchurch conversation among communions with this conviction. From this initiative came the 1967 Louisville Conference on "The Concept of the Believers' Church."[8]

Only very recently has an overture from the W.C.C. Faith and Order Commission reopened the issue with fitting and promising seriousness, marked incidentally by a modest consultation in Louisville in March 1979.[9]

8. Cf. Garrett, *The Concept of the Believers' Church.*
9. Briefly noted by Gunter Wagner, "Baptism from Accra to Lima," pp. 12–32 in Max Thurian, ed., *Ecumenical Perspectives on Baptism, Eucharist and Liturgy,* Faith and Order Paper 116, esp. p. 20.

Religious Liberty and Human Rights

The time is ripe for a restored insistence upon the importance of the churches' freedom from civil authorities and from all the powers of society. We have been spoiled by our North American experience; on the world scale, disestablishment has not yet won the day, even in Europe. Blatant denials of religious liberty by governments continue to abound. Yet, we seem to rest on our credentials as veteran libertarians, slow to push this issue with other Christians. The World Council of Churches' Nairobi Assembly gave dramatic attention to the limits on religious liberty in Eastern Europe, in connection with a discussion of the Helsinki accords, but the advocates of that measure were mostly Reformed church leaders from Western Europe. Switzerland is one exception of which I know; there may be others. In the Swiss inter-church dialogue the issue of establishment is dealt with directly by Baptists and Mennonites; yet, even there, it is not primarily because of the free church witness that a growing number of Reformed theologians are calling for a degree of church/state disengagement.

The new commitment that is called for will not simply be to renew the call of earlier generations to separation. In at least three respects that earlier experience is insufficient. In the American experience it let itself become funneled into a narrow span of symbolic issues, mostly parochial educational funding and school prayers. With regard to much of the rest of the world, it centered upon the freedom to hold religious assemblies (so that repressive regimes can claim to be respecting it as long as they allow the gatherings). By considering religious liberty as a right of believers rather than as a duty of governments, we have lost chances to spread our vision regarding human rights beyond the specifically religious. We will not have renewed our libertarian witness if we accept freedom of religious assembly for church bodies as part of a bargain to keep us silent about basic human rights for all, a trade-off that previously embattled evangelical minorities have found hard to resist in some places.

The Primacy of the Local

The time is ripe for a restored insistence on the primacy of the local gathering as defining the reality of the church and, therefore, also as locating the primary ecumenical agenda. For a long time mainstream denominations have dominated the discussions of church unity with

varying models of how to bring together the agencies of church government at the top. That thrust is now losing steam, not because a counter-
witness of Baptists or Disciples has been heard, but because of its own
inherent top-heaviness. United churches around the globe, the fruit of
great pains of negotiators and mediators, while not breaking up, have
not brought the degree of payoff in either witness credibility or ministering effectiveness that was hoped for, and negotiations toward merger
are slowing. Those mergers work the best that bring together those who
are already closest together. This is no surprise, but it decreases the
usability of that union model for the really important divisions. In the
United States the Consultation on Church Union is moving away from
the federative vision that brought it to birth in favor of a pattern that
will celebrate unity as it already exists and move initiative from the
"brass" to the "grass." Now certainly the response to the challenge of
this time is not to say that a Baptist convention or a Mennonite general
conference or assembly (for which our own stated ecclesiologies have
no clear explanation) are more valid forms for church unity than are
the structures of other denominations. The need would be to find ways
— and they must be new ways — to formulate our forebears' claim that
all over-arching or connectional structures are provisional and derivative (not, as with the Landmarkers and Churches of Christ, that they
are nonexistent — a stance impossible to make credible), so that the
separateness of Christians that is a scandal to the world is not first the
separateness of those agencies. Let congregationalism again be an affirmation instead of a demurrer, and a whole new universe of ecumenical agenda would open up, in which precisely the "free churches"
should be most at their ease.

Scripture and Saving Faith

This time is ripe for a reformulation of the claim that the Scriptures are
a constant power for renewal transcending all post-scriptural creeds
and structures. In the past that claim has often been defended at the
wrong front: literalism versus historical or literary criticism, creationism
versus the scientific world view, Protestant *sola scriptura* versus Catholic
"two sources." Some of those formulations have become obsolete;
others never were helpful or necessary. Now a new generation of biblical theologians — moving beyond the sterility of critical literary-criti-
cal methodologies when practiced for their own sake, illuminated by a
sociology-of-knowledge understanding both of how believing com-

munities came to be and of how Scriptures came to operate as canon — are restoring our ability to find "old treasures and new" in the Bible. That was the original free church vision before it ran shallow in debates about infallibility or about whether there is a univocal "biblical answer" on every issue.

The time will soon be ripe for a restatement of what is and is not meant by the individuality of personal saving faith. Our North Atlantic culture is not yet out of the thicket of false kinds of individualism: narcissism in the search for experience and fulfillment at the cost of commitment and community, selfishness as economically legitimate, the celebrity as role model. Correctives pointing in a more corporate dimension are needed. Those correctives will have to purge us from the past too-close linkage of conversionist preaching with post-enlightenment individualist anthropology. Conversion is, after all, a move from one contextualized identity to another — from one world, one set of bonds, one family, to another. Yet such correctives cannot be an end in themselves. They must clear the way for a new focusing of genuinely personalized conviction. Instead of "massification" like that of the audience of rock concerts and super bowls and media minstrels, in place of the routinization of what a "born-again experience" must look like, who but the free churches should be able to renew the offer of personal appropriation of renewing grace, in the local fellowship where every member is uniquely cherished and every gift needed?

I have been itemizing those points at which a classical free church witness seems to me to be awaiting revival.[10] Let it not be thought that thereby I am claiming "we told you so; we were always right," as a way to call Baptists and other free churches to be less afraid of the ecumenical arena because we need not be ashamed of ourselves in it. We have much to be ashamed of, both for not having let our own light shine and for having been inexcusably deaf to the complementary and corrective traditions of other communities. Within that confession of our inadequacy, I must limit myself to a few specific points at which our failings have most directly undercut our claimed strengths. To identify them will extend into critique the affirmations I have just been renewing.

Our message calls us not simply to want to disengage the church as a legally identifiable association from the state as an administrative agency but to want to disengage the people of God from the structures

10. The list is not exhaustive; the dignity of preaching, the priesthood of the laity, and freedom of worship are among the other differentiae.

of unbelief. Our generation's encounter with the worldwide rhetoric of revolution and liberation — however insufficient some of those slogans may be — summons us to an understanding of disestablishment that will denounce all the principalities and powers, the bondages of ethnocentrism and nationalism, the demonic drives of the arms race and consumerism, the confusion of loyal citizenship with blind provincialism. When the prophetic and priestly roles of the people of God yield to that of the chaplain alone, the treason to the gospel that that reestablishment represents is all the greater if those who fall into it claim to represent a more biblical vision.

What must be said of "separation" as an institutional mark can also be said of "believer's baptism" as the personal one. Baptism for Jesus at the hands of John, and for the first believers at the hands of the first disciples, for Bunyan and Carey, meant a radically new life in the light of the inbreaking of God's reign. Socially defensive child raising, cheaply persuasive evangelizing, a focus on guilt or fear and its relief rather than on God's sovereignty and glory, and negligence of moral catechesis before or after baptism have brought many of our churches to the point where the social impact of a person's baptism is that of a rite of passage deepening his or her rootage in the known world rather than launching him or her onto a new life possible only by grace.

I do not apologize for having slipped from observation into participation. I have not been describing Baptists as a contemporary journalist, social historian, or bureaucrat could observe them performing. I have been identifying the largely unmet challenge opening before all the free churches in tomorrow's ecumenical realignments in which Baptists stand as prototype for us others as well. What matters first is not how Baptists have been doing but what they have to say. Instead of being by the nature of things marginal participants in a game played by someone else's rules, we have a chance and a call to help remake the game according to the imperatives of the gospel itself.

A "Free Church" Perspective on Baptism, Eucharist and Ministry

"A 'Free Church' Perspective on Baptism, Eucharist and Ministry" originated as an invited response by the editors of *Midstream* to the 1982 "Lima Text" on *Baptism, Eucharist and Ministry* Faith and Order Paper No. 111. (BEM) produced by the Faith and Order Commission of the World Council of Churches, meeting in Lima, Peru, chaired by Geoffrey Wainwright. First published in the ecumenical journal *Midstream* 23/3 (July 1984): 270–77, the article is substantially the same as the published version with only minor stylistic changes, corrections, and the addition of some quotations for those not familiar with the BEM document.

The leadership of the Commission on Faith and Order invited various "responses" (official and unofficial) to the BEM document on a series of questions: (1) the extent to which "the faith of the church throughout the ages" can be recognized in BEM; (2) the "consequences" that can be drawn from BEM for the ways in which churches can enter into dialogue and relationship with other churches; (3) the "guidance" that can be taken from BEM for "the worship, educational, ethical, and spiritual life of witness" of the churches; (4) suggestions in relation to BEM for the ongoing work of the Commission on Faith and Order, particularly with respect to the latter's long-range research project "Towards the Common Expression of the Apostolic Faith Today."

Here again, in his unofficial response to BEM, Yoder emphasizes the ecumenical importance of the kind of "dialogical process" embodied within the churches of the free church tradition in contrast to the "procedural" process employed by the Faith and Order Commission in the discussions that led to the Lima text. As Yoder points out, each of the issues discussed in the three sections of BEM "has a different institutional history with regard to free church concerns"; accordingly, his response calls attention to different levels and degrees of objection to the discussions of baptism, Eucharist, and ministry in the Lima text. Given the prominence of ecumenical affirmation of "one baptism" in the Lima text, the greater part of Yoder's response focuses on questions that can be raised about the adequacy of the resolution of this issue in BEM. Yoder attempts to offer clarification about where the believers' church tradition would object to the Lima formulation, particularly with respect to "believer's baptism" and "rebaptism"; he also raises questions about the adequacy of the practice of infant baptism and notes the lack of any acknowledgment in the Lima text of problems in the history of this practice.

On one level Yoder commends the modern ecumenical movement for enabling a "self-defining" dialogical process in which a conversation emerges based not upon "inherited institutional, ritual, or creedal status" but rather the participation of various interlocutors (some of which are participants in the dialogue and others of which, such as the believers' church traditions, are not). However, Yoder also raises serious questions about the way certain traditional areas of disagreement were finessed in the Lima text, particularly with respect to questions of baptism and order. Because of this, Yoder regards the Lima text as "generally disappointing in its avoidance of classically defined issues" such as the relationship of baptism to confirmation, the question of women's ordination, and the ontological status of the elements in the Eucharist. In these matters, what appears to be an agreement is actually a carefully constructed consensus that neither acknowledges nor attends to the historic free church objections. Thus, while Yoder regards some aspects of the Lima text as "promising," at the end of the day his judgment is that only "modest" progress has been made. For Yoder, the Lima text does not represent the kind of discussion to which an *ecumenical* conversation should aspire.

A "Free Church" Perspective on Baptism, Eucharist and Ministry

Already at the time of the Lund Assembly (1952), W. E. Garrison and Henry P. van Dusen commented that in its style and structure the Faith and Order Commission of the World Council of Churches was predisposed by its history and its procedures toward the "high" or "mainline" perspectives and against those of the "free churches." Despite the limits of such broad slogan labels, that reading was neither unfair nor a reproach; it stated a fact of life. The family of communions who by conviction are without central episcopacy and confessional documents are at a disadvantage in conversational processes based on those components of ecclesiological and ecclesiastical identity.

The orientation represented in this article has been variously denominated as "believers' church" by Max Weber, as "free church" by Franklin H. Littell, and as "radical reformation" by George H. Williams. James Wm. McClendon Jr. proposes to call them all "baptist."[1] Most of the people in these movements in the past preferred to call themselves "brethren." A few called themselves "Friends," a few "Christians." Neither the etymological backgrounds nor the emotive overtones of these labels are identical. All of them involve possible debates about whether they are historically precise or invidious: but that is no less true for the people who choose to call themselves "Orthodox," "Catholic," or "Reformed." One can argue that in America all churches are "free." The Lutherans, in submitting a confession to the 1530 Imperial Diet at Augsburg, intended to deny to the Romans their claimed proprietorship of the name "Catholic." Such cavils are linguistically absolutely true, but ecumenically they constitute obfuscation, as they would waste our energies on the avoidance of any words with more than one meaning. Today the term "brethren" will seem sexist to some, the term "baptist" will seem to exclude the Quakers, and the label "radical reformation" seems to center attention on times of schism. "Restoration" centers on a specific, debatable theory of historic origins. Granting that each label has its shortcomings, our choice for the present would seem to have to be with Littell,[2] with "free" designating at the same time (a) voluntary adult membership, (b) the rejection of establishment whether in the sense of state control or of provincialism, and (c) the relativizing of prescribed forms of either ritual or dogma.

The perspective from which I address these questions to the Lima document is not that I would ask that the text should represent a "believers' church" position. I need rather to seek to note those points at

---

1. *Ethics: Systematic Theology*, vol. 1 (Nashville: Abingdon Press, 1986): 7ff.
2. *The Free Church* (Boston: Starr King, 1957); but Littell also uses "Believers' Church" in his keynote address to the Louisville Conference on the concept of the Believers' Church. See James Leo Garrett, *The Concept of the Believers' Church* (Scottdale, Penn.: Herald Press, 1969): 15-32.

which it fails to represent a mediating or synthetic position, i.e., where consciously or unconsciously it has retained a tilt away from recognition of concerns which a believers' church perspective would raise.

One of the ways in which the believers' church family differs from the others is that it has no central institutional definition and no one creedal norm. Thus there is about my task an element of simplification and selectivity that would not be equally appropriate if I were seeking to speak for one of the "mainstream" denominations.

What I shall seek to summarize is at some points the statistical summation of what most Baptists, Mennonites, Plymouth Brethren, Quakers, and some Disciples would hold to, on the basis of what they consider to be their tradition. At other points I shall be representing more an ideal type, and at still others a distillation based in historical origins.

The most helpful context for this conversation would be one in which we could look sentence by sentence at the Lima document's phrasing and reconstruct behind it the arguments that must have led to it. It would represent the symbolic equivalent of having had the opportunity to enter the dialogue earlier and would demonstrate an effort to affirm the understanding of the lines of argument that formed the BEM text. For purpose of the present summary, that amount of care as to detail will not be possible. The Lima text is not up for rewriting. The points where the solutions it suggests are unconvincing are perhaps not best clarified here by a fine-grained reading of a compromise document. The response here must then be more to its general stance than to its wordings.

Dialogical Process

From the believers' church perspective there is strong ground to welcome the kind of process represented by the BEM. The modern ecumenical movement itself is a kind of believers' church, i.e., it begins by relativizing those definitions of unity that depended upon an established hierarchy, one particular body of authoritative creeds, or the rejection of a particular set of heretics. It carries on a conversation in which those parties are qualified to be interlocutors who do, in fact, participate in the dialogue. The dialogical process is thus self-defining rather than having been made possible (or restricted) by an inherited institutional, ritual, or creedal status.

The conversational process that produced these documents had about it some characteristics that fit with the believers' church tradition. The process relativized confessional commitment by the very fact that it invited representatives of all the traditions to converse with one another more than their documentary bases would authorize. A dialogical process reaching beyond one's institution is itself an ecclesiastical reality, although few denominations have adopted a document that enables one to affirm that.

We would, however, doubt the adequacy of the statement that consensus should be "understood as that experience of life and articulation of faith necessary to realize and maintain the Church's visible unity."[3] That common articulation is helpful, and sociologically indispensable, is a different thing from granting that it is theologically imperative. On the other hand, one major gap becomes visible when we compare the text with a believers' church style. Another term used by the historians to refer to the "believers' churches" is, as we noted, "radical reformation." This refers to the conviction that what was needed to come out of the unfaithfulness of medieval establishment was not just a superficial adjustment here or there in the form of the church or its services but a fundamental renewal and redefinition, including judgment upon the unfaithfulness of the past. Unfaithfulness was a reality in the past, and it is a threat today.

The present document is not at all clear about how Christians could discern in themselves, in their own churches, or in sister churches any reality of unfaithfulness. "Reform" is not a widely current theme in the conciliar movement. It gives us the impression of moving forward in a way such as to affirm that everything and everybody is in; I am okay and you are okay, nobody is fundamentally wrong. "Convergence" is the preferred metaphor. Yet we would not be in the mess we are in if there had not been unfaithfulness in the past. The commentary on paragraph 6[4] gives a strong expression to the wrongness of the present divided situation; but it carefully avoids even hypothetically opening for scrutiny the possibility that the wrong use of baptism (or anything else specially wrong that any tradition in particular would need to disavow) could have been part of the reason for this. That is of a piece with the wider strategic tendency of inclusive agency leaders

3. "Baptism, Eucharist and Ministry," Faith and Order Paper 110, 111 (Geneva, 1982): ix.
4. "The inability of the churches mutually to recognize their various practices of baptism . . . and their actual dividedness in spite of mutual baptismal recognition, have given visibility to the broken witness of the church," op. cit., p. 3.

to believe that ecumenical unity can be achieved by going forward together without repentance.

Numerous communions, some of the highly creedal fundamentalist variety, and others of an anti-theological and anti-structural type, concur in labeling "inclusivism," a strategy that on purpose excludes nothing, as a pastoral mistake or even a theological heresy. This theme is not brought into focus in the BEM document, although it is posed implicitly by the process that produced it. It is a consensus document of all of those who were participating; yet, there is no accounting for the absences of others and no indication of consistent attention to unrepresented positions. One senses at several points the writers' awareness of Roman Catholics looking over their shoulders but not of Pentecostals and Plymouth Brethren. Quakers are simply outvoted even though the Society of Friends counts member communions in the WCC: Roman Catholicism is represented strongly and heard although not a member church.

If we assume that the Faith and Order agenda properly should be in some sense "classical," i.e., that it should be dictated by the heritage of schismatic experiences that have left us contradictory creeds and polities, then the steps that the document makes represent epoch-making progress toward understanding, toward relative recognition of the case for contradictory positions, and toward civility within controversy. Should we, on the other hand, be judging it from the perspective of concern to draw into the mainstream dialogue those parties whose absence from it was not dictated by classical creeds nor institutionalized in consistories and chanceries, then this very component of the consensus process hardens a new polarization. If our ultimate goal is to develop shared understandings such that "all in one place" can fully recognize the validity of one another's sacraments and ministries, then this text has to count as marking the end of the beginning rather than the beginning of the end. It states carefully the starting position of those who are the most inclined to cooperative Christianity on the level of style and structure and at the same time the least open to fundamental challenge of the medieval heritage on the level of substance.

Believers' Baptism and "Rebaptism"

The document is right in recognizing baptism as a first issue and in describing the shape of the debate about the baptism of infants as an issue in its own right. It is less clear about the way the baptism question surfaces a difference between a minority-missionary and an established-pedagogical conception of the church. It is vague — and in that sense deceptive — when it presents itself as a breakthrough as to how the evenhanded balancing of paragraphs 12–16 would in reality enable mutual respect.[5]

The text that rejects the idea of "rebaptism" is literally unexceptionable.[6] There is no Mennonite, Baptist, or other believers' community that could not affirm those words. Yet, to let that statement stand alone represents a tilt in what was supposed to be a mediating document, when it is accompanied by no sign of recognizing on the other hand the importance of the kind of theological concern that in the past brought about phenomena that, while not considered "rebaptism" by those who practiced them, were condemned as such by others.

It could have been said, in recognition of the other side of the picture, that when ceremonies purporting to be "baptism" are practiced in ways that do not correspond to what baptism ought to mean, the communities or agencies authorizing such practice make it possible that other people and communities, committed to the notion that sacramental practice must meet specified criteria of validity, will believe that they need to do again validly what was first done invalidly. It is important to note that the notion of sacraments being "valid" is not peculiar to the believers' churches. In fact the ordinary ways of measuring "validity," in terms of ritual form, ministerial orders, or doctrinal or experiential content are usually more at home in the "high" context than in the "radical reformation" tradition where the question is the authenticity of the believer's confession.

Those who in the sixteenth century were labeled "Anabaptist" by their persecutors, in order to use against them the ancient Roman codes' rules against the Donatists, never accepted that description.[7] They denied that the ritual they had undergone in infancy constituted baptism. For that question — distinguishing between a ritual that counts

5. Op. cit., pp. 4–6. By accentuating the commonalities of the two traditions and eliding the arguments, the text supports a mode of generosity but does not advance dialogue about the hard points.

6. Para. 13, p. 4.

7. The Donatists of the fourth century said that ordinations or baptisms by a clergyman who had denied the faith were not valid and should be repeated. As we discussed above, the issue here was the celebrant, not the baptized. Yet the "Holy Roman Empire" used the designation "rebaptism" to justify persecuting the radical protestants of 1525–50 by using the Augustinian rationale for persecution.

as baptism and one that does not — all communions have always had criteria. The Lima document avoids the clash of criteria and proceeds as if that made all rituals valid.

Not only is this one traditional crux avoided. The document is generally disappointing in its evasion of classically defined issues. One wonders whether the writers assumed that if any issue had been a source of division in the past it must have been the result of a misunderstanding, so that it can be resolved better by looking past it than by analyzing it. One such classically defined issue that Lima simply avoids was the practice of confirmation as an identifiable, distinct action, whereby the already "baptized" person appropriates, as an accountable older youth or adult, the implicit meaning of the "baptism" that he or she had received as an infant. Historically this has figured in important ways as a concession or bridge whereby the pedobaptist communions recognized the imperative of explicit commitment on the part of the believer. It correlated with the ways in which the antipedobaptist communions developed other ceremonies than baptism for recognizing the birth of children in Christian families. The document does not help the reader explain the absence of confirmation by providing[8] any arguments. In the place where confirmation is named[8] it appears as just one other component of the single baptismal ritual.

Another such redirection of attention is the generally uncritical and unargued affirmation that it is good for baptism to be surrounded by other kinds of theologically unexplained formalities: charismation, the imposition of hands and other "vivid signs."[9] In the absence of argument it is unconvincing to affirm that additional ceremonies, which are not in the same sense the direct content of a divine mandate, and which in some cases may in fact change its meaning, should be permitted uncritically to proliferate. This was a concern not only of the most radical of the believers' churches (Anabaptists, Baptists, Quaker) but also of the mainstream Zwinglian and Calvinist traditions, who condemned in principle giving normative status to what they called "ceremonies." A particular case may be made for other "vivid signs"; but affirming them in general does not belong in a consensus statement where the case against ritual proliferation has not been heard and the

8. Op. cit., para. 14, pp. 4–6. This sets aside very lightly the many pedobaptist traditions for which for centuries confirmation was a prerequisite of full membership.

9. Para. 14 and 19, p. 6; the sign of the cross is the only other "vivid sign" suggested.

case for those particular signs has not been made. There is a great difference between allowing liberty for whimsical or serious innovation and symbolic behavior in worship, and saying (as this text does so briefly) that such behavior should be integrated into the meaning of the fundamental sacramental celebrations that one communion asks other communities to recognize as constitutive of our unity.

One of the regular patterns of inadequate representation produced by denominationalism is especially visible at the point of baptism. Since Karl Barth's historic stand a sizable theologically responsible minority within the Reformed churches of Switzerland and France challenges or even rejects a baptism of infants. This minority has been growing. In some parts of the Reformed Church of France or that of Geneva the preference for baptism upon confession is the dominant pastoral position. Similar questions came to be raised in the Lutheran churches of East Germany in the 1960s and in West Germany in the 1970s. They are raised today in North American Roman Catholicism, especially in connection with the newly rewritten Ritual for the Christian Initiation of Adults. In each case this challenging of infant baptism has on its side the fruit of biblical, historical, and pastoral studies. Those who have made these changes were not listening to the ecumenical witness of Baptists or Pentecostals. The Lima baptism document leaves no traces of this development because the representatives of the respective denominations who participate in Faith and Order are charged to speak on behalf of their historic positions rather than of their pastorally responsible growing edges.[10]

Eucharist and Ministry

Each of the issues with which the three sections of the report deal has a different institutional history with regard to free church concerns. The issue with regard to adult versus infant baptism is unavoidably on the surface of the document, and what we needed to debate is whether the complementary both/and resolution that it proposes is acceptable to "believers' churches."[11]

10. Cf. my paper "Adjusting to the Changing Shape of the Debate on Infant Baptism," in A. Lambo, ed., *Oecumennisme* (Amsterdam: ADS, 1989): 201–14.
11. One serious contribution to the conversation in response to BEM is Merle D. Strege, ed., *Baptism and Church: A Believers' Church Vision* (Grand Rapids: Sagamore Books, 1986).

The Eucharist, on the other hand, is not an issue concerning which historically the believers' churches (except for the Friends) differed from others as a confessional unity. Some of them have been generally at home in a Zwinglian attitude, but that was not a point of distinctive identity, either in the crises of their origins or during the centuries of their maintaining distinctive identity. For the purposes of this rapid survey I therefore pass to the third section.[12]

Ministry is an issue on which the radical reformation churches would divide among themselves. Some of them, Baptists especially, and many Pentecostals, are accustomed to patterns of pastoral government that are compatible with the rest of Protestantism. Their concern would be only to tone down the sacramental ontology of ordained status, to upgrade the authority of the congregation as a whole in calling and governing the minister, to doubt the claims of a supracongregational episcopacy, and (for some) to include women. A weighty minority within the radical reformation contingents will, however, make a far more radical critique, to which the document pays no attention, on the perfectly natural grounds that by virtue of the process chosen it would not have been represented in the process of consultation. Here my concentration must be upon that particular component of the "baptist" family that is the most constitutively distinctive. With regard to "the ordained ministry" I shall not, therefore, speak for Baptists, who intended no dissent from their Presbyterian and Congregational colleagues, but rather for Friends and Plymouth Brethren, Churches of Christ, Chinese house churches, and the Mukyokai.[13]

These communions, supported by a strong current of contemporary biblical scholarship and an undercurrent of missionary theology, would argue against the fundamental concept of the sacramentally and professionally "set apart" ministry, whether on the grounds that priesthood is done away with in the new covenant, or because all God's people are priests and every one is a charismatic minister.[14] Other times

12. The mainstream process paid no attention to the basic challenges of the physical Eucharist by Quakerism and the Salvation Army. Those communities are given a derisory after-the-fact space of one page in the post-Lima anthology *Ecumenical Perspectives on Baptism, Eucharist and Ministry*, ed. Max Thurian, Faith and Hope Paper No. 116 (Geneva: WCC, 1983): 161ff.

13. Most of the church growth for forty years in China under Mao has taken the form of an indigenous counterpart of the Plymouth Brethren tradition. The "no-church-church" or Mukyokai movement was the most energetic, effective, and indigenously genuine form of Christianity in Japan from the 1940s.

14. Cf. my *The Fullness of Christ* (Elgin: Brethren Press, 1987).

this critique is more pragmatically oriented and would remind us that the professional priesthood is predisposed to social conservatism, that its links with political and economical power support patriarchal styles, and that it fosters dichotomizing between the religion of the rites, for which a professional is needed, and justice issues in the real world.[15] That each of these slogans is debatable does not keep them from amounting cumulatively to a weighty case against priesthood or what some radicals called the "hireling ministry." Compared to that challenge, the issues with which the Lima ministry consensus document struggles are trivial.

Both those churches that retained a central pastorate, like the Baptists, and those like the Plymouth Brethren and the Friends who rejected it linked their understanding of ministry with their generally Zwinglian view on sacraments and ceremonies. Whether speaking statistically for their heirs in general or normatively for what I would consider a responsible contemporary ecumenical posture, it should be said that both the apostolic vision of everyone having a gift (1 Cor. 12, Rom. 12, Eph. 4) and the lessons needing to be learned from the proliferation of superstitions and ceremonies within established Christendom call us to continuing restraint in the temptation to ascribe any ontological status to what happens to the bread and wine in the rituals of consecration or what happens to a minister in the rituals of commissioning. At this first level, namely skepticism about the ontology of sacraments and orders, the BEM document identifies the problem, yet without reproducing the elements of a dialogue that would indicate that the perspective of the Zwinglians or the Quakers had been heard, much less responded to. But my present concern is the second order impact of that issue on the question of orders: this document assumes a qualitative difference between the set-apart ministers and the laity rather than arguing it. The exclusion of most of the people who by grace are bearers of charismatic office from recognition as "ministers," and the exclusion of all women, is too high a price to pay at this early point in the conversation to maintain the appearance of ecumenical "good manners."

Having made a prior commitment to the "high church" rather

15. Another practical advantage is that in some kinds of repressive societies the absence of a visible clergy facilitates the spread and survival of evangelical communities. This has been the advantage of the "Brethren" communities in Latin America and Latin Europe, before it was the case among continental and overseas Chinese.

than the dialectical understandings of inclusiveness, the Lima document has obviously given hostages to Eastern Orthodoxy both at the point of feminine ministry and at that of the ontology of orders. The strongest alternative perspectives were excluded not by dialogue but on procedural grounds. The requirements that would obtain for a negotiated ecclesiastical unity are thereby given priority over the normal ground rules of an open ecumenical dialogue. I have no basis from outside the process to evaluate that strategic decision within Faith and Order. The effect of the decision is to exclude from the conversational process one set of interlocutors, confirming van Dusen's reading.

The Way Forward

A more fine-grained critical reading of the Lima document would have disengaged its varied assumptions about the appeal to Scripture, the authority of the evolution of church practices, and the prognosis for continuing conversations. That would have made issues debatable, whereas the above inventory has merely named them. A deeper analysis would have distinguished between appeals to momentum or "convergence" and other more convincing theological warrants, whereas here I could only point to the places where argument would be needed. We may hope that as the conversations continue ways can be found to involve the hitherto less adequately represented and to move beyond covenants of reciprocal respect to challenges of truth and obedience. That will be a worthy prolongation of these promising though modest beginnings.

The Imperative of Christian Unity

"The Imperative of Christian Unity" originated as a resume of a guest lecture presented to students in a course on "Church and Ministry" at Associated Mennonite Biblical Seminaries, Elkhart, Indiana. It is published here for the first time in substantially the same form as the 1983 transcription of the lecture, with only a few additions and notes for clarification.

Here Yoder is addressing students from his own communion with the call to engage the question of ecumenicity, not on the grounds established by someone else's consensus, but on biblical and theological grounds. In much the same way that Yoder had done this in his early pamphlet *The Ecumenical Movement and the Faithful Church* (Scottdale, Penn.: Herald Press, 1957), he offers a survey of the various approaches to ecumenism that were in evidence at the time and situates the Anabaptist-Mennonite tradition in relation to the "imperative" of Christian unity.

Yoder contrasts the "lazy solution" of pluralism, which presumes that "unity is based on agreement, so that every dispute calls for division," with the more challenging task of reconciliation in the midst of disagreement as called for in the New Testament writings. In particular, Yoder calls into question the "American cafeteria–style" of pluralism with its inadequate conception of diversity as compared with the New Testament conception of diversity in unity. As Yoder spells out, these kinds of misconceptions of "Christian unity" have affected not only mainstream Protestant groups but also the Mennonite denominations as well. The very conception of Mennonites as a "denomination" alongside other denominated groups leads contemporary heirs of the Anabaptist vision to neglect the task of embodying the *visible unity* of the Body of Christ in the world. This concern, in turn, poses problems as well as possibilities for "bilateral conversations" between various denominations and traditions of Christianity.

In the concluding section of this article Yoder takes up two different but related contexts for seeking to embody visible unity of the church: denominational agencies and the local church. "The locus of visibility of most Christians is where they live and go to church. Therefore, the most important locus of concern for unity to be visible should be on the home level, in the relationship between Christians across the back fence, or in the same school district, or between neighboring congregations of different confessions."

The Imperative of Christian Unity

What Is the Ground for Concern for Unity?

For some Christians, concern for the visible unity of Christians is a matter of good manners. In spiritual matters it is not seemly to compete by undercutting one another's claims, to commend oneself as being more right than someone else, to make truth claims that exclude others. The separate existence of sects is not only an offense when someone else separates from us; we also sense it as a failure of good manners when we separate from someone else. Good style, good sportsmanship is a matter of social tone that belongs to the leadership style of the religious community.

For another set of people we need unity for the sake of efficiency. Services and curricula and hymnals are duplicated, programs compete for the support of a limited constituency, parallel bureaucracies draw not only money but personnel, energy, and creativity away from mission to maintenance.

For many, the concern for Christian unity is valuable but dispensable. It is something we do when we can, and which we cut off when we have to. If through generosity and good fortune we find ourself better off at the end of a budget period, we may do something generously ecumenical with our balance; but if we are tight for funds, that is also where we will first cut. To use the old technical phrases, investment in wider Christian unity is part of the *bene esse* or the *plene esse* of the church: it is ultimately good, but it is not essential. If you had to do with less, you would not cut into paying the mortgage on the sanctuary nor paying the salary to the pastor, but you would cut off contributions to councils of churches or to cooperative service programs. They are thereby functionally identified as frills or fringes.

According to the New Testament none of these assumptions is adequate. Until we humbly confess their inadequacy, we will not be ready to understand that the Bible is calling for something that we are far from being open to affirm or to pay for. The unity of Christians is a *theological* imperative first of all in the sense that its reasons arise out of the basic truth commitments of the gospel and the church's intrinsic mission.

Speaking even more precisely, as we turn to the most clearly stated text of the New Testament, it is a Christological imperative: it has to do with who Jesus is. This much we can see, without going into a thorough analysis, in the most precise texts from the New Testament on the subject.

The Johannine text is obviously John 17:20ff. In his prayer for the future believers, Jesus asks of the Father that they may be one as the Father and the Son are one, so that the world might believe that the Son was sent by the Father. That the Son was sent by the Father is obviously the most fundamental statement in John's Gospel about who Jesus was. Likewise, that the Father and the Son are one is a fundamental Johannine confession; and that kind of oneness is the model for the disciples' unity. The function of the unity of the future believers is, therefore, to make credible the fundamental Christian claim ("that the world might believe," said twice) and to reflect the nature of the unity between the Son and Father, to render that credible witness substantial.

The basic Pauline text (Eph. 2–3) is just as dramatic. The apostle claims it as his specific message, the mystery not revealed to others in other ages, nor even to other apostles, but only to and through Paul in his distinctive missionary ministry. The message is that from all eternity the purpose of God was going to be making one humanity out of Jew and Gentile. God's purpose is cosmic: that through the church this new-found wisdom should be made manifest to "the principalities and powers." We need not know exactly what the "principalities and powers" are to know that Paul making a statement of cosmic dimensions. The unity of two kinds of people, those born within the law and those without, is what God was about from all history. It is once again not the mere result of parallel interests or economies of scale: it is their witness itself that is at stake. Where Christians are not united, the gospel is not true in that place.

American religious pluralism denies that gospel truth. By "pluralism" we designate that pattern of independence and toleration whereby each group lets the others exist without coercion or unification, also without agreement. That is the best solution, for politics, when Christians have failed to be a church. When I say "the best solution for politics," I mean that it is the best solution from the perspective of civil government, which should permit all religious communities their liberty. But I also mean that it is the best solution for church politics, when the structure of the church as institution has failed to bring about healing and, instead, has become a set of power relationships without dialogue or reconciliation.

To the words of Paul and John we should add one synoptic Gospel text: the only one where Jesus is reported as using the word "church," namely Matthew 18:15–20. That word is used to describe a process of decision making ("binding and loosing"), that takes place through dialogue with a reconciling intention ("if that person listens, you have won your brother or sister") on the basis of an initial conflict ("your brother or sister has sinned"). The effect is a conclusion that stands before God because Christ was present in people's coming to agreement (*symphonein*). So here again, the knowledge of the presence of Christ is made available to them through a reconciling, deliberative process undertaken in his name in the power of his spirit.

The lazy solution of pluralism reinforces the false view that unity is based on agreement, so that every dispute calls for division. As a matter of fact, disagreement calls not for dividing but for reconciling people. Undertaking that reconciling process at the point of division is more important than affirming common conviction where that can be taken for granted. The difference is more important because it deals with more important issues, namely the ones people differ about. The mandate to be reconciled at the point of difference is the one most often disobeyed by churches in general and especially by pluralistic churches. Thus the functional meaning of church unity is not that people agree and, therefore, work together but that where they disagree they recognize the need to talk together with a view to reconciliation.

When that meaning is not recognized and acknowledged, i.e., where people operate on the assumption that unity is the product of agreement, this is the sociological form of works religion, namely the understanding that the reality of the gospel is the product of human performance. This is to deny the gift quality of the gospel, which is precisely that we have been, despite ourselves, by virtue of grace, made one with people with whom we were not one. It also runs away from the hard, concrete task of working the reconciliation message out from the level of generality to that of concrete action.

A difference of perspective that hides behind the tension between (a) expressing unity because we agree and (b) the mandate to care about one another where we disagree is the contrast of implications that the two perspectives have for the handling of a conflict. If achieving unity through commonality is accented, we will find ourselves in practical negotiations trying to reconcile positions by saying that they are complementary when they are not, or by saying that we agree to differ, since reaching a relative common denominator consensus is a challenge to our own leadership, patience, and ingenuity.

If, on the other hand, we see clash and reconciliation, accusation and repentance as the more fundamental model, we will want to clarify differences rather than to fuzz them over. We will put the truth question and the repentance question at the fundamental point, though being very slow to name that point. No amount of ecumenical good manners can justify refusing to name an error when it is recognized as such. Great amounts of irenic sensitivity need to be devoted to not naming such a crisis where it does not really obtain. However well intentioned Dominic and Torquemada were, the Inquisition was wrong. However fervent "Saint" Bernard was, the Crusades were wrong. However sensitive was the pastoral feeling of the pope and all the bishops he consulted around 1950, the promulgation of the doctrine of the Assumption of the Virgin in that year was hogwash theologically and a sin against the unity of the body of Christ.

The American pluralistic cafeteria is, therefore, a fundamental dodge, avoiding the truth question, ducking the hard duties of reconciliation, postponing long-range investment in tasks that take time and that demand occasional readiness for suffering. This is not to deny that diversity is very important in the church. Pluralism is more than diversity. The diversity that the New Testament celebrates is that of several members of one body, several functions with the same purpose, numerous people doing different things but each in unity with the others. That diversity is accredited by its being within the fundamental unity with purpose and complementarity of function. Pluralism, on the other hand, is diversity without unity, variation without asking the truth question, work at cross purposes without accountable discipline.

The pluralistic cafeteria has the effect of reproducing, in the realm of religious truth, the pattern that Gresham identified in the field of economics. Cheaper currency circulates more. If you have a brand new silver dollar with its original full silver content and other silver dollars with less silver content, you will keep the new one and circulate the old ones. So it is that generally the least valuable currency circulates the most easily. The same applies in the realm of ideas. When people are being solicited on all sides to accept new ideas, there are normal psychological dynamics that push them toward accepting more easily the ideas that are cheaper, that call for less critical perspective, less sacrifice, and less change. The competitive cafeteria, therefore, puts a premium on the less true truths. It puts a special burden on the hard truths that ought to be faced, whether that be the hard words of the gospel or the difficult readings of the way the world really is.

With time, furthermore, the cafeteria approach of old denominations side-by-side becomes more and more wrong. The old identities no longer hold and new divisions arise on new issues, to which the same level of tolerance does not seem to apply. What divided Lutherans from Catholics in the sixteenth century, or Lutherans from Calvinists or Presbyterians from Baptists, becomes less important in our time. At the same time new divisions strike down the middle of the communions. The charismatic experience, the science/religion debate and fundamentalism, political activity, and new social threats like feminism or homosexuality will divide people, who were unquestioningly together before under the common roof, whatever denominational definitions they had inherited from the preceding set of crises. The denomination that accepts separation from people from whom one is not profoundly separated and, on the other hand, tries to hold together people who cannot stand each other is, therefore, a particularly inappropriate instrument for authentic expression of the visible unity of believers.

Since the denomination is itself structurally contradictory, it is no surprise that particular positions taken in defense of the denomination are intrinsically contradictory or paradoxical. When the separatism of a denomination is criticized for being willing to go it alone although recognizing that many other people are Christian "out there," denominational leaders will say, "we know we are in spiritual unity with many other people, who do not join our budget, or participate in our decision making and we sometimes cooperate with them ad hoc when we have common projects." In other words they argue that it is spiritually and theologically adequate to express concrete unity occasionally and that unity should otherwise be invisible or inoperative (which seems to be the main meaning in this connection of the word "spiritual"). Yet when problems arise within the denomination, when someone threatens to take the right wing of the Mennonite denomination off by revitalizing the issues of fundamentalism and nonconformity, or when some other advocacy group like "the women" or the ethnic caucuses raises questions about how deeply they want to be identified with the denomination at large, *then* the loyalty that denominational leaders say they want to defend is not "spiritual" but visible, not ad hoc but institutional, not functional but committed. When explaining why they could not cooperate with other Christian groups they say, "because we do not agree with them deeply enough." Yet when asking for their own dissenters to stay in the fold they say, "but you don't have to agree with us, you can just maintain dialogue."

That same paradoxical tension (which would have to be called bad faith if it were more conscious) is visible also when we look at smaller parts of the picture: i.e., at the specific differentiating marks. When asked why they are not cooperating with other Christians, Mennonites would often say that it is because they do not believe in baptizing babies, or they do not believe in war, or they believe in taking the Bible straight. But when they get a chance, how many of them have spoken how much about the wrongness of baptizing babies when they could talk to Catholics or Lutherans? How often have they made occasions to talk to Christians of different beliefs on the matters they differ about?

Many Mennonite, Mennonite Brethren, or Brethren in Christ leaders would refer immediately to "our peace witness" as a reason that their denomination should not merge with the Baptists or the Free Methodists, yet would not once in a year communicate on the subject of the peace witness to nonpacifist colleagues in the local ministerial group, or do not more than three times in a year teach about the peace position in their own congregational educational programs, and never in the year do they deal institutionally with the non-pacifists in their own church. Are we ourselves as sure of having a solid position on these matters as we would have to be for our using them as a grounds for separation to be credible? After all, sizable numbers of young men from Mennonite churches did serve in the military in World War II. Did our official peace position make us stop fellowshiping with those individuals or with their congregations? At the same time that we maintain a sense of independence by producing our own curricular material and our own hymnbooks, most of what is in the curriculum and most of what is in the hymnbooks is non-Mennonite material.

These paradoxes, if maintained consciously and joked about, would have to be identified as hypocrisy or bad faith. They are not that. They rather show a certain dullness of mind with regard to the seriousness of the gospel challenge that we ought to be facing in this area. Not having quite granted its seriousness, we are not quite able to see that it is being sinned against.

What God Is Doing

Visible unity is not a realm in which the facts will stand still. Major shifts in the lay of the land have taken place in recent years.

1. There is a new "right wing" ecumenicism based in the media, very inclusive within traditional doctrinal areas, so that Baptists and Catholics can work together, yet profoundly doctrinaire and exclusive on social matters. One group recently called itself the "Moral Majority." Several nationwide media agencies spend literally hundreds of millions of dollars for air time to maintain the movement. It is authentically "ecumenical," in the sense that it draws people together in a contemporary missionary cause without regard to denominational origin. It is profoundly divisive, in that the organs of this new unity are themselves ad hoc, personal, politicized, self-contained, and committed to the refusal of dialogue with their adversaries in the churches.

2. Our age has seen the maturation as well of the "high" ecumenism of the major denominations bound together in the councils of churches. The Consultation on Church Unity (COCU) in the United States has lowered its sights. It no longer projects the creation of a centralized super church but does serve a growing degree of mutual recognition among the midstream denominations. The World Council of Churches, in addition to the continuing growth and visibility of its other components that deal with world mission or peace and justice, has also turned a corner in the circulation of its consensus document on *Baptism, Eucharist and Ministry* (Lima, 1982).

The National Council of Churches, with less of the component dealing with "Faith and Order," and therefore more fickle and irregular on matters of common action and witness, is nonetheless surviving through generational changes. The challenge to its inclusiveness by the Metropolitan Community Churches will, however, pose a greater structural crisis than it has faced for a long time.

Neither of these sets of phenomena represents "the ecumenical movement" or the visibility of the body of Christ. Nonetheless Christians, including Mennonite Christians, and including Associated Mennonite Biblical Seminaries students, ought to care enough about these matters to be informed about them. Seminarians expecting to have a place in congregational leadership should see the matter of visible Christian unity, which these phenomena test and represent, as one realm of expert ministerial responsibility.

Apart from the above entities, which seek to gather as many as possible for a particular purpose and which, therefore, tend to downplay the weight of differentiae, another kind of dialogue proceeds in the other direction; namely by bilateral conversations that increasingly are taking place between one Christian body and just one other Christian body. Then instead of needing to itemize a great scope of contested questions or to ignore them, the bilateral conversation enables the participants responsibly to look just at what has been separating their true traditions. Each bilateral constellation will, therefore, have a different agenda. Mennonites will talk about something different depending on whether they are conversing with Disciples or with Lutherans. Such conversations are, therefore, more substantial, more interesting to experts, more likely to produce authentic new light on some subject. They are, however, also deceptive in that those particular Catholics and those particular Lutherans who happen to get together to talk about Catholics and Lutherans will probably come out closer together than those other Catholics and other Lutherans who didn't get to the meeting and who will not consider themselves to have been adequately represented. Thus the apparent consensus is not as strong, when measured by the churches represented, as it seemed to be in that particular meeting under the blessing of authentic dialogical progress.

Institutional Meanings: Local Responsibility and Special Agency

The assigned reading for this class session[1] centered upon the problem of interchurch relations as institutional challenge. Therefore, it talked about what we can do together as a denomination, being what we are. That was a natural focus in view of the assignment. It, however, represents a spiritual and pastoral foreshortening, which ought to be corrected if the matter is to be pursued further in the churches.

I already argued earlier that we need to take unity seriously at the point of our differences and not only where we are in sufficient agreement to be able to do something positively together. This is one needed corrective.

Another is the importance of the local church. The locus of visibility of most Christians is where they live and go to church. Therefore, the most important locus of concern for unity to be visible should be

---

1. The background reading for the session had been a document digesting several unpublished "think pieces" produced 1967–71 by a denominational study committee.

on the home level, in the relationship between Christians across the back fence, or in the same school district, or between neighboring congregations of different confessions. Partly this is a heartening statement, because there are many kinds of mutual recognition already going on, between Christians of different traditions who listen to the same radio broadcast or attend the same revivalist events in the local community. Yet, on another level it is also disheartening because most of the things that people do separately in their separate local congregations/parish structures are things that they could just as well do together. Visible unity is the exception when it should be the rule. That, of course, is not only the case between a Mennonite church and a Lutheran church. It is often the case between two Mennonite churches, even of the same conference.

The priority of the local congregation is an imperative both theologically and tactically. It should be recognized as such more easily by Mennonites than by Catholics. Yet, to argue about the priority of the local congregation is no excuse for Mennonites, when what we are talking about is the self-sufficiency of denominational bureaucracies in Elkhart, Lombard, Newton, Hillsboro.[2]

One of the defenses of inaction in this area is to say that interchurch relations are being done by everybody: local congregations do whatever they do, mission boards cooperate with other mission boards, and service agencies maintain linkage with cognate agencies, so that without having a special office or committee for the subject we by definition are doing what we believe in in this area. There is an element of factual truth in this statement, of course: very little that Christians do does not have *some* dimension or relations to other Christians. But that is a far cry from doing it consciously, doing it credibly, doing it accountably, and doing it coherently.

It would be just as possible to argue that everything we do is education. Mission boards educate congregations, mothers educate, fathers educate, *Christian Living* magazine educates . . . and yet we have created not only primary schools and colleges. We have created a "Board of Education," which does not even operate a school but only educates about education, coordinates thinking, coordinates institutions, so that the general realm of education shall be dealt with consciously and accountably by all of the many agencies that educate, some of them under the formal jurisdiction of the Mennonite Board of Education,

2. These were in 1983 the addresses of the central offices of the three largest Mennonite denominations.

some of them informally under its counseling jurisdiction, some of them not at all under its jurisdiction but open to its testimony. It brings together information, analytical tools, specialized consulting skills, trouble shooting. It does no education at all itself: it coordinates thinking about the place of education in the denominational community.

In this sense, the Inter-Church Relations Committee of the Mennonite General Conference[3] proposed that there be a *standing* agency under the new General Board, within (or under the oversight of) the Council on Faith, Life and Strategy, which would be the clearing house for information, education, and coordination with regard to relations between Mennonites and the rest of the body of Christ. It would seem that something like that would make sense more than the present assignment of most responsibility in the area to decisions made by default.

The 1971 text centers its attention on the analysis of the theological profiles of different agencies. Thereby it gives a degree of credence to the mistaken or at least unbalanced notion that what makes an agency's identity is a doctrinal stance. That is true, but it is also not as true as we assume. My argument elsewhere has made more clear than the 1971 text does that to identify an agency with a theological stance may be both positively and negatively a shortcut: it is just as important to know the agency's ethnic composition, the psychological style of its chief executive, the deliberative patterns of its decision-making groups, and how much of the money comes from which donors.

3. This was the name of the study committee named in the first note. It was phased out in 1971.

Catholicity in Search of Location

"Catholicity in Search of Location" originated in an invitation to John H. Yoder to give a lecture at Church Divinity School of the Pacific, Berkeley, California (5 April 1990), on the occasion of the departure of James William McClendon, Jr., from that institution. The article is published here, with revisions, for the first time.

In several ways, the audience and setting of this lecture influenced the way Yoder chose to proceed. Some of the examples used are particular to the community and constituency of Church Divinity School of the Pacific. Yoder also chose to converse especially with the Anglican tradition since the host institution serves the Protestant Episcopal Church in America. In addition, the attention to catholicity as the particular theme was provoked by a debate in *Journal of Ecumenical Studies* about "catholicity" in which the approach to ecumenism common to the works of John H. Yoder and James William McClendon, Jr., had been criticized by David Wayne Layman, a Mennonite graduate student in the Department of Religion at Temple University. Layman argued that "the particular reading of the Christian tradition" articulated by McClendon and Yoder calls into question "the inner character of the Christian tradition — and thus short-circuits interreligious discussion." For the full exchange on this topic, see David Wayne Layman's article "The Inner Ground of Christian Theology: Church, Faith and Sectarianism," *Journal of Ecumenical Studies* 27/3 (Summer 1990): 480–503, and "Christian Identity in Ecumenical Perspective: A Response to David Wayne Layman" by Yoder and McClendon in the same issue, pp. 561–80.

Apart from the particularities of this occasion and its setting and audience, this essay displays many of the themes that Yoder explored in earlier essays such as those found in *The Priestly Kingdom*. Here again, Yoder engages the arguments of veteran ecumenists ranging from Eugene Carson Blake to the late Albert Outler not by offering a polemic but by challenging the basis of ecumenical dialogue. "The logical alternative to someone else's design for merger is not my design for a merger; it is rather a search for modes of dialogue that do not begin by asking which structures are right." Yoder's conception of how to proceed challenges the adequacy of the conception of catholicity used by many ecumenists as well as their conception of dialogue itself. "It is thus fitting not only procedurally but also substantially that we begin with the role of discernment. It is not as if liturgy or works of love were less characteristic of catholic faith than is discerning dialogue; yet, they are less representative of the challenge of location. Catholic existence will not be achieved by one decisive act but asymptotically, cumulatively, through communication processes that fulfill more or less our common calling." In so doing, Yoder sketches a vision of the Christian tradition that is, at one and the same time, radically reformed and radically catholic.

Catholicity in Search of Location

When they saw him they fell down before him, though some
hesitated. Jesus came up and spoke to them. He said,
  "All authority in heaven and on earth has been given to me.
  Go therefore; make disciples of all nations;
  Baptize them in the name of the Father
  and of the Son
  and of the Holy Spirit;
  teach them to observe all the commands I gave you;
  Know that I am with you always, yea to the end of time."
                                        (Matthew 28:17–20)

I have lifted most of my title, with grateful acknowledgement, from a paper published in the 1969 *Journal of Ecumenical Studies* by José Míguez

Bonino, then one of the presidents of the World Council of Churches.[1] Dr. Míguez Bonino there wrote: "Neither the study of unity nor the search for patterns of unity seems to have successfully overcome the Constantinian presupposition that we all disclaim in theory. . . ." By "Constantinian presupposition" he meant the tacit assumption that the entity whose "catholic" quality one seeks to test is primordially a structure of ecclesiastical government or a structure of dogmatic elucidation. I suspect that some of you might hear this warning more readily from José Míguez Bonino than if it were James McClendon, Jr., or I using the same words.

Yet, one word of my title differs from his. Dr. Míguez Bonino was writing about "Christian Unity in Search of Locality." "Unity" in that usage drives more rapidly to institutional definition, whereas "catholicity," being a notch more abstract, can live longer with the acknowledgement that there may in fact exist today no one valid instantiation of its imperatives. It is that acknowledgement that I need first to spell out. To ask "What does catholicity look like?" or "Where must one look for catholicity?" need not, in order to be a necessary question, have a ready answer. The "search" we are called to may best be characterized not by asking "How will we know it when we see it?" but rather "When we cannot locate it, how can we nonetheless know what we are looking for?"

"Catholicity" is neither a Platonic idea nor a humanistic ideal; it is a reality and an imperative flowing down through human history, ever since Pentecost, or if you will ever since Abraham. But that it is real does not save us the effort of locating it. To "locate," in the language of logic and geometry, does not mean (as it does in colloquial parlance) to go out looking around for something that one will recognize when one sees it. It means rather to define on fundamental grounds the proper place of that something, the locus where it ought by definition to be found.[2] The locus of points equidistant from a given point "A"

1. José Míguez Bonino, "Christian Unity in Search of Locality," *Journal of Ecumenical Studies* 6/2 (Spring 1969): 185–99.
2. Nor do I intend the commonsense meaning used by Geoffrey Wainwright in his chapter "Ecclesial Location and Ecumenical Vocation" in *The Ecumenical Moment* (Grand Rapids: Eerdmans, 1983): 189ff. What Wainwright does is to "locate" Methodism so to speak by finding where it is on the map of world Christianity. When Methodism is defined by Wesley's legacy and Wainwright's best vision, it is in the center of that picture. Wainwright's description both of Methodism and of the mainstream ecumenical conversations in which he has been a leader is very attractive and helpful; but his method is the opposite of the "geometric" or defini-

is in two-dimensional space a circle, in three-dimensional space a sphere.

If we fail appropriately to define the locus of a value, we may talk past each other not because it is that value itself we disagree about but because our uncriticized assumptions about its location divert us.

I. Shall We Argue by Definition?

Whoever looks at only a brief sampling of the past intrachurch and interchurch debates on our subject knows that the conceptual confusion is considerable. One longs to find — or to have the right to decree — a simple non-question-begging classification of the diverse prevalent usages so as to be able to point it out when people are with good intentions using the same word with different meanings.[3] Such a classification, once agreed upon, would certainly be helpful; yet, it cannot be my task this evening to provide it, for several reasons.

The first reason is that to provide an adequate glossary would demand gathering inductively the record of usages from across a vast universe of discourse. The second is that in arenas where some of the established positions have been hardened over the centuries, questions of the very definition of terms have come to be part of the debate, in such a way that any choice of how to distribute the categories across the scale risks being already vitiated by bias.

But the third reason is yet more serious. Careful analysis of the scope of contrasting usages would demand that we look not only at the variety of *substantial* definitions in the ordinary sense of the terms; i.e., descriptions of what it would take for an entity or a position to live up to it. The *Oxford English Dictionary* provides a standard spectrum of

---

tional one advanced by his fellow Methodist Míguez Bonino, which I propose here. It would not work for a tradition less able to claim to be in the center of the map.

Nor does my use of "locus" have much to do with the old intraprotestant debate about what Methodists call "connection," i.e., the role of bishops and conferences, as traditionally challenged by Disciples and Baptists.

3. James McClendon, Jr., and I attempted to use such a stipulative mode in our paper in the *Journal of Ecumenical Studies* article cited in the introduction. There we sought to disentangle by means of subscripts three different notions of "catholic." That approach was dictated by the particular confusions in the paper to which we were responding. The readers of that paper will have to judge whether that move clarified helpfully. For the present paper, the field needing to be illuminated is much wider and the problem more basic.

a half-dozen ways the word "catholic" is in fact used, though it still omits some of those for which some specified dogmatic content is decisive. We must also distinguish among variations in the function of a term within value-laden debate. Sometimes a term is relatively neutral or trans-subjective in its ("substantial") readiness to serve as shared language. We confirm that our definitions are compatible by being able to converse without talking past each other.

Yet, what matters are the times where the simplicity of description and ascription is complicated by value commitments. Once valuation enters the arena the debate changes. It is not that — as seemed to be suggested by some debates among philosophers — we could distinguish cleanly between fact terms and value terms, or between purely factual usage and valuational usage. It is that the presence of value commitments robs the previously apparently agreed meanings of their obvious utility as tools of conversation. Someone who liturgically recites "I believe the Catholic Church" has by this confessional act modified the terms of the discussion of the meaning of the adjective. They are not proposing a non-question-begging definition of a word. Such a confessor is less free than an "ideal observer" to recognize variations in the content of the term. Someone who polemically claims "the ecclesiastical institution of which I am a member is catholic as the others are not" has put yet another valuational spin on the language. Now the term is used as self-description for a denomination — logically a contradiction in terms, even though we do it all the time.

Then once the language is spinning, yet another level of usage arises. Participants in the conversation seek to move to another level of abstraction and objectivity, asking, as it were from above the debate, what might be the metadefinitional or catholic-making qualities whereby one could choose among the clashing substantial visions without being simply petitionary. Here we have the Vincentian definition,[4] or people appeal to words and codes of the notion of wholeness, or the Lambeth quadrilateral.[5] These are not definitions but locational metadefinitions. They try to tell us how in a contested setting we can recognize which usage of the adjective is accredited.

4. Vincent of Lérins (early fifth century) defined catholic faith as *quod ubique, quod semper, quod omnibus creditus est:* "what has been believed everywhere, always, by everyone." He meant this as a way to validate doctrines, not a church.

5. The "Lambeth" formulation for what Anglicans consider the irreducible prerequisites is modern: Scripture, the Creeds, the historic episcopate, and the two sacraments. The so-called "Wesleyan quadrilateral" is Scripture, tradition, reason, and experience.

Different answers to the "ordinary substantial" definition questions, as well as to the metadefinitional ones, are not merely different but contradictory. A definition centered on the adequacy of a particular past historical instantiation (e.g., episcopal succession as defined by Rome) is structurally contradictory to functional "catholicity" not only in the formal sense of rejecting other sees but even more by virtue of the criterion's inaccessibility to others. This observation also applies to those definitions that intend to identify what is peculiarly characteristic of "the Roman obedience"; as when James Gustafson points to the concept of the natural law,[6] or Richard McBrien the notions of "sacramentality," "mediation," and "communion."[7]

I do not despair at all of the possibility that careful analysis *might* be able to bring order to all of the above varieties; I do, however, decline to make that abstract and encyclopedic exercise my task. If there were a way to sort out all the shapes of the claim to universality or catholicity, without anyone's being accused of using the clarification in the interest of her own "spin," it would clarify the lay of the land but would not advance any particular thesis. I must, therefore, resign myself to walking with you through the conceptual minefield without naming or taming beforehand all the hazards.

II. The Ordinary Appearance of the Minefield

The classical functional metadefinition ascribed to Vincent of Lerins is that we should believe "what has been believed always, everywhere, by everyone" — a neat formula, but of no real help. Like the four negatives of Chalcedon,[8] it may be right in what it excludes. A faith can hardly be claiming catholicity that ignores or excludes a priori some times, some places, or some people. Yet we would need no criteria, if

---

6. James Gustafson, *Protestant and Roman Catholic Ethics* (University of Chicago Press, 1978).

7. Richard McBrien, *Catholicism* (Minneapolis: Winston, 1981): 1180–83. McBrien calls these "theological foci." When experts like Gustafson and McBrien illuminate present identity discussions with higher-order metadoctrinal abstractions like these, whereby "catholic" tends to coincide with a contemporary liberal consensus, it is unclear what light they think that should throw on older identity markers like papal infallibility, transsubstantiation, or the Assumption of Mary.

8. The Ecumenical Council of Chalcedon (451) said that "We confess the same Son, our Lord Jesus Christ, . . . of two natures, unmixed, unconfused, undivided, unseparated. . . ."

in simple fact everyone everywhere always had believed the same things.

Nonetheless, in its very formal emptiness the Vincentian formula enables us to make a first point. If it is to be meaningful to apply a criterion of catholicity, by asking concerning any question what most people in most times and most places have believed, that will have to happen *locally*. It will have to be done in each time and place. It cannot have to be decided elsewhere than where one is, by sending off to some authority at Rome or Lambeth, Geneva or 475 Riverside Drive[9] for a ruling.

III. Dismantling the Magisterial Stance

The heritage that Dr. Míguez Bonino called "Constantinian" has been defined more functionally by George Huntston Williams as "magisterial."[10] The adjective has two facets, both of them present in all the mainstream Western churches. One is the place of civil government in the origins and government of the visible church. The reformations of Zwingli and Luther would probably not have survived, and that of England would not have begun, if it had not been for the decisive authority claimed by Constantine's local heirs, the autocrats of the several Western nations, and willingly ascribed to them by the theologians in their employ. We describe this today as the question of church and state and rejoice that (except for some Swiss cantons, some West German Länder, three departments of Eastern France, and the Church of England) that linkage belongs to the past, as does the Roman imperial form of the same with which the story had begun with the first Constantine.

But what does not belong to the past at all is the assumption that it is theologically proper to qualify as "church" the governmental institutions created by that linkage. To apply for membership in the World Council of "Churches," a "church" must possess a central bureaucracy

9. Until recently the same ecumenical center in northern Manhattan housed the offices not only of the National Council of Churches but also of the United Methodist and United Presbyterian churches and the United Church of Christ.

10. George Huntston Williams, *The Radical Reformation* (Philadelphia: Westminster, 1968), gave currency to this term. It points to the two dimensions, common to Anglicanism, Lutheranism, and Zwinglianism, which the text above spells out. I would have preferred the term "official" to designate what the three streams had in common, since in addition to magistracy and magisterium, whose definitional weight Williams describes, they also affirmed the centrality of the clerical office, even though they had different definitions of what the priest/preacher was to do.

of a certain size and reliability. Practically always such a "church" is a national body; i.e., its membership is defined by a political border and a state sovereignty claim. Only in rare cases is it larger. Some "churches" have in the past straddled the U.S./Canada border, but that is rapidly being remedied by Canadian nationalists. One Anglican province, namely in East Africa, encompasses more than one nation, but that is because it existed before the several colonies became separate nations. Yet, the general rule remains that a "church" about whose "catholicity" one can ask, is assumed to be a central bureaucracy on the geographic scale of a nation state.

The other definitional facet of the magisterial reformation was the magisterium. Each branch of the reformation looks back to the normative contribution of a professional theologian, who replaced the bishop as definer of true doctrine. Either he was based in the university, like Luther or the early Cranmer, or he founded one, like Zwingli and Calvin. Preaching was conceived as a magisterial function. True faith was defined by university-style documents ratified by the prince and used to control access both to the parish pulpit and to the university chair. Ever since, intellectualized border-defining formulations have taken priority, in the search for definitions of the parameters of communion, over the fuzzier terms of the Scriptures and the creeds.

Obviously neither civil control nor university theology is seen by most of us today as defining the ecumenical agenda. Yet, it remains the case that the problems we do most readily recognize are the legacy of those origins. When the Faith and Order Movement began in the 1920s, "Faith" was the code term designating the concern to affirm the search for unity in the face of the divisions defined by confessional writings. "Order" was the code term for concern for the differences about theologically warranted structures of national bureaucracy. Both parts of the agenda, in other words, both foci of differentiation, were magisterial, as were almost all of the churchmen coming together to talk about them. The definitional concerns of Baptists, Quakers, Disciples, or Pentecostals were simply not on the agenda, as Wilfried Garrison and Henry Pitney van Dusen said of "Faith and Order" as late as Lund (1952).[11]

---

11. Henry P. van Dusen, "Will Lund Be Ecumenical?" *Christian Century* (July 23, 1952): 848–51. Wilfred Ernest Garrison was one of those who spoke at Lund in a section on "Nontheological Factors Affecting the Ecumenical Movement." The illumination provided by that section has not been made much of since then in WCC circles. Garrison's own theme was the heritage of the state church connection: "Free Church and State Church," *Christian Century* (November 5, 1952): 1281–83.

The agenda of the ecumenical enterprise then seemed to be a search for the criteria whereby the several churches could recognize one another's claims to be validly "church." The criteria were to apply to doctrinal formulations ("faith") and to hierarchies ("order"); i.e., to magisterial structures. In the past, such criteria had served to reject one another as unfaithful; but it was thought that perhaps with better manners those schismatic decisions could be revoked. It was assumed that "the unity we seek," with those from whom we are divided, will be modeled for each communion on the nature of the unity we think we already have, with those from whom we think we are not divided. Thereby the structures of our present dividedness become both the paradigm for and the agents of the unity we say we want.

Perhaps the highwater mark of that vision in America was the sermon presented by Eugene Carson Blake, then the chief executive officer of the United Presbyterians, soon to be general secretary of the World Council, at the invitation of Anglican bishop James Pike, here in San Francisco's Grace Cathedral in December 1960. The proposal was for a majestic merger, at the top, of the virtues of what Blake considered to be the three main streams of American churchmanship: catholic, reformed, and evangelical.[12]

I could continue the narrative by watching the history of the Consultation on Church Union, which arose out of this proposal, as it moved from a 1970 document confidently called "Plan" to the one drafted in 1976, revised in 1980, more modestly called "In Quest." I could elaborate on how odd it was that it should so broadly have been taken for granted at the outset that the agencies qualified and willing to bring about the unification of the separated churches should be the structures of their present dividedness. We could review the wisdom of the developments within COCU between 1970 and 1980, as continuing conversations moved from a top-down merger model to a locally-based movement vision, whose participants would be accredited by the fact of their sharing in the process, not by their meeting someone else's previously defined requirements or by their joining someone else's organization or repeating someone else's confession.

Or I could move from here to supporting the Míguez Bonino argument cited at the outset by detailing the counterproductive effects of the magisterial bias on the politics of mainline ecumenism.

12. Paul A. Crow, Jr., and William Jerry Boney, *Church Union at Midpoint* (New York: Association Press, 1972); Gerald F. Moede, *Oneness in Christ: The Quest and Questions* (Princeton: Minute Press, 1981).

But it may be better for our purpose to drop the narrative here and to begin again with argument. We have followed the story far enough to see how widely the prevalent visions of that Christian unity that could authentically claim "catholicity" had initially been given their decisive shape by the historically unself-critical acceptance of the Constantinian settings within which those structures were created.

The logical alternative to someone else's design for merger is not my design for a merger; it is rather a search for modes of dialogue that do not begin by asking which structures are right. There have been such efforts; some helpful and some not. I propose to look at three of them.

The last words of the Gospel according to Matthew, cited above, projected, in the imperative mode, five dimensions of universality:

- the ascending Lord claimed all authority in heaven and on earth;
- the eleven were to make disciples of all the nations;
- they were to baptize them in the Triune name;
- they were to teach them all the commands he had given them;
- he would be with them always.

These five dimensions of "allness" or wholeness may suffice for now to state the metadefinitional catholic-making qualities we want to locate.

IV. Samples of Another Style

1. The late Albert Outler, in addition to being an interpreter of John Wesley, arguably the most catholic Anglican of the eighteenth century, was also a leader in the Faith and Order conversations of the World Council of Churches and an observer at the Second Vatican Council. His 1957 book *The Christian Tradition and the Unity We Seek*[13] is an early testimony to the insights later formulated by Míguez Bonino.

Outler demonstrated that the foundation of "The Unity We Seek" is the reality of a community presupposed by our efforts to express it, not the goal of our negotiations. That very phrase "the Unity We Seek" was the theme of a North American Faith and Order Conference, which was at that time being planned for Oberlin, Ohio, in September 1957.[14]

---

13. (New York: Oxford University Press).
14. The Oberlin theme was reflected in J. Robert Nelson, ed., *Christian Unity in North America* (St. Louis: Bethany Press, 1958). In that connection Albert Outler has an article "The Church Unity We Have," pp. 73–80, making the same point

The use of the phrase begins to delineate the relativizing of classical "Faith and Order" issues that Lund in 1952 had begun. Outler wrote,

> We deceive ourselves if we suppose that what we are waiting for . . . is an ecclesiological formulary so neat, so ingenious, and so imposing that we can all assent to it and then move easily into the ecumenical age. The time is not yet ripe for any such sort of theological "break through."[15]

No already present formula for reunion is sufficient. Communion with Rome, or with Lambeth, or with any given hierarchy or patriarchate, cannot be definitional, unless in the oddly backhanded and improbable way that one patriarch *might* abdicate his claims in favor of acknowledging other criteria of unity over which he has no control. Likewise there is no hope in reviewing past doctrinally frozen schisms, like the *filioque* controversy, in order to decide either which side was right or how to state a middle ground between them.

There is hope, on the contrary, Outler shows, in digging deep for the residual agreements that both parties at the time of schism retained from their common history. Outler continues,

> These agreements are almost always greater and more important than the controversialists had thought. . . . One is certain to find that the issues were ambiguous in themselves and that they had been disastrously constricted in the heat of doctrinal battle.[16]

Far from letting the great landmarks of reciprocal anathematization, even including Nicea or Chalcedon, define orthodoxy, we might let them define the agenda for reconciliation. Outler rejects any "primitivism" that would think that doctrinal development could be undone by reaching behind it to the Scriptures alone; yet, he affirms an ever renewed critical pertinence for the common witness to Christ at the center of the Scriptures,

> to measure all the traditions of any and every church by the single Christian tradition. By this standard, we might find a way to discriminate between those additive traditions which are necessary to the

---

reviewed above. My chapter, "A Historic Free Church View," pp. 89–97 in the same symposium (see pp. 222–30 above), represents an early effort to make the same point as this lecture.

15. Outler, op. cit., p. 148.
16. Outler, op. cit., p. 13.

effectual transmission of the Christian tradition, and those which are indifferent, superfluous, or misleading.[17]

There is, in other words, a perennial recourse to the Scriptures. They are never to be left behind; what Outler calls "additive traditions," like what others call "development of doctrine," may be legitimate, but they need to be validated case by case by the demonstration that they are necessary to ensure faithfulness.

In sum: there is no way to locate the unity we seek before the process of seeking together. We can name no see, no symbol, no compendium of propositions that would not be part of the debate. Within the debate itself, the Scriptures will have decisive authority. This will not occur in a naive way, as if later development should not have happened or could have not happened; that would be to make the Bible itself a frozen compendium of propositions. (Some use the term "primitivist" to designate this kind of antihistorical naiveté; but that petitionary name-calling is just as dysfunctional as are the petitionary uses of "catholic.") But neither can any post-apostolic trajectory be permitted to leave the Bible behind as a launching pad, from which, once in orbit, the spaceship church no longer needs to get its signals.

What we need to "locate" is then the dialogical process itself, where the shared backgrounds and the divergent developments nourish a common contemporary confession.

2. A commission of fourteen Anglo-Catholics, named by the archbishop of Canterbury in 1945 and reporting to him in 1947, were asked to project a vision of "catholicity" in the face of the dividedness of the Protestant and Catholic traditions in the West.[18] These fourteen men transcended their mandate and corrected it wisely by noting the need to consider not only magisterial protestantism but also the liberalism derived from the renaissance. Thereby they relativized, in a way I applaud, the original assumption that all that is needed is for two separated establishments to renegotiate their reunion. They did not, I regret, with equal independence and attentiveness, include in the picture the non-magisterial streams of renewal and mission, which have been important in British Christian history for three and one-half centuries. They very properly rejected any simple vision of "synthesis by

17. Outler, op. cit., p. 127.
18. E. S. Abbott, H. J. Carpenter, et al., *Catholicity: A Study in the Conflict of Christian Traditions in the West* (London: Dacre Press, 1947). I am grateful to professors J. McClendon, Jr., and Guy Lytle of CDSP for the suggestion that this document would be helpful.

way of fastening broken pieces together," as well as the "common denominator" approach of meeting around what we agree on and declaring unimportant what we disagree about.

The fourteen men did not, as I noted, attend to the presence of the free churches within catholic and protestant reality. Even less did they attend to the substantive witness of the free churches at the points where magisterial protestants and catholics historically have agreed among themselves; infant baptism, the linkage of church and state, the morality of war, the concern of the church for religious liberty and political democracy, the place of subjective experience, the place of world missions. These are concerns many Anglicans now share, though historically they would not have been part of a "Catholic" list of criteria. It would, therefore, be out of place for me to evaluate, as a contribution to our conversation, the substantive positions they held on those matters *tacitly* but did not bother to argue. I doubt that all Anglo-Catholics would agree today, on *all* of those matters, with the Church of England and against the Baptists and Quakers. Noting the fact of their silence on these matters is important. It demonstrates that anyone's vision of the "wholeness" they seek is inevitably parochial, contained and constrained by particular past phrasings of what is at stake.

Nor did the commission face with any critical distance the challenge of the rules of advocacy. Having been chosen from and asked to work within one narrow field, they assumed the rightness of their *via media* as the place from which to name the errors of Luther, Calvin, Trent, and liberalism.[19] Much of the time I would agree with their (historically descriptive) judgments (on those matters); but it would be more important to know how they would further have sustained their consensus if the interlocutors had been present and alive. Generally the wrongness of those other views (when taken alone) is rather asserted than argued, in ways by which the Lutherans, Calvinists, and Tridentines I know would not be convinced.

What especially qualifies the fourteen Anglo-Catholic men to figure in this discussion is, however, a position they stated that I have not yet mentioned; namely, that they unapologetically describe the wholeness they seek as "primitive" (their word).[20] They find it instantiated in the New Testament more adequately than in any later time or

19. In this sense what they do is like the Wainwright volume cited above; they describe the world in such a way that they are at the center.

20. Pp. 11ff.

place. They do not argue this normativeness of the apostolic age; they simply take it for granted.

They distinguish their scriptural appeal from that of later protestant biblicism, as Outler did with his scriptural appeal; but they do not, as did the Roman stance canonized at Trent, affirm a second competing or corrective channel of revelation. They do identify three "inevitable tensions" within the apostolic witness, which over the centuries were to demand change beyond the shape of the apostolic churches and were (unfortunately) to produce schism; but they do not claim that in some medieval or Elizabethan synthesis a normative post-biblical resolution of those tensions was ever achieved. Nor do they invite all other Christians to institutional "reunion" with some specific see, whether Rome or Canterbury as now self-defined, as the cure we need.

The cure we need, they say, is on the level of vision. It is not representativity according to the Vincentian canons but a many-dimensional wholeness as contrasted to partiality or fragmentation. Its accomplishment in the modern world is ahead of us, and they do not locate the path to it.

3. Beside these first two serious testimonies, I propose to place in comic relief a more recent and less responsible one, which came to hand while I was preparing this study. The Jesuit journal *America* published an article entitled "Being Catholic — Even If You Can't Become One."[21] The very title represents the semantic complexity of the concept. "You can't become one" refers specifically to Roman Catholic membership, which is inaccessible to the author because, he says, he "does not feel called" to that — not a very canonical criterion. On the other hand, "catholic" "with a small c" denotes a normative quality of openness that the author defines in three ways:

- "putting a priority on collegiality," which he in turn defines as not imposing one's beliefs on others by force;
- "learning to feel 'at home' in church, regardless of the distinctive practices of the particular congregation in whose midst we worship" and despite one's not communicating in the Eucharist one observes; and
- "accepting the boundlessness of the church," refusing to be "segregated by the divisions that human beings have invented."

21. *America* 24 (February 1990): 173.

All three of these traits, native to a loose and modernizing construal of the author's Disciples of Christ tradition, feel as warm to me as they are fuzzy; but there is no way to explain, and it does not occur to the author to bother to explain, why they should constitute the definition of "catholic." If they seem attractive to the readers of *America* it is because they fit with the inclusive civility of our liberal culture, not because the author has provided some accountable procedure to validate them as metacriteria, even less to put them in the place of all the other more traditional marks.

He then proceeds to suggest, not as the marks of his own (small-c) catholicity, but as possible gestures of reciprocal good manners, a handful of practical though superficial ways in which Roman Catholic worship might be so managed as to make noncommunicants feel more at home. He does not take note of the issue, openly contested in Faith and Order circles at least since Montreal (1963), of whether noncommunicant spectators belong at all to the meaning of Eucharist, or (to turn the same question around) why it should qualify me as "catholic" that I be spectator at the performance of a liturgy from which I accept being excluded.

V. The Marks of Another Solution

I hope that this survey of the insufficiency of past patterns of analysis may have indicated where we should look next in the light of the risen Lord's mandates with which I began.

A. If our claim is that the Word we serve is everywhere accredited by the Holy Spirit, then a mark of its authenticity will be our renouncing any of the tools of privilege and power in defining it. What is wrong with the use of the sanctions of Caesar to support the uniformity of the church is not that it sins against some modern vision of the separation of the realms of church and state; it is that it qualifies the universal authority of the risen Lord and short-circuits the dialogical freedom whereby God the Spirit brings her people to unity. It thereby imposes in a given time and place formulations from other times and places, which could not make their way in the open kind of conversation reported in Acts 15 and prescribed by 1 Corinthians 14. It is fascinating that in the report of the fourteen Anglo-Catholic men, despite the disestablishment witness borne in England since the age of Elizabeth and acceded to *by governments* since 1689, there is not a word about the way in which the role of England's Parliament and Crown has been a cause of ecclesiastical division.

B. If we acknowledge that our witness and ministry are imperfect, fallible, in need of correction, then a mark of our honesty will be the affirmation of reformation as a constant need. Calvin is credited with the dictum, *ecclesia reformata semper reformanda* — the church even when reformed always still needs reforming. Reformation is not something which had to happen once, or which might need to happen in a time of emergency once every several centuries, between which the established authorities properly should manage the legacy of the last reform in prudently conservative ways. There is no time when there is not a contemporary issue demanding critical scrutiny and structural change. The challenges addressed today by feminism to patriarchal visions of ministry, or by the base communities to ritualistic notions of sacrament, or to absentee notions of episcopacy, are contributions to, not criticisms of, catholicity properly conceived.

C. If we give to the Vincentian *ubique*, "everywhere," or to Jesus' naming "all the nations," a positive rather than a negative definition, then the functional definition of faith must be local; it must occur in each place freely. At the outset I used the noun "locality" in the geometric sense; now I use it in the colloquial, geographic sense. In a formulation derived from the Faith and Order study process, drafted at St. Andrew's just before then and approved at New Delhi in 1961, it is said that "the unity we seek" is that

> all in each place who are baptized into Jesus Christ and confess him as Lord and Savior are brought by the Holy Spirit into one fully committed fellowship, breaking the one bread, joining in common prayer, and having a corporate life reaching out in witness and service to all and who at the same time are united with the whole Christian fellowship in all places and all ages in such wise that ministry and members are accepted by all, and that all can act and speak together as occasion requires for the tasks to which God calls his people.[22]

As compromise committee documents tend to do, this one left to others to define some of the terms. How large can a "place" be? Could it be as large as the city of Geneva? The great Anglican missionary bishop Stephen Neill defined it as an agglomeration small enough that one can get to open fields by walking twenty minutes, which (then, he thought) was a criterion Geneva met. Can a "place" really be larger

---

22. W. A. Visser 't Hooft, ed., *The New Delhi Report*, alternate title *Jesus Christ the Light of the World* (New York: Association Press, 1962). The report of the section on unity runs pp. 116–34, and the quoted section is on p. 116.

than a parish and do the things the statement describes? Might it have to be smaller than a parish?

The St. Andrew's wording is at least open to the stronger reading, namely that "each place" must be functionally so defined that the people who thus meet together can do so repeatedly, regularly, if not daily or weekly, so as responsibly to support and govern the ministries exercised in their name. The normal designation used by historians for that position since the late sixteenth century is "congregationalism." It is, however, not incompatible with the theological case that can be made for episcopacy or for presbyterianism, as long as the geographical or numerical size of the diocese or synod is not unmanageably large.[23]

C.1. A subfield in the application of this criterion of locality is that whatever be the definition one holds of any pertinent ecclesiological criterion, it must be patient of being so formulated that it can be met everywhere. As the Anglican missionary Roland Allen showed in East Africa three generations ago, Anglicans were giving the lie to their official affirmations about the indispensable place of the priesthood, and of the Eucharist, when they so defined access to the priestly office (namely in terms of British graduate education) that most villages in East Africa could not be served by a resident ordained priest.

The same point is being made again today in the Latin American base communities; Roman Catholics do not really believe that frequent eucharistic communion is necessary to the Christian life, if they so define the sacramental priesthood (in terms of education and celibacy) that most believers will most of the time not have a priest in their midst.

The claim that episcopacy is normatively constitutive of valid ecclesiastical experience — at least as that claim can be based on the "primitive unity" of the first centuries — is singularly weakened if the diocese is permitted to be so large that fewer than one percent of the faithful can regularly worship with their bishop present.

C.2. A second subset in the meaning of locality is the concern for the rules of dialogue in decision making; something that neither Albert Outler nor the fourteen Englishmen overtly attend to. Paul wrote to the Corinthians that the authority of the Holy Spirit would be functionally discernible locally in two ways:

---

23. The free church tradition would find nothing wrong with the notion of "bishops," since the word is biblical, if it were not given an antibiblical definition on post-biblical grounds. Cf. my "Could There Be a Baptist Bishop?" in *Ecumenical Trends* 9/7 (July/August 1980): 104–7.

a. in that every member of the body would know herself bearer of a particular charismatic empowerment to be exercised in the unity of the body,[24] and

b. in that in a meeting everyone would have the authority to take the floor and everyone would listen.[25]

To these the Gospels add a third:

c. According to the only passages of the Gospels where Jesus speaks of the church, the Spirit works through a local procedure of "binding and loosing," or reconciling admonition. "If your brother or sister sins, talk to him or her." The Reformers of the sixteenth century, probably standing on the shoulders of pre-reformation renewal communities, referred to this guidance as "The Rule of Christ."[26] For both Martin Luther and Martin Bucer it was a mandatory practice, distinct from the Roman practice of penitence and absolution in not being the possession of the clergy. Long after Luther and Bucer had abandoned hope of seeing such a practice realized, it remained constitutive in the "baptist" wing of the reformation they had helped to begin.

Each of these modes of spirit working was, in the twelfth or sixteenth or eighteenth century as in the first, countercultural and socially subversive, yet in no sense ahistorical or anarchic. Each demands congregational location.[27] None is according to the New Testament description the possession of clergy. The kind of "wholeness" they represent is denied by any clericalism that claims that being "church" can be authenticated by criteria applying only to priestly leadership. They have been denied systematically, although not always expressly, by the magisterial definers of ecumenical priorities. These

24. Most simply in Rom. 12:3–13, 1 Cor. 12, Eph. 4:4–16; cf. my *The Fullness of Christ* (Elgin: Brethren Press, 1987).

25. Most simply in 1 Cor. 14. Cf. "the Rule of Paul" in my "The Hermeneutics of the Anabaptists," pp. 11–28 in Willard Swartley, ed., *Essays on Biblical Interpretation* (Elkhart, Ind.: Institute of Mennonite Studies, 1984), and in my *Body Politics* (Nashville: Discipleship Resources, 1993): 61ff.

26. "Rule of Christ" is a sixteenth-century usage for the process of moral discernment described in both of the texts cited in note 25. For a discussion of this practice, see Ervin A. Schlabach, "The Rule of Christ among the Early Swiss Anabaptists," Th.D. diss., Chicago Theological Seminary, 1977.

27. As I indicated in notes 2 and 23, the old debate about "connections" versus congregationalism is misdirected. There is no place where this quality of conversation is excluded. Whenever it happens it is in some place, i.e., local. The crucial problem is not what "local" means but what happening we are looking for.

three procedural marks of locality are undeniably part of the wholeness normatively described in the apostolic Scriptures. They — and other functionally definable local marks we could add[28] — are the requisites of survival and mission in a setting, whether before or after the Constantinian age, where central powers are not on our side.

A first, formal and superficial reading of where these comments leave us, would be that I have simply set before you yet one more typical and typological polarity between two definitions of wholeness, with the standard claim that my definition is better. I could argue that my free church vision of wholeness is more whole than that of the reader,[29] just as the fourteen Englishmen could make the same petitionary argument in the other direction. I could claim for the "baptist" vision a greater missionary effectiveness in a hostile world, and the fourteen could claim greater cultural success in the Western world from Constantine to Churchill; then we could raise the circularity to a higher level by challenging each others' views of "effectiveness." I would claim greater fidelity to the social shape of the apostolic community life, and they would claim greater breadth in unfolding the evolutionary potential of the apostles' concepts. I would claim greater resilience in the cause of liberation and they would claim greater respect for the cultural achievements of Christendom. Each party would claim the capacity to envelope the other.

Even with all its frustrating circularity this debate would be preferable to some other debates. Both sides would agree on some important matters. Neither party names as vehicle of its vision a single extant bureaucracy. Not doing so costs me or James McClendon, Jr., very little,[30] whereas for the fourteen appointees of Canterbury it took some integrity to avoid that shortcut.

Neither formally advocates caesaropapism, although the fourteen Anglo-Catholics weaken singularly their rejection of it by saying that only the Byzantine church "became too dependent on the civil power" while "the West has never allowed Caesar to make law in the things of God."[31] This statement is simply false, unless some of the terms be

28. Some of the additional functional marks are also described in *Body Politics* (n. 25 above).

29. Or than that of the predominantly Anglican audience of the Berkeley lecture.

30. The "free church" or "baptist" vision is not opposed to the existence of denominational agencies, although it denies that they are the privileged bearers of legitimacy. Thus the statement just cited from the fourteen Anglicans is a greater concession on their part than agreeing with them is on ours.

31. P. 19.

given very special definitions. Nonetheless, I rejoice that behind the misstatement of fact there is an implied intent to disavow the Erastian stance,[32] without whose power in the sixteenth and seventeenth centuries Anglicanism as we know it might not exist.

The difference that matters, wherein my formulation is not countered by any alternative in the 1947 Anglo-Catholic text, is that mine has location in both senses of the term. It says in a systematic and formal way what must happen, namely that there must be substantial contemporary dialogue in the light of Scripture. Catholicity has been located, in that formal sense, wherever and whenever everyone concerned converses about everything they do and should believe and do as they respond to the Lord who sent them to all the nations with all that he had taught them. Such formal catholicity is denied if any people, or any subjects, are excluded from that conversation.

Catholicity has secondly been "located" in that no one place, not Rome or Canterbury, Geneva or Rhodes is privileged; such conversation must take place everywhere. Normative criterion for these conversations, as for the others a fuller list might add, will be the common loyalty to the Scriptures, setting aside (as Outler and the fourteen agree with me in doing) both the caricature of primitivist fundamentalism and that of progressivist evolutionism. The procedural criterion will be the game rules cited above,[33] grounded in the enablement of the Holy Spirit. All may speak, in orderly ways, and all must listen.

It is not a shortcoming for this vision, as it would be for some others, that it is primarily procedural. Does it necessarily include the wording of Nicea? Episcopal succession? A specific understanding of the Eucharist or of predestination? The "Lambeth quadrilateral"? The so-called Wesleyan Quadrilateral? The six "marks of the church" articulated by Anglican bishop Stephen Neill?[34] The other six of Visser 't Hooft? We'll have to see. No such formula and no set of four of them can be stipulated from outside as prerequisite to the conversational process; each of them, if validly "catholic," should be able to stand up to fraternal scrutiny. It is thus fitting not only procedurally but also substantially that we begin with the role of discernment. It is not as if

---

32. Thomas Erastus, 1524–83, a Swiss-born physician teaching in Heidelberg, participant in debates about reform, came to be recognized as the most able advocate of the view that the church should be reformed by civil rulers, as happened most simply in Zurich and in England.

33. Cf. above notes 24–26.

34. The lists from Neill and Visser 't Hooft are interpreted more fully in "A People in the World" (pp. 65–101 above).

liturgy or works of love were less characteristic of catholic faith than is discerning dialogue; yet, they are less representative of the challenge of location. Catholic existence will not be achieved by one decisive act but asymptotically, cumulatively, through communication processes that fulfill more or less our common calling.

This conversation must, as an activity of the *ecclesia semper reformanda,* denounce present and future as well as past unfaithfulness. Future agenda may reopen the issue of infant baptism, as Romans, Anglicans, Lutherans, and Reformed have been doing recently, not because they have listened to the Baptists or "the baptists" — as James McClendon, Jr., uses the term — but because they have begun to be pastorally honest about the breakdown of establishment. It will have to reopen the issue of justifiable war, as the Romans, the Methodists, and the World Council of Churches have been doing, not because they have been listening to Quakers or Mennonites, but because they have begun to be more honest about the demands arising from their own avowal of "just war" categories. It will have to reopen the issue of sacerdotal paternalism, not because of having heard George Fox or William Booth or Alexander Campbell, but because the yet unheard witness of the Apostle Paul to the charismatic endowment of all members coincides with the Freirian imperative of underdog empowerment.[35]

Catholicity is not "looking for a home" in the sense of a vagabond who "once lodged will no longer roam"; it is a lived reality that will have its place or "location" wherever all comers participate, in the power of the Triune God, in proclaiming to all nations (beginning where they are) all that Jesus taught. Only if the avowed agenda is that broad and that open can we claim the promises of the Lord who pledged that he would accompany us to the end of the age.

35. Paulo Freire, *A Pedagogy of the Oppressed* (New York: Seabury, 1970).

IV. Radical Catholicity

Binding and Loosing

"Binding and Loosing" originated in a study outline designed to explicate the practice of church discipline described in Matthew 18:15–20. It was published as a whole for the first time in *Concern* 14 (February 1967): 2–32. In that publication, it was paired with a treatise (pp. 33–43) by Balthasar Hubmaier, "On Fraternal Admonition: 'Where this is lacking there is certainly no church even if Water Baptism and the Supper of Christ are practiced'" (1527).[1] This latter document has since been made available in a scholarly collection of Hubmaier's writings, *Balthasar Hubmaier: Theologian of Anabaptism*, translated and edited by H. Wayne Pipkin and John H. Yoder for the Classics of the Radical Reformation series (Scottdale, Penn.: Herald Press, 1989): 372–85. After the last copies of the *Concern* pamphlet were sold, mimeograph copies of the study outline were circulated upon request for many years. In 1985, it was reprinted as an appendix to John White and Ken Blue, *Healing the Wounded: The Costly Love of*

---

1. Dr. Balthasar Hubmaier was one of the most striking figures in the Reformation of the 1520s. A trained theologian, once vice-rector of the University of Ingolstadt, he was the only Anabaptist to come out of the official Roman Catholic intellectual circles. A most gifted and popular preacher, he was in his Catholic days cathedral preacher at Regensburg and could with his preaching touch off anti-Semitic violence and create a center of Marian pilgrimages.

Expert popularizer, he produced in his "On the Christian Baptism of Believers" (1525) the first and classic tract on baptism, and in his several catechetical and liturgical writings translated the concept of the believer's church into the flesh and bones of church order. By far the most prolific Anabaptist writer of the 1520s (nineteen printed works in a little over two years), he has been underestimated by Mennonites because of his acceptance of the sword.

Church Discipline (Downers Grove, Ill.: InterVarsity Press, 1985): 211–38. For the most part, the text appears here in substantially the same form as in *Healing the Wounded*. The translation of the text of Matthew 18:15–20 has been revised and section XIII, "Cavils and Caveats: Retrospect on Binding and Loosing," has been added to address questions that have been raised in the last twenty-five years about the practice of admonition.

Here we find Yoder working at a very practical task: spelling out the issues surrounding the practice of fraternal admonition or "the rule of Christ" as it is sometimes known in believers' church circles. Yoder presumed that the readership of this "study outline" would be primarily, if not exclusively, members of church congregations. For this reason, the text is largely unencumbered by textual apparatus; questions for discussion were included should groups want to use them for that purpose. Although widely used in Mennonite circles in the 1960s, this study outline has also been used by non-Mennonites in the decades since it was written. In fact, this piece is authentically ecumenical, in the sense that it challenges *all* Christian groups. At the same time, Yoder is aware that the discussion does constitute a kind of "position" with which the reader may well debate. As he states early in the discussion, the position is hard to pigeonhole precisely because "[i]t gives more authority to the church than does Rome, trusts more to the Holy Spirit than does Pentecostalism, has more respect for the individual than humanism, makes moral standards more binding than puritanism, is more open to the given situation than the 'new morality.' "

Although one might be tempted to regard this piece as primarily oriented toward the practical, and therefore not necessarily theologically provocative, Yoder does articulate several ecclesiological insights in this piece that are notable for both their brevity and pithiness. For example, Yoder specifies the distinctiveness of the character of the gathered community where mutual admonition is practiced. "*The process of binding and loosing in the local community of faith* provides the practical and theological foundation for the centrality of the local congregation. It is not correct to say, as some extreme Baptists and Churches of Christ do, that only the local gathering of Christians can be called 'the church.' The Bible uses the term church for all of the Christians in a large city or even in a province. The concept of local congregational autonomy has, therefore, been misunderstood when it was held to deny mutual responsibilities between congregations or between Christians of different congregations." As this passage suggests, and as Yoder himself notes, the practice of fraternal admonition should not be associated only with traditions characterized by congregational polities; the "rule of Christ" also involves the kind of "connectional" relationships found in the Wesleyan and Roman Catholic traditions, as well as with diverse Christian renewal movements.

As can be seen in the essay on "Catholicity in Search of Location" in this collection (pp. 300–320), Yoder has continued to explore the tensions between the primary relationships of Christians within a covenanted congregation and the connectional relationship of Christians in different congregations. In this way, Yoder raises serious questions about what it would mean to maintain ecumenical relationships across denominational lines as well as within historical traditions of Christianity.

Binding and Loosing

> Better a frank word of reproof than the love that will not speak;
> Faithful are the wounds of a friend.
>
> Proverbs 27:5–6 (Moffatt)

A study outline is intentionally a skeleton, unevenly filled out. It is not written for smooth and easy reading nor for completeness and balance. The careful reader, evaluating it as an essay, will find the presentation fragmentary. The theologically alert reader will resent the absence of efforts to relate to the range of current schools of thought. Questions of historical or textual criticism are avoided. Texts are taken straightforwardly in a way that may seem naive. "How-to-do-it" concerns are mixed with the meaning of atonement with no respect for pigeonholing. No energy has been invested in explaining how this simplification differs from fundamentalism in method or motive.

The position suggested here may seem to gather together the dangers of several ecclesiastical scarecrows. It gives more authority to the church than does Rome, trusts more to the Holy Spirit than does Pentecostalism, has more respect for the individual than humanism, makes moral standards more binding than puritanism, is more open to the given situation than the "new morality." If practiced it would change the life of churches more fundamentally than has yet been suggested by the perennially popular discussions of changing church structures.

Thus the path to the rediscovery of Christian faithfulness may lead right through some positions modern Christian "moderates" have been trying to avoid. The concern expressed here does not fit at any one point on the "map" of traditional denominational positions — which may just show that something is wrong with the map. The positions taken will seem strange to Christians of many schools of thought — and yet it echoes a conviction historically present in many Christian traditions.

In leaving to one side other aspects of the problem of church renewal, and in opening up this one particular topic in this simple, generally accessible, apparently dogmatic way, I imply no claim that oversimplification is generally a way to solve problems. The naive form is a discussion-starting method and not a theological stance.

I. The Key Text — Matthew 18:15–20

15 If your brother or sister sins,
      go† and reprimand that person
      between the two of you, alone;

16 If that person listens,
      you have won your brother or sister.

17 If not, take with you one or two more,
      so that every matter may be established
      by the mouth of two or three witnesses.*
    If the person will not listen to them,
      tell it to the church.
      If the person will not listen to the church either,
      let such a person be to you as a pagan or a taxgatherer.

18 I tell you‡ truly,
      whatever you bind on earth shall be bound in heaven
      and whatever you loose on earth shall be loosed in heaven;

†In the first four verses the "you" is always singular.
*Deut. 19:15.
‡For the rest of the text, "you" is the plural.

326

Discussion questions on Matthew 18:15–20.

- Note your first impressions of the passage under consideration before continuing with further study.
- What is the purpose of dealing with a brother or sister in this way?
- Is this way of dealing with a fellow Christian the responsibility of every Christian? Or only of the one sinned against? Or only of church officers?
- What do you take "binding" and "loosing" in verse 18 to mean?
- Can you think of other New Testament texts on this subject or is it an isolated idea?
- Has the practice that Jesus describes here been a part of your experience as a Christian?

II. The Twofold Meaning of "Binding" and "Loosing"

In the sweeping summary authorization that he gives the church, Jesus uses the verbs "bind" and "loose" in a way that takes for granted that their meaning is clear to his listeners. Centuries later, when neither secular nor religious usage has retained the pair of terms, we must resurrect their meaning. Perhaps the very fact that the terms no longer have a customary sense in current language may permit us to use them now as a "technical" label for the practice Jesus commanded.

A. *Two aspects of meaning.* There are clearly two dimensions to the meaning of these verbs;

(1) Forgiveness: to "bind" is to withhold fellowship, to "loose" is to forgive. This is supported by the parallel texts in Luke 17:3 (based in turn on Lev. 19:17; note the other elements in Luke 17:14 that are also parallel to Matt. 18:14 and 18:21–22) and in John 20:25. It is supported as well by the other portions of Matthew 18 (10–14, the hundredth sheep; 21–22, seventy times seven; 23–35, the unmerciful servant).

(2) Moral discernment: To "bind" is to enjoin, to forbid or make obligatory; to "loose" is to leave free, to permit. We recognize the root *ligare* "to bind" in *obligate, ligament, league.* Thus the New English Bible translates "forbid" and "allow."

This was the current, precise technical meaning that the terms "bind" and "loose" (i.e., their Aramaic equivalents) probably had in the language of the rabbis of Jesus' time. Moral teaching and decision making in Judaism took the form of rulings by the rabbis on problem cases brought to them, either "binding" or "loosing" depending on how they saw the Law applying to each case.[2]

Out of these decisions there accumulated a fund of precedents and principles called the *halakah*, the moral tradition, which continued from one generation to the next to be useful in relating the Law to current problems. By taking over these terms from rabbinic usage, Jesus assigns to his disciples an authority to bind and loose previously claimed only by the teachers in Israel.

This dimension of meaning is the one emphasized in the parallel phrasing of Matthew 16:19 and is further confirmed when we look at Matthew 18:15–20 more closely. Verses 15–17, describing the direct dealings with the brother, are spoken in the singular; but the following verses shift to the plural. This suggests that the authorization of 18–20 may have a broader import for the church than that of the immediate disciplinary context.

B. *The relation of forgiveness and discernment.* At first sight these two activities would seem not to be closely related; yet, on closer analysis their intimate interrelation becomes clear:

(1) Forgiving presupposes prior discernment. Jesus' words startle the modern reader with the simplicity of his beginning: "If your brother or sister sins. . . ." In our age of tolerance and confusion we are not used to thinking of "sin" as that easily identifiable. Jesus assumes that the moral standards by which sin is to be identified are knowable and known. He further assumes that the offender and those who reprove him share a common moral yardstick.

(2) Forgiving furthers discernment. If the standards appealed to by those who would reprove someone are inappropriate, the best way to discover this is through the procedure of person-to-person conversation with reconciling intent. Thus the group's standards can be challenged, tested and confirmed, or changed as is found necessary, in the course of their being applied. The result of the process, whether it ends with the standards being changed or reconfirmed, is to record a new decision as part of the common background of the community, thus accumulating further moral insights by which to be guided in the future.

(3) Discernment necessitates forgiveness. There is in every serious problem a dimension of personal offense or estrangement. This is the case even when the issue at stake is quite "impersonal" or "technical" or "objective." Therefore, in every right decision there must be an

2. Cf. pp. 357–58 below, XIV/A.

element of reconciliation. The idea that questions of right and wrong could best be studied somehow "objectively" or "disinterestedly" is in itself an unrealistic misunderstanding of the personal character of every decision-making process.

(4) Forgiving concern sets the limits of our responsibility for one another's decisions. If I am a Christian at all, what I do is my brother's and my sister's business. We owe one another counsel and, sometimes, correction and pardon. Yet, it is neither possible nor desirable for my brother or sister to be concerned with or responsible for all that I do. What then is the point where the search for a common mind ends and individual variation and personal responsibility begins?

The most current answer is that big sins are the church's business and small ones are not. Yet, every effort to draw that line leads to legalism, and to concern with the deed rather than the doer, with guilt rather than restoration.

The correlation of the two concerns of forgiveness and discernment provides another answer, though not an abstract one, to this question. Differences of conviction and behavior are unacceptable *when they offend*. The "line" is not drawn theoretically but in terms of personality and interpersonal concern. If the difference destroys fellowship, it is for that reason a topic for reconciling concern. Any variance not dealt with, on the grounds that it is unimportant, becomes increasingly important with the passage of time. Unattended, it magnifies the next conflict as well.

But if, on the other hand, Christians have been accustomed to dealing with one another in love and have been finding that they are able to be reconciled whenever they deal with a matter in love, then they find as well that their "tolerance threshold" rises. A spirit of mutual trust grows, in which fewer differences offend.

Thus both the necessity of dealing with some differences and the possibility of leaving other matters to individual liberty are rooted in the very process of the reconciling approach.

"Forgiveness" and "discernment" do not point to two alternative meanings of the same words, whereby one would always need to choose which meaning applies. Forgiveness and discernment are not two poles of a tension but two sides of a coin. Each presupposes and includes the other. In the following pages we shall deal predominantly with the "forgiveness" face of the coin but never as if this excluded the other aspect of moral discernment.

329

Discussion questions on the meaning of binding and loosing.

- Before reading further, note your first reactions on reading that Jesus authorizes his disciples: (a) to forgive sins; and (b) to make binding moral decisions.
- What place has forgiveness had until now in your concept of what the church is for in your experience of church?
- Can you be deeply reconciled with your brother or sister while disagreeing on moral decisions?
- Can you tolerate disagreement with someone you have forgiven or who has forgiven you?
- Can you agree on moral issues with someone you have not forgiven? Are you more critical of someone you have not forgiven?

III. The Source of the Authority to Bind and Loose

A. *The authority given the church is parallel to the authority of Christ himself* (John 20:19–23). Throughout Jesus' ministry, especially as recorded in the fourth Gospel, Jesus scandalized the authorities by his claims to have been sent by the Father in a unique way (5:18ff., 6:30ff., 7:28ff., 8:36ff., 10:25ff.). Now he tells his disciples, "Just as the Father sent me, so I send you."

If it was possible to be yet more offensive to official reverence, it was when Jesus took it upon himself to forgive sins (Mark 2:7; Luke 7:48ff.); yet, this too is what the disciples are charged to do. He lays upon them, and thereby upon us, the same power he claimed for himself.

B. *The scandal of the divine mandate.* We do not fully understand the grandeur of this commission if we are not first shocked by it as were Jesus' contemporaries. Not only were his contemporaries shocked (Mark 1:7, they called it blasphemy); Protestants today are shocked, too. Reacting against the abuses of Roman Catholic penitential practice (see below, section IX/E), Protestants have for centuries been arguing that "only God can forgive." and that the believer receives reassurance of forgiveness not from another person but in the secret of his or her own heart.

In the later development of Judaism as well, a distinction developed between interpersonal adjudication or reconciliation or forgiveness, which the community deals with, and Atonement, accorded by God alone, which is the theme of the annual Holy Day.

The heat and vigor of this old Protestant-Catholic debate point us to the difficulty we have in conceiving, and in believing, that God really can authorize ordinary humans to commit him, that is, to forbid and to forgive on his behalf with the assurance that the action stands "in heaven." How can it be, and what can it mean, that such powers are placed in the hands of ordinary people the likes of Peter? The jealous concern of religious leaders, and of all religion, for the transcendence of God, for his untouchability and his distance from us, might have been able to adjust, or to make an exception, for arrogant claims like this made on behalf of some most exceptional person, a high priest or a grand rabbi, a prophet or king. But the real scandal of the way God chose to work among humans — what we call the Incarnation — is that it was an ordinary working man from Nazareth who commissioned a crew of ordinary people — former fishermen and taxgatherers — *to forgive sins.*

C. *The church is empowered by the Holy Spirit.* The text in John 20 links the imparting of the Holy Spirit directly with the commission to forgive. According to John 14:16, the functions of the promised Spirit will be to "convince," to "lead into all truth," and to remind believers of teachings of Jesus that they had not grasped before.

In Acts 1 and 2 the function of the Spirit is to empower the disciples to be witnesses; but in the rest of the story of Acts, notably in the decisions of chapters 13 and 15, but also in the modest details of Paul's travel arrangements, the Spirit is active especially in making decisions. If the proportionate space given to various themes is indicative, the basic work of the Holy Spirit according to Acts is to guide in discernment. Prophecy, testimony, inward conviction, and empowerment for obedience are subordinate aspects of that work.

The promise of the presence of Christ "where two or three are gathered in my name" is often understood in modern Protestantism as meaning either that there are grounds for belief in the efficacy of prayer or that the gathered congregation may sense a spiritual presence in their midst. Yet, in the original context of Matthew 18:19–20 its application is to the consensus (the verb is *sumphonein,* from which we get "symphony") reached by the divinely authorized process of decision.[3] The "two or three others" are the witnesses required in the Mosaic law for a judicial proceeding to be formally valid (Deut. 17:6; 19:15; applied in Num. 35:30; 2 Cor. 13:1; 1 Tim. 5:19; Heb. 10:28).

3. Rabbi Hananjah ben Teradion (d. 135) said, "when two sit and there are between them words of Torah, the Shechinah rests between them . . . " (*Aboth* Sayings of the Fathers III/3; other looser parallels in III/4, III/7, IV/10; brought to my attention by Michael Signer).

D. *This mandate makes the church the church.* The Greek word *ekklesia* ("church") is found only twice in the Gospels coming from Jesus' lips; the two times are the two "bind and loose" passages. The word *ekklesia* itself (like the earlier Hebrew term and the Aramaic equivalent that Jesus probably used) does not refer to a specifically religious meeting nor to a particular organization; rather it means the "assembly," the gathering of a people into a meeting for deliberation or for a public announcement. It is no accident that in Matthew 16 the assignment by Jesus of the power to bind and loose follows directly upon Peter's first confession of Christ as Messiah. The confession is the basis of the authority; the authorization given is the seal upon the confession. The church is where, because there Jesus is confessed as Christ, men and women are empowered to speak to one another in God's name.

Discussion questions on the church's authorization.

- Are there many different activities, or only a few, that Jesus specifically ordered the church to carry out in his name?
- Read John 16 and the story in Acts to check on the statements made in Section C, above, concerning the work of the Holy Spirit.
- What teaching do you remember in the past about who can forgive sin?

IV. The Way of Dealing with the Brother or Sister Is Determined by the Reconciling Intent

A. *The reconciling approach is personal.* The entire section 18:15–18 is in the singular: it is a command to the individual. The point of the passage is not that there must be just three steps (rather than four or five) but that (1) the first encounter is "between the two of you alone"; and that (2) still another small group effort at mediation is made, if the first attempt has failed, before (3) the matter becomes public.

The personal approach first of all guarantees that the matter remains confidential. This is the scriptural prohibition of gossip and defamation. Anyone knows that there is something wrong with talebearing. But sometimes one may think it wrong only because it reveals secrets, or only when the reports one passes on are not true, or when the intention in passing them on is to hurt someone. Each of these explanations of what is wrong with gossip leaves a loophole. Each would permit some kinds of talking about the neighbor's faults to continue.

But if Jesus' command is that the thing to do with an unfavorable report is to go to the person herself/himself, then all one's temptations to pass the word along are blocked and confidentiality is demanded by the concern for the offender.

Second, it is hereby assured that the process is closely bound to the local situation. Either party can bring into the discussion aspects of the picture that would not be taken into account in general statements of rules. Thus there is a safeguard against the danger of legalism, which promulgates ethical generalities apart from the context where they must apply and then applies them strictly and uniformly to every case.

When dealing personally with the offender, in view of that person's problems, it is not possible to identify as virtues or vices whole categories of behavior without taking part with that person in the struggle and the tension of applying them to his or her situation. It is that person who must determine how to behave when he or she really faces the difficult choice. It may be that the one accused will be able to demonstrate that the action criticized as "sin" was right after all. Or perhaps the one admonishing may be able to help the accused find a better solution he or she had not seen.

This is a built-in way to assure that churches will not continue to proclaim rules that are no longer capable of application. Standards must constantly be tested by whether it is possible to show the brother or sister how he or she has sinned. If no one can show that person how he or she should have done differently, then the rules are inadequate and that person has been accused unfairly. The very process of conversation with that person is then the way to change the rules. If, on the other hand, the standards continue to be correct, it is in the conversation with the offending individual that the church will be obliged and enabled to give the most fruitful attention to finding other ways of meeting his or her needs and the temptations that led that person to fall.

Yet, at the same time that legalism must be avoided, there is an equal danger of letting the situation provide its own rules. What modern writers call "situation ethics" or "relevance" or "contextualism" may mean simply allowing every individual full liberty to make his or her own decisions. This approach ends by sacrificing all moral bindingness and all community, adopting in advance, in a general way, a general "rule-against-rules." Binding and loosing achieves the same flexibility to fit each context, without being too sweepingly permissive.

The approach is made in a "spirit of meekness" (Gal. 6:1); i.e., in recognition of the mutual need of all members for one another and for forgiveness. "Bearing one another's burdens" in Galatians 6:2 is centered not on economic needs, as it is often read, but on the need for this kind of mutual moral support.

B. *Everyone in the church shares responsibility for the reconciling approach.*

(1) The command of Matthew 18 assigns the initiative to anyone aware of the offense. The words "against thee," present in most older translations, are missing in the most reliable ancient manuscripts; no such limitation is present in Luke 17:3, Galatians 6:1–2, James 5:19–20.

Those who interpret the instructions to apply only to the person sinned against would shift the attention from the offender's need for reconciliation to the resentment of the person hurt in order to give vent to his or her feelings. If this shift is taken seriously, it could mean that for certain sins where there is no one specific person offended, or the offended person is absent, there would be nothing for anyone to do. Such a limiting interpretation would also lead the more "mature" or "tolerant" or "accepting" person to absorb the offense and suffer without response, claiming to be adult enough or magnanimous enough not to need to "blow off steam." However, according to Galatians 6, it is the spiritually mature person who is especially responsible to act in reconciliation.

(2) The instructions of Matthew 5:23ff. assign the same responsibility to the person who has offended, if that person becomes aware of the offense. His or her obligation to be reconciled is prior to any other righteous works, however worthy. If your fellow Christian has something against you, don't bring your sacrifice to the altar. It is thus the responsibility of every person — of the offender, of the offended, of every informed third party in the Christian fellowship when aware of any kind of offense, to take initiative toward the restoration of fellowship.

(3) There is no indication that this responsibility belongs in any particular way to "the ministry." "Forgiving" is never indicated in the New Testament as one of the "gifts" distributed within the congregation, nor as a specific responsibility of the pastor, elder, bishop, or deacon.

Now there are good commonsense reasons for assuming that anyone who is responsible for leadership in the life of the church will also be concerned for the proper exercise of this reconciling discipline. Thus church leaders might well be included among the "two or three" of Matthew 18:16, or the "wise among you" of 1 Corinthians 6:5, who seek to mediate in the second effort, or among the "more spiritual" of

Galatians 6:1. Nevertheless these are only relative, commonsense considerations. They may be properly applied only after the first attempt at reconciliation: for to inform church leaders before that first attempt is counter to the letter and the intent of the demand for initial confidentiality: "between you and him or her alone."

For the pastor, the teacher, the elder, the preacher, or the deacon to be normally or exclusively the disciplinarian, to the extent that others no longer share in bearing the same burden, undermines both the reconciling process and this person's other leadership ministries. It is one of the main reasons for both the loss of authentic discipline in the churches and the discrediting of some kinds of ministerial leadership.

C. *This process belongs in the church.* The church's responsibility may not be turned over to the state (as in the age of the Reformation, according to the convinced theological opinions of Huldrych Zwingli and his followers) or to any other agency representing the total society.

Something like this is happening in our society. Although legalism in churches is going out of style, we are accustomed to the FBI and the draft board exercising moral oversight; we expect schools and social workers to develop the character of the persons they work with.[4]

Nor can the reconciling process in the church be properly replaced by secular psychotherapy. This study makes no attempt to investigate the complex interrelationships between the church and the mental health institution, between moral guilt and psychotic anxiety, etc. There clearly can and should be no fixed wall between mental health and the church, yet neither may one be absorbed into the other. No definition of the interrelation of these areas can be accepted that takes the matter of guilt and grace completely away from the congregation, or that excludes conscious confession and forgiveness for known willful offenses, or that dissolves all moral measurement into self-adjustment. Not psychiatry and psychology but the caricature of these professions as secular agencies of forgiveness is the abuse we need to avoid.

D. *Reconciliation and restoration is the only worthy motive.* Any textbook discussion of "church discipline" aligns several other reasons for its application by the church:

---

4. Concerning the way the nation takes over the moral authority of the church, see John Edwin Smylie, "The Christian Church and the National Ethos," in *Biblical Realism Confronts the Nation*, ed. Paul Peachey (Nyack, N.Y.: Fellowship Publications, 1963): 33–44.

- the purity of the church as a valuable goal in its own right;
- protecting the reputation of the church before the outside world;
- testifying to the righteous demands of God;
- dramatizing the demands of church membership, especially to new or young members, assumed more likely to be tempted;
- safeguarding against relativization and the loss of common Christian moral standards.

Real as they are as byproducts, and logical as they may well be in motivating the church, it is striking that these concerns are not part of the New Testament picture. These reasonings all put the church in a posture of maintaining its own righteousness, whereas the New Testament speaks of shared forgiveness.

Nevertheless there is, beyond Jesus' simple "you will have won your sister or brother," one deeper way of phrasing the motivation. 1 Corinthians 5:6ff. speaks of the discipline process in the image of "leaven": the church is the lump of dough, all of which will be caused to ferment by the presence of a few yeast cells within it. Paul thus says that there is a kind of moral solidarity linking all the members of the body so that if individuals persist in disobedience within the fellowship, their guilt is no longer the moral responsibility of those individuals alone but becomes a kind of collective blame shared by the whole body. I should deal with my fellow believer's sin because that person and I are members one of another; unless I am the agent of that person's sharing in restoration, he or she is the agent of my sharing guilt.

Discussion questions on the reconciling approach.

- Would it be possible to maintain self-righteousness or judgmental attitudes if the principle of going directly to the offender were respected?
- Would the concern for discipline be more effectively taken care of if it were assigned to one particular officer in the church?
- Are there certain kinds of questions to which the instructions of Matthew 18 should not apply? Certain sins that should not be so easily forgiven? Or certain others that do not call for this much attention?

336

V. The Centrality of This Forgiving Function in the New Testament

A. *Reference to "binding and loosing"* occurs at the only places in the Gospels where the word "church" is reported as used by Jesus. The church is, therefore, most centrally defined as the place where "binding and loosing" takes place. Where this does not happen, "church" is not fully present.

B. *This is the only connection* in which it is said of the church that it is authorized to "commit God." "What you bind on earth stands bound in heaven." The image is that of the ambassador plenipotentiary or of the "power of attorney"; the signature of the accredited representative binds the one who gave the commission.

C. *It is in the context* of this activity of the church that the promise is given (Matt. 18:19–20; John 14:26; 16:12ff., 20–23) that Christ (or the Spirit) is present where his followers meet in his name. It can be argued that in the New Testament the gift of the Spirit is more often spoken of in connection with discerning and forgiving than (as in Acts 1:8) in relation to witnessing.

D. *This practical application* of forgiveness (18:15–18) is the center of the teaching of the entire chapter 18 on forgiveness.

E. *The only condition* in the Lord's Prayer (Matt. 6:12) and the only commentary of Jesus on the prayer (Matt. 6:15) both limit God's forgiveness to those who forgive others (also said in Matt. 18:35; Mark 11:25; Eph. 4:32; Col. 3:13; Sirach 28:2).

F. *The reconciliation* with one's brother or sister is prerequisite to valid worship (Matt. 5:23f.).

G. *The promise* of the presence of the Holy Spirit is related especially closely to binding and loosing as we saw above (III/C., Matt. 18:19, 20).

H. *It is a function* of the "spiritual" people in the church that in a spirit of meekness they restore offenders; this is called "bearing one another's burdens" (Gal. 6:1–2). It is also described as "covering a multitude of sins" (James 5:19–20).

337

Discussion questions on the New Testament.

- Do you see in the passages cited any localizing of this function as a "ministry" of specific officers of the church?
- Do you see in the narrative elements of the New Testament that this function was exercised?
- Do you see in the letters of the New Testament that the writer "admonishes" his readers in this way?
- As you pray the Lord's Prayer does the phrase "as we forgive" draw your mind to whether you are in fact forgiving others as you ask to be forgiven?

VI. The Centrality of Binding and Loosing in the Life of Free-Church Protestantism

A. *The small group of followers* of Huldrych Zwingli who after 1525 came to be known as Anabaptists are usually thought of as having begun their search for the form of the faithful church around the question of the state church or around infant baptism. It is, however, just as correct to say that the point at which the group of brethren became conscious of identity was a concern for dealing with offenders according to the pattern of Matthew 18. The term *rule of Christ,* with which they referred to the instructions of Matthew 18, was already a fixed phrase in their vocabulary in 1524, before they had reached any final conclusions about the form of the church, the practice of adult baptism, or the church's independence from the state.

The first Anabaptists did not say that infants should not be baptized because they cannot have an experience of faith and the new birth, nor did they reject infant baptism only because there was no biblical text commanding it.[5] Their belief was rather that one who requests baptism submits to the mutual obligation of giving and receiving counsel in the congregation; this is what a child cannot do.

In the first clear statement rejecting infant baptism, in September 1524, before going on to discuss whether water has a saving effect or whether unbaptized children are lost, Conrad Grebel wrote "even an adult is not to be baptized without Christ's rule of binding and loosing."

5. These are the reasons that most contemporary Baptists, Pentecostals, or Disciples of Christ would give.

Thus the issue is not the age of the one baptized but the commitment that person makes, entering into the covenant community with a clear understanding of its claims upon him or her.

Balthasar Hubmaier, the theologian of Anabaptism and the only first-generation leader to have the opportunity to draw up printed patterns of church order, likewise put the commitment character of baptism at the center of his view of reformation. It is clear in his catechism:

Q. What is the baptismal pledge?
A. It is a commitment which one makes to God publicly and orally before the church, in which he renounces Satan, and his thoughts and works. He pledges as well that he will henceforth set all his faith, hope and trust alone in God, and direct his life according to the divine Word, in the power of Jesus Christ our Lord and in case he should not do that, he promises hereby to the church that he desires virtuously to receive fraternal admonition from her members and from her, as is said above.

. . . .

Q. What power do those in the church have over one another?
A. The authority of fraternal admonition.

Q. What is fraternal admonition?
A. The one who sees his brother sinning goes to him in love and admonishes him fraternally and quietly that he should abandon such sin. If he does so he has won his soul. If he does not, then he takes two or three witnesses with him and admonishes him before them once again. If he follows him, it is concluded, if not, he says it to the church. The same calls him forward and admonishes him for the third time. If he now abandons his sin, he has saved his soul.

Q. Whence does the church have this authority?
A. From the command of Christ, who said to his disciples, "all that you bind on earth shall be bound also in heaven and all that you loose on earth shall also be loosed in heaven."

Q. But what right has one brother to use this authority on another?

339

A. From the baptismal pledge in which one subjects oneself to the Church and all her members according to the word of Christ.[6]

Far from being the extreme expression of individualism, the baptism of believers is thus the foundation of the most sweeping communal responsibility of all members for the life of all members.

B. *The Wesleyan revival* may stand as a sample for the numerous renewal movements since the sixteenth century. John Wesley and his colleagues had some particular doctrinal emphases and some unique personal gifts. Their ministry came at a time of great need. Yet the fundamental local experience that the "methodist" believer had week by week, and the real reason for the movement's practical success, was the regular encounter with the "class." This was a circle of persons meeting regularly, committed to one another and bearing one another's burdens in every way, with special attention to reproof and restoration.[7]

This has been true of movements of revival and renewal in every age; they restore a new freedom in forgiving relationships within the local fellowship and a renewed ethical earnestness born not out of rigorous law but out of mutual concern.

C. *Contemporary examples* may be found in the revivalism of Keswick and of East Africa, and in most renewal movements. By the nature of the case such movements, without fixed denominational authority, are open to various organizational, doctrinal, and personal peculiarities. Some of these are novel and some perhaps may be questionable. Yet, what keeps these movements alive and lively is the renewed experience of the gift of openness, the capacity given by grace to be transparent with the brother about one's own sins and the brother's and thereby to make concrete the assurance of forgiveness.

---

6. For the entirety of Hubmaier's "A Christian Catechism," see H. Wayne Pipkin and J. Yoder, eds., *Balthasar Hubmaier: Theologian of Anabaptism* (Scottdale, Penn.: Herald Press, 1989): 339–71; the portions cited here are from pp. 350–53 of this volume. Another translation is available in Denis Janz, ed., *The Reformation Catechisms* (New York: Edwin Mellen Press, 1982): 135ff. Cf. Ervin Schlabach, "The Rule of Christ among the Early Swiss Anabaptists," Th.D. diss., Chicago Theological Seminary, 1977.

7. See "The Nature, Design and General Rules of the United Societies . . ." (1743) in *The Works of John Wesley*, vol. 9 of *The Methodist Societies: History, Nature, and Design*, ed. Rupert Davies (Nashville: Abingdon, 1989): 69–73; and "Rules of the Band Societies," 77–78.

Thus every revival and every renewal movement has begun by reestablishing among estranged brethren, by repentance, a possibility of communication that had been broken off by the pride and the power-hunger of those within the churches. This kind of renewal may happen at any time or place and within any kind of Christian group; but for the free churches it is constitutive, it defines their specific character. The free church is not simply an assembly of individuals with a common spiritual experience of personal forgiveness received directly from God; nor is it merely a kind of working committee, a tool to get certain kinds of work carried out. The church is also, as a social reality right in the midst of the world, that people through whose relationships God makes forgiveness visible.

Discussion questions on the histories of renewal.

- What has been the record of breakthrough experiences of forgiveness and dialogical discernment in the history of your own community? In the biographies and novels you have read?
- What has been the place of failure to dialogue reconcilingly in the failures to "be church" that you have seen?

VII. The Congregational Method of Decision Making

The mandate to forgive and to decide makes no formal prescriptions about how small or large groups (the "two or three with you" or "the church") are to discuss and decide. Shall the decisions for the group be made by authority personages, entitled by age or ordination to speak for all? Or by a numerical majority? This question applies not only to "discipline" but to other kinds of "discerning" decision making as well. This study does not seek to go deeply into this formal matter.

A. *From the narrower realm* of the forgiving process, we must carry over into the broader discussion of churchly decision making several elements that are not usually emphasized in discussions of church organization: (1) the abiding awareness that all decision involves elements of conflict and resentment that need to be dealt with in an atmosphere of abiding forgiveness; and (2) the situation-bound movement of an issue from the two through the few to the congregation.

341

B. *From the few descriptions* of congregational meetings we have in the New Testament, especially 1 Corinthians 12–14, it seems clear that every member has a right, perhaps a duty, to share in the process. This is not to say that the Corinthian type of church life, charismatically effervescent to the border of disorder, is normative in any formal way.

C. *It is clear that specific "gifts"* contribute to the Spirit-led decision process; it is an orderly and not a formless movement. Some "prophesy," others "preside" and "oversee" and "administer."[8]

D. *The decision process*, although it is often "illuminated" by some immediate inspiration, cannot go forward validly in a knowledge vacuum. There must be, if a decision is to be faithful, a way of informing it with full access to the biblical and theological heritage of Christian insight. If it is to be relevant, it must be equally informed about all the factual dimensions of the current problem. There is no basis for any dichotomy between "religious" and "secular" information, as if either could make decision making superfluous or as if Spirit guidance could get along without either. Holy Spirit guidance is not an alternative to correct information.

Discussion questions on decision making.

- Does it ever happen that "religious knowledge" is held to settle a question so that no decision is needed?
- Does the same thing ever happen with "secular" knowledge? Do the "authorities" or the "law" settle a question without decision making?
- Do current ways of assigning tasks to individuals in our churches reflect the teaching of Romans 12, Ephesians 4, 1 Corinthians 12?

VIII. Misunderstandings of the Concept of "Discipline"

As central as is the commission to bind and to loose, both in the New Testament and in any sober view of the mission of the church, it has nevertheless been widely misunderstood, distorted, and neglected. How can this have come about? So universal a loss of so fundamental

8. For a discussion of the "gifts" in the New Testament context, see my *The Fullness of Christ* (Elgin: Brethren Press, 1989).

a function must be understood and evaluated. Otherwise we may well fall into the same traps and be unable to recover it, or, having grasped it, rapidly lose it again. We shall, therefore, have to devote a sizable part of our study to the encounter with other points of view.

We look first at misunderstandings connected to the word "discipline," the label by which this work of community maintenance is most often designated.

A. *The attention may move from the reconciliation of the offender to his or her punishment.* Under this misunderstanding, instead of restoration, one seeks to inflict on the guilty party some suffering to compensate for the suffering caused; at least the suffering of public humiliation. This may be thought of as a right, or a need, of the offended people or group for some kind of vengeance; or it may be thought that the "moral order" somehow demands it, or that the guilty one himself needs chastisement.

B. *The attention may move from the person to the offense.* Big offenses call for big punishment, small ones for lesser measures. These standards are the same regardless of the person involved. Concern for "fairness," i.e., uniformity in application, replaces the unpredictability of dealing with one offense at a time.

C. *Concern may move from the offender to the "standards."* Strict observance of the rules is thought of as necessary to reassure the group of its righteousness, or to teach other members the seriousness of the offense, or to justify to the surrounding world of the church's seriousness. The brother is then less important to the church than its identity and reputation and standards or even than the power of its leaders that is threatened by the offender's not conforming.

D. *Responsibility moves from the brother or sister to the church disciplinarian;* the bishop or the deacon (in Protestantism), the priest (in Catholicism) is charged *ex officio* with the duty of reprimand: (1) this depersonalizes the process, for the official disciplinarian will be farther from the offense and will be concerned to demonstrate fairness by treating all alike; (2) this furthermore undermines the other ministries that that minister should be exercising in the church; and (3) such delegation of power bypasses the express instruction of Matthew 18:15 to the effect that the first approach made to the guilty one by anyone should be "between the two of you, alone," i.e., such an approach should exclude any discussion with a third party.

E. *In line with these misunderstandings, there may well develop the idea of a distinction between several categories of sin.* Public and scandalous offenses (sexual sins, theft, and murder) or ritual taboos (alcohol and dancing in pioneer Protestantism) can be dealt with in a depersonalized, puritan discipline. But talebearing, pride, and avarice cannot. The sins of the weak and sensual are magnified; those of the proud and strong are not named. Now if the New Testament authorizes any distinction at all between the several levels of different kinds of sin — which is challengeable — it would be the other way around.

We may sum up this constant temptation to deform the binding and loosing experience with the word "puritan." It is this abuse that has given to terms like "discipline," "admonish" and "reprove" a distasteful ring in our ears. The puritan is concerned to impose the right standards on a whole society; Jesus and the free church are concerned to see the fellow believer grow freely in the integrity with which he or she lives out the meaning of a freely made commitment to Christ.

Discussion questions on the misunderstanding of discipline.

- Can you illustrate from experience any of the reformations listed above?
- Talk back; are there any understandings listed above as "misunderstandings" that you think are correct? Why?
- Can you see some other reasons for the repeated loss, with the passage of time, of the practice of fraternal discipline?
- Is the above outline right in rejecting the idea of "punishment"? Does society need to punish the offender? Does the offender need to feel punishment? Does the moral order call for it?

IX. Misunderstandings of the Meaning of Love

The expression of evangelical forgiveness and discernment can just as easily be lost in the reaction against puritanism, which in the name of love leaves the individual alone with his or her struggles, guilt, uncertainty, and mistaken certainties. Once the puritanical approach has been discredited by its friends and undermined by the pressure of the larger society (which in its demands for conformity at other points is, however, also a backhanded kind of puritanism), the undiscerning and adolescent reaction that comes most easily is that of letting every individual be his or her own master.

A. *This failure to intervene* may be explained (sincerely or in cowardice) in terms of "love" or "acceptance" or "respect for individual difference" or "leaving him or her free to work it out for himself or herself." There is an element of truth in this feeling; it is understandable to the extent to which puritanism is assumed to be the only alternative. But the procedure commanded by Jesus is also an expression of "love" and "acceptance" and still "lets him or her work it out himself or herself."

During the first generation of reaction against a puritanical heritage, people may have sufficient moral rigor built into their reflexes that they may seem to be able to get along with a great degree of individual autonomy and still not loose their moorings. Yet, once the backlog of puritanical certainties is no longer there to lean upon and to react against, it again becomes visible that individual freedom is a most deceptive and loose kind of conformity to the world.

B. *There is the excuse of modesty.* Who am I to say that he or she has sinned because I, too, am a sinner, because I don't know his or her situation ("sin" is, after all, a relative matter) or because everyone must find his or her own way?

We can agree that no one knows the offender's situation quite as he or she does. This is why the one who reproves him or her must "go to him or her alone" instead of judging him or her a priori for what he or she is thought to have done. This approach thus safeguards all the valid concerns of what is currently advertised as "situation ethics."

It is true as well that we are all sinners; but Jesus does not let the duty to forgive depend on one's own sinlessness; he precisely says that it is those who are forgiven who must forgive.

C. *The excuse of "maturity"*: if I am emotionally strong I can forgive and forget without bothering the brother, the sister, or the church. This attitude, which can be the sincere expression of a forgiving spirit and of wholesome emotional resilience, is based on the mistaken assumption (see above, IV/B/1) that the concern of the process is for the one offended rather than for the offender.

D. *The idea of blanket forgiveness* by virtue of theological understanding or by liturgy:

1. Forms that prescribe the phrases for the routine confession of sin and the assurance of forgiveness are part of the regular liturgies of the Anglican and Lutheran communions.

2. Anyone who knows, as any Christian should know, that God is a forgiving God, can apply this knowledge to herself or himself as a purely mental operation and thus have the assurance of one's own reconciliation.

3. Anyone accustomed to the diluted "lay" forms of popular contemporary psychology knows that "self-acceptance" is for the contemporary person a possibility, a virtue, or even a duty. Thus, knowing it should be done and therefore must be possible, one may seek consciously to "forgive himself."

E. *The anti–Roman Catholic argument* that forgiveness is not within the authority of the church. As at other points, some Protestants have been driven by their anti-Catholicism to become unbiblical. The medieval Catholic penitential practice involved some definite abuses:

1. Limiting the forgiving function to a sacramentally authorized priest.

2. Tying it to a prescribed set of acts of penance.

3. Trying to make it consistent, legal, impersonal, impartial, so as to apply in the same way to all without favoritism (the same deformation as in puritan Protestantism).

4. Leaving room for the idea that the sin is "made right" not wholly by forgiveness but also partly by reparation or penance.

5. Linking absolution to the church hierarchy's control of the means of grace.

There is in all these abuses no reason to reject the offering of words of pardon from one believer to another.

F. *Individualism seen in its various forms:* as a modern humanist philosophy making each person a law unto himself; or as an antipuritan reaction denying that it is the business of the church to reach common decisions about contemporary faithfulness; or as a spiritualist glorification of guidance or illumination received immediately by the individual.

G. *Arguing that the church should preach about sin* or sinfulness but not deal with specific sins or specific sinners.

H. *All of the above distortions* relate to the application of reconciling concern to moral offense; the other possibility is to call into question the principle of morality itself as a common concern. Many contemporary currents of thought, within and without the church, challenge whether a common Christian moral position is attainable, or desirable, or binding.

This argument needs to be faced honestly. But for present purposes we must only recognize that it is a quite different question from the ones we have been dealing with thus far. The New Testament and Christians until modern times agreed that such moral consensus is desirable. With those who challenge this, the argument must be carried out on a different basis and a different level from the present outline.

X. Diversions and Evasions

A. *The mechanical detour.* Since as we have seen the two dimensions of discernment and forgiveness, or decision making and reconciliation, are intimately mingled, every estrangement between people also has about it a difference in discernment: a conflict about fact or about proper procedures or wrong policies. Differences in opinion or policy are both causes and effects of personal disharmony.

It is, therefore, no surprise that the "detour" of attention to mechanics is frequently resorted to. Divided about principles or people and unwilling to face the strain and threat of reconciliation, we concentrate instead on procedures. The prospect of loving frankness, with admonition and forgiveness flowing freely both ways, is threatening by its unfamiliarity. Ours is an age of great psychological and sociological self-awareness, which heightens the consciousness of the threat. Ours is also an age of great organizational concern, which increases our ability to find ways to avoid such an open meeting of souls.

1. There is evasion by compromise, bypassing an issue without resolving it, hoping it will resolve itself.

2. There is evasion by superior power, overcoming the other not by reconciliation but by maneuvering, by parliamentary or administrative methods.

3. There is evasion by appeal to outside authority. That authority may be an expert in sociological theory or management methods, or in theological correctness or empirical research, who is called in to provide us an answer without opening up the personal dimensions.

Calling in the outsider depersonalizes the issue. Should the outsider take "our side," this is powerful confirmation of our rightness that we can ask everyone to submit to, whatever may have been the personal feelings. Should he or she take "the other side," we can bow to authority with less "loss of face" than would have been involved in listening and submitting to the sister or brother.

B. *The therapy detour.* A detour is also possible by taking the matter to a counselor whose solution is felt to be preferable because it is given by a "doctor figure" rather than a sister or brother:

1. One is not otherwise personally or socially related to the healer figure; both "doctor" and "patient" deal with one another as roles rather than as people.

2. The "doctor's" very involvement in the problem labels the trouble as "illness" rather than "blame," so that one feels less responsible.

3. The "doctor" is sure to accept me, for that is his or her role.

4. The "doctor" solves my problem by virtue of technical competence and not through personal commitment to me.

5. The "doctor" serves me for payment; once payment is made there is no more hold on me, and I need feel no debt of commitment to the person or of gratitude.

6. I can trust the "doctor" to keep my problem confidential.

This characterization of the therapeutic counselor is not meant to be an evaluation; our only point here is that this resource is different in kind and in function from that of the community.

C. *Evaluations related to an incomplete view of human nature.* In one way or another all of the misunderstandings that stand in the way of a confident and loving binding and loosing are variations on a basic misconception of human nature. If we think of ourselves as normally not in need of admonition and restoration and guidance from the brotherhood, then we think of the procedure described in Matthew 18 as exceptional, for use only in extreme cases.

1. We would hope not to have to apply it often, and then only after other means of evasion or of indirect pressure had failed.

2. We would hope, as serious, well-intentioned Christians, not to need such treatment ourselves.

3. We would withdraw from exercising this ministry to others if in need of it ourselves.

4. We would "hesitate to make an issue" of another's peculiarities, as long as they were within the limits of the tolerable.

5. We consider the need for this admonition to be itself a sign of blameworthy weakness. We tend to look down on the person who

needs it and respect instead the irreproachable person. Thus we are on the way toward the puritan deformation again.

6. We see no direct connection between this matter and the gospel, since by *gospel* we mean a kind of general graciousness of God toward sinfulness in general rather than concrete forgiveness for oneself or one's sister or brother. We seek instead to fix a great gulf between divine and human forgiveness.

7. We concentrate our attention on an initial Christian experience of conversion and regeneration, or on a specific second experience of sanctification brought about by God alone. These emphases in many cases can become a denomination's special emphasis and can be identified and spoken about more easily. They may even help us to think that, following this divine work, daily forgiveness should be less necessary.

D. *Hindrances in unbelief:* Thus far, our analysis of how churches lose the reality of forgiving fellowship has assumed the best of intentions, as if misinformation were keeping Christians from doing what would otherwise be easily attained. It certainly is possible that misunderstandings and erroneous teachings can stand in the way of knowing and thereby in the way of doing right. Yet, ignorance or misinformation only complicate the problem; they do not create it. The real reason we do not go to our brother or sister lies in disobedience; that of the individual or of the community.

The individual neither loves sufficiently nor believes sufficiently in the renewing power of the Holy Spirit, to go to the other when it is one's duty, when both the outer command and the inner awareness are clear despite all misunderstandings.

XI. The Price of the Neglect of This Function of the Church

A. *We are not faithful.* This failure to be the real church in which the Spirit works shows up in a sense of formality and unreality in the life of the congregation. More and more we have the feeling that we are going through the motions of what was meaningful in another age and that the real depths of concern and of motivation are not touched in what we speak about when we are together.

In the absence of clear devotion to this central working of the Spirit by which the church is defined we tend to take refuge in other good works and other manifestations of the presence of the Spirit, which, although good, constructive, and proper in their place, are nevertheless not equally indispensable.

In the more "respectable" segments of Christendom these secondary works are focused in the areas of Christian nurture and social action. In the more "enthusiastic" portions of the church the concentration is on the outwardly ecstatic aspects of the Spirit's working. The concentration on the "respectable" or on the "enthusiastic" works of the Spirit (as well as the almost universally accepted assumption that the two are mutually exclusive) is but a sign of the loss of the living center in which a functioning congregation would hold in genuine unity the entire range of the Spirit's gifts.

B. *We are not forgiven, and we are not guided.* The widespread success of secular and sub-Christian sources of forgiveness and guidance in society (psychiatry, Peale-ism, astrology, Ann Landers and Abigail Van Buren) are testimony to the lostness of living without the forgiving and discerning resources of fellowship. Here we see the desperate and irrational lengths to which people will go to find a substitute.

C. *But the real tragedy* is not that individuals within the larger society are without guidance and without forgiveness; it is that as *church* we have come to respect as a sign of maturity the willingness to live with directionlessness and with unreconciled divisions and conflicts. We reject as immature or impatient those who would argue that something definitely must or must not be done.

We make a virtue of the "acceptance" of intolerable situations rather than of the obedience in openness and forgiveness that could transform situations. Especially we have come to "live with" a situation in which, as a defense against "defenders of the faith" whose methods in the past were less than redemptive, we are satisfied with trying to do a decent job day by day without taking responsibility for the direction in which churches and their institutions are evolving. A sense of not knowing where to turn next is pervasive among denominational leaders.

D. *The church that does not forgive is not a missionary church.* A great mass of contradictory testimony springs out of the widespread recognition of the ineffectiveness of the Christian churches before their missionary task. For some, the corrective should be a renewed dedication to the forms of message and ministry found effective in other ages, in the confidence that it is adequate if preached with conviction.

For others, the message must be "translated" into another more relevant idiom in order to "communicate." For others, it is the "struc-ture" of church activity that must change to fit the new urban world. For still others *mission* itself must be redefined to refer to all the whole-some contributions the church makes to society, independently of win-ning the allegiance of additional individuals.

These discussions are worthwhile in their own right, yet the danger is great that they become a substitute for the church's being the forgiving and discerning fellowship of which we are speaking. No juggling of vocabulary or of agencies or of times and places and forms of meeting can fill the vacuum where fellowship is missing. Yet, where believers do interact in reconciling love, the tool is at hand for changing both societies and personalities.

XII. Wider Implications

This outline has intentionally been kept simple and practice-oriented, since it is on the level of simple obedience to a clear duty that we usually go astray. Yet, if this task were tested by and related to broader kinds of theological meditation, or other ways of understanding and helping humanity, the import of what we have been discussing would be all the stronger.

A. *The human is a social being,* not by error nor by compromise but by nature and by divine intent.

After centuries of trying best to understand the person as a spirit in a hostile body or an individual in a hostile world, both theology and psychology are seeing that what one is is not separable from the net-work of one's social relationships. Thus healing, whether from sin or from sickness, is inseparable from the healing of human relationships.

B. *The work of God in the whole biblical story,* from Abraham to Pentecost and from Adam to the New Jerusalem, is the creation of covenant community, in which the loving relationships are the outworking of people's obedience to the reconciliation worked for them by God. Sal-vation is not just fishing single souls out of the mass for a privileged destiny; salvation is loving human relationships under God.

C. *The witness of the church* is not only the verbal message of public preaching; in a day of cheapened words this may become the least important language, especially for the outsider. The witness of the church always includes and may sometimes center upon the quality of personal relationships that even the outsider may observe.

D. *We may be humiliated,* but we should not be surprised to discover that Christian duty is also secular good sense. Current techniques in institutional and industrial management replacing hierarchical authority by group decision processes, commending frankness as more efficient than deviousness, are now recognized as good (i.e., efficient) practice.

E. *The readiness not only to forgive* but to make forgiveness the instrument and the standard of all church experience is of a piece with the broader theme of suffering servanthood, the theme that stretches from Hosea and Isaiah 42, 49, 52–53 through Christ himself to the cross bearing of his disciples.

Forgiveness is not a generally accessible human possibility; it is the miraculous fruit of God's own bearing the cost of human rebellion. Forgiveness among us also costs a cross. One can go to one's brother or sister only as God came to us: not counting our trespasses against us. Forgiveness does not brush the offense off with a "think nothing of it"; it absorbs the offense in suffering love.

F. *The process of binding and loosing in the local community of faith* provides the practical and theological foundation for the centrality of the local congregation. It is not correct to say, as some extreme Baptist and Churches of Christ do, that only the local gathering of Christians can be called "the church." The Bible uses the term church for all of the Christians in a large city or even in a province. The concept of local congregational autonomy has, therefore, been misunderstood when it was held to deny mutual responsibilities between congregations or between Christians of different congregations.

We understand more clearly and correctly the priority of the congregation when we study what it is that it is to do. It is only in the local face-to-face meeting, with brothers and sisters in Christ who know one another well, that this process can take place of which Jesus says that what it has decided stands decided in heaven. Whether the outcome be the separating of fellowship or its restoration, the process is not one that can be carried on in a limited time and by means of judicial formalities; it demands conversation of a serious, patient, sustained, loving character. Only when people live together in the same city, meet together often, and know each other well can this "bearing of one another's burdens" be carried out in a fully loving way.

The church is defined by this process; not by a legal organization nor by a purely spiritual doctrinal criterion. The church is where two or three or more are gathered in the name of Jesus around this kind of need. The synod, or the overseer from outside the congregation, may very well be of real assistance and may very well share something of the character of the "church"; but there is no way whereby such people or mechanisms could replace the process of loving and binding fraternal conversation.

G. *If we understand deeply enough* the way in which the promise of the Holy Spirit is linked to the church's gathering to bind and loose (Matt. 18:19–20), this may provide us as well with a more wholesome understanding of the use and authority of Scripture. One of the most enduring subjects of unfruitful controversy over the centuries has been whether the words of Scripture, when looked at purely as words, isolated from the context in which certain people read them at a certain time and place, have both the clear meaning and the absolute authority of revelation.

To speak of the Bible apart from people reading it and apart from the specific questions that those people reading need to answer is to do violence to the very purpose for which we have been given the Holy Scriptures. There is no such thing as an isolated word of the Bible carrying meaning in itself. It has meaning only when it is read by someone and then only when that reader and the society in which he or she lives can understand the issue to which it speaks.

Thus the most complete framework in which to affirm the authority of Scripture is the context of its being read and applied by a believing people that uses its guidance to respond to concrete issues in their witness and obedience. Our attention should center not on what theoretical ideas a theologian (isolated from the church) can dissect out of the text of Scripture in order to relate them to one another in a system of thought. As the apostle Paul says, it is for teaching, reproof, correction, and instruction in right behavior.

Let us, therefore, not be concerned, as amateur philosophers, to seek for truth "in itself," as if it were more true by its being more distant from real life. The Bible is the book of the congregation, the source of understanding and insight as, with the assistance of the same Spirit under whose guidance the apostolic church produced these texts, the congregation seeks to be the interpreter of the divine purpose in the church's own time and place.

XIII. Cavils and Caveats

Retrospect on Binding and Loosing

The above basic outline has been found useful in the same form for a quarter century, with only minimal corrections needed. There has been no reason to change its account of the place of the message of Matthew 18 in the mainstream Protestant Reformation[9] or in the Anabaptist movement.

There would, however, be reason to move farther along in three directions than the original outline intended to do. None of these can be pursued at depth here, but each should be noted.

If taken seriously, simply in the practical life of Christian communities, would it work? The original outline intentionally left this question in the form of a simple exposition of the biblical message; but that should not mean that significant objections as to realistic feasibility would not need to be taken account of.

A. *In the nineties there is* a much more widespread awareness than obtained in the sixties concerning the way in which human relations are predisposed by considerations of power and status. The initial imperative, "Go to your brother or sister, between the two of you" may now be thought by some to be unrealistic. It seems to presuppose that the brothers and sisters are equals, so that anyone who is aware of an offense is empowered to admonish and anyone who needs admonition is committed, by virtue of the baptismal covenant, to be addressable. But if the offense itself involved an abuse of power, how can one expect the victim to have the courage to address the perpetrator? Does such a requirement not merely reinforce the offender's control of a skewed relationship? In settings where the recovery of concern for reconciliation overlaps with awareness of power abuse, there are thus many who simply would set aside Jesus' guidance as not relevant. The issue is worthy of analysis.

1. The level of dialogue where this point tends to be made is often superficial. One often sees the point argued in short letters to church papers, in which there is no serious wrestling with the possibility that behind the literal meaning of the words of Jesus (which the children of naive biblicists or fundamentalists enjoy setting aside) there might be

---

9. John H. Yoder, "Martin Luther's Forgotten Vision," in *The Other Side* (April 1977): 66–70.

a deep understanding of the nature of reconciling social process. "We need not take it literally" is just as naive a way of reading texts as is "we must take it literally."

2. It is not the case that to respect Jesus' words would obligate the victim to make herself vulnerable to being overpowered again by the offender. As was already spelled out in the original version of the above text, it is a mistake to think that the first purpose of admonition is to meet the victim's need to purge her pain or resentment. In either of two ways, the straightforward meaning of Jesus' guidance compensates directly for that weakness.

The very first imperative empowers the victim with the mandate to confront; but the second imperative heightens the corrective. "If your brother or sister will not listen, take with you two or three." Here the power imbalance is radically reversed. Or one could also understand (1.B.2) that the intervention of a third party, if informed about an offense whose victim does not feel capable to talk back, would constitute the first step of reconciling address.

3. Those who so easily set aside the direct approach to the offender usually do not make clear what other alternatives are thereby opened up. Is the better recourse to call on the state? the press? a discreet ecclesiastical agency? Any other path decreases the likeliness of convincing and/or healing. Some alternative recourses might retain Jesus' stated concern for ultimate reconciliation and for the implicit room for truth-finding as to the original offense, which Jesus' guidance provides; but some do not. Some seek to correct for one unilateral use of power by another use, equally unilateral, of even greater power. Thereby what is sacrificed is not merely (as we were told at first) a superficial part of Jesus' procedural guidance but also Jesus' ultimate reconciling intention.

B. *The procedure Jesus called for* is radically decentralized, as was the life of the synagogue in the age of Jesus. "Tell it to the church" means that every local community is responsible. Will that not make for diversity that will confuse people and in fact even discredit the process?

1. One pitfall under the heading of "decentralization, diversity" arises when we take stock of the fact that the criteria, whereby people will state their belief that "your brother or sister has sinned," are often matters on which sincere believers differ. Killing in war is a sin for a Mennonite congregation and not for a Lutheran one. Knowing of the presence of other churches with different standards may well undercut the readiness of the person being admonished to grant the nature of the offense.

A part of the answer to this worry is the fact that the admonition is based on the covenant of the congregation that the individual voluntarily joined. If he or she voluntarily joined a Mennonite congregation and not a Lutheran one, he or she is asking for pacifism to be part of the discipline.

Yet, the membership covenant cannot involve a full prior catalog of all possible offenses to avoid. There may and should well be cases where the individual admonished does not grant the wrongness of the deed. This is not much of a problem in the first generation of the life of a very cohesive community. It becomes more delicate if the community in question maintains cooperative and fraternal relations with other Christian bodies who think otherwise. The problem may also get worse in the measure in which leadership separates the meaning of discipleship from the meaning of membership; i.e., if the notion is accepted that some components of Christian obedience are optional, matters of idealism rather than obligation. This is a set of questions that Jesus was not addressing. It may well be that there will be some issues in the divided church on the modern scene where the Rule of Christ will not suffice to resolve all questions.

2. A weightier handicap of local autonomy is the possibility that the regular application of this procedure might quash valid prophetic vocation. At first view the procedure seems to be biased in favor of enforcing recent customs, which often have much wisdom behind them but cannot be infallible. The process is also biased in favor of the squeaky wheel; it will give more of a hearing to those persons who are more ready to complain and to intervene. The history of discipline procedures that have gone wrong in the past should be sufficient to warn us that this danger is real.

The corrective for this danger is, however, not to abandon the vision (in favor of what alternative?) but to implement it with still greater understanding and sensitivity. To provide for ways to respect the rare but real possibility of the utterly isolated dissenting individual being right, the community must have ways to record the nuances of the more difficult decisions. Sometimes it should be recorded that a member submitted without being convinced, in the interest of the peace and the ongoing momentum of the community. Then the community thanks the member for that submissiveness and recognizes that he or she might in fact be right. Thereby the door is held open for reviewing the question later, especially if new evidence should arise. Sometimes the strong dissent of an individual, who refuses to be convinced and also refuses simple withdrawal, might be dealt with by a postponement.

This does not mean, however, that the communal decision structure would be crippled by every case of dissent or that some other mode of locating responsibilities (an absentee bishop? a synod?) would be more fair, more sure, or more loving.

C. *One more reason*, both practical and moral, for not bypassing the sinner in the process of admonition is that there needs to be a concern for clarifying the truth of the accusation. There are truths that are not "the whole truth" or "nothing but the truth." There are cases of dramatic memory, especially if the memory is retrieved after the passage of time or in a process of therapy, where the offense is seen in the light of other times or places or persons. Some accusations are only partly true by no fault of the accuser; even more so if the accounts are received indirectly.

Some sincerely intended accusations deal not only with what happened but also with what was intended; sometimes that is surmised rather than known firsthand. The guilty person should be allowed to say "that was not what I meant" as well as "that is not what happened." Some accusations are in fact inflated or slanderous or malevolent.

In this setting the secular courts recognize a truth-finding obligation that includes the accused's opportunity to "confront the accuser." If in a society aware of the psychodynamic biases the notion of "confronting" is less apt, out of concern for the victim's vulnerability, the concern for truth finding should be no less. The accused has a claim, and the stated reconciling intention of the process of admonition has a stake, in giving the accused an opportunity to test the fullness and the fairness of the accusation. If for special reasons the accuser and the accused cannot *at first* converse "between the two of you, alone" then the other parties who become involved in the second or the third phase have an obligation to make up for the gap in the process, rather than leapfrogging over the truth-finding phase.

XIV. Textual Fine Points

A. *The phrases "to bind," la'asor, "to loose," lehatir:*
The classic scholarly summary of the usage of this pair of terms in the rabbinic Judaism is provided in the (German) commentary of Strack and Billerbeck (Munich 1923, pp. 738ff. dealing with Matt. 16:18f.).

In the *Theological Dictionary of the New Testament* (ed. R. Kittel

[Grand Rapids: Eerdmans, 1964], vol. 2, p. 20) Prof. Büchsel, author of a very brief article on "binding and loosing," agrees that the *halakah* meaning of moral decision making was the standard usage yet denies that Jesus could have meant this. The denial is dictated, however, not by dictionary considerations but by Büchsel's own theology.

The article by J. Jeremias on "keys" is more helpful (*TDNT*, vol. 3, pp. 749ff.). He points out that the scribes claimed this same authority (Matt. 25:13).

B. *The tense of Matthew 18:18:*

The future perfect tense twice used in this verse would be rendered literally: "What you bind on earth shall have been bound in heaven; what you loose on earth shall have been loosed in heaven."

A few interpreters have sought to restrict considerably the scope of Jesus' mandate by using the future perfect restrictively, so as to mean "You should bind on earth only what has already been bound in heaven." Their practical pastoral and theological motivation is clear: a fear lest human office bearers speak unduly in God's name.

What "has already been bound in heaven" would be hard to know from the original context, but for the twentieth-century evangelicals who argue this point (with motivations like those cited in sections VIII–X above, especially IX/E) it probably means "what is in the Bible."

This reading has been applied only in the modern version of the New Testament, translated by Charles B. Williams and printed by Moody Press (Chicago, 1952). It was argued most fully by J. R Mantey, "The Mistranslation of the Perfect Tense. . . ." *Journal of Biblical Literature* 58 (1939): 243ff., and refuted convincingly by Henry J. Cadbury, "The Meaning of John 20:23, Matthew 16:19 and Matthew 18:18" (ibid., pp. 251ff.).

Sacrament as Social Process:
Christ the Transformer of Culture

"Sacrament as Social Process: Christ the Transformer of Culture" originated in a lecture at The Divinity School of Duke University in February 1986. It was subsequently given as Yoder's Presidential Address delivered to the Western Regional Meeting of the Society of Christian Ethics meeting at Loma Linda, California, on February 20, 1987, and presented as a lecture at Boston University (Apr. 1987), Eden Theological Seminary (Oct. 1987), and Bangor Theological Seminar (Feb. 1988). It was first published under the title "Sacrament as Social Process: Christ the Transformer of Culture" in *Theology Today* 48/3 (April 1991): 33–44. It is reprinted here without substantial change, with only a few typographical changes having been made to the text.

This essay marks the first published articulation of a suggestion first made by Yoder in the "Stone Lectures" delivered at Princeton Theological Seminary in February 1980. In fact, it might be argued that here Yoder provides the fullest counter-example to H. Richard Niebuhr's typology of "Christ and Culture" by offering an analysis of the practices of the apostolic community or church that serves the purpose of validating his more general claim that the Christian community is "a sociological entity in its own right." The five social practices that are discussed in this essay — fraternal admonition, the universality of charisma, the Spirit's freedom in the meeting, breaking bread, and induction into the new humanity — have since been discussed in an expanded version (but with different headings) in Yoder's book *Body Politics: Five Practices of the Christian Community before the Watching World* (Nashville: Discipleship Resources, 1993). The first practice, fraternal admonition, is discussed more fully in Yoder's newly revised study outline on "Binding and Loosing" (see above, pp. 323–58).

Far from seeing this set of social practices as relevant only for the church, Yoder contends that they each offer models for how other groups and peoples in the world might be ordered. ". . . Each of these practices [of the apostolic community] can function as a paradigm for ways in which other social groups might operate. . . . People who do not share the faith or join the community can learn from them. 'Binding and loosing' can provide models for conflict resolution, alternatives to litigation, and alternative perspectives on 'corrections.' Sharing bread is a paradigm, not only for soup kitchens and hospitality houses, but also for social security and negative income tax. 'Every member of the Body has a gift' is an immediate alternative to vertical 'business' models of management. Paul's solidarity models of deliberation correlate with the reasons that the Japanese can make better cars than Detroit."

The conclusion of this essay, which constitutes a reworked version of the fifth Stone Lecture, offers a good summary of what Yoder believes to be the eschatological significance of each of these "evangelical" social practices: "It is an a posteriori political practice that tells the world something it did not know and could not believe before. It tells the world what is the world's own calling and destiny, not by announcing either a utopian or a realistic goal to be imposed on the whole society, but by pioneering a paradigmatic demonstration of both the power and the practices that define the shape of restored humanity. The confessing people of God is the new world on its way."

Sacrament as Social Process: Christ the Transformer of Culture

Ever since Paul Ramsey spoke to the 1979 session of the Society of Christian Ethics on "Liturgy and Ethics"[1] there has been within the ethics guild a rising awareness of the need to think more clearly about the interrelationship of worship and morality. For some it may even have displaced the earlier routine question of the relationship between Scripture and ethics. The connections between worship and ethics have

1. *Journal of Religious Ethics* 7/2 (1979): 139ff.

been tested in various directions. Some say that what worship does is to form the character of the person or of the community, and then that character determines the style of moral discernment. For others worship contributes to ethics something less precise but more foundational: love or hope — what ordinary usage might call "motivation." What these varied efforts have in common is that they begin with the problem of a qualitative distance between the two realms of liturgy and ethics and maintain that a bridge of some kind needs to be built. With gratitude and great respect for those efforts, but not satisfied by them, I propose to set beside them a simpler account, one that at least complements them and might partially correct them.

I

Observe a commonality underlying five practices described in the New Testament, practices explicated mostly in the Pauline writings but rooted as well in the Gospels and paralleled in the other epistles. What they have in common is that each of them concerns *both* the internal activities of the gathered Christian congregation *and* the ways the church interfaces with the world. Thus, each of the five practices described and mandated in the New Testament exemplifies a link between ecclesiastical practice and social ethics that is usually undervalued or ignored.[2] For each of them, I must dispense with detailed exegesis of the texts' linguistic and contextual dimensions, but not because more attention to the scholar's resources would not be corroborative.

(1) Fraternal Admonition

In a key passage of Matthew's Gospel, Jesus tells his disciples that, as they carry out a particular practice under his instructions, they do the activity of God: "What you bind on earth is bound in heaven," he says (Matt. 18:18). A specific human activity is mandated, and its form is prescribed in some detail. The context in Matthew, reinforced by the parallels in Luke and in John, makes it evident that one objective of the

2. In grouping them in this way I am pursuing a suggestion made in the "Stone Lectures" at Princeton Theological Seminary in February 1980 and in my essay "The Kingdom as Social Ethic" in *The Priestly Kingdom* (Notre Dame: University of Notre Dame Press, 1984): 93.

procedure is forgiveness, "remitting" an offense — i.e., reconciliation, restoring to the community a person who had offended. Jesus' choice of a pair of rabbinic technical terms indicates, however, that more than that is involved: "To bind" is to respond to a question of ethical discernment (we still have the root in our word "obligate"), and to "loose" is to free from obligation (in the beginning of the Sermon on the Mount Jesus had warned that whoever does that with any commandment will be "the least in the Kingdom").

Into the interlocking of the dialogue of reconciliation ("remitting") with the dialogue of moral discernment ("binding" and "loosing"), Jesus inserts yet another element of classical due process: the participants who "harmonize" in this process (the verb is *symphonein,* which we recognize in the noun form "symphony") are described in juridical terms as the "two or three witnesses" who according to Mosaic law[3] make a serious deliberation valid.

Paul referred to this process as "the law of Christ" (Gal. 6:2). The Reformers of the sixteenth century (Martin Luther, Martin Bucer, and some of the so-called Anabaptists) called it *Regnum Christi,* "the rule of Christ." They looked to this process to move the Reformation from the university lecture hall and the scholar's office to the life of the parish and the family.[4]

A process of human interchange combining the mode of reconciling dialogue, the substance of moral discernment, and the authority of divine empowerment deserves to be considered one of the sacramental works of the community. Only a few of the Reformation traditions came near to saying that, and the "Catholic" practices carried on under the rubric of "absolution" or "reconciliation" have long since come to have a much thinner meaning.

(2) *The Universality of Charisma*

The Paul of Ephesians uses the term "the fullness of Christ" to describe a new mode of group relationships in which every member of a body

---

3. Num. 35:30; Deut. 17:6, 19:15; John 8:17.

4. Cf. my review of the New Testament witness in "Binding and Loosing," (pp. 323–58 in this volume). On the sixteenth-century place of this practice, see Ervin A. Schlabach, *The Rule of Christ among the Early Swiss Anabaptists* (Chicago: Chicago Theological Seminary Th.D Thesis, 1977), and my "Hermeneutics of the Anabaptists," in W. Swartley, ed., *Essays on Biblical Interpretation* (Elkhart, Ind.: Institute of Mennonite Studies, 1984): 23ff.

(it is to him that we owe the currency of the noun "body" to describe a social group) has a distinctly identifiable, divinely validated, and empowered role. The Paul of 1 Corinthians says literally that every member is the bearer of such a "manifestation of the Spirit for the common good," and he prescribes quite detailed counter-intuitive and counter-traditional guidelines for how this understanding leads to ascribing the greater value to the less honored members. The Paul of Romans instructs his readers about their ability and duty to think of themselves in such a way as to conform to "the grace that had been meted out" to each of them. He saw all this (there is Petrine corroboration that indicates that the entire thought pattern was not original or peculiar to Paul) as a specific working of God the Spirit, present in, with, and under a particular pattern of social process, profoundly different both from contemporarily available social models and from most of what later Christian history has done with the notions of "charisma" and "ministry."[5]

(3) *The Spirit's Freedom in the Meeting*

In the context of this already described vision of body process, yet distinguishable within it by its narrower focus, Paul instructs the Corinthians about how to hold a meeting in the power of the Spirit. Everyone who has something to say can have the floor, with only a relative priority being given to the mode of prophecy because it speaks "to improve, to encourage, and to console." The others "weigh" what the prophet has said.[6] The same assumptions were operative behind the narrative of Acts, where a foundational problem of missionary strategy yielded to a conversational process[7] of whose conclusions the moderator could say that they had "seemed good to the Holy Spirit and to us."

5. The apostolic testimony is summarized in my *The Fullness of Christ* (Elgin, Ill.: Brethren Press, 1987).

6. Cf. the section on "The Rule of Paul" in Yoder, "Hermeneutics of the Anabaptists."

7. I hesitate to use routinely and uniformly the term "practice" for fear that it be taken too technically as having a special meaning defined by ethicists. There are some who do this with the definition offered by Alasdair MacIntyre in his *After Virtue* (Notre Dame: University of Notre Dame Press, 1981): 175. There is nothing wrong with MacIntyre's description, but some take it as transforming a commonsensical meaning into a recondite one.

I interrupt the listing to note that I began with these three specimens of apostolically prescribed social process because they do *not* fall
within what ordinarily is called "worship," even less "liturgy." Yet, why
should they not be so designated? Each speaks of practices carried out
when believers gather for reasons evidently derived from their faith
and capable of being illuminated by doctrinal elaboration. These practices are described as involving both divine and human action and as
mandatory. It makes a difference whether they are done rightly or
wrongly. Are these not the characteristics of what we ordinarily call
"worship"?

What New Testament believers were doing in these several practices — the three listed so far — can be spoken of in social process terms
easily translated into nonreligious terms. The multiplicity of gifts is a
model for the empowerment of the humble and the end of hierarchy
in social process. Dialogue under the Holy Spirit is the ground floor of
the notion of democracy. The admonition to bind or loose at the point
of offense is the foundation for what now would be called conflict
resolution and consciousness raising.

The social-process meaning of the other two practices to which I
now turn, more traditionally called "sacraments," has been less evident
until recently. Part of the reason for not looking at them as social
practices over the years may well be the special aura cast around them
by the word "sacrament." Now, however, there is a veritable wave of
writings connecting the Eucharist with economics; Orbis Press has
several books making such a point. That this juxtaposition is now
popular does not prove, of course, that it is exegetically warranted;
many fads are not. In this case, though, others had been making this
juxtaposition since long before the fad, but it was less noted because it
was not in a Catholic frame of reference.[8]

(4) Breaking Bread

Fourth, then, the Eucharist is an act of economic ethics. In the passages
to which later generations gave the technical label "words of institution" Jesus says, "Whenever you do this, do it in my memory." Do *what*

8. See Arthur Cochrane, *Eating and Drinking with Jesus* (Philadelphia: West-
minster Press, 1974); Norman Fox, *Christ in the Daily Meal: The Ordinance of the
Breaking of Bread* (New York: Fords, Howard and Hulbert, 1898); and William H.
Willimon, *Sunday Dinner* (Nashville: The Upper Room, 1981).

in his memory? It cannot mean "whenever you celebrate the Mass" because there was then no such thing as a Mass. He might mean "whenever you celebrate the Passover," but that is not what the hearers took him to mean. That would have called for an annual celebration. He must have meant (and the record indicates that they took him to mean) "whenever you have your common meal." The meal he blessed and claimed as his memorial was their ordinary partaking together of food for the body. Only because it was that communal meal of the disciples' fellowship could it provide the occasion for their organization of the ministering structures reported in Acts 7.

We commit the hermeneutical sin of anachronism when we look in the New Testament for any light on the much later eucharistic controversies. All of those later controversies were about something of which the apostolic generation had no notion, namely about the detailed theoretical definition of the meaning of specific actions and things ("sacraments") within the special set-apart world of the "religious" in a frame of reference that the later churches took over from paganism when the latter replaced Judaism as their cultural soil. What the New Testament is talking about in "breaking bread" is believers actually sharing with one another their ordinary day-to-day material substance. It is not the case, as far as understanding the New Testament accounts is concerned, that, in an act of "institution" or symbol making, God or the church would have said "let bread stand for daily sustenance." It is not even merely that, in many settings, as any cultural historian would have told us, eating together already stands for values of hospitality and community formation, these values being distinguishable from the signs that refer to them. It is that bread is daily sustenance. Bread eaten together *is* economic sharing. Not merely symbolically but in actual fact it extends to a wider circle the economic solidarity that normally is obtained in the family. When, in most of his post-Resurrection appearances, Jesus takes the role of the family head distributing bread (and fish) around his table, he projects into the post-Passion world the common purse of the wandering disciple band whose members had left their prior economic bases to join his movement.

A rationalistic or Zwinglian understanding of symbol says that a symbolic act has a "meaning" distinguishable from the act itself and that, for certain purposes, it is in fact helpful to disentangle the "meaning" from the act. This is in order to define it, to derive from it additional derivative meanings, and perhaps to resymbolize it into other forms in other settings. In this frame of reference, one can say (although no one did for a long time) that breaking bread together *means* economic solidarity, so that forms of social life that transcend individualism and share with larger communities are preferable to those that name as agents only independent individuals. But such an action of derivation is an intellectual operation, arbitrary and unaccountable. This we might call the "Zwinglian" way of access to an economic meaning of the Eucharist.

At the other end of the scale, what we may call the "sacramentalist" view of a sign says that by a distinct divine act of definition, a specific set of practices is pulled up out of daily life and given, by gracious decree, a distinctive meaning, one best served by accentuating the distance between the special meaning and the ordinary one. A separate "theology of sacraments" then develops a corpus of dogma about that special realm. The bread no longer looks or tastes like the bread one shares with children and guests or that is owed to cousins and to the beggar. It is not broken nor (classically) even put into the mouth the same way as ordinary, real-world food. Its most important meaning is the one that forces us to debate in what sense the bread has now become the body of the Lord and in what sense our eating it mediates to us the grace of salvation. I submit that (although this is no place to spread out the argument) there is no direct path from this point to economics. The Roman Catholic authors who establish such a connection have to start over again from somewhere else.[9]

What I propose, for present purposes, to call the sacramental (as distinct from the sacramentalistic) view spares us those abstracted definitions and articulations of how the sign signifies. When the family head feeds you at his or her table, the bread for which he or she has given thanks, you are part of the family. The act does not merely *mean* that you are part of the family. To take the floor in a community dialogue does not mean that you are part of the group; it *is* operational group membership. To be immersed and to rise from the waters of the *mikvah* may be said to symbolize death and resurrection, but really it makes you a member of the historical community of the new age. This was the case, not only for Jesus, but also for John and for the other Jewish proselytizers and revivalists who used the baptism of repentance before him. This leads us to the fifth social-ethical ritual.

9. Tissa Balasuriya, *The Eucharist and Human Liberation* (Maryknoll: Orbis Press, 1979), makes the argument most directly. See also Geevarghese Osthathios, *Theology of a Classless Society* (Maryknoll: Orbis Press, 1979); Rafael Avila, *Worship and Politics* (Maryknoll: Orbis Press, 1981); Joseph A. Grassi, *Broken Bread and Broken Bodies* (Maryknoll: Orbis Press, 1981); and, from another press, Monika Hellwig, *The Eucharist and the Hunger of the World* (New York: Paulist Press, 1976).

(5) Induction into the New Humanity

Baptism inducts people into a new people, and one of the distinguishing marks of this new people is that all prior given or chosen definitions of identity are transcended. When Paul writes "if anyone is in Christ the whole world is new" so that "worldly standards have ceased to count in my estimate of a person" (2 Cor. 5:16, 17), the concrete social-functional meaning of these statements is that social definitions based upon class and category are no longer basic. The phrase in Galatians, "neither slave nor free, neither male nor female . . . you are one in Christ Jesus" (Gal. 3:28), is explicitly a description of what baptism does, parallel to Ephesians 2 ("new humanity") or to 2 Corinthians 5 ("new creation") in its substance. The fundamental breakthrough at the point of the Jew-Gentile barrier, which generated these texts, demands and produces congruent breakthroughs where the barrier is slavery, gender, or class.[10]

There is, of course, a sacramentalist understanding of baptism, defining the salvation it mediates in terms of original sin. Egalitarianism or interethnic reconciliation cannot be part of its meaning. There is no clear reason not to do it to a newborn infant. There is no reason it was wrong to do it coercively in the Middle Ages.

Of course, there is also, at the other end of the scale, a Zwinglian understanding of what baptism properly "signifies." This is most widely represented today by Baptists, that is, by radicalized Zwinglians. If baptism signifies the new birth as an inward individual experience, it is obvious why we should disavow administering it coercively or to infants, but there is still no natural access to egalitarianism.

If, on the other hand, we can resurrect a sacramental realism, whereby baptism is the constitution of a new people whose newness and togetherness explicitly relativize prior stratifications and classification, then we need no path to get from there to egalitarianism. We start egalitarian, and the reasons to disavow any nonvoluntary practice of the act are built in.

---

10. I have spelled out further the importance of the interethnic meaning of baptism in my "The Apostle's Apology Revisited" in William Klassen, ed., *The New Way of Jesus* (Newton, Kans.: Faith and Life Press, 1980): 115–34, and in "The Social Shape of the Gospel" in Wilbert Shenk, ed., *Exploring Church Growth* (Grand Rapids: Eerdmans, 1983): 277–84.

II

We have now described five social practices, each with an underlying meaning given in the action itself:

(1) There is the interweaving of forgiveness and moral discernment, operative at the point of offense, driven by the intent to forgive, reflecting and also conditioning the reality of divine forgiveness. Jesus' word for this was "binding and loosing"; ours is sometimes "reconciliation," sometimes "discernment."

(2) There is the universalization of giftedness, with every member having his or her charismatic role, whose exercise the community helps define, celebrates, and monitors. It destroys patriarchalism but not in the interest of anarchy or some other "-archalism." It equalizes, but it is the opposite of leveling. I am not sure we have a word for it. I am not sure we have ever seen it practiced with any approximation of the innovative depth and power that Paul was writing about, though several of our modern forms of social organization, role differentiation, and mutuality provide pale images of it.[11]

(3) There is decision making by open dialogue and consensus; everyone can have the floor. Commonsense ground rules assure due process and continuity with the rest of the church, past and present. I have described this process most sociologically in my essay "The Hermeneutics of Peoplehood."[12] I would call this "democracy" but with the recognition that that word has other definitions for some people.[13]

11. There are approximations of it in the Friends' rejection of a standard sacerdotal class or in that of the ("Plymouth") Brethren, but in neither case is the affirmative notion of universal empowerment carried through.

12. John H. Yoder, *The Priestly Kingdom* (Notre Dame: University of Notre Dame Press, 1985): 15–36. Reviewing its contribution to the development of democratic forms in the civil order would be a separate study. Specimens of the way "binding and loosing" and "everyone takes the floor" contribute to the origins of democracy would include (a) the way Calvin's vision of society is said to have had its roots in conciliarism; (b) A. D. Lindsay's rooting of the democracy of England and New England in the experience of the Puritan meeting; and (c) the fact that, even though Calvinist theory was at first elitist and in favor of government's repressing dissent, with time Reformed communities contributed, in fact, to the growth of civil rights, having found themselves in positions not of government but of dissent.

13. I shall return later to the notion that we should eschew the use of words that "might be misunderstood," i.e., that others would use differently. This concern is understandable, but if we took it seriously there would not be many words left. The meaning of incarnation hardly permits avoiding the ambivalence of all particular meanings.

(4) There is the sharing of the simple wherewithal of human life, with the table as its instrument, a practice by its nature decentralized, particular, personal. The simplest word for this is family; another is socialism, although for some that has other meanings.

(5) There is status equality, acted out by baptism, defined as relativizing (not denying) social differences, rejecting their discriminatory impact.

My concern here is not to exposit further any one of these functions, either its "inner" meaning in the body of the community or its example for the world. My purpose in looking at the five specimens in parallel was to identify the lessons to be learned from their formal commonality, as they illuminate the way we see social ethics. Quite separate from one another with regard to subject matter, to where they appear in the New Testament, and to their respective agenda, vocabulary, and procedures, these five practices have much in common. The commonalities qualify my grouping them as an authentic induction.

III

What are the implications for ethics of these five practices? Each of them, first of all, is a wholly human, empirically accessible practice — nothing esoteric. Yet each is, according to the apostolic writers, an act of God. God does not merely authorize or command them. *God is doing* them in, with, and under the human practice: "What you bind on earth is bound in heaven."

Second, all of them are practices that constitute the believing community as a social body. To see them in operation we need to do sociology, not semantics or philosophy. Together (though other dimensions could yet be added) they offer a well-rounded picture of the believing community; that is, of specific, datable, nameable, local, first-century, messianic synagogues as a form of human life together demonstrating not only far-reaching continuities with earlier history and culture but also foundational innovations.

Third, each of these practices can function as a paradigm for ways in which other social groups might operate. These forms are derived from and illuminated by reference to specific components of the faith stance of the first century's messianic synagogues, yet they are accessible to the public. People who do not share the faith or join the community can learn from them. "Binding and loosing" can provide models for conflict resolution, alternatives to litigation, and alternative perspectives on "corrections." Sharing bread is a paradigm, not only for soup kitchens and hospitality houses, but also for social security and negative income tax. "Every member of the body has a gift" is an immediate alternative to vertical "business" models of management. Paul's solidarity models of deliberation correlate with the reasons that the Japanese can make better cars than Detroit. It was not by accident or whim that I could use as labels the modern secular handles "egalitarianism," "democracy," and "social-ism," although each of these terms needs to be taken in a way different from their secularistic and individualistic usages.

Some have warned me that it is dangerous to borrow such worldly words as "egalitarianism" or "freedom" since those concepts are not only hard to define but are the property of the liberal establishment, which is an oppressive elite. These friends are right in thus warning me. If I were to think that those contemporary terms have a univocal normative meaning, and if I were proposing that they simply be "bap-tized," I should have sold out. But those warning friends are wrong if they suggest that some other, less liberal words (for example "virtue," "narrative," "community") would be safer from abuse. The right cor-rective is not to seek fail-safe words never yet corrupted but rather to renew daily the action of preempting the extant vocabulary, rendering every creature subject to God's rule in Christ. What is needed is to surface the criteria whereby we can tell whether, in the appropriation of each new language, the meaning of Jesus is authentically reenacted or abandoned.

Fourth, the reason for their paradigmatic accessibility to others and their translatability into other terms is that they are not "religious" or "ritual" activities at bottom. They are by nature "lay" or "public" phenomena. The two, from among the five, that did become "sacra-ments" in the later "Catholic" synthesis, after the divorce with Judaism and the remarriage with Constantine, had to change their basic meaning for that to be carried through.

Fifth, these practices are enabled and illuminated by Jesus of Nazareth, who is confessed as Messiah and as Lord. They are part of the order of redemption, not of creation. Hereby we loop back to the difference between the New Testament parallels and the standard ac-count of the relations of particular and general truths, or of revelation and reason. The standard account of these matters had told us that in order for Christians to be able to speak to others we need to look less to redemption and more to creation, or less to revelation and more to nature and reason. In only slightly different ways recent Reformed thinkers (for example Emil Brunner, Reinhold Niebuhr, and H. Richard

Niebuhr)[14] play the Creator/Father off against the Redeemer/Son in such a way that the will of God as Father (known reliably by means of reason) counts for the social realm, as the words and example of the Son do not.

In the practices I am describing (and the thinking underlying them), the apostolic communities did it the other way around. The multiplicity of gifts is described in Ephesians 4 in analogy to the booty generously dispensed by a victorious champion (appropriating the military victory march hymn of Psalm 68). The ascended Lord Christ pours out the gifts. Binding and loosing makes us participants of the reconciling work of God in Christ. Egalitarianism is enabled by the "new creation," which baptism signs and seals.

In other words, all of these social/ethical/sacramental practices are formally rooted in the order of redemption. That by no means makes them less public. It makes them more realistic about sin and more hopeful about reconciliation than those approaches that trust the reason/nature/creation complex to derive our knowledge of what should be from what is.

Sixth, and also in contrast to the standard account, none of these practices makes the individual the pivot of change. The individual is in no way forgotten or relativized; nothing could be more particularly tailored to measure than the notion of every member's possessing (or being possessed by) a distinctive charisma. Nothing empowers more potently than saying that in the meeting everyone can take the floor. But no trust is placed in the individual's changed insights (as liberalism does) or on the believer's changed insides (as does pietism) to change the world. The fulcrum for change and the forum for decision is the moral independence of the believing community as social body. The dignity of the individual is his or her uniqueness as specific member of that body.

Seventh, none of these five practices was revealed from above or created from scratch; each was derived from already existent cultural models. Table fellowship, baptism, and the open meeting were not new ideas, yet in the gospel setting they have taken on new meanings and a new empowerment.

Eighth, it is hard to link this picture with our guild's standard

---

14. H. R. Niebuhr, "The Doctrine of the Trinity and the Unity of the Church," one of the few texts to be published twice in *Theology Today*, in October 1946 and in July 1983. According to this modalistic trinitarianism, God the Father is more competent for ethical guidance in the realm of "culture" than is the Son.

meta-ethical discussions of consistent moral discourse. Some ethicists believe that the most important, and the procedurally prior, task of the ethicist is to disentangle the varieties of modes of moral argument and to argue that one of them is right. Do these apostolic models of social-ethical creativity reason consequentially or deontologically? Do they prefer the modes of story or of virtue? As far as I can tell, the questions are impertinent.[15] Not only would the apostolic writers not have understood what these questions mean, had they understood them, they would have refused to answer. They would have seen no reason to choose among those incommensurate kinds of resources; why not use them all? The originality and the specificity of their stance lies elsewhere than within the reach of that traditional but abstract methodological debate. Methodological analysis is helpful to illuminate problems of structure, but it is not the prerequisite for the community's right or capacity to reason morally.

Ninth, the apostolic model transcends some other dichotomies as well. It clearly assumes rootage in the normative events that some epistemological analysis calls "revelation," yet without selling reason short, contrary to those who play the orders of "redemption" and "reason" off against one another. Nothing could be more reasonable than the dialogue modes described in Acts 15 and 1 Corinthians 14. Were we to try to lay over it the Catholic/Protestant typological grid of James Gustafson, or the fivefold typology of his mentor H. Richard Niebuhr, it would fit nowhere. The apostolic model trusts a living magisterium more than does Rome and needs no special theories about the epistemological status of its sources. In that way it is not "Protestant." It places little trust in non-congregational or supra-congregational office bearers, and it has no place to locate the notion that there would be a body of "general" moral knowledge accessible without dialogue or context by means of "reason" or "nature." In that way it is not "Catholic." This is analogous to the way that, as I said, some have warned me of the danger of borrowing such worldly words as "egalitarianism" or "freedom" because those concepts are the property of the liberal establishment. The early communities do not let themselves be held at a distance by hermeneutic grids like "Protestant/Catholic" or "radical/liberal."

15. My doubts about the standard methodological disjunctions were already stated in my *Priestly Kingdom*, pp. 113ff. See also John H. Yoder, "Walk and Word: The Alternatives to Methodologism" in *Theology without Foundations: Religious Practice and the Future of Theological Truth*, ed. Nancey Murphy, Mark Nation, and Stanley Hauerwas (Nashville: Abingdon, 1994): 77–90, with notes on pp. 311–16.

IV

The last few of these inductive observations have been polemic. I have identified some currently popular analytical perspectives that, while helpful for other purposes, cannot box in the apostolic experience. I also maintain that the apostolic model is "evangelical" in the functional sense. For some the label "evangelical" points to a checklist of traditional doctrines and for others to a key inner experience. I mean neither.

For a practice to qualify as "evangelical" in the functional sense means first of all that it communicates *news*. It says something particular that would not be known and could not be believed were it not said. Second, it must mean functionally that this "news" is attested as *good*; it comes across to those whom it addresses as helping, as saving, and as *shalom*. It must be public, not esoteric, but the way for it to be public is not an a priori logical move that subtracts the particular. It is an a posteriori political practice that tells the world something it did not know and could not believe before. It tells the world what is the world's own calling and destiny, not by announcing either a utopian or a realistic goal to be imposed on the whole society, but by pioneering a paradigmatic demonstration of both the power and the practices that define the shape of restored humanity. The confessing people of God is the new world on its way.

If the good is new, it will have to be said in new contexts, where there is no adequate language for it, until that language is crafted.[16] Since the new is good, it will have to be said in such a creative, loving, and pertinent way that the hearers' acceptance of it is not obligatory but the product of the fit between the news and the hearers' awareness of their lostness.

On the other hand, the search for a general language that people should have to believe does not want to have to depend upon faith or to avow lostness. Its wanting to avoid the risk of deniability is psychically coercive in intent. The credibility of that which is both "good" and "news" consists precisely in its vulnerability, its refusability. That weakness marks all five of the incarnational processes I have been describing. They are not ways to administer the world; they are modes of vulnerable but also provocative, creative presence in its midst. That is the primordial way in which they transform culture.

---

16. "To craft" is the fitting verb. We are not concerned with creation ex nihilo; language is not created that way. A craft works out of living familiarity with the material it transforms.

Selected Bibliography of John H. Yoder on Ecclesiology and Ecumenism

COMPILED BY MARK K. NATION

The following selected bibliography has been prepared with several different kinds of readers in mind: (1) the general interest reader who is interested in reading more of John H. Yoder's work; (2) the church leader (lay or clergy) who may read these essays out of concern for church renewal; (3) the scholarly researcher who may want to trace the development of John H. Yoder's ecclesiology and ethics. This bibliography is organized chronologically under three headings: books, published articles, and other unpublished lectures and papers. In case of repetition, entries for a particular year are alphabetized. Editorial comments for the purpose of offering guidance to readers have been placed in [ ] brackets to distinguish these remarks from the bibliographical information.

Books

1962   *Täufertum und Reformation in der Schweiz: I. Die Gespräche zwischen Täufern und Reformatoren 1523–1538.* Schriftenreihe des Mennonitischen Geschichtsvereins, no. 6. Karlsruhe: Buchdruckerei und Verlag H. Schneider.

1964   *The Christian Witness to the State.* Newton, Kans.: Faith and Life Press. [Third printing, 1977, has updated footnotes]

1968   *Täufertum und Reformation im Gesprach: Dogmengeschichtliche Untersuchung der frühen Gesprache zwischen Schweizerischen Täufern und Reformatoren.* Zurich: EVZ-Verlag. [Esp. sections III and IV]

1970   *Karl Barth and the Problem of War*. Nashville: Abingdon Press.
1971   *Nevertheless: The Varieties and Shortcomings of Religious Pacifism*. Scottdale, Penn.: Herald Press. (Second edition, 1976, revised and expanded edition, 1992)
1972   *The Politics of Jesus*. Grand Rapids: Eerdmans. (1972, revised 1994)
1981   *Preface to Theology: Christology and Theological Method*. Elkhart, Ind.: Goshen Biblical Seminary. (Distributed, in photocopied form, by Cokesbury Bookstore, Duke Divinity School, Durham, N.C.)
1983   *Christian Attitudes to War, Peace, and Revolution: A Companion to Bainton*. Elkhart, Ind.: Goshen Biblical Seminary. (Distributed, in photocopied form, by Cokesbury Bookstore, Duke Divinity School, Durham, N.C.)
1984   *The Priestly Kingdom: Social Ethics As Gospel*. Notre Dame: University of Notre Dame Press. [Esp. chaps. 1, 4, 5, 6, & 7]
1985   *He Came Preaching Peace*. Scottdale, Penn.: Herald Press.
1987   *The Fullness of Christ: Paul's Vision of Universal Ministry*. Elgin, Ill.: Brethren Press.
1991   Gwyn, Douglas; George Hunsinger; Eugene F. Roop; and John Howard Yoder. *A Declaration on Peace: In God's People the World's Renewal Has Begun*. Scottdale, Penn.: Herald Press.
1992   *Body Politics: Five Practices of the Christian Community before the Watching World*. Nashville: Discipleship Resources.

Published Pamphlets, Articles, and Chapters in Books

1954   "The Anabaptist Dissent: The Logic of the Place of the Disciple in Society." *Concern* 1 (June): 45–68.
1954   "Let Evanston Speak on War!" *The Christian Century* 71 (August 18): 973–74. [This article happened to be printed on adjoining pages with Reinhold Niebuhr's article "Co-Existence or Total War?" The two articles addressed different perspectives on war and ecumenics (971–73).]
1955   "The New Testament View of the Ministry." *Gospel Herald* 48 (February 8): 121–22, 124.
1955   "Reinhold Niebuhr and Christian Pacifism." *Mennonite Quarterly Review* 29 (April): 101–17.
1958   *The Ecumenical Movement and the Faithful Church*. Scottdale, Penn.: Herald Press. Focal Pamphlet Series #3: 43pp.

1959   "The Two Kingdoms." *Christus Victor* 106 (September): 3–7.

1961   *As You Go: The Old Mission in a New Day.* Scottdale, Penn.: Herald Press. Focal Pamphlet Series #5: 36pp.

1964   "Christian Discipline." *Gospel Herald* 57 (August 18): 709–10.

1964   "The Pacifism of Karl Barth." Washington, D.C.: The Church Peace Mission. (pamphlet): 30pp.

1967   "A Summary of the Anabaptist Vision." *An Introduction to Mennonite History.* Edited by Cornelius J. Dyck. Scottdale, Penn.: Herald Press, 103–11. [Revised 1981: 136–45]

1969   "The Unique Role of the Historic Peace Churches." *Brethren Life and Thought* 14 (Summer): 132–49.

1970   "Anabaptist Vision and Mennonite Reality." *Consultation on Anabaptist-Mennonite Theology: Papers Read at the 1969 Aspen Conference.* Edited by A. J. Klassen. Fresno, Calif.: The Council of Mennonite Seminaries, 1–46.

1970   "A Non-Baptist View of Southern Baptists." *Review and Expositor* 67 (Spring): 219–28.

1973   "Church Growth Issues in Theological Perspective." *The Challenge of Church Growth: A Symposium.* Edited by Wilbert R. Shenk. Elkhart, Ind: Institute of Mennonite Studies, 25–47. (Missionary Studies No. 1.)

1973   "Jesus and Power." *The Ecumenical Review* 25 (October): 447–54. [The same as "Jesus and Power" in *On Earth Peace*, edited by Donald F. Durnbaugh (Elgin, Ill.: The Brethren Press), 365–72.]

1973   "What Do Ye More Than They?" *Gospel Herald* 66 (January 23): 72–75. [Lecture at Conference on Evangelism.]

1974   "The Biblical Mandate." *The Chicago Declaration.* Edited by Ronald J. Sider. Carol Stream, Ill.: Creation House, 88–116; and "Evangelicals at Chicago: A New Openness to Prophetic Social Critique." *Christianity and Crisis* 34 (February 18): 23–25.

1977   "Martin Luther's Forgotten Vision." *The Other Side* 13 (April 1977): 66–70.

1978   "Church and State According to a Free Church Tradition." *On Earth Peace.* Edited by Donald F. Durnbaugh. Elgin, Ill.: The Brethren Press, 279–88.

1978   "On Divine and Human Justice." *On Earth Peace.* Edited by Donald F. Durnbaugh. Elgin, Ill.: The Brethren Press, 197–210.

1978   "Epilogue: The Way Ahead." *On Earth Peace.* Edited by Donald F. Durnbaugh. Elgin, Ill.: The Brethren Press, 390–93.

1978	"The Theological Basis of the Christian Witness to the State." *On Earth Peace.* Edited by Donald F. Durnbaugh. Elgin, Ill.: The Brethren Press, 136–43.
1979	"The Believers' Church: Global Perspectives." *The Believers' Church in Canada.* Edited by J. Zeman and W. Klaassen. Winnipeg: The Baptist Federation and The Mennonite Central Committee, 3–15.
1979	"The Contemporary Evangelical Revival and the Peace Churches." *Mission and the Peace Witness: The Gospel and Christian Discipleship.* Edited by Robert L. Ramseyer. Scottdale, Penn.: Herald Press, 68–103, 137.
1979	"Discerning the Kingdom of God in the Struggles of the World." *International Review of Missions* 68 (October): 366–72.
1980	"The Apostle's Apology Revisited." *The New Way of Jesus.* Edited by William Klassen. Newton, Kans.: Faith and Life Press, 115–34.
1980	"Could There Be a Baptist Bishop?" *Ecumenical Trends* 9 (July–August): 104–7.
1982	"Einfachere Einheit für knappere Zeiten." *Möglichkeiten und Grenzen der Ökumene Heute.* Edited by Karlfried Frölich. Tübingen: Mohr, 107–11. [Festschrift for Oscar Cullmann.]
1983	"The Social Shape of the Gospel." *Exploring Church Growth.* Edited by Wilbert R. Shenk. Grand Rapids: Eerdmans, 277–84.
1985	"A Critique of North American Evangelical Ethics." *Transformation* 2 (Jan./March): 28–31.
1985	"The Prophetic Task of Pastoral Ministry: The Gospels." *The Pastor as Prophet.* Edited by Earl E. Shelp and Ronald H. Sunderland. New York: Pilgrim Press, 78–98.
1985	"Reformed Versus Anabaptist Social Strategies: An Inadequate Typology." *TSF* [Theological Students' Fellowship] *Bulletin* 8 (May–June): 2–10.
1986	"Calling a Council for Peace." *Ecumenical Trends* 15 (November): 157–60.
1986	"The Challenge of Peace: A Historic Peace Church Perspective." *Peace in a Nuclear Age: The Bishops' Pastoral Letter in Perspective.* Edited by Charles J. Reid, Jr. Washington, D.C.: The Catholic University of America Press, 273–90.
1986	"Karl Barth: How His Mind Kept Changing." *How Karl Barth Changed My Mind.* Edited by Donald K. McKim. Grand Rapids: Eerdmans, 166–71.

1986   "A 'Peace Church' Perspective on Covenanting." *The Ecumenical Review* 38 (July): 318–21.

1988   "The Anabaptist Shape of Liberation." *Why I Am a Mennonite: Essays on Mennonite Identity.* Edited by Harry Loewen. Scottdale, Penn.: Herald Press, 338–48.

1988   "Armaments and Eschatology." *Studies in Christian Ethics* 1/1. Edinburgh: T & T Clark, 43–61.

1988   "The Reception of the Just War Tradition by the Magisterial Reformers." *History of European Ideas* 9:1–23. [Cf. I, 1983, pp. 97–112.]

1988   "Theological Revision and the Burden of Particular Identity." *James M. Gustafson's Theocentric Ethics: Interpretations and Assessments.* Edited by Harlan R. Beckley and Charles M. Swezey. Macon, Ga.: Mercer University Press, 63–89; discussion: 89–94.

1989   "Adjusting to the Changing Shape of the Debate on Infant Baptism." *Oecumennisme: Opstellen aangeboden an Henk B. Kossen.* . . . Edited by Arie Lambo. Amsterdam: Algemene Doopsgezinde Societeit, 201–14.

1989   Richard J. Mouw and. . . . "Evangelical Ethics and the Anabaptist-Reformed Dialogue." *The Journal of Religious Ethics* 17 (Fall): 121–37.

1989   "The Historic Peace Churches: Heirs to the Radical Reformation." *Peace, War and God's Justice.* Edited by Thomas D. Parker and Brian J. Fraser. Toronto, Canada: The United Church Pub. House, 105–22.

1990   "Ethics and Eschatology." *Ex Auditu* 6:119–28.

1990   James Wm. McClendon, Jr. and. . . . "Explorations and Responses: Christian Identity in Ecumenical Perspective: A Response to David Wayne Layman." *Journal of Ecumenical Studies* 27 (Summer): 561–80.

1990   "The Free Church Syndrome." *Within the Perfection of Christ: Essays on Peace and the Nature of the Church.* Edited by Terry L. Brensinger and E. Morris Sider. Nappanee, Ind.: Evangel Press, 169–76.

1990   "The One or the Many? The Pauline Vision [of Ministry] and the Rest of the Reformation" and "Epilogue." *Servants of the Word: Ministry in the Believers Churches.* Edited by David B. Eller. Elgin, Ill.: Brethren Press, 51–64, 201–12.

1991   "The Believers' Church Conferences in Historical Perspective." *Mennonite Quarterly Review* 65 (January): 5–19.

1991   "Conscientious Objection" and "Peace." *Dictionary of the Ecumenical Movement.* Edited by Geoffrey Wainwright, et al. Geneva: WCC Pub./Grand Rapids: Eerdmans, 221, 786–89.

1991   "Thinking Theologically from a Free-Church Perspective." *Doing Theology in Today's World: Essays in Honor of Kenneth S. Kantzer.* Edited by John D. Woodbridge and Thomas Edward McComiskey. Grand Rapids: Zondervan Publishing House, 251–65.

1992   "On Not Being Ashamed of the Gospel: Particularity, Pluralism and Validation." *Faith and Philosophy* 9 (July): 285–300.

1993   "The Burden and Discipline of Evangelical Revisionism." *Nonviolent America: History through the Eyes of Peace.* Edited by Louise Hawkley and James C. Juhnke. North Newton, Kans.: Bethel College, 21–37.

1994   "How H. Richard Niebuhr Reasons: A Critique of *Christ and Culture.*" *Authentic Transformation: A New Vision of Christ and Culture* by John Howard Yoder, Diane Yeager, and Glenn Stassen. Nashville: Abingdon, 1994.

1995   "Walk and Word: The Alternatives to Methodologism." *Theology without Foundations: Religious Practice and the Future of Theological Truth.* Edited by Nancey Murphy, Mark Nation, and Stanley Hauerwas. Nashville: Abingdon, 77–90, with notes on 311–16. Forthcoming.

Lectures, Papers, and Other Unpublished Works

1959   "The Nature of the Church's Responsibility in the World." Contribution to a study conference of Mennonite Central Committee Peace Section, Chicago, Mimeo. 7pp.

1960   "Mennonites and Contemporary Ecumenical Movements." From: Centennial Study Conference, General Conference Mennonite Church, "Christian Unity in Faith and Witness," Donnellson High School Auditorium, Donnellson, Iowa, June 20–23; this lecture: June 23. 8pp.

1963   "Believer's Baptism as Representative and Constitutive of a Specific and Coherent View of the Church and Her Place in the World." A programmatic concept draft written after conversations with Prof. J. A. Oosterbaan at Montreal in 1963. 13pp.

1964   "Christian Life Week Lectures." Eight lectures, with the individual titles: (1) "We Have No Choice," (2) "Faith Is Foreign," (3) "To Save Our Lives," (4) "Faith Is Resurrection," (5) "To Make Sense," (6) "Faith Is Coherent," (7) "Once For All," and (8) "Faith Is Fellowship." Delivered at Bethel College, Newton, Kans., January 19–22. 51pp. (Mimeographed and bound by Bethel College.)

1965   "Issues in Ecclesiology." Notes taken by John Paul Wenger and typed by Harvey Graber from class of same title taught in spring. 28pp.

1966   "Lecture Series in South America." (Delivered in Spanish.) Three Series.

Series I: The Believers' Church
Individual Titles:
(a) "Only Believers." 8pp.;
(b) "Commission to Bind and to Loose." 8pp.;
(c) "The Mandate to Share." 9pp.;
(d) "Walking in the Resurrection." 9pp.

Series II: Peace
Individual Titles:
(a) "Discipleship in the Sermon on the Mount." 8pp.;
(b) "The Cross as a Social Fact." 9pp.;
(c) "Love and Responsibility." 10pp.;
(d) "The Doctrine of the 'Just War': Its Values and Its Limits." 6pp.;
(e) "A Biblical View of History." 9pp.

Series III: Church in a Revolutionary World
Individual Titles:
(a) "The Otherness of the Church." 10pp.;
(b) "Christ and the Powers." 12pp.;
(c) "Constantinianism Old and New." 9pp.;
(d) "Revolution and Gospel." 10pp.;
(e) "The Meaning of Our Revolutionary Age." 8pp.
[Manuscripts of these exist in Spanish and English.]

1967   "Anabaptist Understandings of the Nature and Mission of the Church, with Implications for Contemporary Mennonite Church Organization." Paper presented to the Study Commission on Church Organization, Consultation of Nature and Mission of Mennonite Church, Pittsburgh, April 10–11. 19pp., with at least four "exhibits" attached.

1967   "Christian Unity within a Divided North American Protestantism." Memorandum on Mennonite Board of Missions and Charities stationery. March 1. 13pp.

1968 "Proposal for a Group of 'Believers' Church' Theologians." August. 5pp.

1968 "Second Draft of 'Theses' on the Definition of the Free Church Vision." Presentation to the Dean's Seminar, May 30. 8pp.

1973 "Fuller Definition of 'Violence.'" Memo to: Cooper/Cardiff Study Group, March 28. 7pp.

1976 "Alternative to Violence." Lecture given for the South Africa Council of Churches, early 1976. 12pp.

1977 "Experiencing Joy and Unity: A Communion Meditation." Bulletin of the Mennonite Biblical Seminaries, Elkhart, Ind., 40 (January). 5pp.

1977 "Tertium Datur: Refocusing the Jewish-Christian Schism." Read before the Notre Dame Graduate Theological Union, October 13. 42pp.

1978 "The Believers' Church and the Arms Race." Address delivered at Goshen College as part of "No More War Week" activities, March 15. 8pp.

1978 "The Basis of Barth's Social Ethics." Lecture at Constitutive Meeting of the Midwestern Section of the Karl Barth Society at Elmhurst, Ill., September 29–30. 11pp.

1978 "The Lord's Supper in Historical Perspective." A teaching given at the Assembly, Goshen, Ind., November 26. 8 pp.

1979 "The Church and Change: Violence and Its Alternatives." Lecture presented at the annual conference, South African Council of Churches, Hammanskraal, July 24. 35pp.

1980 "The Stone Lectures." Unpublished manuscripts of five lectures delivered at Princeton Theological Seminary, February. [Partially repeated as "The Morgan Lectures" at Fuller Theological Seminary.]
    Lecture 1: "Why Ecclesiology Is Social Ethics." 39pp.
    Lecture 2: "The Scandal of Apocalypse." 39pp.
    Lecture 3: "Behold, My Servant Shall Prosper." 28pp.
    Lecture 4: "Sacrament as Social Process." 20pp.
    Lecture 5: "Body Politics." 18pp.

1982 "The Menno Simons Lectures." Presented at Bethel College, North Newton, Kans. [Also presented at Earlham School of Religion, Richmond, Ind., April 1985.] (One sermon and five lectures.)

Sermon: "Salvation Is of the Jews." 4pp.

Lecture 1: "It Did Not Have to Be." 24pp.

Lecture 2: "Judaism as the Original Peace Church." 21pp.

Lecture 3: "The Jewishness of the Free Church Vision." 15pp.

Lecture 4: "Paul the Judaizer." 7pp.

Lecture 5: "The Jewishness of Anabaptism." 3pp.

A post-Newton fragment: "Another Way Jews and Christians Are Not So Different." 2pp.

A post-Earlham fragment: "Bias? Co-option?" 5pp.

1983   "The Finality of Jesus Christ and Other Faiths." Collected from material from several earlier prepared lectures and essays. Reproduced in the fall for the AMBS course "Ecclesiology in Missional Perspective." 33pp.

1988   "Methodological Miscellany #2: Have You Ever Seen a True Church?" April. 5pp.

1988   "The Christological Presuppositions of Discipleship." [Paper on Dietrich Bonhoeffer] presented at the Annual Meeting of the American Academy of Religion in Chicago, Ill., November 11. 27 pp.

1992   "Methodological Miscellany, Moral Theology #1: Is an Ethic of Discipleship 'Absolute'?" September. 14pp. [Revised several times since 1982.]

Index

Index of Scripture References

Index of Names

Abbot, E. S., 311n
Abraham, 115, 116, 117, 149, 157, 172, 174, 302
Allen, Roland, 316
Anselm, 120
Augustine, 57, 58, 62, 89, 154, 214n, 245
Avila, Rafael, 366n
Bainton, Roland, 23, 25, 67n, 68n, 135n, 214n
Balasuriya, Tissa, 366n
Barbour, Hugh, 87n
Barth, Karl, 4, 15, 16-18, 61, 102-3, 104-10, 113, 116, 120-21, 125, 139, 164n, 166, 183, 252, 285
Barth, Markus, 73
Bartsch, Hans-Werner, 73
Bellah, Robert, 36n
Ben Teradion, Rabbai Hananjah, 331n
Ben Zakki, Johanan, 134
Bender, Harold, 15, 79
Bender, Ross T., 12, 14, 77n
Benson, Lewis, 232n
Berkhof, Hendrikus, 38, 134n, 194
Bethge, Eberhard, 45n
Betsworth, Roger, 35n
Billerbeck, P., 357
Blake, Eugene Carson, 301, 308
Blue, Ken, 323
Boney, William Jerry, 308n

Bonhoeffer, Dietrich, 30n, 44n, 45n, 114, 138-39, 197, 252
Bonino, José Míguez, 15, 17n, 301-2, 303n, 306, 308, 309
Booth, William, 320
Bridston, Keith, 233n
Brunner, Emil, 114, 370
Bucer, Martin, 133, 135, 317, 362
Büchsel, F., 358
Bullinger, J. H., 71
Bultmann, R., 35, 61, 73
Bunyan, J., 276
Butterfield, Herbert, 124, 154, 159, 160n
Cadbury, Henry J., 358
Caesar, 130
Calvin, John, 70, 71, 80, 82, 114, 307, 315, 368n
Campbell, Alexander, 266n, 320
Carey, W., 276
Carlson, C. Emanuel, 27n, 65
Carpenter, H. J., 311n
Cartwright, Michael G., 28n
Charlemagne, 254
Charles V, 59
Chelcickyz, Peter, 71
Churchill, W., 318
Cicero, 58
Coalter, Milton J., 42n
Cochrane, Arthur C., 183n, 364n
Congar, Yves, 242, 256-57